BLACK&DECKER®

THE COMPLETE PHOTO GUIDE TO

HOME REPAIR

Creative Publishing
international

MINNEAPOLIS, MINNESOTA
www.creativepub.com

Creative Publishing international

Copyright © 2008
Creative Publishing international, Inc.
400 First Avenue North, Suite 300
Minneapolis, Minnesota 55401
1-800-328-0590
www.creativepub.com

Printed at R.R. Donnelley
10 9 8 7 6 5 4 3 2

Library of Congress Cataloging-in-Publication Data

The complete photo guide to home repair : with 350 projects and over 2000 photos.
   p. cm.
 Includes index.
 Summary: "Features more than 200 essential home repair projects, including common wiring, plumbing, interior and exterior repairs"--Provided by publisher.
 ISBN-13: 978-1-58923-417-8
 ISBN-10: 1-58923-417-0
 1. Dwellings--Maintenance and repair--Amateurs' manuals. I. Title.

TH4817.3.C655 2008
643'.7--dc22

2008016520

President/CEO: Ken Fund
VP for Sales & Marketing: Kevin Hamric

Home Improvement Group

Publisher: Bryan Trandem
Managing Editor: Tracy Stanley
Senior Editor: Mark Johanson
Editor: Jennifer Gehlhar

Creative Director: Michele Lanci-Altomare
Senior Design Managers: Jon Simpson, Brad Springer
Design Manager: James Kegley

Lead Photographer: Steve Galvin
Photo Coordinator: Joanne Wawra
Shop Manager: Bryan McLain
Shop Assistant: Cesar Fernandez Rodriguez

Production Managers: Linda Halls, Laura Hokkanen

Page Layout Artist: Danielle Smith

The Complete Photo Guide to Home Repair
Created by: The Editors of Creative Publishing international, Inc., in cooperation with Black & Decker.
Black & Decker® is a trademark of The Black & Decker Corporation and is used under license.

NOTICE TO READERS

For safety, use caution, care, and good judgment when following the procedures described in this book. The publisher and Black & Decker cannot assume responsibility for any damage to property or injury to persons as a result of misuse of the information provided.

    The techniques shown in this book are general techniques for various applications. In some instances, additional techniques not shown in this book may be required. Always follow manufacturers' instructions included with products, since deviating from the directions may void warranties. The projects in this book vary widely as to skill levels required: some may not be appropriate for all do-it-yourselfers, and some may require professional help.

    Consult your local building department for information on building permits, codes, and other laws as they apply to your project.

Contributing Editors, Art Directors, Set Builders, and Photographers

Phil Aarrestad, Glenn Austin, Randy Austin, Kim Bailey, Mark Biscan, Stewart Block, Rose Brandt, Gary Branson, Greg Breining, Dave Brus, Keith Bruzelius, Ron Bygness, Jennifer Caliandro, Rudy Calin, Tom Carpenter, Dan Cary, Julie Caruso, Janice Cauley, Tate Carlson, Marcia Chambers, Scott Christiansen, Tom Cooper, Paul Currie, Cy DeCosse, Jim Destiche, Doug Deutsche, Diane Dreon, Arthur Durkee, Barbara Falk, Jerri Farris, Mary Firestone, Steve Galvin, Jennifer Gehlhar, Abby Gnagey, Patricia Goar, Paul Gorton, Lynne Hanauer, Barbara Harold, Carol Harvatin, Rebecca Hawthorne, Tom Heck, Jon Hegge, Mike Hehner, Tami Helmer, Paul Herda, John Hermansen, Jonathan Hinz, Sara Holle, Lori Holmberg, Jim Huntley, Rex Irmen, Mark Johanson, Troy Johnson, Kari Johnston, Rob Johnstone, William B. Jones, Phil Juntti, Andrew Karre, Patrick Kartes, James Kegley, Geoffrey Kinsey, Tony Kubat, Michele Lanci-Altomare, Marcus Landram, Karl Larson, John Lauenstein, Thomas Lemmer,

Bill Lindner, Earl Lindquist, Daniel London, Barbara Lund, Curtis Lund, Mark Macemon, Bernice Maehren, Dave Mahoney, Paul Markert, Brett Martin, Jamey Mauk, Bryan McLain, John Nadeau, Paul Najlis, Bill Nelson, Charles Nields, Mette Nielsen, Kristen Olson, Carol Osterhus, Brad Parker, Mike Parker, Christian Paschke, Mike Peterson, Greg Pluth, Anne Price-Gordon, John Riha, Cesar Rodriguez, Tom Rosch, Susan Roth, Andrea Rugg, Karen Ruth, Gary Sandin, Dave Schelitzche, Joel Schmarje, Philip Schmidt, Joel Schnell, Mark Scholtes, Ned Scubic, Gina Seeling, Cathleen Shannon, Mike Shaw, Hugh Sherwood, Jon Simpson, Michelle Skudlarek, Steve Smith, Angela Spann, Brad Springer, Dick Sternberg, Lori Swanson, Andrew Sweet, Dianne Talmage, Glenn Terry, Keith Thompson, Vryan Trandem, Gregory Wallace, Kevin Walton, Joanne Wawra, Robert Weaver, John Webb, Brad Webster, Wayne Wendland, John Whitman, Dan Widerski, Christopher Wilson, Mike Woodside

Contents

The Complete Photo Guide
to Home Repair

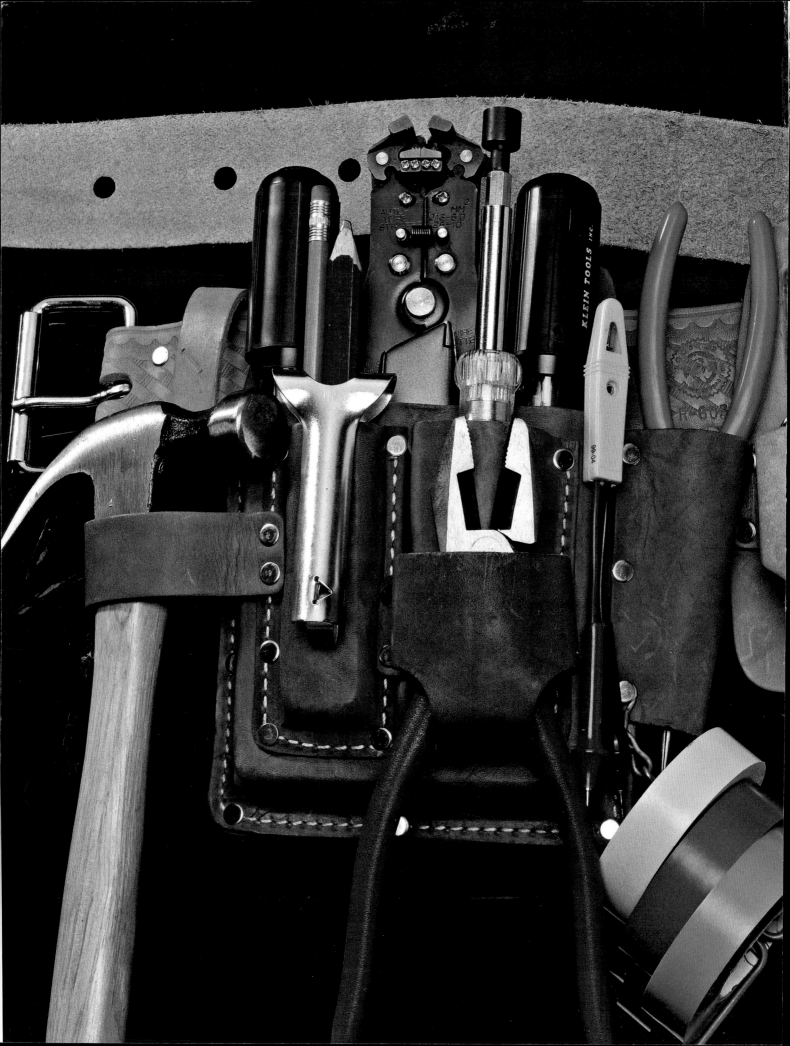

Introduction

As millions of homeowners have discovered over the years, there's a good reason for the enduring popularity of *The Complete Photo Guide to Home Repair*: it's got everything. Every major system and surface in and around the house is covered with in-depth how-to text and detailed photos. No filler, nothing you don't need—it's full of hundreds of projects and thousands of photos to help you keep your home in top shape. It's no wonder this is the bestselling home repair book on the market.

This third edition includes all the best of previous editions, as well as new repair projects for every area of the house. All projects include:

- Step-by-step instructions full of pro tips and techniques. Our home improvement experts give you clear, concise directions to help you from start to finish.
- Color photos of every stage of a project. Clear, realistic photos illustrate every step of the project so you'll know exactly hat to expect.
- Detailed anatomy photos and illustrations. We go to great lengths to show all the aspects of tool, system, or project, so you won't be left in the dark.

Every area of the house is covered. In the interiors section, you'll find comprehensive repairs for basements, walls, floors, and ceilings. There's detailed information on minor and major repairs to flooring materials from carpet to contemporary laminate materials. You'll learn everything from how to make your existing windows more energy efficient to replacing old windows with the latest high-efficiency windows.

When it comes to exterior repairs, we've got you covered for all essential maintenance and repairs to your home's exterior, including tips for winterizing and improving energy efficiency. We'll show you how to patch a leaky roof and repair and restore a worn patio, deck, or sidewalk. Repairs to every major siding material are also covered.

Repairs to wiring, plumbing, and heating-ventilation-and-air-conditioning systems can be the most intimidating for homeowners, and they're almost always the most expensive to hire out. Armed with this book, you'll have all the information and direction you need to tackle common wiring and plumbing projects with confidence. Whether you've got a running toilet or a problem with old wiring, odds are you'll find a clear, effective solution in this book—without a call to an electrician or a plumber.

As a homeowner, you know your home is your biggest investment. *The Complete Photo Guide to Home Repair* is your indispensable resource for maximizing your return on that investment .

Interior

In this chapter:

Repairing Floors

Floor coverings wear out faster than other interior surfaces because they get more wear and tear. Surface damage can affect more than just appearance. Scratches in resilient flooring and cracks in grouted tile joints can let moisture into the floor's underpinnings. Hardwood floors lose their finish and become discolored. Loose boards squeak.

Underneath the finished flooring, moisture ruins wood underlayment and the damage is passed on to the subfloor. Bathroom floors suffer the most from moisture problems. Subflooring can pull loose from joists, causing floors to become uneven and springy.

You can fix these problems yourself, such as squeaks, a broken stair tread, damaged baseboard and trim, and minor damage to floor coverings, with the tools and techniques shown on the following pages.

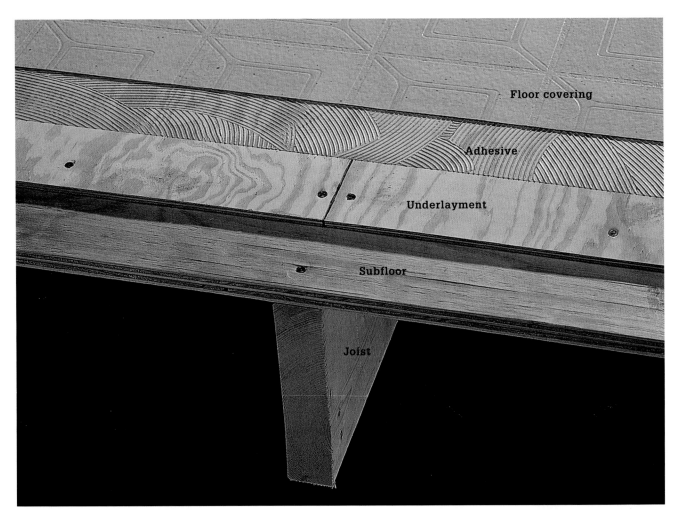

A typical wood-frame floor consists of layers that work together to provide the required structural support and desired appearance: 1. At the bottom of the floor are the joists, the 2 × 10 or larger framing members that support the weight of the floor. Joists are typically spaced 16" apart on center. 2. The subfloor is nailed to the joists. Most subfloors installed in the 1970s or later are made of ¾" tongue-and-groove plywood; in older houses, the subfloor often consists of 1"-thick wood planks nailed diagonally across the floor joists. 3. On top of the subfloor, most builders place a ½" plywood underlayment. Some flooring materials, especially ceramic tile, require cementboard for stability. 4. For many types of floor coverings, adhesive or mortar is spread on the underlayment before the floor covering is installed. Carpet rolls generally require tackless strips and cushioned padding. 5. Other materials, such as snap-fit laminate planks or carpet squares, can be installed directly on the underlayment with little or no adhesive.

Tips for Evaluating Floors

When installing new flooring over old, measure vertical spaces to make sure enclosed or under-counter appliances will fit once the new underlayment and flooring are installed. Use samples of the new underlayment and floor covering as spacers when measuring.

High thresholds often indicate that several layers of flooring have already been installed on top of one another. If you have several layers, it's best to remove them before installing the new floor covering.

Buckling in solid hardwood floors indicates that the boards have loosened from the subfloor. Do not remove hardwood floors. Instead, refasten loose boards by drilling pilot holes and inserting flooring nails or screws. New carpet can be installed right over a well-fastened hardwood floor. New ceramic tile or resilient flooring should be installed over underlayment placed on the hardwood flooring.

Loose tiles may indicate widespread failure of the adhesive. Use a wallboard knife to test tiles. If tiles can be pried up easily in many different areas of the room, plan to remove all of the flooring.

Air bubbles trapped under resilient sheet flooring indicate that the adhesive has failed. The old flooring must be removed before the new covering can be installed.

Cracks in grout joints around ceramic tile are a sign that movement of the floor covering has caused, or has been caused by, deterioration of the adhesive layer. If more than 10% of the tiles are loose, remove the old flooring. Evaluate the condition of the underlayment (see opposite page) to determine if it also must be removed.

Repairing Joists

A severely arched, bulged, cracked, or sagging floor joist can only get worse over time, eventually deforming the floor above it. Correcting a problem joist is an easy repair and makes a big difference in your finished floor. It's best to identify problem joists and fix them before installing your underlayment and new floor covering.

One way to fix joist problems is to fasten a few new joists next to a damaged floor joist in a process called sistering. When installing a new joist, you may need to notch the bottom edge so it can fit over the foundation or beam. If that's the case with your joists, cut the notches in the ends no deeper than ⅛" of the actual depth of the joist.

Tools & Materials ▸

4-ft. level
Reciprocating saw
Hammer
Chisel
Adjustable wrench
Tape measure
Ratchet wrench

3" lag screws
  with washers
Framing lumber
16d common nails
Hardwood shims
Metal jack posts

How to Repair a Bulging Joist

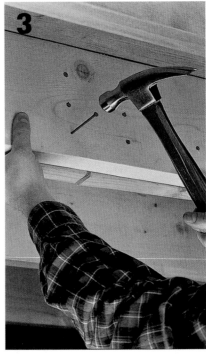

Find the high point of the bulge in the floor using a level. Mark the high point and measure the distance to a reference point that extends through the floor, such as an exterior wall or heating duct.

Use the measurement and reference point from the last step to mark the high point on the joist from below the floor. From the bottom edge of the joist, make a straight cut into the joist just below the high point mark using a reciprocating saw. Make the cut ¾ of the depth of the joist. Allow several weeks for the joist to straighten.

When the joist has settled, reinforce it by centering a board of the same height and at least 6 ft. long next to it. Fasten the board to the joist by driving 12d common nails in staggered pairs about 12" apart. Drive a row of three nails on either side of the cut in the joist.

How to Repair a Cracked or Sagging Joist

Identify the cracked or sagging joist before it causes additional problems. Remove any blocking or bridging above the sill or beam where the sister joist will go.

Place a level on the bottom edge of the joist to determine the amount of sagging that has occurred. Cut a sister joist the same length as the damaged joist. Place it next to the damaged joist with the crown side up. If needed, notch the bottom edge of the sister joint so it fits over the foundation or beam.

Nail two 6-ft. 2 × 4s together to make a cross beam, then place the beam perpendicular to the joists near one end of the joists. Position a jack post under the beam and use a level to make sure it's plumb before raising it.

Raise the jack post by turning the threaded shaft until the cross beam is snug against the joists. Position a second jack post and cross beam at the other end of the joists. Raise the posts until the sister joist is flush with the subfloor. Insert tapered hardwood shims at the ends of the sister joist where it sits on the sill or beam. Tap the shims in place with a hammer and scrap piece of wood until they're snug.

Drill pairs of pilot holes in the sister joist every 12", then insert 3" lag screws with washers in each hole. Cut the blocking or bridging to fit and install it between the joists in its original position.

Eliminating Floor Squeaks

Floors squeak when floorboards rub against each other or against the nails securing them to the subfloor. Hardwood floors squeak if they haven't been nailed properly. Normal changes in wood make some squeaking inevitable, although noisy floors sometimes indicate serious structural problems. If an area of a floor is soft or excessively squeaky, inspect the framing and the foundation supporting the floor.

Whenever possible, fix squeaks from underneath the floor. Joists longer than 8 feet should have X-bridging or solid blocking between each pair to help distribute the weight. If these supports aren't present, install them every 6 feet to stiffen and help silence a noisy floor.

Tools & Materials ▶

Drill	Wood putty
Hammer	Graphite powder
Nail set	Dance-floor wax
Putty knife	Pipe straps
Wood screws	Hardwood shims
Flooring nails	Wood glue

How to Eliminate Floor Squeaks

1

If you can access floor joists from underneath, drive wood screws up through the subfloor to draw hardwood flooring and the subfloor together. Drill pilot holes and make certain the screws aren't long enough to break through the top of the floorboards. Determine the combined thickness of the floor and subfloor by measuring at cutouts for pipes.

2

When you can't reach the floor from underneath, surface-nail the floor boards to the subfloor with ring-shank flooring nails. Drill pilot holes close to the tongue-side edge of the board and drive the nails at a slight angle to increase their holding power. Whenever possible, nail into studs. Countersink the nails with a nail set and fill the holes with tinted wood putty.

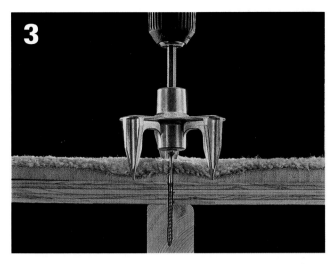

Eliminate squeaks in a carpeted floor by using a special floor fastening device, called a Squeeeeek No More, to drive screws through the subfloor into the joists. The device guides the screw and controls the depth. The screw has a scored shank, so once it's set, you can break the end off just below the surface of the subfloor.

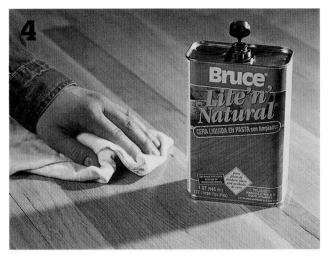

Eliminate squeaks in hardwood floors with graphite powder, talcum powder, powdered soap, mineral oil, or liquid wax. Remove dirt and deposits from joints, using a putty knife. Apply graphite powder, talcum powder, powdered soap, or mineral oil between squeaky boards. Bounce on the boards to work the lubricant into the joints. Clean up excess powder with a damp cloth. Liquid wax is another option, although some floor finishes, such as urethane and varnish, are not compatible with wax, so check with the flooring manufacturer. Use a clean cloth to spread wax over the noisy joints, forcing the wax deep into the joints.

In an unfinished basement or crawl space, copper water pipes are usually hung from floor joists. Listen for pipes rubbing against joists. Loosen or replace wire pipe hangers to silence the noise. Pull the pointed ends of the hanger from the wood, using a hammer or pry bar. Lower the hanger just enough so the pipe isn't touching the joist, making sure the pipe is held firmly so it won't vibrate. Renail the hanger, driving the pointed end straight into the wood.

The boards or sheeting of a subfloor can separate from the joists, creating gaps. Where gaps are severe or appear above several neighboring joists, the framing may need reinforcement, but isolated gapping can usually be remedied with hardwood shims. Apply a small amount of wood glue to the shim and squirt some glue into the gap. Using a hammer, tap the shim into place until it's snug. Shimming too much will widen the gap, so be careful. Allow the glue to dry before walking on the floor.

Replacing Trim Moldings

There's no reason to let damaged trim moldings detract from the appearance of a well-maintained room. With the right tools and a little attention to detail, you can replace or repair them quickly and easily.

Home centers and lumber yards sell many styles of moldings, but they may not stock moldings found in older homes. If you have trouble finding duplicates, check salvage yards in your area. They sometimes carry styles no longer manufactured. You can also try combining several different moldings to duplicate a more elaborate version.

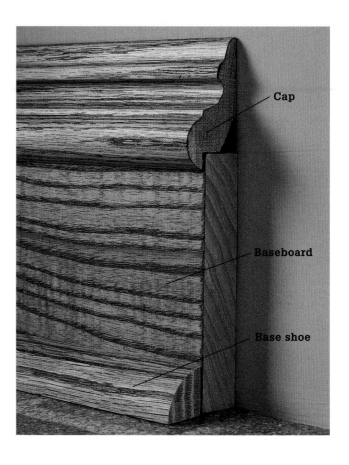

Tools & Materials ▸

Flat pry bars (2)
Coping saw
Miter saw
Drill
Hammer
Nail set

Wood scraps
Replacement moldings
2d, 4d, and 6d
    finish nails
Wood putty

How to Remove Damaged Trim

Even the lightest pressure from a pry bar can damage wallboard or plaster, so use a large, flat scrap of wood to protect the wall. Insert one bar beneath the trim and work the other bar between the baseboard and the wall. Force the pry bars in opposite directions to remove the baseboard.

To remove baseboards without damaging the wall, use leverage rather than force. Pry off the base shoe first, using a flat pry bar. When you feel a few nails pop, move farther along the molding and pry again.

How to Install Baseboards

Start at an inside corner by butting one piece of baseboard securely into the corner. Drill pilot holes, then fasten the baseboard with two 6d finish nails, aligned vertically, at each wall stud. Cut a scrap of baseboard so the ends are perfectly square. Cut the end of the workpiece square. Position the scrap on the back of the workpiece so its back face is flush with the end of the workpiece. Trace the outline of the scrap onto the back of the workpiece.

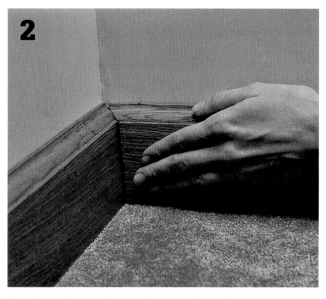

Cut along the outline on the workpiece with a coping saw, keeping the saw perpendicular to the baseboard face. Test-fit the coped end. Recut it, if necessary.

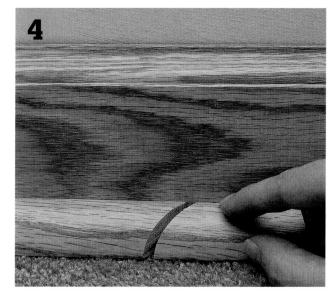

To cut the baseboard to fit at outside corners, mark the end where it meets the outside wall corner. Cut the end at a 45° angle, using a power miter saw. Lock-nail all miter joints by drilling a pilot hole and driving 4d finish nails through each corner.

Install base shoe molding along the bottom of the baseboards. Make miter joints at inside and outside corners, and fasten base shoe with 2d finish nails. Whenever possible, complete a run of molding using one piece. For long spans, join molding pieces by mitering the ends at parallel 45° angles. Set nail heads below the surface using a nail set, and then fill the holes with wood putty.

Repairing Hardwood

A darkened, dingy hardwood floor may only need a thorough cleaning to reveal an attractive, healthy finish. If you have a fairly new or prefinished hardwood floor, check with the manufacturer or flooring installer before applying any cleaning products or wax. Most prefinished hardwood, for example, should not be waxed.

Water and other liquids can penetrate deep into the grain of hardwood floors, leaving dark stains that are sometimes impossible to remove by sanding. Instead, try bleaching the wood with oxalic acid, available in crystal form at home centers or paint stores. When gouges, scratches, and dents aren't bad enough to warrant replacing a floorboard, repair the damaged area with a latex wood patch that matches the color of your floor.

Identify surface finishes using solvents. In an inconspicuous area, rub in different solvents to see if the finish dissolves, softens, or is removed. Denatured alcohol removes shellac, while lacquer thinner removes lacquer. If neither of those work, try nail polish remover containing acetone, which removes varnish but not polyurethane.

Tools & Materials ▸

Vacuum	Hardwood cleaning kit	Latex wood patch	Hammer
Buffing machine	Paste wax	Sandpaper	Caulk gun
Hammer	Rubber gloves	Drill	Spine-shank
Nail set	Oxalic acid	Spade bit	flooring nails
Putty knife	Vinegar	Circular saw	Nail set
Cloths	Wood restorer	Chisel	Wood putty

How to Clean & Renew Hardwood

Vacuum the entire floor. Mix hot water and dishwashing detergent that doesn't contain lye, trisodium phosphate, or ammonia. Working on 3-ft.-square sections, scrub the floor with a brush or nylon scrubbing pad. Wipe up the water and wax with a towel before moving to the next section.

If the water and detergent don't remove the old wax, use a hardwood floor cleaning kit. Use only solvent-type cleaners, as some water-based products can blacken wood. Apply the cleaner following the manufacturer's instructions.

When the floor is clean and dry, apply a high-quality floor wax. Paste wax is more difficult to apply than liquid floor wax, but it lasts much longer. Apply the wax by hand, then polish the floor with a rented buffing machine fitted with synthetic buffing pads.

How to Remove Stains

1

Remove the finish by sanding the stained area with sandpaper. In a disposable cup, dissolve the recommended amount of oxalic acid crystals in water. Wearing rubber gloves, pour the mixture over the stained area, taking care to cover only the darkened wood.

2

Let the liquid stand for one hour. Repeat the application, if necessary. Wash with 2 tablespoons borax dissolved in one pint water to neutralize the acid. Rinse with water, and let the wood dry. Sand the area smooth.

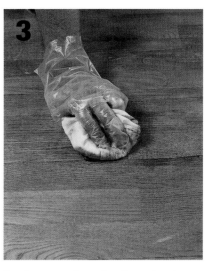

3

Apply several coats of wood restorer until the bleached area matches the finish of the surrounding floor.

How to Patch Scratches & Small Holes

1

Before filling nail holes, make sure the nails are securely set in the wood. Use a hammer and nail set to drive loose nails below the surface. Apply wood patch to the damaged area, using a putty knife. Force the compound into the hole by pressing the knife blade downward until it lies flat on the floor.

2

Scrape excess compound from the edges, and allow the patch to dry completely. Sand the patch flush with the surrounding surface. Using fine-grit sandpaper, sand in the direction of the wood grain.

3

Apply wood restorer to the sanded area until it blends with the rest of the floor.

Replacing a Damaged Floorboard

When solid hardwood floorboards are beyond repair, they need to be carefully cut out and replaced with boards of the same width and thickness. Replace whole boards whenever possible. If a board is long, or if part of its length is inaccessible, draw a cutting line across the face of the board, and tape behind the line to protect the section that will remain.

Tools & Materials ▸

Drill	Replacement boards
Spade bit	Masking tape
Circular saw	Construction
Chisel	adhesive
Hammer	Spiral-shank
Caulk gun	flooring nails
Nail set	Wood putty

How to Replace Damaged Floorboards

Draw a rectangle around the damaged area. Determine the minimal number of boards to be removed. To avoid nails, be sure to draw the line ¾" inside the outermost edge of any joints.

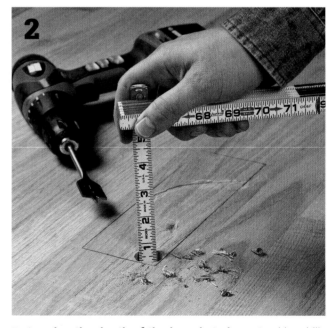

Determine the depth of the boards to be cut. With a drill and ¾"-wide spade bit, slowly drill through a damaged board. Drill until you see the top of the subfloor. Measure the depth. A common depth is ⅝" or ¾". Set your circular saw to this depth.

To prevent boards from chipping, place masking tape or painter's tape along the outside of the pencil lines. To create a wood cutting guide, tack a straight wood strip inside the damaged area (for easy removal, allow nails to slightly stick up). Set back the guide the distance between the saw blade and the guide edge of the circular saw.

Align the circular saw with the wood cutting guide. Turn on the saw. Lower the blade into the cutline. Do not cut the last ¼" of the corners. Remove cutting guide. Repeat with other sides.

Complete the cuts. Use a hammer and sharp chisel to completely loosen the boards from the subfloor. Make sure the chisel's beveled side is facing the damaged area for a clean edge.

Remove split boards. Use a scrap 2 × 4 block for leverage and to protect the floor. With a hammer, tap a pry bar into and under the split board. Most boards pop out easily, but some may require a little pressure. Remove exposed nails with the hammer claw.

(continued)

Use a chisel to remove the 2 remaining strips. Again, make sure the bevel side of the chisel is facing the interior of the damaged area. Set any exposed nails with your nail set.

Cut new boards. Measure the length and width of the area to be replaced. Place the new board on a sawhorse, with the section to be used hanging off the edge. Draw a pencil cutline. With saw blade on waste side of mark, firmly press the saw guide against the edge of a framing square. Measure each board separately.

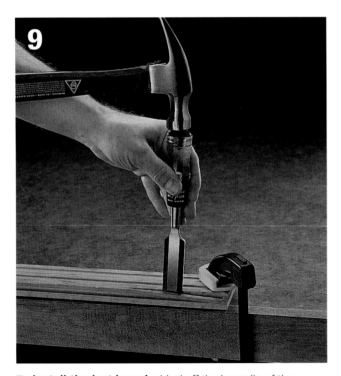

To install the last board, chisel off the lower lip of the groove. Remove the tongue on the end of the board, if necessary. Apply adhesive to the board, and set it in place, tongue first.

Pick a drill bit with a slightly smaller diameter than an 8-penny finish nail, and drill holes at a 45° angle through the corner of the replacement piece's tongue every 3" to 4" along the new board. Hammer a 1½"-long, 8-penny finish nail through the hole into the subfloor. Use a nail set to countersink nails. Repeat until the last board.

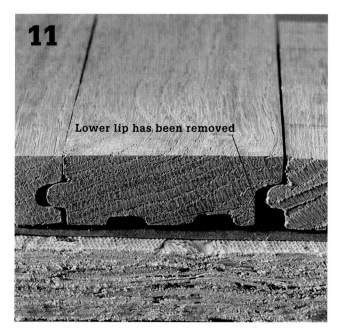

Lay the last board face down onto a protective 2 × 4 and use a sharp chisel to split off the lower lip. This allows it to fit into place.

To install the last board, hook the tongue into the groove of the old floor and then use a soft mallet to tap the groove side down into the previous board installed.

Drill pilot holes angled outward: two side-by-side holes about ½" from the edges of each board, and one hole every 12" along the groove side of each board. Drive 1½"-long, 8-penny finish nails through the holes. Set nails with a nail set. Fill holes with wood putty.

Once the putty is dry, sand the patch smooth with fine-grit sandpaper. Feather-sand neighboring boards. Vacuum and wipe the area with a clean cloth. Apply matching wood stain or restorer, then apply 2 coats of matching finish.

How to Repair Splinters

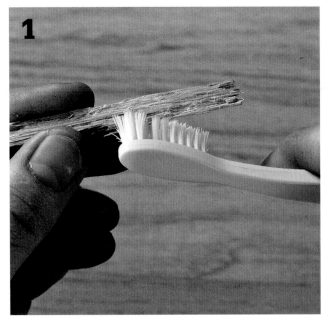

If you still have the splintered piece of wood, but it has been entirely dislodged from the floor, it's a good bet that the hollowed space left by the splinter has collected a lot of dirt and grime. Combine a 1:3 mixture of distilled white vinegar and water in a bucket. Dip an old toothbrush into the solution and use it to clean out the hole left in the floor. While you're at it, wipe down the splinter with the solution, too. Allow the floor and splinter to thoroughly dry.

If the splinter is large, apply wood glue to the hole and splinter. Use a Q-Tip or toothpick to apply small amounts of wood glue under smaller splinters. Soak the Q-Tip in glue; you don't want Q-Tip fuzz sticking out of your floor once the glue dries.

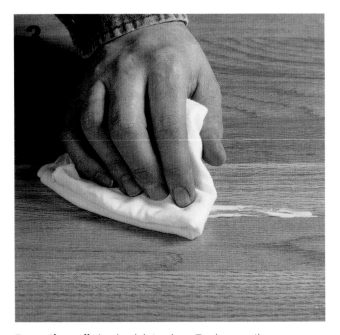

Press the splinter back into place. To clean up the excess glue, use a slightly damp, lint-free cloth. Do not oversoak the cloth with water.

Allow the adhesive to dry. Cover the patch with wax paper and a couple of books. Let the adhesive dry overnight.

How to Patch Small Holes in Wood Floors

Repair small holes with wood putty. Use putty that matches the floor color. Force the compound into the hole with a putty knife. Continue to press the putty in this fashion until the depression in the floor is filled. Scrape excess compound from the area. Use a damp, lint-free cloth while the putty is still wet to smooth the top level with the surrounding floor. Allow to dry.

Sand the area with fine (100- to 120-grit) sandpaper. Sand with the wood grain so the splintered area is flush with the surrounding surface. To better hide the repair, feather sand the area. Wipe up dust with a slightly damp cloth.

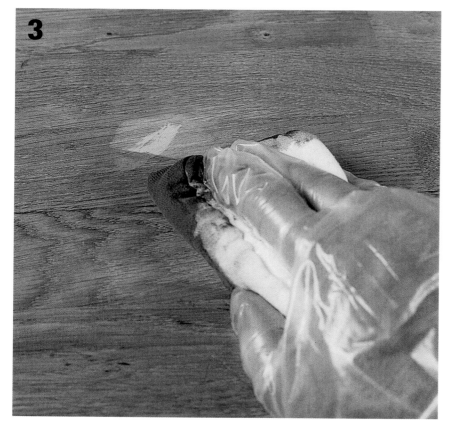

With a clean, lint-free cloth, apply a matching stain (wood sealer or "restorer") to the sanded area. Read the label on the product to make sure it is appropriate for sealing wood floors. Work in the stain until the patched area blends with the rest of the floor. Allow area to completely dry. Apply two coats of finish. Be sure the finish is the same as that which was used on the surrounding floor.

Replacing Sections of Wood Floors

When an interior wall or section of wall has been removed during remodeling, you'll need to patch gaps in the flooring where the wall was located. There are several options for patching floors, depending on your budget and the level of your do-it-yourself skills.

If the existing flooring shows signs of wear, consider replacing the entire flooring surface. Although it can be expensive, an entirely new floor covering will completely hide any gaps in the floor and provide an elegant finishing touch for your remodeling project.

If you choose to patch the existing flooring, be aware that it's difficult to hide patched areas completely, especially if the flooring uses unique patterns or finishes. A creative solution is to intentionally patch the floor with material that contrasts with the surrounding flooring (opposite page).

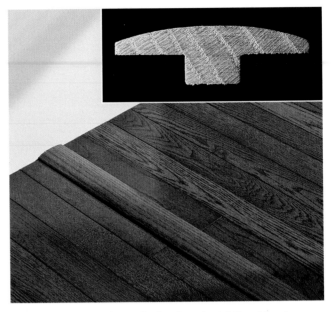

A quick, inexpensive solution is to install T-molding to bridge a gap in a wood strip floor. T-moldings are especially useful when the surrounding boards run parallel to the gap. T-moldings are available in several widths and can be stained to match the flooring.

When patching a wood-strip floor, one option is to remove all of the floor boards that butt against the flooring gap using a pry bar and replace them with boards cut to fit. This may require you to trim the tongues from some tongue-and-groove floorboards. Sand and refinish the entire floor so the new boards match the old.

How to Use Contrasting Flooring Material

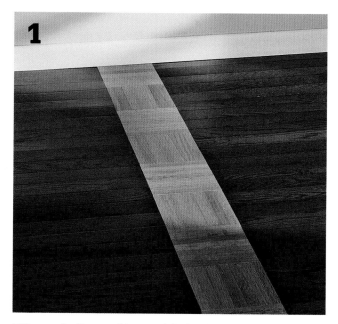

Fill gaps in floors with materials that have a contrasting color and pattern. For wood floors, parquet tiles are an easy and inexpensive choice (above, left). You may need to widen the gap with a circular saw set to the depth of the wood covering to make room for the contrasting tiles. To enhance the effect, cut away a border strip around the room and fill these areas with the same contrasting flooring material (above, right).

Tips for Patching Floors ▸

Build up the subfloor in the patch area, using layers of thin plywood and building paper, so the new surface will be flush with the surrounding flooring. You may need to experiment with different combinations of plywood and paper to find the right thickness.

Make a vinyl or carpet patch by laying the patch material over the old flooring, then cutting through both layers. When the cut strip of old flooring is removed, the new patch will fit tightly in its place. If flooring material is patterned, make sure the patterns are aligned before you cut.

Install a carpet patch using heatactivated carpet tape and a rented seam iron. Original carpet remnants are ideal for patching. New carpet, even of the same brand, style and color, will seldom match the original carpet exactly.

Replacing Laminate Flooring

In the event that you need to replace a Laminate plank, you must first determine how to remove the damaged plank. If you have a glueless "floating" floor it is best to unsnap and remove each plank starting at the wall and moving in until you reach the damaged plank. However, if the damaged plank is far from the wall it is more time-efficient to cut out the damaged plank. Fully-bonded laminate planks have adhesive all along the bottom of the plank and are secured directly to the underlayment. When you remove the damaged plank you run the risk of gouging the subfloor, so we recommend calling in a professional if you find that your laminate planks are completely glued to the subfloor.

Tools & Materials ▸

Circular saw	Chisel
Underlayment	Rubber mallet
½" spacers	Drawbar
Tapping block	Finish nails
Scrap foam	Nail set
Speed square	Strap clamps
Manufacturer's glue	Threshold
Painter's tape	and screws

As indestructible as laminate floors may seem, minor scratches caused by normal day-to-day wear and tear are unavoidable. Whether the damaged plank is close to a wall or in the middle of the floor, this project will show you how to replace it.

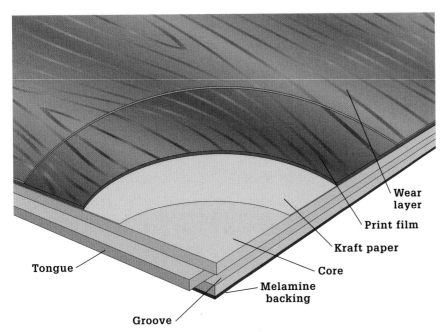

Tongue

Groove

Melamine backing

Core

Kraft paper

Print film

Wear layer

From bottom to top, laminate planks are engineered to resist moisture, scratches, and dents. A melamine base layer protects the inner core layer, which is most often HDF (high-density fiberboard). This is occasionally followed by kraft paper saturated in resins for added protection and durability. The print film is a photographic layer that replicates the look of wood or ceramic. The surface is a highly protective wear layer. The tongue-and-groove planks fit together tightly and may be (according to manufacturer's instructions) glued together for added stability.

How to Replace Laminate Planks

Draw a rectangle in the middle of the damaged board with a 1½" border between the rectangle and factory edges. At each rectangle corner and inside each corner of the plank, use a hammer and nail set to make indentations. At each of these indentations, drill ³⁄₁₆" holes into the plank. Only drill the depth of the plank.

To protect the floor from chipping, place painter's tape along the cutlines. Now, set the circular saw depth to the thickness of the replacement plank. (If you don't have a replacement plank, see page 20, Step 2 to determine the plank thickness.) To plunge cut the damaged plank, turn on the saw and slowly lower the blade into the cutline until the cut guide rests flat on the floor. Push the saw from the center of the line out to each end. Stop ¼" in from each corner. Use a hammer to tap a pry bar or chisel into the cutlines. Lift and remove the middle section. Place a sharp chisel between the two drill holes in each corner and strike with a hammer to complete each corner cut. Vacuum.

To remove the remaining outer edges of the damaged plank, place a scrap 2 × 4 wood block along the outside of one long cut and use it for leverage to push a pry bar under the flooring. Insert a second pry bar beneath the existing floor (directly under the joint of the adjacent plank) and use a pliers to grab the 1½" border strip in front of the pry bar. Press downward until a gap appears at the joint. Remove the border piece. Remove the opposite strip and then the two short end pieces in the same manner.

Place a scrap of cardboard in the opening to protect the underlayment foam while you remove all of the old glue from the factory edges with a chisel. Vacuum up the wood and glue flakes.

(continued)

To remove the tongues on one long and one short end, lay the replacement plank face down onto a protective scrap of plywood (or 2 × 4). Clamp a straight cutting guide to the replacement plank so the distance from the guide causes the bit to align with the tongue and trim it off. Pressing the router against the cutting guide, slowly move along the entire edge of the replacement plank to remove the tongue. Clean the edges with sandpaper.

Dry-fit the grooves on the replacement board into the tongues of the surrounding boards and press into place. If the board fits snugly in between the surrounding boards, pry the plank up with a manufacturer suction cup. If the plank does not sit flush with the rest of the floor, check to make sure you routered the edges off evenly. Sand any rough edges that should have been completely removed and try to fit the plank again.

Set the replacement plank by applying laminate glue to the removed edges of the replacement plank and into the grooves of the existing planks. Firmly press the plank into place.

Clean up glue with a damp towel. Place a strip of wax paper over the new plank and evenly distribute some books on the wax paper. Allow the adhesive to dry for 12 to 24 hours.

Variation: Floating Floors ▸

If your damaged plank is close to the wall and the laminate floor is glueless, follow these steps:

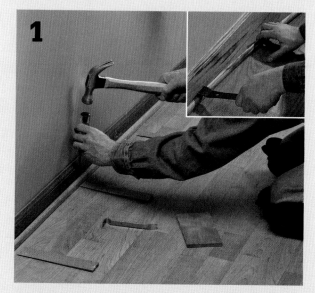

To remove shoe molding, wedge a chisel between the shoe molding and baseboards to create a gap and maintain that gap with wood shims. Continue this process every 6" along the wall. Locate the nails that are holding the shoe to the baseboard and use a pry bar at those locations to gently pull the shoe away from the baseboard (inset).

To remove the first plank closest to the wall, use a pry bar to lift it just enough to get your hands under it and then slowly lift up and away from the adjacent plank. Continue to remove the planks that are between the shoe molding and the damaged plank with your hands. Finally, remove the damaged plank.

Snap in a new replacement plank and then continue to replace the rest of the boards until you reach the wall in the same manner.

Lay the shoe molding back in place along the wall. Using a nail set and hammer, countersink finish nails into the top of the shoe molding every 6 to 12" along the wall. Fill the holes with wood putty.

How to Replace a Parquet Tile

For the initial plunge cut, set the depth of a circular saw to the thickness of the parquet tile. (If you don't know the thickness, see Here's How, this page.) Hold the saw so that only the top of the guide plate touches the surface of the wood; the blade, when lowered, will cut into the damaged wood block. Turn on the saw. Slowly lower the blade into the cutting line until the saw's cut guide rests flat on the floor. Make a series of four plunge cuts into the damaged tile—1" inside each edge—to make a square cutout.

Use a hammer and a sharp, 1"-wide chisel to chip out the cut pieces in the center of the damaged tile. When you're removing the pieces around the edge of the cutout, make sure the beveled side of the chisel is facing the damaged area so that a clean flat edge is left along the adjacent tiles. If you need some elbow grease to remove the center pieces, use a hammer to tap a pry bar under the damaged cutout and then lean it over a scrap of 2 × 4 for leverage.

Here's How ▶

Use a putty knife to scrape away the remaining adhesive on the underlayment so that the new tile will sit flush with the surrounding floor.

If you don't have a replacement tile, and therefore don't know how thick the tiles are, you can determine the thickness by slowly drilling through the damaged tile with a ¾" hole saw or ¾"-wide spade drill bit. Very slowly drill through the damaged tile. Drill only a bit at a time until you bore all the way through the flooring and can see the top of the subfloor, then you can measure the depth of the board with a measuring tape. The depth will range from 5⁄16" to ¾" thick.

Remove lower lip of groove in replacement tile. If the replacement wood block has a tongue-and-groove structure, remove the lower lip of the groove so that you can press it into place. Lay the replacement block face down onto a protective scrap of wood and use a sharp chisel to split off the lower lip. Lightly sand the edges.

Apply adhesive. Use a ⅛" notched trowel to spread a thin layer of floor adhesive onto the back of the replacement tile and the floor. The ridges should be about ⅛" high on the replacement tile. The adhesive on the floor is only to make sure the tiles are completely covered on all edges. You want a secure bond, but you do not want adhesive to squeeze up between the tiles.

Warning ▶

Whenever cutting or drilling wood, be sure to wear protective eyewear. Eyeglasses made of safety glass will suffice as protective eyewear.

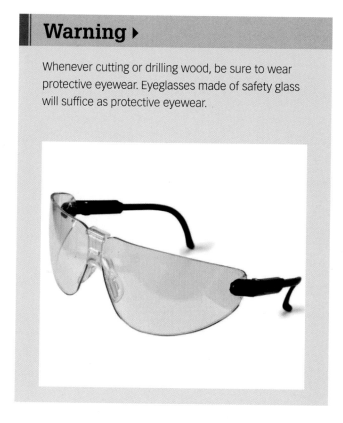

Install replacement block. Hook the tongue of the replacement block into the groove of an adjacent block and then use a soft mallet to gently tap the groove side of the new block down into place. If adhesive happens to squeeze up onto any of the block, clean it immediately with the cleaning solvent recommended by the adhesive manufacturer. You're done!

Repairing Vinyl

Repair methods for vinyl flooring depend on the type of floor as well as the type of damage. With sheet vinyl, you can fuse the surface or patch in new material. With vinyl tile, it's best to replace the damaged tiles.

Small cuts and scratches can be fused permanently and nearly invisibly with liquid seam sealer, a clear compound that's available wherever vinyl flooring is sold. For tears or burns, the damaged area can be patched. If necessary, remove vinyl from a hidden area, such an the inside of a closet or under an appliance, to use as patch material.

When vinyl flooring is badly worn or the damage is widespread, the only answer is complete replacement. Although it's possible to add layers of flooring in some situations, evaluate the options carefully. Be aware that the backing of older vinyl tiles made of asphalt may contain asbestos fibers. Consult a professional for their removal.

Tools & Materials ▸

Carpenter's square	Masking tape
Utility knife	Scrap of
Putty knife	matching flooring
Heat gun	Mineral spirits
J-roller	Floor covering adhesive
Notched trowel	Wax paper
Marker	Liquid seam sealer

How to Patch Sheet Vinyl

Measure the width and length of the damaged area. Place the new flooring remnant on a surface you don't mind making some cuts on—like a scrap of plywood. Use a carpenter's square for cutting guidance. Make sure your cutting size is a bit larger than the damaged area.

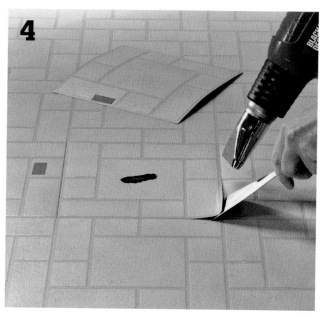

Lay the patch over the damaged area, matching pattern lines. Secure the patch with duct tape. Using a carpenter's square as a cutting guide, cut through the new vinyl (on top) and the old vinyl (on bottom). Press firmly with the knife to cut both layers.

Use tape to mark one edge of the new patch with the corresponding edge of the old flooring as placement marks. Remove the tape around the perimeter of the patch and lift up.

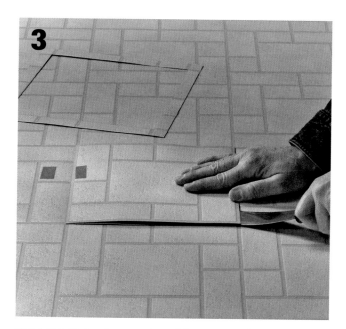

Soften the underlying adhesive with an electric heat gun and remove the damaged section of floor. Work from edges in. When the tile is loosened, insert a putty knife and pry up the damaged area.

(continued)

Scrape off the remaining adhesive with a putty knife or chisel. Work from the edges to the center. Dab mineral spirits (or Goo Gone) or spritz warm water on the floor to dissolve leftover goop, taking care not to use too much; you don't want to loosen the surrounding flooring. Use a razor-edged scraper (flooring scraper) to scrape to the bare wood underlayment.

Apply adhesive to the patch, using a notched trowel (with ⅛" V-shaped notches) held at a 45° angle to the back of the new vinyl patch.

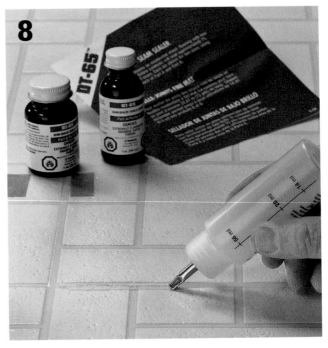

Set one edge of the patch in place. Lower the patch onto the underlayment. Press into place. Apply pressure with a J-roller or rolling pin to create a solid bond. Start at the center and work toward the edges, working out air bubbles. Wipe up adhesive that oozes out the sides with a clean, damp cloth or sponge.

Let the adhesive dry overnight. Use a soft cloth dipped in lacquer thinner to clean the area. Mix the seam sealer according to the manufacturer's directions. Use an applicator bottle to apply a thin bead of sealer onto the cutlines.

How to Replace Resilient Tile

Use an electric heat gun to warm the damaged tile and soften the underlying adhesive. Keep the heat source moving so you don't melt the tile. When an edge of the tile begins to curl, insert a putty knife to pry up the loose edge until you can remove the tile. *Note: If you can clearly see the seam between tiles, first score around the tile with a utility knife. This prevents other tiles from lifting.*

Scrape away remaining adhesive with a putty knife or, for stubborn spots, a floor scraper. Work from the edges to the center so that you don't accidentally scrape up the adjacent tiles. Use mineral spirits to dissolve leftover goop. Take care not to allow the mineral spirits to soak into the floor under adjacent tiles. Vacuum up dust, dirt, and adhesive. Wipe clean.

When the floor is dry, use a notched trowel—with ⅛" V-shaped notches—held at a 45° angle to apply a thin, even layer of vinyl tile adhesive onto the underlayment. *Note: Only follow this step if you have dry-back tiles.*

Set one edge of the tile in place. Lower the tile onto the underlayment and then press it into place. Apply pressure with a J-roller to create a solid bond, starting at the center and working toward the edge to work out air bubbles. If adhesive oozes out the sides, wipe it up with a damp cloth or sponge. Cover the tile with wax paper and some books, and let the adhesive dry for 24 hours.

Repairing Ceramic Tile Floors

Although ceramic tile is one of the hardest floor coverings, problems can occur. Tiles sometimes become damaged and need to be replaced. Usually, this is simply a matter of removing and replacing individual tiles. However, major cracks in grout joints indicate that floor movement has caused the adhesive layer beneath the tile to deteriorate. In this case, the adhesive layer must be replaced in order to create a permanent repair.

Any time you remove tile, check the underlayment. If it's no longer smooth, solid, and level, repair or replace it before replacing the tile. When removing grout or damaged tiles, be careful not to damage surrounding tiles. Always wear eye protection when working with a hammer and chisel. Any time you are doing a major tile installation, make sure to save extra tiles. This way, you will have materials on hand when repairs become necessary.

How to Replace Ceramic Tiles

With a carbide-tipped grout saw, apply firm but gentle pressure across the grout until you expose the unglazed edges of the tile. Do not scratch the glazed tile surface. If the grout is stubborn, use a hammer and screwdriver to first tap the tile (Step 2).

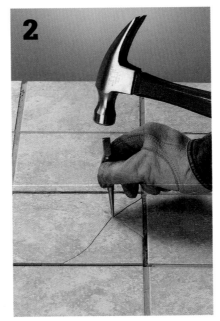

If the tile is not already cracked, use a hammer to puncture the tile by tapping a nail set or center punch into it. Alternatively, if the tile is significantly cracked, use a chisel to pry up the tile.

Insert a chisel into one of the cracks and gently tap the tile. Start at the center and chip outward so you don't damage the adjacent tiles. Be aware that cement board looks a lot like mortar when you're chiseling. Remove and discard the broken pieces.

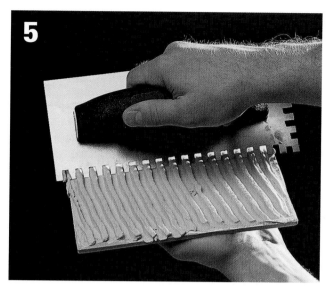

Use a putty knife to scrape away old thinset adhesive; use a chisel for poured mortar installation. If the underlayment is covered with metal lath, you won't be able to get the area smooth; just clean it out the best you can. Once the adhesive is scraped from the underlayment, smooth the rough areas with sandpaper. If there are gouges in the underlayment, fill them with epoxy-based thinset mortar (for cementboard) or a floor-leveling compound (for plywood). Allow the area to dry completely.

Use a ¼" notched trowel to apply thinset adhesive to the back of the replacement tile. Set the tile down into the space, and use plastic spacers around the tile to make sure it is centered within the opening.

Set the tile in position and press down until it is even with the adjacent tiles. Twist it a bit to get it to sit down in the mortar. Use a mallet or hammer and a block of wood covered with cloth or a carpet scrap (a "beater block") to lightly tap on the tile, setting it into the adhesive. Use a level or other straight surface to make sure the tile is level with the surrounding tiles. If necessary, continue to tap the tile until it's flush with the rest of the surrounding tiles.

Remove the spacers with needlenose pliers. Get the mortar or thinset adhesive out of the grout joints with a small screwdriver and a cloth. Also, wipe away any adhesive from the surface of the tiles, using a wet sponge. Let the area dry for 24 hours (or according to the manufacturer's recommendations).

Use a putty knife to apply grout to the joints. Fill in low spots by applying and smoothing extra grout with your finger. Use the round edge of a toothbrush handle to create a concave grout line, if desired. You must now grout the joint.

Repairing Carpet

Burns and stains are the most common carpeting problems. You can clip away the burned fibers of superficial burns using small scissors. Deeper burns and indelible stains require patching by cutting away and replacing the damaged area.

Another common problem, addressed on the opposite page, is carpet seams or edges that have come loose. You can rent the tools necessary for fixing this problem.

Tools & Materials ▶

Cookie-cutter tool
Knee kicker
4" wallboard knife
Utility knife
Seam iron
Replacement
  carpeting

Double-face
  carpet tape
Seam adhesive
Heat-activated
  seam tape
Boards
Weights

How to Repair Spot Damage

1

Remove extensive damage or stains with a "cookie-cutter" tool, available at carpeting stores. Press the cutter down over the damaged area and twist it to cut away the carpet.

2

Using the cookie-cutter tool again, cut a replacement patch from scrap carpeting. Insert double-face carpet tape under the cutout, positioning the tape so it overlaps the patch seams.

3

Press the patch into place. Make sure the direction of the nap or pattern matches the existing carpet. To seal the seam and prevent unraveling, apply seam adhesive to the edges of the patch.

How to Restretch Loose Carpet

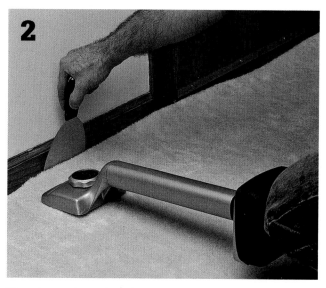

Adjust the knob on the head of the knee kicker so the prongs grab the carpet backing without penetrating through the padding. Starting from a corner or near a point where the carpet is firmly attached, press the knee kicker head into the carpet, about 2" from the wall.

Thrust your knee into the cushion of the knee kicker to force the carpet toward the wall. Tuck the carpet edge into the space between the wood strip and the baseboard using a 4" wallboard knife. If the carpet is still loose, trim the edge with a utility knife and stretch it again.

How to Glue Loose Seams

Remove the old tape from under the carpet seam. Cut a strip of new seam tape and place it under the carpet so it's centered along the seam with the adhesive facing up. Plug in the seam iron and let it heat up.

Pull up both edges of the carpet and set the hot iron squarely onto the tape. Wait about 30 seconds for the glue to melt. Move the iron about 12" farther along the seam. Quickly press the edges of the carpet together into the melted glue behind the iron. Separate the pile to make sure no fibers are stuck in the glue and the seam is tight. Place weighted boards over the seam to keep it flat while the glue sets. Remember, you have only 30 seconds to repeat the process.

How to Patch Major Carpet Damage

Use a utility knife to cut four strips from a carpet remnant, each a little wider and longer than the cuts you plan to make around the damaged part of your carpet. Most wall-to-wall carpet is installed under tension; so to relieve that tension, set the knee kicker 6" to 1 ft. from the area to be cut out and nudge it forward (toward the patch area). If you create a hump in the carpet, you've pushed too hard and need to back off. Now place one of the strips upside down in front of the knee kicker and tack it to the floor at 2" to 4" intervals. Repeat the same process on the other three sides.

Use a marker to draw arrows on tape. Fan the carpet with your hand to see which direction the fibers are woven, and then use the pieces of tape to mark that direction on both the carpet surrounding the damaged area and the remnant you intend to use as a patch. Place a carpet remnant on plywood and cut out a carpet patch slightly larger than the damaged section, using a utility knife. As you cut, use a Phillips screwdriver to push carpet tufts or loops away from the cutting line. Trim loose pile, and then place the patch right side up over the damaged area.

Tool Tip ▶

Knee kickers have teeth that grab the carpet backing. These teeth should be set to grab the backing without grabbing the padding. There is an adjustable knob to do this. You can tell if the knee kicker is grabbing the padding by the increased pressure needed to move it forward. To release the tension just before a damaged area of carpet you intend to patch, place the feet on the floor and use your knee to press it toward the damaged area.

Tack one edge of the patch through the damaged carpet and into the floor, making sure the patch covers the entire damaged area. Use a utility knife to cut out the damaged carpet, following the border of the new patch as a template. If you cut into the carpet padding, use duct tape to mend it. Remove the patch and the damaged carpet square.

Cut four lengths of carpet seam tape, each about 1" longer than an edge of the cut out area, using a utility knife or scissors. Cover half of each strip with a thin layer of seam adhesive and then slip the coated edge of each strip, sticky side up, along the underside edges of the original carpet. Apply more adhesive to the exposed half of tape, and use enough adhesive to fill in the tape weave.

Line up your arrows and press the patch into place. Take care not to press too much, because glue that squeezes up onto the newly laid carpet creates a mess. Use an awl to free tufts or loops of pile crushed in the seam. Lightly brush the pile of the patch to make it blend with the surrounding carpet. Leave the patch undisturbed for 24 hours. Check the drying time on the adhesive used and wait at least this long before removing the carpet tacks.

What If . . . ▶

If you have cushion-backed, fully-bonded carpet, you can follow the instructions above to make a large patch, except:

1. You won't need a knee kicker.
2. You don't need to nail outline strips around the patch area.
3. Use a putty knife to scrape away any dried cement from the hole you make. Some glues may require heat or chemical solvents to effectively remove them.
4. Apply multi-purpose flooring adhesive to the floor with a ³⁄₃₂" trowel.
5. Instead of seam tape, just use a thin bead of cushion-back seam adhesive along the perimeter of the hole.

Sealing Interior Concrete Floors

Concrete is a versatile building material. Most people are accustomed to thinking of concrete primarily as a utilitarian substance, but it can also mimic a variety of flooring types and be a colorful and beautiful addition to any room.

Whether your concrete floor is a practical surface for the garage or an artistic statement of personal style in your dining room, it should be sealed. Concrete is a hard and durable building material, but it is also porous. Consequently, concrete floors are susceptible to staining. Many stains can be removed with the proper cleaner, but sealing and painting prevents oil, grease, and other stains from penetrating the surface in the first place; thus, cleanup is considerably easier.

Prepare the concrete for sealer application by acid etching. Etching opens the pores in concrete surfaces, allowing sealers to bond with it. All smooth or dense concrete surfaces, such as garage floors, should be etched before applying stain. The surface should feel gritty, like 120-grit sandpaper, and allow water to penetrate it. If you're not sure whether your floor needs to be etched or not, it's better to etch. If you don't etch when it is needed, you will have to remove the sealer residue before trying again.

Tools & Materials ▸

Garden hose
  or pressure washer
  (for outdoors
  and garages only)
Stiff bristle broom
Acid-tolerant bucket
Sprinkling can
  or acid-tolerant
  pump spray

4-in.-wide synthetic
  bristle paint brush
Paint tray
Soft-woven roller cover
  with ½" nap
Long-handle
  paint roller
Wet/dry shop vacuum

Long pants and
  long-sleeve shirt
Rubber boots
Rubber gloves
Safety goggles
Chlorine respirator
Acid etcher

Alkaline-base
  neutralizer
  (ammonia,
  gardener's lime,
  baking soda,
  or Simple Green
  cleaning solution)
Concrete sealer

Tips for Acid Etching Concrete Floors

A variety of acid etching products is available: Citric acid is a biodegradable acid that does not produce chlorine fumes. It is the safest etcher and the easiest to use, but it may not be strong enough for some very smooth concretes. Sulfamic acid is less aggressive than phosphoric acid or muriatic acid, and it is perhaps the best compromise between strength of solution and safety. Phosphoric acid is a stronger and more noxious acid than the previous two, but it is considerably less dangerous than muriatic acid. It is currently the most popular etching choice. Muriatic acid (hydrochloric acid) is an extremely dangerous acid that quickly reacts and creates very strong fumes. This is an etching solution of last resort. It should only be used by professionals or by the most serious DIYers. Never add water to acid—only add acid to water.

Acids of any kind are dangerous. Use caution when working with acid etches; it is critical that there be adequate ventilation and that you wear protective clothing, including: safety goggles, rubber gloves, rubber boots, long pants and a long-sleeve shirt. In addition, wear a chlorine respirator—the reaction of any base and acid can release chlorine or hydrogen gas.

Even after degreasing a concrete floor, residual grease or oils can create serious adhesion problems for coatings of sealant or paint. To check whether your floor has been adequately cleaned, pour a glass of water on to the floor. If it is ready for sealing, the water will soak into the surface quickly and evenly. If the water beads, clean the floor again.

How to Acid Etch a Concrete Floor

Clean and prepare the surface by first sweeping up all debris. Next, remove all surface muck: mud, wax, and grease. Finally, remove existing paints or coatings.

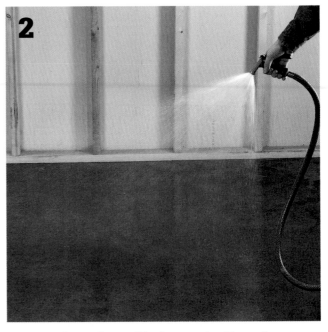

Saturate the surface with clean water. The surface needs to be wet before acid etching. Use this opportunity to check for any areas where water beads up. If water beads on the surface, contaminants still need to be cleaned off with a suitable cleaner or chemical stripper.

Test your acid-tolerant pump sprayer with water to make sure it releases a wide, even mist. Once you have the spray nozzle set, check the manufacturer's instructions for the etching solution and fill the pump sprayer with the recommended amount of water.

Add the acid etching contents to the water in the acid-tolerant pump sprayer (or sprinkling can). Follow the directions (and mixing proportions) specified by the manufacturer. Use caution.

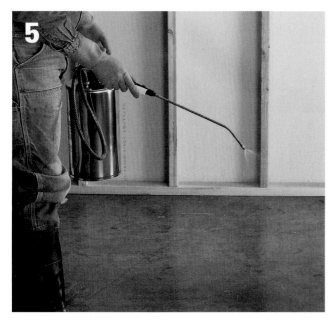

Apply the acid solution. Using the sprinkling can or acid-tolerant pump spray unit, evenly apply the diluted acid solution over the concrete floor. Do not allow acid solution to dry at any time during the etching and cleaning process. Etch small areas at a time, 10 × 10 ft. or smaller. If there is a slope, begin on the low side of the slope and work upward.

Use a stiff bristle broom or scrubber to work the acid solution into the concrete. Let the acid sit for 5–10 minutes, or as indicated by the manufacturer's directions. A mild foaming action indicates that the product is working. If no bubbling or fizzing occurs, stop the process and re-clean the surface thoroughly.

When the fizzing stops, the acid has finished reacting with the alkaline concrete surface. Neutralize any remaining acid by adding a gallon of water to a 5-gallon bucket and then stirring in an alkaline-base neutralizer (options include 1 cup ammonia, 4 cups gardener's lime, a full box of baking soda, or 4 oz. of "Simple Green" cleaning solution).

Use a stiff bristle broom to distribute the neutralizing solution over the entire floor area. Sweep the water around until the fizzing stops and then spray the surface with a hose to rinse it.

(continued)

Use a wet-dry shop vacuum to clean up the rinse water. Although the acid is neutralized, it's a good idea to check your local regulations regarding proper disposal of the neutralized spent acid.

When the floor dries, check for residue by rubbing a dark cloth over a small area of concrete. If any white residue appears, continue the rinsing process. Check for residue again. An inadequate acid rinse is even worse than not acid etching at all when it's time to add the sealant.

If you have any leftover acid you can make it safe for your disposal system by mixing more alkaline solution in the 5-gallon bucket and carefully pouring the acid from the spray unit into the bucket until all of the fizzing stops.

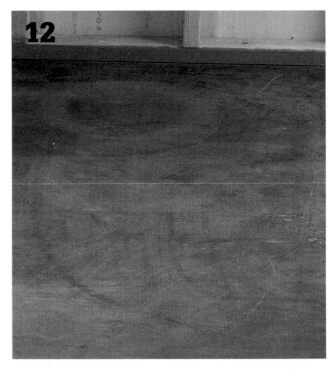

Let the concrete dry for at least 24 hours and sweep it thoroughly. The concrete should now have the texture of 120-grit sandpaper and be able to accept concrete sealant. Mask any exposed sill plates or base trim before sealing.

How to Seal a Concrete Floor

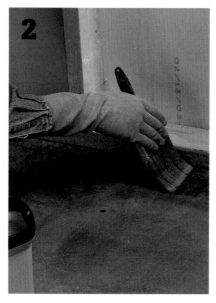

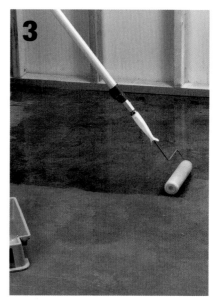

Etch, clean, and dry concrete.
Mix the sealer in a bucket with a stir stick. Lay painter's tape down for a testing patch. Apply sealer to this area and allow to dry to ensure desired appearance. *Note: Because concrete sealers tend to make the surface slick when wet, add an anti-skid additive to aid with traction, especially on stairs.*

Use wide painter's tape to protect walls and then, using a good quality 4"-wide synthetic bristle paintbrush, coat the perimeter with sealer.

Use a long-handled paint roller with a ½" nap to apply an even coat to the rest of the surface. Do small sections at a time (about 2 × 3 feet). Work in one orientation. Avoid lap marks by always maintaining a wet edge. Do not work the area once the coating has partially dried; this could cause it to lift from the surface. Allow surface to dry according to the manufacturer's instructions, usually 8 to 12 hours.

After the first coat has dried, apply the second coat at an orientation 90° from the first coat.

Clean tools according to manufacturer's directions.

Repairing Wallboard

Patching holes and concealing popped nails are common wallboard repairs. Small holes can be filled directly, but larger patches must be supported with some kind of backing, such as plywood. To repair holes left by nails or screws, dimple the hole slightly with the handle of a utility knife or wallboard knife and fill it with spackle or joint compound.

Use joint tape anywhere the wallboard's face paper or joint tape has torn or peeled away. Always cut away any loose wallboard material, face paper, or joint tape from the damaged area, trimming back to solid wallboard material.

All wallboard repairs require three coats of joint compound, just like in new installations. Lightly sand your repairs before painting, or adding texture.

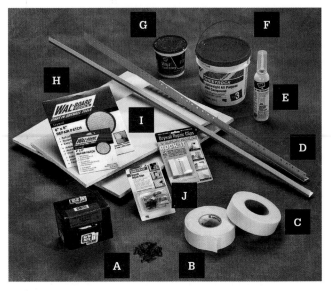

Most wallboard problems can be remedied with basic wallboard materials and specialty materials: (A) wallboard screws; (B) paper joint tape; (C) self-adhesive fiberglass mesh tape; (D) corner bead; (E) paintable latex or silicone caulk; (F) all-purpose joint compound; (G) lightweight spackling compound; (H) wallboard repair patches; (I) scraps of wallboard; (J) and wallboard repair clips.

Tools & Materials ▸

Drill or screwgun	Wallboard saw	All-purpose	Paper joint tape
Hammer	Rasp	joint compound	Self-adhesive fiberglass
Utility knife	Hacksaw	Lightweight spackle	mesh joint tape
Wallboard knives	Fine metal file	150-grit sandpaper	Wallboard repair patch
Framing square	1¼" wallboard screws	Wood scraps	Wallboard repair clips

To repair a popped nail, drive a wallboard screw 2" above or below the nail, so it pulls the panel tight to the framing. Scrape away loose paint or compound, then drive the popped nail ¹⁄₁₆" below the surface. Apply three coats of joint compound to cover the holes.

If wallboard is dented, without cracks or tears in the face paper, just fill the hole with lightweight spackling or all-purpose joint compound, let it dry, and sand it smooth.

How to Repair Cracks & Gashes

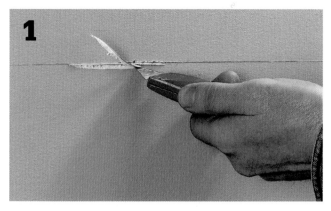

Use a utility knife to cut away loose wallboard or face paper and widen the crack into a "V"; the notch will help hold the joint compound.

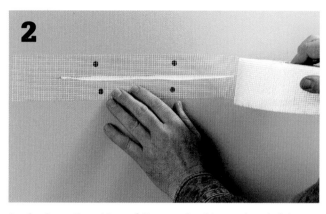

Push along the sides of the crack with your hand. If the wallboard moves, secure the panel with 1¼" wallboard screws driven into the nearest framing members. Cover the crack and screws with self-adhesive mesh tape.

Cover the tape with compound, lightly forcing it into the mesh, then smooth it off, leaving just enough to conceal the tape. Add two more coats, in successively broader and thinner coats to blend the patch into the surrounding area.

For cracks at corners or ceilings, cut through the existing seam and cut away any loose wallboard material or tape, then apply a new length of tape or inside-corner bead and two coats of joint compound.

Variation: For small cracks at corners, apply a thin bead of paintable latex or silicone caulk over the crack, then use your finger to smooth the caulk into the corner.

How to Patch Small Holes in Wallboard

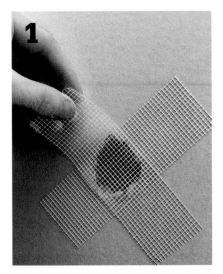

Trim away any broken wallboard, face paper, or joint tape around the hole, using a utility knife. Cover the hole with crossed strips of self-adhesive mesh tape.

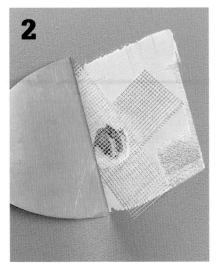

Cover the tape with all-purpose joint compound, lightly forcing it into the mesh, then smooth it off, leaving just enough to conceal the tape.

Add two more coats of compound in successively broader and thinner coats to blend the patch into the surrounding area. Use a wallboard wet sander to smooth the repair area.

Other Options for Patching Small Holes in Wallboard

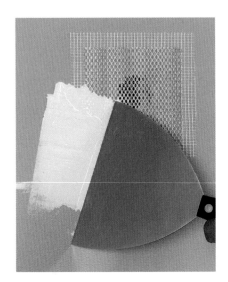

Wallboard repair patches: Cover the damaged area with the self-adhesive patch; the thin metal plate provides support and the fiberglass mesh helps hold the joint compound.

Beveled wallboard patch: Bevel the edges of the hole with a wallboard saw, then cut a wallboard patch to fit. Trim the beveled patch until it fits tight and flush with the panel surface. Apply plenty of compound to the beveled edges, then push the patch into the hole. Finish with paper tape and three coats of compound.

Wallboard paper-flange patch: Cut a wallboard patch a couple inches larger than the hole. Mark the hole on the backside of the patch, then score and snap along the lines. Remove the waste material, keeping the face paper "flange" intact. Apply compound around the hole, insert the patch, and embed the flange into the compound. Finish with two additional coats.

How to Patch Large Holes in Wallboard

  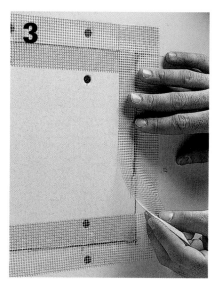

Outline the damaged area, using a framing square. (Cutting four right angles makes it easier to measure and cut the patch.) Use a drywall saw to cut along the outline.

Cut plywood or lumber backer strips a few inches longer than the height of the cutout. Fasten the strips to the back side of the drywall, using 1¼" drywall screws.

Cut a drywall patch ⅛" smaller than the cutout dimensions, and fasten it to the backer strips with screws. Apply mesh joint tape over the seams. Finish the seams with three coats of compound.

How to Patch Large Holes with Repair Clips

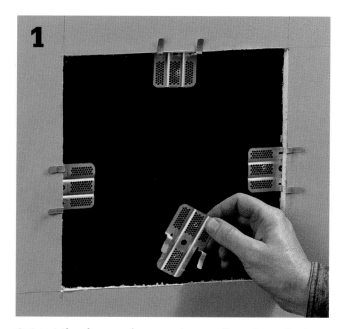 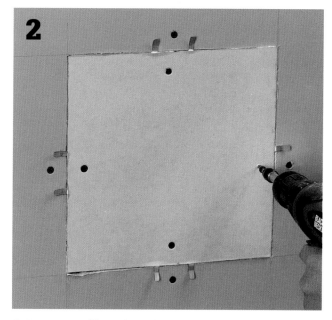

Cut out the damaged area, using a wallboard saw. Center one repair clip on each edge of the hole. Using the provided wallboard screws, drive one screw through the wall and into the clips; position the screws from the edge and centered between the clip's tabs.

Cut a new wallboard patch to fit in the hole. Fasten the patch to the clips, placing wallboard screws adjacent to the previous screw locations and ¾" from the edge. Remove the tabs from the clips, then finish the joints with tape and three coats of compound.

How to Patch Over a Removed Door or Window

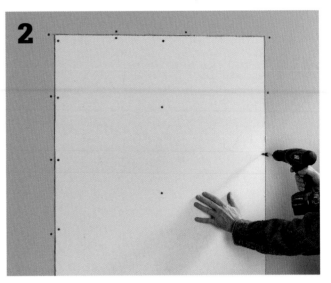

Frame the opening with studs spaced 16" O.C. and partially beneath the existing wallboard—the new joints should break at the center of framing. Secure the existing wallboard to the framing with screws driven every 12" around the perimeter. If the wall is insulated, fill the stud cavity with insulation.

Using wallboard the same thickness as the existing panel, cut the patch piece about ¼" shorter than the opening. Position the patch against the framing so there is a ⅛" joint around the perimeter, and fasten in place with wallboard screws every 12". Finish the butt joints with paper tape and three coats of compound.

How to Repair Metal Corner Bead

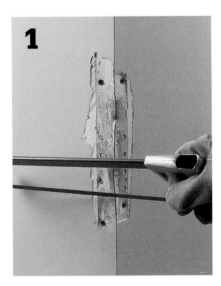

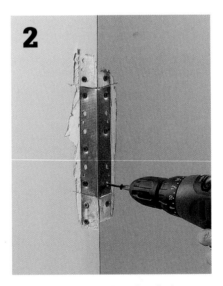

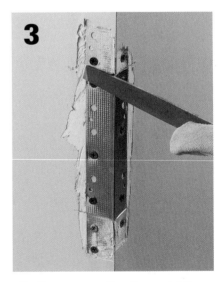

Secure the bead above and below the damaged area with 1¼" wallboard screws. To remove the damaged section, cut through the spine and then the flanges, using a hacksaw held parallel to the floor. Remove the damaged section, and scrape away any loose wallboard and compound.

Cut a new corner bead to fit the opening exactly, then align the spine perfectly with the existing piece and secure with wallboard screws driven ¼" from the flange edge; alternate sides with each screw to keep the piece straight.

File the seams with a fine metal file to ensure a smooth transition between pieces. If you can't easily smooth the seams, cut a new replacement piece and start over. Hide the repair with three coats of wallboard compound.

Repairing Plaster

Plaster walls are created by building up layers of plaster to form a hard, durable wall surface. Behind the plaster itself is a gridlike layer of wood, metal, or rock lath that holds the plaster in place. Keys, formed when the base plaster is squeezed through the lath, hold the dried plaster to the ceiling or walls.

Before you begin any plaster repair, make sure the surrounding area is in good shape. If the lath is deteriorated or the plaster in the damaged area is soft, call a professional.

Use a latex bonding liquid to ensure a good bond and a tight, crack-free patch. Bonding liquid also eliminates the need to wet the plaster and lath to prevent premature drying and shrinkage, which could ruin the repair.

Tools & Materials ▸

Wallboard knives
Paintbrush
Utility knife
Lightweight spackle
All-purpose
   joint compound

Patching plaster
Fiberglass mesh tape
Latex bonding liquid
150-grit sandpaper
Paint

Spackle is used to conceal cracks, gashes, and small holes in plaster. Some new spackling compounds start out pink and dry white so you can see when they're ready to be sanded and painted. Use lightweight spackle for low-shrinkage and one-application fills.

How to Fill Dents & Small Holes in Plaster

1

Scrape or sand away any loose plaster or peeling paint to establish a solid base for the new plaster.

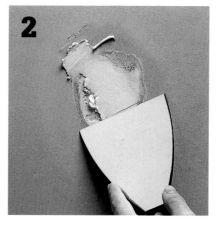

2

Fill the hole with lightweight spackle. Apply the spackle with the smallest knife that will span the damaged area. Let the spackle dry, following the manufacturer's instructions.

3

Sand the patch lightly with 150-grit production sandpaper. Wipe the dust away with a clean cloth, then prime and paint the area, feathering the paint to blend the edges.

How to Patch Large Holes in Plaster

Sand or scrape any texture or loose paint from the area around the hole to create a smooth, firm edge. Use a wallboard knife to test the plaster around the edges of the damaged area. Scrape away all loose or soft plaster.

Apply latex bonding liquid liberally around the edges of the hole and over the base lath to ensure a crack-free bond between the old and new plaster.

Mix patching plaster as directed by the manufacturer, and use a wallboard knife or trowel to apply it to the hole. Fill shallow holes with a single coat of plaster.

For deeper holes, apply a shallow first coat, then scratch a crosshatch pattern in the wet plaster. Let it dry, then apply second coat of plaster. Let the plaster dry, and sand it lightly.

Use texture paint or wallboard compound to recreate any surface texture. Practice on heavy cardboard until you can duplicate the wall's surface. Prime and paint the area to finish the repair.

Variation: Holes in plaster can also be patched with wallboard. Score the damaged surface with a utility knife and chisel out the plaster back to the center of the closest framing members. Cut a wallboard patch to size, then secure in place with wallboard screws driven every 4" into the framing. Finish joints as you would standard wallboard joints.

How to Patch Holes Cut in Plaster

Cut a piece of wire mesh larger than the hole, using aviation snips. Tie a length of twine at the center of the mesh and insert the mesh into the wall cavity. Twist the wire around a dowel that is longer than the width of the hole, until the mesh pulls tight against the opening. Apply latex bonding liquid to the mesh and the edges of the hole.

Apply a coat of patching plaster, forcing it into the mesh and covering the edges of the hole. Scratch a cross-hatch pattern in the wet plaster, then allow it to dry. Remove the dowel and trim the wire holding the mesh. Apply a second coat, filling the hole completely. Add texture. Let dry, then scrape away any excess plaster. Sand, prime, and paint the area.

How to Repair Cracks in Plaster

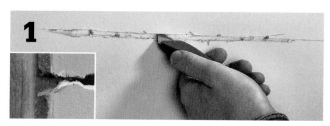

Scrape away any texture or loose plaster around the crack. Using a utility knife, cut back the edges of the crack to create a keyway (inset). The keyway will help lock the patch in place and prevent recracking.

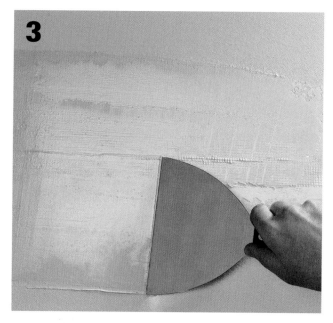

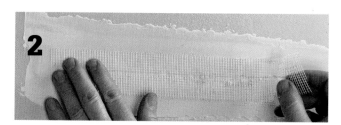

Work joint compound into the keyway using a 6" knife, then embed mesh tape into the compound, lightly forcing the compound through the mesh. Smooth the compound, leaving just enough to conceal the tape.

Add two more coat of compound, in successively broader and thinner coats, to blend the patch into the surrounding area. Lightly sand, then retexture the repair area to match the wall. Prime and paint it to finish the repair.

Replacing Sheet Paneling

Despite its durability, prefinished sheet paneling occasionally requires repairs. Many scuff marks can be removed with a light coat of paste wax, and most small scratches can be disguised with a touchup stick.

Paneling manufacturers do not recommend trying to spot-sand or refinish prefinished paneling.

The most common forms of significant damage to paneling are water damage and punctures. If paneling has suffered major damage, the only way to repair it is to replace the affected sheets.

If the paneling is more than a few years old, it may be difficult to locate matching pieces. If you can't find any at lumber yards or building centers, try salvage yards. Buy the panels in advance so that you can condition them to the room before installing them. To condition the paneling, place it in the room, standing on its long edge. Place spacers between the sheets so air can circulate around each one. Let the paneling stand for 24 hours if it will be installed above grade, and 48 hours if it will be installed below grade.

Before you go any further, find out what's behind the paneling. Building Codes often require that paneling be backed with wallboard. This is a good idea, even if Code doesn't require it. The support provided by the wallboard keeps the paneling from warping and provides an extra layer of sound protection. However, if there is wallboard behind the paneling, it may need repairs as well, particularly if you're dealing with water damage. And removing damaged paneling may be more difficult if it's glued to wallboard or a masonry wall. In any case, it's best to have a clear picture of the situation before you start cutting into a wall.

Finally, turn off the electricity to the area and remove all receptacle covers and switch plates on the sheets of paneling that need to be replaced.

Most scuffs in paneling can be polished out using paste wax. To use, make sure the panel surface is clean and dust free, then apply a thin even coat of paste wax using a clean soft cloth. Work in small areas using a circular motion. Allow to dry until a paste becomes hazy (5 to 10 minutes), then buff with a new cloth. Apply a second coat if necessary.

Touch-up and fill sticks can help hide most scratches in prefinished paneling. Wax touch-up sticks are like crayons—simply trace over the scratch with the stick. To use a fill stick, apply a small amount of the material into the surface and smooth it over the scratch using a flexible putty knife. Wipe away excess fill with a clean, soft cloth.

Tools & Materials ▸

Wallboard knife	Replacement panels
Putty knife	Spray paint
Flat pry bar	Panel adhesive
Framing square	Color-matched
Linoleum knife	paneling nails
Hammer	Shims
Chisel	Finish nails
Caulk gun	Putty sticks
Rubber mallet	Wood filler
Nail set	

How to Replace a Strip of Paneling

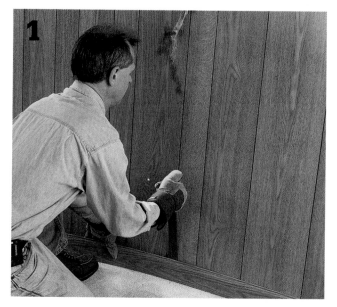

Carefully remove the baseboard and top moldings. Use a wallboard or putty knife to create a gap, then insert a pry bar and pull the trim away from the wall. Remove all the nails.

Draw a line on the panel from top to bottom, 3-in. to 4-in. from each edge of the panel. Hold a framing square along the line and cut with a linoleum knife. Using a fair amount of pressure, you should cut through the panel within two passes. If you have trouble, use a hammer and chisel to break the panel along the scored lines.

Insert a pry bar under the panel at the bottom, and pull up and away from the wall, removing nails as you go. Once the center portion of the panel is removed, scrape away any old adhesive, using a putty knife. Repair the vapor barrier if damaged; below-grade applications may require a layer of 4mil polyethylene between outside walls and paneling. Measure and cut the new panel, including any necessary cutouts, and test-fit the panel.

On the back of the panel, apply zigzag beads of panel adhesive from top to bottom every 16", about 2" in from each edge, and around cutouts. Tack the panel into position at the top, using color-matched paneling nails. When the adhesive has set up, press the panel to the wall and tap along stud lines with a rubber mallet, creating a tight bond between the adhesive and wall. Drive finish nails at the base of the panel to hold it while the adhesive dries. Replace all trim pieces and fill nail holes with wood filler.

Maintaining Wall Tile

As we've said throughout this book, ceramic tile is durable and nearly maintenance-free, but like every other material in your house, it can fail or develop problems. The most common problem with ceramic tile involves damaged grout. Failed grout is unattractive, but the real danger is that it offers a point of entry for water. Given a chance to work its way beneath grout, water can destroy a tile base and eventually wreck an entire installation. It's important to regrout ceramic tile as soon as you see signs of damage.

Another potential problem for tile installations is damaged caulk. In tub and shower stalls and around sinks and backsplashes, the joints between the tile and the fixtures are sealed with caulk. The caulk eventually deteriorates, leaving an entry point for water. Unless the joints are recaulked, seeping water will destroy the tile base and the wall.

In bathrooms, towel rods, soap dishes, and other accessories can work loose from walls, especially if they weren't installed correctly or aren't supported properly. For maximum holding power, anchor new accessories to wall studs or blocking. If no studs or blocking are available, use special fasteners, such as toggle bolts or molly bolts, to anchor the accessories directly to the surface of the underlying wall. To hold screws firmly in place in ceramic tile walls, drill pilot holes and insert plastic sleeves, which expand when screws are driven into them.

Tools & Materials ▸

Awl	Tile adhesive
Utility knife	Masking tape
Trowel	Grout
Grout float	Cloth or rag
Hammer	Rubbing alcohol
Chisel	Mildew remover
Small pry bar	Silicone or latex caulk
Eye protection	Sealer
Replacement tile	Sponge

How to Regrout Wall Tile

Use an awl or utility knife to scrape out the old grout completely, leaving a clean bed for the new grout.

Clean and rinse the grout joints, then spread grout over the entire tile surface, using a rubber grout float or sponge. Work the grout well into the joints and let it set slightly.

Wipe away excess grout with a damp sponge. When the grout is dry, wipe away the residue and polish the tiles with a dry cloth.

How to Recaulk a Joint

1

Start with a completely dry surface. Scrape out the old caulk and clean the joint with a cloth dipped in rubbing alcohol. If this is a bathtub or sink, fill it with water to weight it down.

2

Cut the tip off caulk cartridges at a 45° angle and then make a flat cut at the top with a utility knife. This will allow you to deliver a smooth bead that is not too thin or too heavy.

2

Clean the joint with a product that kills mildew spores; let it dry. Fill the joint with silicone or latex caulk.

3

Wet your fingertip with cold water, then use your finger to smooth the caulk into a cove shape. After the caulk hardens, use a utility knife to trim away any excess.

How to Replace Built-in Wall Accessories

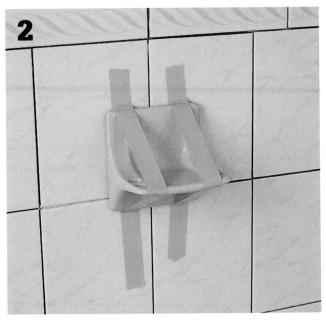

Carefully remove the damaged accessory. Scrape away any remaining adhesive or grout. Apply dry-set tile adhesive to the back side of the new accessory, then press it firmly in place.

Use masking tape to hold the accessory in place while the adhesive dries. Let the mortar dry completely (12 to 24 hours), then grout and seal the area.

How to Replace Surface-mounted Accessories

Lift the accessory up and off the mounting plate. If the mounting plate screws are driven into studs or blocking, simply hang the new accessory. If not, add hardware such as molly bolts, toggle bolts, or plastic anchor sleeves.

Put a dab of silicone caulk over the pilot holes and the tips of the screws before inserting them. Let the caulk dry, then install the new fixture on the mounting plate.

How to Remove & Replace Broken Wall Tiles

Carefully scrape away the grout from the surrounding joints, using a utility knife or an awl. Break the damaged tile into small pieces, using a hammer and chisel. Remove the broken pieces, then scrape away debris or old adhesive from the open area.

If the tile to be replaced is a cut tile, cut a new one to match. Test-fit the new tile and make sure it sits flush with the field. Spread adhesive on the back of the replacement tile and place it in the hole, twisting it slightly. Use masking tape to hold the tile in place for 24 hours so the adhesive can dry.

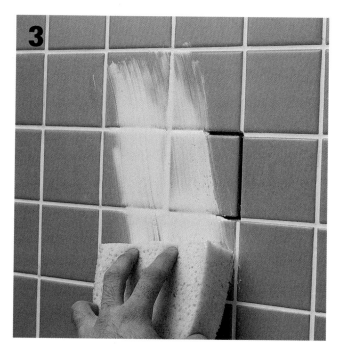

Remove the tape, then apply premixed grout, using a sponge or grout float. Let the grout set slightly, then tool it with a rounded object such as a toothbrush handle. Wipe away excess grout with a damp cloth.

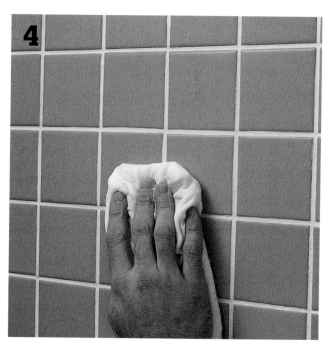

Let the grout dry for an hour, then polish the tile with a clean, dry cloth.

Repairing Wallcovering

Loosened seams and bubbles are common wallcovering problems, but both are easy to remedy using a little adhesive and a sponge. For papers that are compatible with water, use a clean, damp sponge. For other types of papers (grasscloth or flocked wallcoverings, for example), clean fingers are probably the best choice.

Scratches, tears or obvious stains can be patched so successfully that the patch is difficult to spot. Whenever you hang wallcoverings, save remnants for future repairs. It's also a good idea to record the name of the manufacturer as well as the style and run numbers of the wallcoverings. Write this information on a piece of masking tape and put it on the back of a switchplate in the room.

If you need to patch an area of wallcovering but don't have remnants available, you can remove a section of wallcovering from an inconspicuous spot, such as inside a closet or behind a door. You can camouflage the spot by painting the hole with a color that blends into the background of the wallcovering.

Tools & Materials ▸

Edge roller
Syringe-type
   adhesive applicator
Sponge
Utility knife

Adhesive
Removable tape
Wallcovering
   remnants

How to Fix a Bubble

Cut a slit through the bubble, using a sharp razor knife. If there is a pattern in the wallcovering, cut along a line in the pattern to hide the slit.

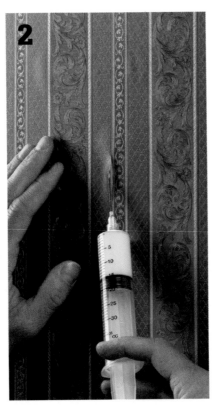

Insert the tip of a glue applicator through the slit and apply adhesive sparingly to the wall under the wallcovering.

Press the wallcovering gently to rebond it. Use a clean, damp sponge to press the flap down and wipe away excess glue.

How to Patch Wallcovering

1

Fasten a scrap of matching wallcovering over the damaged portion with drafting tape, so that the patterns match.

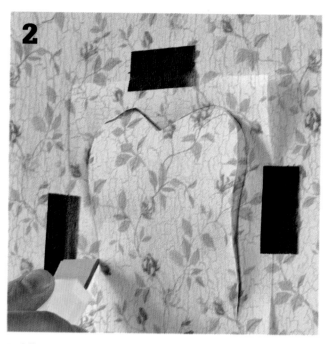

2

Holding a razor knife blade at a 90° angle to the wall, cut through both layers of wallcovering. If the wallcovering has strong pattern lines, cut along the lines to hide the seams. With less definite patterns, cut irregular lines.

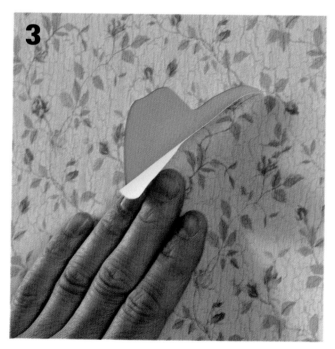

3

Remove the scrap and patch, then peel away the damaged wallcovering. Apply adhesive to the back of the patch and position it in the hole so that the pattern matches. Rinse the patch area with a damp sponge.

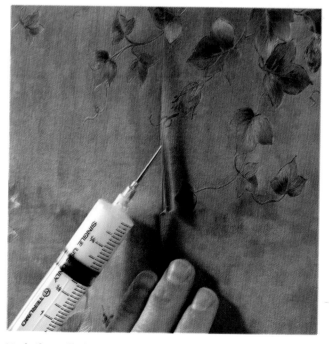

Variation: Lift the edge of the wallcovering seam and insert the tip of a glue applicator under it. Squirt adhesive onto the wall and gently press the seam flat. Let the repair stand for ½ hour, then smooth the seam lightly with a seam roller. Wipe the seam lightly with a damp sponge.

Repairing Ceilings

Most ceiling repairs are relatively simple: the techniques used to repair wallboard walls apply to ceilings as well, while sagging panels can be refastened or replaced easily; the tongue-and-groove edges of acoustical tiles make it easy to remove and replace a single tile; and textures such as acoustical "popcorn" can be matched with a little practice on a scrap of cardboard or simply removed altogether.

However, plaster, by contrast, is difficult to work with, and replastering is not an option for most homeowners. While minor repairs are manageable, widespread failure of the bond between the plaster coating and the lath foundation can be dangerous. If you find large spongy areas or extensive sags in your plaster ceiling, consult a professional.

Aerosol touch-up products are available for small repairs to ceilings with popcorn and orange peel textures. Use a wallboard knife to scrap away the existing texture at the damaged area and slightly around it. Make any necessary repairs, then spray on the aerosol texture carefully to blend the new texture with the existing ceiling.

How to Remove Popcorn Ceiling Texture

To protect floors and ease cleanup later, line floors with 6-mil plastic, then cover with corrugated cardboard to provide a non-slip surface. Caution: Popcorn ceilings in houses built prior to 1980 may contain asbestos. Contact your local building department for regulations governing asbestos removal.

Using a pressure sprayer, dampen the ceiling with a mixture of a teaspoon of liquid detergent per gallon of water. Allow 20 minutes for the mixture to soak in, rewetting as necessary.

Scrape texture from the ceiling using a 6-in. wallboard knife. Be careful not to cut into the wallboard surface. After all texture is removed, sand rough spots, then carefully roll up and dispose of the plastic and debris. Patch any damaged areas with joint compound, then prime and paint.

How to Replace Acoustical Ceiling Tile

Cut out the center section of the damaged tile with a utility knife. Slide the edges away from the surrounding tiles.

Trim the upper lip of the grooved edges of the new tile, using a straightedge. If necessary, also remove one of the tongues.

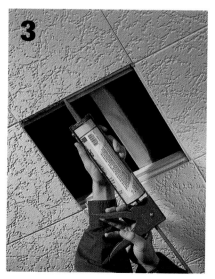

At the ceiling, apply construction adhesive to the furring strips. Install the new tile, tongue first, and press it into the adhesive. *Tip: To hold large tiles in place while the glue dries, lay a flat board across the tile, then prop a 2 × 4 post between the board and the floor.*

How to Raise a Sagging Wallboard Ceiling

Position a T-brace under the lowest point of the sagging area with the bottom end on a piece of plywood or hardboard on the floor. Nudge it forward until the sagging panels are tight to the joists. If fasteners pop through the surface, drive them back in.

Remove loose tape and compound at joints between loose panels. Starting at one end, drive wallboard screws with broad, thin washers every 4" through the center of the joint and into the joists. In the field of panel, drive screws 2" from existing fasteners.

When the area is securely fastened, remove the T-brace. Scrape off any loose chips of paint or wallboard around joints and screws, then fill with compound. Cover large cracks or gaps with fiberglass tape before applying the compound.

Repairing Water Damaged Walls & Ceilings

A sure sign of a water problem is discoloration and bubbling on the ceiling surface. Water from a leaky roof or pipe above will quickly find a low spot or a joint between wallboard panels, soaking through to a visible surface in a matter of minutes. Water in joints is especially damaging because it ruins the edges of two panels at once. If you have a water problem, be sure to fix the leak and allow the damaged wallboard to dry thoroughly before making any repairs.

Whenever water or moisture infiltrates a house, there is always a concern regarding mold. Mold grows where water and nutrients are present—damp wallboard paper can provide such an environment. You can use a damp rag and baking soda or a small amount of detergent to clean up small areas of mold (less than one square yard), though you should wear goggles, rubber gloves, and a dust mask to prevent contact with mold spores. If mold occupies more area than this, you may have a more serious problem. Contact a mold abatement specialist for assessment and remediation. To help prevent mold growth, use exhaust fans and dehumidifiers to rid your home of excess moisture and repair plumbing leaks as soon as they are found.

If damaged wallboard requires extensive repair, resurfacing walls and ceiling with a layer of new wallboard may be the best option. Resurfacing is essentially the same installation as hanging multiple layers of wallboard, and results in a smooth, flat surface. However, the added wall thickness can affect the appearance of window and door trim, which may need to be extended. Use ⅜" wallboard for resurfacing—while ¼" wallboard is thinner, it's fragile and can be difficult to work with.

Tools & Materials ▸

Utility saw	Wallboard (for patching
Utility knife	or resurfacing)
Drill or screwgun	Construction adhesive
Wallboard knives	Stain-blocking primer/
150-grit sandpaper	sealer
Paint roller and tray	Paper tape
Wallboard screws	Joint compound

How to Repair Water Damaged Wallboard

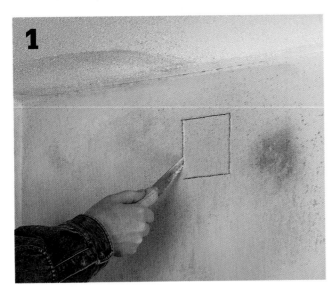

After the source for the water leak has been fixed, cut 4-in. holes at each end of joist and stud bays to help ventilation. Where possible, remove wet or damp insulation to dry out. Use fans and dehumidifiers to help speed up the drying process.

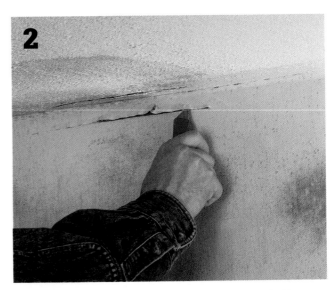

Remove loose tape and compound using a utility knife. Cut back areas of soft wallboard to solid material. To prevent sagging, prop waterlogged ceiling panels against joists with T-braces.

3

Once wallboard is dry, refasten ceiling panels to framing or remove panels that are excessively bowed. Reinforce damaged wall panels with wallboard screws driven 2-in. from the existing fasteners.

Tip ▶

If wallboard contains small areas (less than one square yard) of mold on the panel surface, clean with a damp rag and baking soda or detergent. Allow to dry, then continue the repair. Wear protective eyewear, rubber gloves, and a disposable dust mask when cleaning mold. Caution: Larger areas containing mold must be evaluated and treated by a mold abatement specialist.

4

Patch all vent holes and damaged areas with wallboard and replace insulation. Apply a quality stain-blocking primer/sealer to the affected area. Use an oil-based sealer; latex-based sealers may allow water stains to bleed through.

5

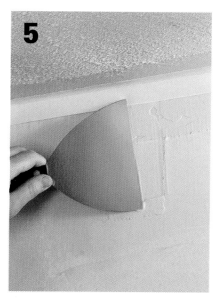

After the primer/sealer has dried, finish all joints and repairs with paper tape and three coats of compound. If water stains bleed through, reseal prior to final priming and painting.

Variation: Where damage is severe, resurface with a new layer of ¼" or ⅜" wallboard. Hang new panels perpendicular to existing wallboard, and use panel adhesive to strengthen the bond.

Removing Wall & Ceiling Surfaces

If a wall or ceiling surface is damaged or deteriorated beyond repair or if your remodeling project requires framing alterations or additional utility lines, you may need to remove the wall and ceiling surfaces.

Removing any wall surface is a messy job, but it's not a difficult one. But before you tear into a wall with a hammer or power saw, you need to know what lies inside. Start by checking for hidden mechanicals in the project area. Wiring that's in the way can be moved fairly easily, as can water supply pipes and drain vents. If it's gas piping, drain pipe, or ducting, however, you'll probably have to call a professional before you can move to the next step.

It's also a good idea to locate all of the framing members in the project area. Marking all of the studs, plates, and blocking will help guide your cuts and prevent unpleasant surprises.

When you're ready to begin demolition, prepare the work area to help contain dust and minimize damage to flooring and other surfaces—tearing out wallboard and plaster creates a very fine dust that easily finds its way into neighboring rooms. Cover doorways (even closed ones) and openings with plastic sheeting. Tape plastic over HVAC registers to prevent dust from circulating through the system. Protect floors with cardboard or hardboard and plastic or drop cloths. Also, carefully remove any trim from the project area, cutting painted joints with a utility knife to reduce the damage to the finish.

As an added precaution, turn off the power to all circuits in the work area, and shut off the main water supply if you'll be making cuts near water pipes.

Tools & Materials ▸

- Utility knife
- Pry bar
- Circular saw with demolition blade
- Straightedge
- Maul
- Masonry chisel
- Reciprocating saw with bimetal blade
- Heavy tarp
- Hammer
- Protective eyewear
- Dust mask

Locate framing members using a stud finder or by knocking on the wall and feeling for solid points. Verify the findings by driving finish nails through the wall surface. After finding the center of one stud, measure over 16" to locate neighboring studs.

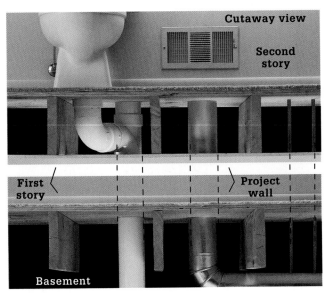

Check for hidden plumbing lines, ductwork, wiring, and gas pipes before cutting into a wall. To locate the lines, examine the areas directly below and above the project wall. In most cases, pipes, utility lines, and ductwork run through the wall vertically between floors. Original blueprints for your house should show the location of many of the utility lines.

Lead Paint ▸

Before removing any surface in a home built before 1980, test for lead, a hazardous substance. (Lead paint additives were banned in 1978, but supplies on hand were sold and used beyond that time.) You can find inexpensive test kits at hardware stores and home centers. If tests indicate lead, get expert advice. Most paint stores and the paint department in larger home centers carry free brochures on what's known as "lead abatement procedures." You can also find information at www.epa.gov.

How to Remove Wallcovering

Find a loose edge and try to strip off the wallcovering. Vinyls often peel away easily. If the wallcovering does not strip by hand, cover the floor with layers of newspaper. Add wallcovering remover fluid to a bucket of water, as directed by the manufacturer.

Pierce the wallcovering surface with a wallpaper scorer (inset) to allow remover solution to enter and soften the adhesive. Use a pressure sprayer, paint roller, or sponge to apply the remover solution. Let it soak into the covering, according to the manufacturer's directions.

Peel away loosened wallcovering with a 6-in. wallboard knife. Be careful not to damage the plaster or wallboard. Remove all backing paper. Rinse adhesive residue from the wall with remover solution. Rinse with clear water and let the walls dry completely.

How to Remove Ceramic Wall Tile

Be sure the floor is covered with a heavy tarp, and the electricity and water are shut off. Knock a small starter hole into the bottom of the wall, using a maul and masonry chisel.

Begin cutting out small sections of the wall by inserting a reciprocating saw with a bimetal blade into the hole, and cutting along grout lines. Be careful when sawing near pipes and wiring.

Cut the entire wall surface into small sections, removing each section as it is cut. Be careful not to cut through studs.

How to Remove Wallboard

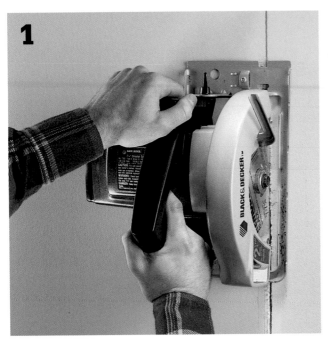

Remove baseboard and other trim, and prepare the work area. Set a circular saw to the thickness of the wallboard, then cut from floor to ceiling. Use a utility knife to finish the cuts at the top and bottom and to cut through the taped horizontal seam where the wall meets the ceiling surface.

Insert the end of a pry bar into the cut, near a corner of the opening. Pull the pry bar until the wallboard breaks, then tear away the broken pieces. Take care to avoid damaging the wallboard outside the planned rough opening.

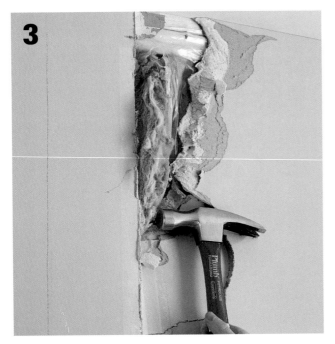

Strike the wallboard with the side of a hammer, then pull it away from the wall with the pry bar or your hands.

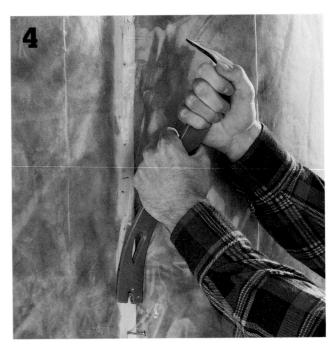

Remove nails, screws, and any remaining wallboard from the framing members, using a pry bar or drill (or screwgun). Check the vapor barrier and insulation for damage and replace if necessary.

How to Remove Plaster

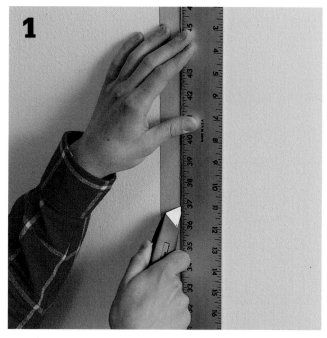

Remove baseboards and other trim and prepare the work area. Score the cutting line several times with a utility knife, using a straightedge as a guide. The line should be at least ⅛" deep.

Break the plaster along the edges by holding a scrap piece of 2 × 4 on edge just inside the scored lines, and rapping it with a hammer. Use a pry bar to remove the remaining plaster.

Cut through the lath along the edges of the plaster, using a reciprocating saw or jigsaw. Remove the lath from the studs using a pry bar. Pry away any remaining nails. Check the vapor barrier and insulation for damage and replace if necessary.

Variation: If the wall has metal lath laid over the wood lath, use aviation snips to clip the edges of the metal lath. Press the jagged edges of the lath flat against the stud. The cut edges of metal lath are very sharp; be sure to wear heavy work gloves.

Final Inspection & Fixing Problems

After the final coat of joint compound has dried but before you begin sanding, inspect the entire finish job for flaws. If you discover scrapes, pitting, or other imperfections, add another coat of joint compound. Repair any damaged or overlooked areas such as cracked seams and over-cut holes for electrical boxes prior to sanding.

During your inspection, make sure to check that all seams are acceptably feathered out. To check seams, hold a level or 12-in. taping knife perpendicularly across the seam; fill concave areas with extra layers of compound and correct any convex seams that crown more than $\frac{1}{16}$".

Tools & Materials ▸

6" and 12" taping knives
Sanding block or pole sander
All-purpose joint compound
Self-adhesive fiberglass mesh tape
220-grit sanding screen or 150-grit sandpaper

How to Fix Common Taping Problems

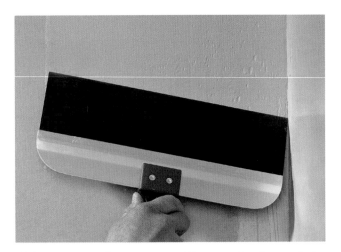

Pitting occurs when compound is overmixed or applied with too little pressure to force out trapped air bubbles. Pitting can be corrected easily with a thin coat of compound. If trapped air bubbles are present, sand lightly before covering with compound.

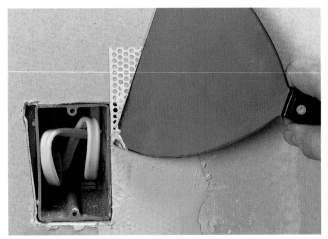

Mis-cut holes for electrical boxes can be flat-taped. Cover the gap with self-adhesive mesh tape and cover with three coats of all-purpose compound. Pre-cut repair patches are also available.

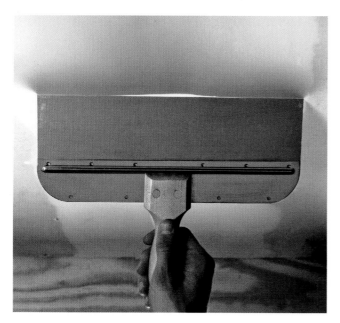

Concave seams can be filled with an extra layer or two of all-purpose compound. Let dry and sand lightly between coats.

For seams crowned more than 1/16", carefully sand along the center, but do not expose the tape.Check the seam with a level. If it's still crowned, add a layer of compound with a 12" knife, removing all of it along the seam's center and feathering it out toward the outside edges. After it dries, apply a final coat, if necessary.

Bubbled or loose tape occurs when the bed layer is too thin, which causes a faulty bond between the tape and compound. Cut out small, soft areas with a utility knife and retape. Large runs of loose tape will have to be fully removed before retaping.

Cracked seams are often the result of compound that has dried too quickly or shrunk. Retape the seam if the existing tape and compound is intact; otherwise, cut out any loose material. In either case, make sure to fill the crack with compound.

Ladders & Scaffolds

Two quality stepladders and an extension plank are all you need to paint most interior surfaces. For painting high areas, build a simple scaffold by running the plank through the steps of two stepladders. It can be easy to lose your balance or step off the plank, so choose tall ladders for safety; the upper part of the ladders can help you balance and will keep you from stepping off the ends of the plank. Buy a strong, straight 2" × 10" board no more than 12 feet long, or rent a plank from a material dealer or rental outlet.

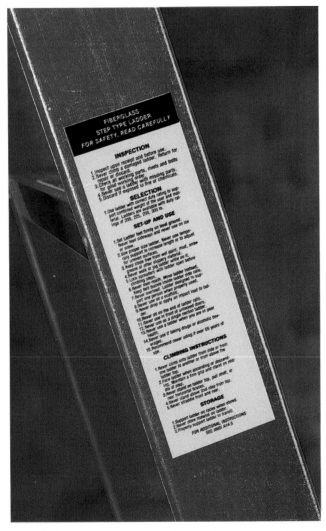

A manufacturer's sticker provides weight ratings and instructions for the correct use of the ladder. Read it carefully when shopping for a ladder. Choose a ladder that will easily accommodate your weight plus the additional weight of any tools or materials you plan to carry up the ladder.

Rent extension planks from a paint dealer or from a rental center.

Keep steps tight by periodically checking them and tightening the braces when they need it.

Keep the ladder in front of you when working. Lean your body against the ladder for balance.

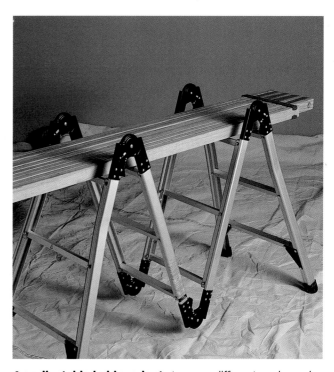

An adjustable ladder adapts to many different work needs. It can be used as a straight ladder, a stepladder, or a base for scaffold planks.

Paint Safety

Always read and follow the label information on paint and solvent containers. Chemicals that pose a fire hazard are listed (in order of flammability) as: combustible, flammable, or extremely flammable. Use caution when using these products and remember that the fumes are also flammable.

The warning "use with adequate ventilation" means that there should be no more vapor buildup than there would be if you were using the material outside. Open doors and windows, use exhaust fans, and wear an approved respirator if you can't provide adequate ventilation.

Save a small amount of paint for touchups and repairs, and then safely dispose of the remainder. Dispose of alkyd (oil-based) paint according to local regulations regarding hazardous materials; if possible, recycle latex paint at your local hazardous waste disposal facility or allow it to dry out completely and set it out with your regular trash.

Paint chemicals do not store well. Buy only as much as is needed for the project and keep them away from children and pets.

Read label information. Chemicals that are poisonous or flammable are labeled with warnings and instructions for safe handling.

Wear safety goggles when using chemical stripper or cleaning products. Use goggles when painting overhead.

Do not use chemicals that are listed as combustible or flammable, such as paint strippers, near an open flame. Store paint chemicals out of the reach of children and away from appliances with pilot lights, such as a furnace or gas oven.

Open windows and doors and use a fan for ventilation when painting indoors. If a product label has the warning "harmful or fatal if swallowed," assume that the vapors are dangerous to breathe.

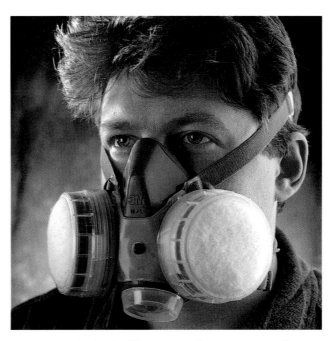

Wear a respirator to filter vapors if you cannot ventilate a work area adequately. If you can smell vapors, the ventilation is not adequate.

Pour paint thinner into a clear jar after use. When the solid material settles out, pour off the clear thinner and save it to reuse later. Dispose of the sediment as hazardous waste.

Dispose of leftover latex primers and paint safely. Let the container stand uncovered until the paint dries completely. In most communities, dried latex paint can be put into the regular trash. (Alkyd primers and paint must be disposed of as hazardous waste.)

Preparation Tools & Materials

It's as simple as it is unavoidable: Good preparation produces a professional-looking job. In the old days, preparation could be difficult and time consuming, but with the help of the new tools and materials on the market today, it's easier than ever.

New cleaners and removal agents help prepare surfaces for paint and wallcovering; new patching products help you create virtually invisible wall repairs; ingenious new masking and draping materials take the tedium out of keeping the paint where it belongs; primers and sealers provide good coverage and help paint bond properly. While you're in the planning stages of a painting or decorating project, take a stroll down the aisles at a local home center or hardware store. Consider the project ahead of you and evaluate which products will make the job simpler and more enjoyable.

Smooth, even surfaces are easy to achieve with tools such as these: sanding sponges (A), sandpaper (B), sanding block (C), a drywall-corner sanding sponge (D), microfiber tack cloth (E), and synthetic steel wool (F).

Tools for preparation include some ordinary home workshop tools and some specialty items. All are available at home improvement centers, as well as at better decorating supply stores.

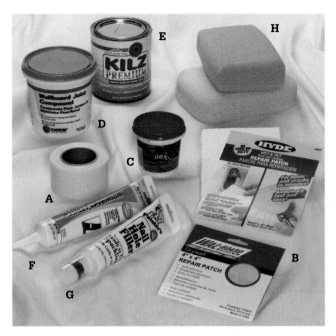

Wall repair materials include: self-adhesive seam tape (A), hole-patching kits (B), crack-repair compound (C), joint compound (D), stainblocking primer/sealer (E), and sink and tub caulk (F). Some new spackling compounds (G) start out pink and dry white so you can see when they're ready to be sanded and painted. Sponges (H) are useful for smoothing damp joint compound to reduce the amount of sanding that's necessary later.

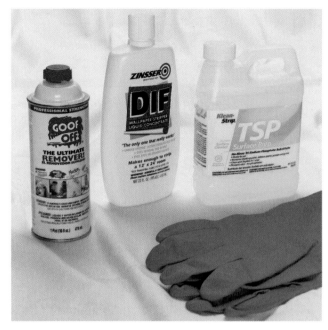

Walls must be clean, smooth, and free of grease before a painting project. If wallpaper is to be removed, a wallpaper removal agent is extremely helpful. Clockwise from top left are: cleanup solution to remove old drips and splatters, wallcovering remover to strip old wallcoverings, trisodium phosphate (TSP) for washing the walls, and rubber gloves, which should be worn when using chemicals such as these.

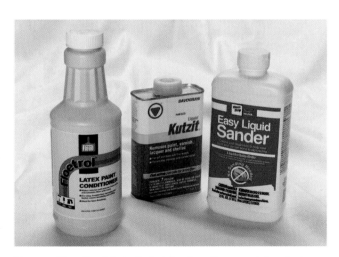

Preparation liquids include latex bonding agent for plaster repairs; paint remover; and liquid deglosser, for dulling glossy surfaces prior to painting.

Primers provide maximum adhesion for paint on any surface. There are many specialty primers available, including mold-resistant primers that are especially useful in areas that tend to be damp, such as bathrooms (A), primers made for plaster and new drywall (B), stainblocking primers (C), and tinted primers that reduce the need for multiple coats of paint (particularly for deep colors) (D).

Room Preparation

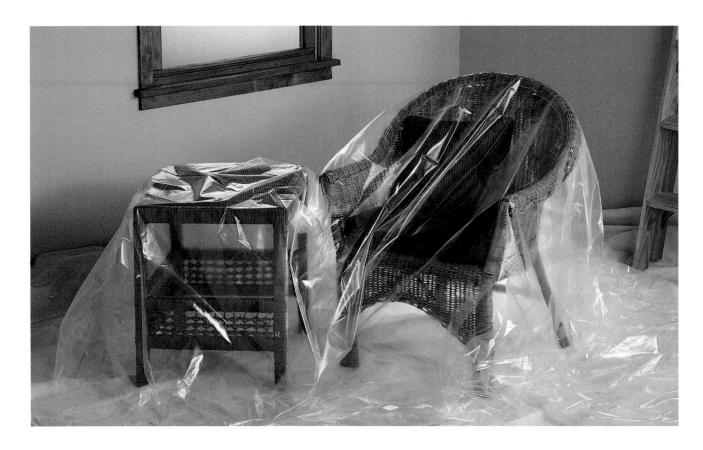

Before painting, your first step is to protect everything that could be covered by dust or splattered by paint. Remove all window and door hardware, light fixtures, and coverplates on outlets and wall switches. Drape furniture and cover the floors. Remove heating and air conditioning duct covers. Mask off wood moldings with self-adhesive paper or masking tape. Painting time can be a good opportunity to upgrade with new hardware, like window pulls and cabinet knobs.

Tip ▸

When removing hardware, mark the pieces with masking tape for identification so that they can easily be replaced.

How to Prepare a Room

Remove all hardware, such as window handles and cabinet catches, from surfaces to be painted. If you will be installing new hardware, buy it now and drill new screw holes if needed.

Remove all nails, screws, and picture hangers from surfaces to be painted. To prevent damage to the plaster or wallboard, use a block of wood under the head of the hammer.

Remove covers from heating and air-conditioning ducts to protect them from splatters. Remove thermostats, or use masking tape to protect them against paint drips.

Move furniture to the center of the room and cover it with plastic sheets. In large rooms, leave an alley through the center for access if you are painting the ceiling. Cover floors with 9-ounce canvas drop cloths. Canvas absorbs paint spills.

Turn off the electricity. Remove the coverplates from outlets and switches, then replace the cover screws. Lower light fixtures away from electrical boxes, or remove the fixtures. Cover hanging fixtures with plastic bags.

Primers & Sealers

A sealer should be applied to wood surfaces before they are varnished. Wood often has both hard and soft grains, as well as a highly absorbent end grain. Applying a sealer helps close the surface of the wood so the varnish is absorbed evenly in different types of wood grain. If the wood is not sealed, the varnish may dry to a mottled finish.

Primers are used to seal surfaces that will be painted. Wallboard seams and patched areas absorb paint at a different rate than surrounding areas. Joints and patch areas often show or "shadow" through the finished paint if the walls are not adequately primed.

Choose a primer designed for the project: mildew-resistant primers are excellent for bathrooms and laundry rooms, stain-blocking primers cover smoke and other hard-to-cover stains, and tinted primers provide good bases for deep colors, such as red or purple.

Tinted primers provide an excellent base for finish coats, especially for deep colors that might otherwise require several coats to cover adequately. Color base is available to tint white primers if necessary.

Tips for Priming & Sealing ▶

Seal raw wood by applying a primer before painting or a clear sealer before varnishing. Unsealed wood can produce a spotty finish.

Roughen gloss surfaces with fine sandpaper, then prime them to provide good bonding between the new and the old paint. Primers provide "tooth" for the new coat of paint.

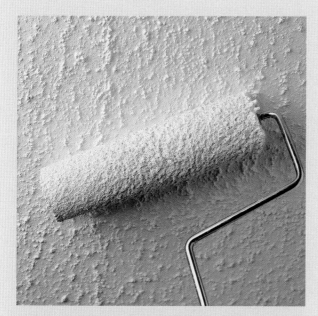

Seal textured surfaces with a PVA or alkyd primer, then apply a finish coat with a long-nap roller. Textured walls and ceilings soak up a lot of paint and make it difficult to apply paint evenly.

Prime repair areas on plaster with high-quality primer.

How to Use a Paint Roller

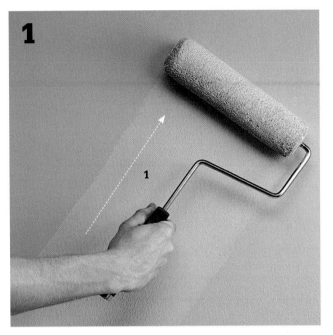

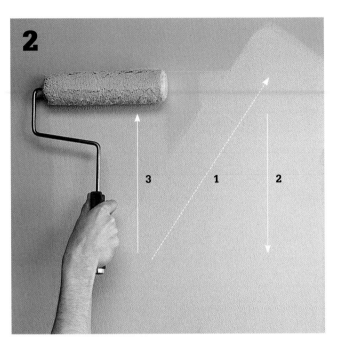

Wet the roller cover with water (for latex paint) or mineral spirits (for alkyd enamel), to remove lint and prime the cover. Squeeze out excess liquid. Dip the roller fully into the paint pan reservoir and roll it over the textured ramp to distribute the paint evenly. The roller should be full, but not dripping. Make an upward diagonal sweep about 4 ft. long on the surface, using a slow stroke to avoid splattering.

Draw the roller straight down (2) from the top of the diagonal sweep made in step 1. Lift and move the roller to the beginning of the diagonal sweep and roll up (3) to complete the unloading of the roller.

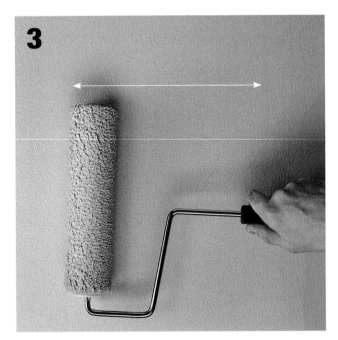

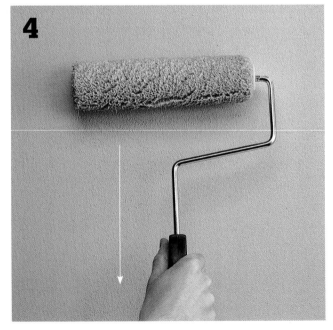

Distribute the paint over the rest of the section with horizontal back-and-forth strokes.

Smooth the area by lightly drawing the roller vertically from the top to the bottom of the painted area. Lift the roller and return it to the top of the area after each stroke.

How to Use a Paintbrush

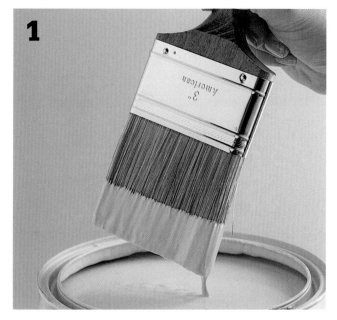

1

Dip the brush into the paint, loading one-third of its bristle length. Tap the bristles against the side of the can to remove excess paint, but do not drag the bristles against the lip of the can.

2

Paint along the edges (called "cutting in") using the narrow edge of the brush, pressing just enough to flex the bristles. Keep an eye on the paint edge, and paint with long, slow strokes. Always paint from a dry area back into wet paint to avoid lap marks.

3

Brush wall corners using the wide edge of the brush. Paint open areas with a brush or roller before the brushed paint dries.

4

To paint large areas with a brush, apply the paint with 2 or 3 diagonal strokes. Hold the brush at a 45° angle to the work surface, pressing just enough to flex the bristles. Distribute the paint evenly with horizontal strokes.

5

Smooth the surface by drawing the brush vertically from the top to the bottom of the painted area. Use light strokes and lift the brush from the surface at the end of each stroke. This method is best for slow-drying alkyd enamels.

Trim Techniques

When painting an entire room, paint the wood trim first, then paint the walls. Start by painting the inside portions of the trim, and work out toward the walls. On windows, for instance, first paint the edges close to the glass, then paint the surrounding face trim.

Doors should be painted quickly because of the large surface. To avoid lap marks, always paint from dry surfaces back into wet paint. On baseboards, cut in the top edge and work down to the flooring. Plastic floor guards or a wide broadknife can help shield carpet and wood flooring from paint drips.

Alkyds and latex enamels may require two coats. Always sand lightly between coats and wipe with a tack cloth so that the second coat bonds properly.

How to Paint a Window

To paint double-hung windows, remove them from their frames if possible. Newer, spring-mounted windows are released by pushing against the frame (see arrow).

Drill holes and insert two 2" nails into the legs of a wooden step ladder. Mount the window easel-style for easy painting. Or, lay the window flat on a bench or sawhorses. Do not paint the sides or bottom of the window sashes.

3

Using a tapered sash brush, begin by painting the wood next to the glass. Use the narrow edge of the brush, and overlap the paint onto the glass to create a weatherseal.

4

Remove excess paint from the glass with a putty knife wrapped in a clean cloth. Rewrap the knife often so that you always wipe with clean fabric. Overlap paint from the sash onto the glass by 1/16".

5

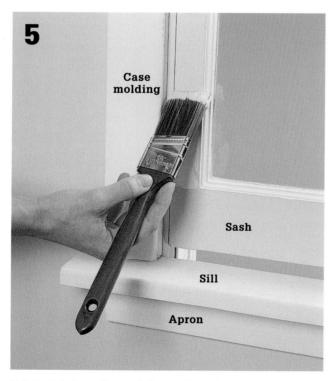

Case molding

Sash

Sill

Apron

Paint all flat portions of the sashes, then the case moldings, sill, and apron. Use slow brush strokes, and avoid getting paint between the sash and the frame.

6

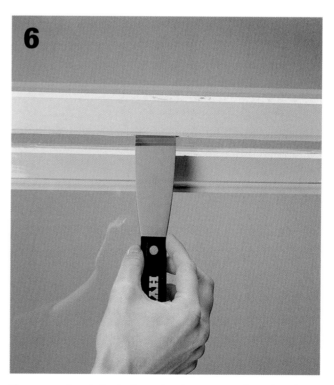

If you must paint windows in place, move the painted windows up and down several times during the drying period to keep them from sticking. Use a putty knife to avoid touching the painted surfaces.

How to Paint Doors

Remove the door by driving out the lower hinge pin with a screwdriver and hammer. Have a helper hold the door in place. Then, drive out the middle and upper hinge pins.

Place the door flat on sawhorses for painting. On paneled doors, paint in the following order, using a brush rather than a roller: 1) recessed panels, 2) horizontal rails, and 3) vertical stiles.

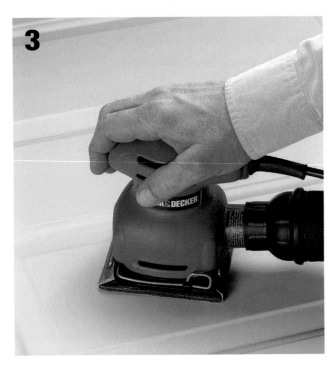

Let the painted door dry. If a second coat of paint is needed, sand the first coat lightly and wipe the door with tack cloth before repainting.

Seal the unpainted edges of the door with a clear wood sealer to prevent moisture from entering the wood. Water can cause wood to warp and swell.

Protect wall and floor surfaces with a wide wallboard knife or a plastic shielding tool.

Wipe all of the paint off of the wallboard knife or shielding tool each time it is moved.

Paint both sides of cabinet doors. This provides an even moisture seal and prevents warping.

Paint deep patterned surfaces with a stiff-bristled brush, like this stenciling brush. Use small circular strokes to penetrate recesses.

Ceiling & Wall Techniques

For a smooth finish on large wall and ceiling areas, paint in small sections. It's best to paint both the edges and expanses of each wall, one at a time, rather than edge the entire room before rolling. First use a paintbrush to cut in the edges, then immediately roll the section while it is still wet before moving on. If brushed edges dry before the area is rolled, lap marks will be visible on the finished wall. Working in natural light makes it easier to spot missed areas.

Choose high-quality paint and tools and work with a full brush or roller to avoid lap marks and to ensure full coverage. Roll slowly to minimize splattering.

Tips for Painting Ceilings & Walls ▶

Paint to a wet edge. Cut in the edges on small sections with a paintbrush, then immediately roll the section. (Using a corner roller makes it unnecessary to cut in inside corners.) With two painters, have one cut in with a brush while the other rolls the large areas.

Minimize brush marks. Slide the roller cover slightly off of the roller cage when rolling near wall corners or a ceiling line. Brushed areas dry to a different finish than rolled paint.

How to Paint Ceilings

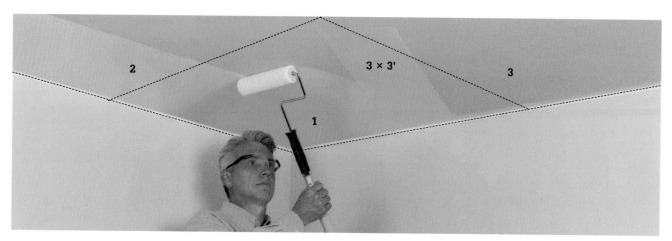

Paint ceilings with a roller handle extension. Use eye protection while painting overhead. Start at the corner farthest from the entry door. Paint the ceiling along the narrow end in 3 × 3' sections, cutting in the edges with a brush before rolling. Apply the paint with a diagonal stroke. Distribute the paint evenly with back-and-forth strokes. For the final smoothing strokes, roll each section toward the wall containing the entry door, lifting the roller at the end of each sweep.

How to Paint Walls

Paint walls in 2 × 4' sections. Start in an upper corner, cutting in the ceiling and wall corners with a brush, then rolling the section. Make the initial diagonal roller stroke from the bottom of the section upward, to avoid dripping paint. Distribute the paint evenly with horizontal strokes, then finish with downward sweeps of the roller. Next, cut in and roll the section directly underneath. Continue with adjacent areas, cutting in and rolling the top sections before the bottom sections. Roll all finish strokes toward the floor.

Painting Cabinets

If your kitchen cabinets are in good shape structurally and you are happy with their configuration but not their appearance, a coat of paint may be all it takes to update your kitchen in a dramatic way. You can brighten dark wood, freshen up previously painted cabinet surfaces, or create a new look with faux finish techniques. Any wood, metal or previously painted cabinets can be painted.

As with any painting project, your final results depend on careful and thorough preparation and use of high-quality products. Remove doors, drawers and all hardware so you can paint the surfaces in a flat position, eliminating many drips and sags.

Choose a high-quality enamel paint in either satin, low-luster or semi-gloss finish. A high gloss finish will highlight surface defects and create glare. Latex paint is suitable for this project. Using an alkyd (oil-based) paint may result in a smoother finish with fewer brush marks, but the cleanup is more involved and the fumes may require that you wear a respirator.

Cabinets with matte surfaces in good condition need only be washed with trisodium phosphate (TSP) or another appropriate detergent for preparation. But if the surface is smooth or glossy, as when varnished or painted with a gloss enamel, you'll need to sand and/or chemically degloss before you apply paint. An undercoat of primer improves adhesion and reduces stain-through. If the previous paint was dark or a highly saturated color, or bare wood has been exposed, an undercoat is also necessary. Do not spot-prime because the top coat will not cover evenly in those areas. Avoid applying two layers of top coat, but if you do, make sure to sand or degloss the first coat to get good adhesion of the second coat.

If you are also changing hardware, determine whether you will be using the same screw holes. If not, fill the existing holes with wood putty before sanding.

Painted cabinets are re-emerging as a popular design element in kitchens. Bright paint adds liveliness and fun, while more neutral tones are soothing and let other kitchen elements have the spotlight.

How to Paint Cabinets

Remove doors and drawers. Wash all surfaces to be painted with TSP or other degreaser. Scrape off any loose paint. Sand or chemically degloss all surfaces. Wipe away sanding dust and prime varnished surfaces, dark colors or bare wood with primer.

Remove shelves, when possible, to create access for painting cabinet interiors. Paint the cabinet backs first, followed by the tops, sides and then the bottoms. Paint the face frames last (so you won't need to reach over them when painting the interior).

Paint both sides of doors beginning with the interior surfaces. With raised panel doors, paint the panel inserts first, then the horizontal rails. Paint the vertical stiles last.

Eliminating Stair Squeaks

This staircase has center stringers to help support the treads. The 2 × 4s nailed between the outside stringers and the wall studs serve as spacers that allow room for the installation of skirt boards and wall finishes.

Like floors, stairs squeak when the lumber becomes warped or loose boards rub together. The continual pounding of foot traffic takes its toll on even the best built staircases. An unstable staircase is as unsafe as it is unattractive. Problems related to the structure of a staircase, such as severe sagging, twisting, or slanting, should be left to a professional. However, you can easily complete many common repairs.

Squeaks are usually caused by movement between the treads and risers, which can be alleviated from above or below the staircase.

Tools & Materials ▸

Drill	Caulk gun
Screwdriver	Hardwood shims
Hammer	Wood plugs
Utility knife	Wood glue
Nail set	Quarter-round molding
Wood screws	Finish nails
Wood putty	Construction adhesive

Tread

Risers

Center stringer

Outside stringer

How to Eliminate Squeaks from Below the Stairs

Glue wood blocks to the joints between the treads and risers with construction adhesive. Once the blocks are in place, drill pilot holes and fasten them to the treads and risers with wood screws. If the risers overlap the back edges of the treads, drive screws through the risers and into the treads to bind them together.

Fill the gaps between stair parts with tapered hardwood shims. Coat the shims with wood glue and tap them into the joints between treads and risers until they're snug. Shimming too much will widen the gap. Allow the glue to dry before walking on the stairs.

How to Eliminate Squeaks from Above the Stairs

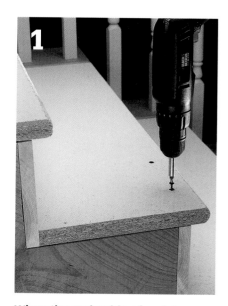

When the underside of a staircase is inaccessible, silence noisy stairs from above. Drill pilot holes and drive screws down through stair treads into the risers. Countersink the screws and fill the holes with putty or wood plugs.

Support the joints between treads and risers by attaching quarter-round molding. Drill pilot holes and use finish nails to fasten the molding. Set the nails with a nail set.

Tap glued wood shims under loose treads to keep them from flexing. Use a block to prevent splitting, and drive the shim just until it's snug. When the glue dries, cut the shims flush, using a utility knife.

Replacing a Broken Stair Tread

A broken stair tread is hazardous because we often don't look at steps as we climb them. Replace a broken step right away. The difficulty of this job depends on the construction of your staircase and the accessibility of the underside. It's better to replace a damaged tread than to repair it. A patch could create an irregular step that surprises someone unfamiliar with it.

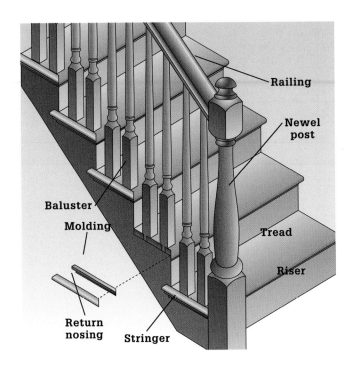

Tools & Materials ▸

Flat pry bar
Hammer
Combination square
Circular saw
Drill
Nail set
Caulk gun

Stair tread
Construction
  adhesive
Screws
Wood putty
Finish nails
Nail set

How to Replace a Broken Stair Tread

Carefully remove any decorative elements attached to the tread. Pull up carpeting and roll it aside. Remove trim pieces on or around the edges of the tread. Remove the balusters by detaching the top ends from the railing and separating the joints in the tread. Some staircases have a decorative hardwood cap inlaid into each tread. Remove these with a flat pry bar, taking care to pry from underneath the cap to avoid marring the exposed edges.

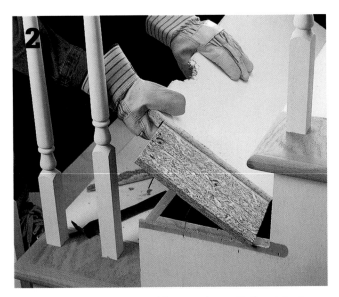

If possible, hammer upward from underneath the stairs to separate the tread from the risers and stringers. Otherwise, use a hammer and pry bar to work the tread loose, pulling nails as you go. Once the tread is removed, scrape the exposed edges of the stringers to remove old glue and wood fragments.

Measure the length for the new tread and mark it with a combination square so the cut end will be square and straight. If the tread has a milled end for an inlay, cut from the plain end. Cut the new tread to size, using a circular saw, and test-fit it carefully.

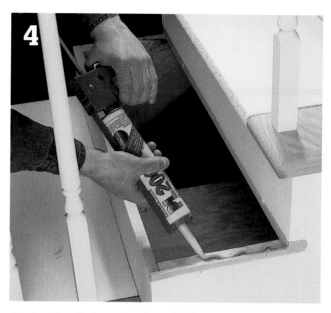

Apply a bead of construction adhesive to the exposed tops of the stringers. The adhesive will strengthen the bond between the tread and stringer and will cushion the joint, preventing the parts from squeaking.

Set the tread in place. If you have access to the step from underneath, secure the tread to the riser above it by driving screws through the riser into the back edge of the tread. To fasten it from the top side, drill and countersink pilot holes and drive two or three screws through the tread into the top edge of each stringer. Also drive a few screws along the front edge of the tread into the riser below it. Fill the screw holes in the tread with wood putty or plugs.

Reinstall any decorative elements, using finish nails. Set the nails with a nail set. Reinstall the balusters, if necessary.

Maintaining Windows & Doors

In this chapter:

Solving Common Door Problems

The most common door problems are caused by loose hinges. When hinges are loose, the door won't hang right, causing it to rub and stick and throwing off the latch mechanism. The first thing to do is check the hinge screws. If the holes for the hinge screws are worn and won't hold the screws, try the repair on the next page.

If the hinges are tight but the door still rubs against the frame, sand or plane down the door's edge. If a door doesn't close easily, it may be warped; use a long straightedge to check for warpage. You may be able to straighten a slightly warped door using weights, but severe warpage can't be corrected. Instead of buying a new door, remove the doorstop and reinstall it following the curve of the door.

Door latch problems occur for a number of reasons: loose hinges, swollen wood, sticking latchbolts, and paint buildup. If you've addressed those issues and the door still won't stay shut, it's probably because the door frame is out of square. This happens as a house settles with age; you can make minor adjustments by filing the strike plate on the door frame. If there's some room between the frame and the door, you can align the latchbolt and strike plate by shimming the hinges. Or, drive a couple of extra-long screws to adjust the frame slightly.

Common closet doors, such as sliding and bifold types, usually need only some minor adjustments and lubrication to stay in working order.

Door locksets are very reliable, but they do need to be cleaned and lubricated occasionally. One simple way to keep an entry door lockset working smoothly is to spray a light lubricant into the keyhole, then the key in and out a few times. Don't use graphite in locksets, as it can abrade some metals with repeated use.

Tools & Materials ▸

Screwdrivers	Spray lubricant
Nail set	Wooden golf tees
Hammer	or dowels
Drill	Wood glue
Utility knife	Cardboard shims
Metal file	3" wood screws
Straightedge	Finish nails
Pry bar	Paint or stain
Plane	Sandpaper
Paintbrush	Wood sealer

Tip ▸

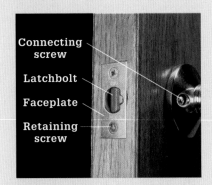

Latchbolts stick when they are dirty or in need of lubrication. Clean and lubricate locksets, and make sure the connecting screws aren't too tight—another cause of binding.

Connecting screw
Latchbolt
Faceplate
Retaining screw

A misaligned latchbolt and strike plate will prevent the door from latching. Poor alignment may be caused by loose hinges, or the door frame may be out of square.

Strike plate
Latchbolt

Sticking doors usually leave a mark where they rub against the door frame. Warped doors may resist closing and feel springy when you apply pressure. Check for warpage with a straightedge.

How to Remove a Door

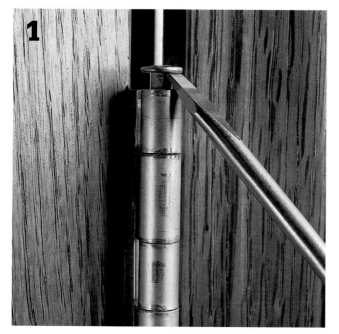

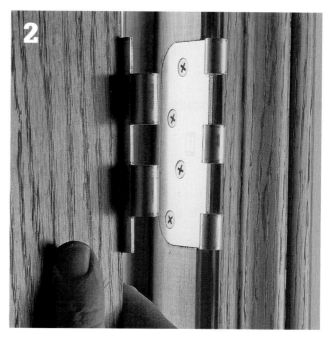

Drive the lower hinge pin out using a screwdriver and hammer. Have a helper hold the door in place, then drive out the upper (and center, if applicable) hinge pins. To help get the screwdriver tip under the pin head, use a nail set or small punch to tap the pin up from underneath.

Remove the door and set it aside. Clean and lubricate the hinge pins before reinstalling the door.

How to Tighten a Loose Hinge Plate

Remove the door from the hinges. Tighten any loose screws. If the wood won't hold the screws tightly, remove the hinges.

Coat wooden golf tees or dowels with wood glue, and drive them into the worn screw holes. If necessary, drill out the holes to accept dowels. Let the glue dry, then cut off excess wood.

Drill pilot holes in the new wood, and reinstall the hinge.

Tips for Aligning a Latchbolt & Strike Plate ▸

Check the door for a square fit. If the door is far out of square with the frame, remove it and shim the top or bottom hinge (right). Or, drive long screws into one of the hinges (below).

Install a thin cardboard shim behind the bottom hinge to raise the position of the latchbolt. To lower the latchbolt, shim behind the top hinge.

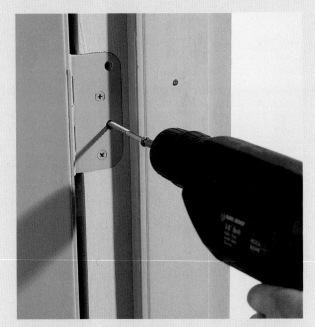

Remove two hinge screws from the top or bottom hinge, and drive a 3" wood screw into each hole. The screws will reach the framing studs in the wall and pull the door jamb upward, changing the angle of the door. Add long screws to the top hinge to raise the latchbolt or to the bottom hinge to lower it.

Fix minor alignment problems by filing the strike plate until the latchbolt fits.

How to Straighten a Warped Door

Check the door for warpage using a straightedge. Or, close the door until it hits the stop and look for a gap (see below). The amount of gap between the door and the stop reveals the extent of the warpage. The stop must be straight for this test, so check it with a straightedge.

If the warpage is slight, you can straighten the door using weights. Remove the door, and rest the ends of the door on sawhorses. Place heavy weights on the bowed center of the door, using cardboard to protect the finish. Leave the weights on the door for several days, and check it periodically with a straightedge.

How to Adjust for a Severely Warped Door

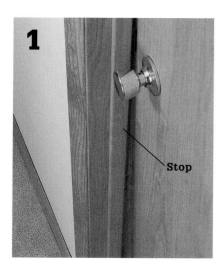

Stop

A severe warp cannot be corrected. Instead, you can adjust the doorstop to follow the shape of the door. If you touch up the door jamb with paint or stain after you've finished, no one will notice the repair.

Remove the doorstop using a small pry bar. If it's painted, cut the paint film first with a utility knife to prevent chipping. Avoid splintering by removing nails from the stop by pulling them through the back side of the piece. Pull all nails from the door jamb.

Close the door and latch it. Starting at the top, refasten the stop, keeping the inside edge flush against the door. Drive finish nails through the old holes, or drill new pilot holes through the stop. Set the nails with a nail set after you've checked the door's operation.

How to Free a Sticking Door

Tighten all of the hinge screws. If the door still sticks, use light pencil lines to mark the areas where the door rubs against the door jamb.

During dry weather, remove the door. If you have to remove a lot of material, you can save time by planing the door (step 3). Otherwise, sand the marked areas with medium-grit sandpaper. Make sure the door closes without sticking, then smooth the sanded areas with fine-grit sandpaper.

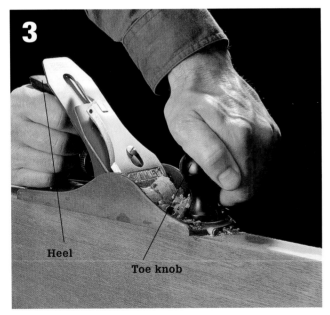

Heel

Toe knob

Secure the door on-edge. If the door has veneered surfaces, cut through the veneers with a utility knife to prevent splintering. Operate the plane so the wood grain runs "uphill" ahead of the plane. Grip the toe knob and handle firmly, and plane with long, smooth strokes. To prevent dipping, press down on the toe at the start of the stroke, and bear down on the heel at the end of the stroke. Check the door's fit, then sand the planed area smooth.

Apply clear sealer or paint to the sanded or planed area and any other exposed surfaces of the door. This will prevent moisture from entering the wood and is especially important for entry doors.

How to Maintain a Sliding Door

Clean the tracks above and below the doors with a toothbrush and a damp cloth or a hand vacuum.

Spray a greaseless lubricant on all the rollers, but do not spray the tracks. Replace any bent or worn parts.

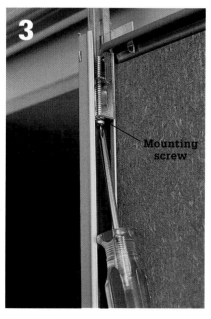

Mounting screw

Check the gap along the bottom edge of the door to make sure it is even. To adjust the gap, rotate the mounting screw to raise or lower the door edge.

How to Maintain a Bifold Door

Track Pins

Open or remove the doors and wipe the tracks with a clean rag. Spray the tracks and rollers or pins with greaseless lubricant.

Pivot block

Check closed doors for alignment within the door frame. If the gap between the closed doors is uneven, adjust the top pivot blocks with a screwdriver or wrench.

Pivot block

Adjustable pivot blocks are also found at the bottom of some door models. Adjust the pivot blocks until the gap between the door and the frame is even.

Weatherizing Basics

No matter whether you live in a hot or a cold climate, weatherizing your home's windows and doors can pay off handsomely. Heating and cooling costs may account for over half of the total household energy bill.

Since most weatherizing projects are relatively inexpensive, you can recover your investment quickly. In fact, in some climates, you can pay back the cost of a weatherproofing project in one season.

If you live in a cold climate, you probably already understand the importance of weatherizing. The value of keeping warm air inside the house during a cold winter is obvious. From the standpoint of energy efficiency, it's equally important to prevent warm air from entering the house during summer.

Weatherizing your home is an ideal do-it-yourself project, because it can be done a little at a time, according to your schedule. In cold climates, the best time of the year to weatherize is the fall, before it turns too cold to work outdoors.

Whether you're concerned about the environment or want to spend less on your utility bills, some simple adjustments around your home can help you accomplish your goal.

Most weatherizing projects deal with windows and doors, because these are the primary areas of heat loss in most homes. Here are a few simple suggestions you might consider for the exterior of your home:

Before buying a basement window well cover, measure the widest point of the window well and note its shape.

Use a caulk that matches your home exterior to seal the window and door frames.

A felt door sweep can seal out drafts, even if you have an uneven floor or a low threshold.

Minimize heat loss from basement window wells by covering them with plastic window well covers (left, top). Most window well covers have an upper flange designed to slip under the siding. Slip this in place, then fasten the cover to the foundation with masonry anchors and weigh down the bottom flange with stones. For extra weatherizing, seal the edges with caulk.

Adding caulk is a simple way to fill narrow gaps in interior or exterior surfaces. It's also available in a peelable form that can be easily removed at the end of the season.

When buying caulk, estimate half a cartridge per window or door, four for an average-sized foundation sill, and at least one more to close gaps around vents, pipes, and other openings.

Caulk around the outside of the window and door frames to seal any gaps. For best results, use a caulk that matches or blends with the color of your siding.

There are many different types of caulk and weather stripping materials. All are inexpensive and easy to use, but it's important to get the right materials for the job, as most are designed for specific applications.

Generally, metal and metal-reinforced weather stripping is more durable than products made of plastic, rubber, or foam. However, even plastic, rubber, and foam weather stripping products have a wide range of quality. The best rubber products are those made from neoprene rubber—use this whenever it's available.

A door sweep (previous page, bottom) attaches to the inside bottom of the door to seal out drafts. A felt or bristle sweep is best if you have an uneven floor or a low threshold. Vinyl and rubber models are also available.

A threshold insert fits around the base of the door. Most have a sweep on the interior side and a drip edge on the exterior side to direct water away from the threshold.

A threshold insert seals the gap between the door and the threshold. These are made from vinyl or rubber and can be easily replaced.

Self-adhesive foam strips (below) attach to sashes and frames to seal the air gaps at windows and doors. Reinforced felt strips have a metal spine that adds rigidity in high-impact areas, such as doorstops.

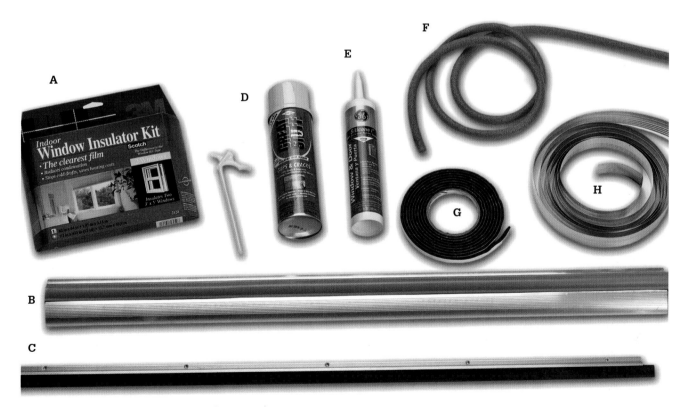

Weatherizing products commonly found in home centers include: A clear film, heat-shrink window insulator kit (A); an aluminum door threshold with vinyl weatherstripping insert (B); a nail-on, rubber door sweep (C); minimal expanding spray foam (D); silicone window and door caulk (E); open-cell foam caulk-backer rod (F); self-adhesive, closed-cell foam weatherstripping coil (G); flexible brass weatherstripping coil, also called V-channel, (H).

Tips for Weatherizing Doors ▶

Door weather stripping is prone to failure because it undergoes constant stress. Use metal weather stripping that is tacked to the surfaces whenever you can—especially around door jambs. It is much more durable than self-adhesive products. If your job calls for flexible weather stripping, use products made from neoprene rubber, not foam. Replace old door thresholds or threshold inserts as soon as they begin to show wear.

Install a storm door to decrease drafts and energy loss through entry doors. Buy an insulated storm door with a continuous hinge and seamless exterior surface.

Adjust the door frame to eliminate large gaps between the door and jamb. Remove the interior case molding and drive new shims between the jamb and framing member on the hinge side, reducing the size of the door opening. Close the door to test fit, and adjust as needed before reattaching the case molding.

Patio door: Use rubber compression strips to seal the channels in patio door jambs, where movable panels fit when closed. Also install a patio door insulator kit (plastic sheeting installed similarly to plastic sheeting for windows) on the interior side of the door.

Garage door: Attach a new rubber sweep to the bottom outside edge of the garage door if the old sweep has deteriorated. Also check the door jambs for drafts, and add weather stripping, if needed.

How to Weatherize an Exterior Door

Cut two pieces of metal tension strip or V-channel the full height of the door opening, and cut another to full width. Use wire brads to tack the strips to the door jambs and door header on the interior side of the doorstops. *Tip: Attach metal weather stripping from the top down to help prevent buckling.* Flare out the tension strips with a putty knife to fill the gaps between the jambs and the door when the door is in the closed position (do not pry too far at a time).

Add reinforced felt strips to the edge of the doorstop on the exterior side. The felt edge should form a close seal with the door when closed. *Tip: Drive fasteners only until they are flush with the surface of the reinforcing spine—overdriving will cause damage and buckling.*

Attach a new door sweep to the bottom of the door on the interior side (felt or bristle types are better choices if the floor is uneven). Before fastening it permanently, tack the sweep in place and test the door swing to make sure there is enough clearance.

Tip ▶

Fix any cracks in wooden door panels with epoxy wood filler or caulk to block air leaks. If the door has a stain finish, use tinted wood putty, filling from the interior side. Sand and touch up with paint or stain.

Tips for Weatherizing a Window ▶

Sliding windows: Treat side-by-side sliding windows as if they were double-hung windows turned 90°. For greater durability, use metal tension strips, rather than self-adhesive compressible foam, in the sash track that fit against the edge of the sash when the window is closed.

Casement windows: Attach self-adhesive foam or rubber compression strips on the outside edges of the window stops.

Storm windows: Create a tight seal by attaching foam compression strips to the outside of storm window stops. After installing the storm window, fill any gaps between the exterior window trim and the storm window with caulk backer rope (left). Check the inside surface of the storm window during cold weather for condensation or frost buildup (facing page). If moisture is trapped between the storm window and the permanent window, drill one or two small holes through the bottom rail (right) to allow moist air to escape. Drill at a slightly upward angle.

How to Weatherstrip a Window

Cut metal V-channel to fit in the channels for the sliding sash, extending at least 2" past the closed position for each sash (do not cover sash-closing mechanisms). Attach the V-channel by driving wire brads (usually provided by the manufacturer) with a tack hammer. Drive the fasteners flush with the surface so the sliding sash will not catch on them.

Flare out the open ends of the V-channels with a putty knife so the channel is slightly wider than the gap between the sash and the track it fits into. Avoid flaring out too much at one time—it is difficult to press V-channel back together without causing some buckling.

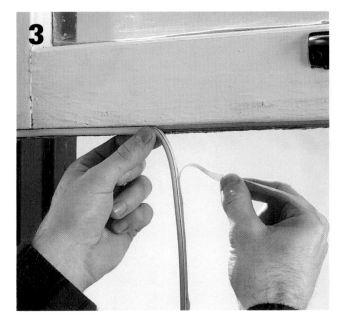

Wipe down the underside of the bottom window sash with a damp rag, and let it dry; then attach self-adhesive compressible foam or rubber to the underside of the sash. Use high-quality hollow neoprene strips, if available. This will create an airtight seal when the window is locked in position.

Bottom sash (raised)

Top sash (lowered)

Seal the gap between the top sash and the bottom sash on double-hung windows. Lift the bottom sash and lower the top sash to improve access, and tack metal V-channel to the bottom rail of the top sash using wire brads. *Tip: The open end of the "V" should be pointed downward so moisture cannot collect in the channel. Flare out the V-channel with a putty knife to fit the gap between the sash.*

Shortening Interior Doors

There should be a ⅜ to ¾" gap between the bottom of interior doors and the finished floor. This lets the door swing without binding on new carpet or other floor coverings. But eventually, you may decide to recarpet or add new tile or wood flooring beneath an existing door, and you'll need to shorten the door to create the proper gap again. If you own a circular saw with a fine-tooth blade, it's a simple project for a do-it-yourselfer.

Most newer homes have solid-wood interior doors these days, but hollow-core doors are still fairly common, and they're typical on older homes. Shortening either door type is a similar task, but hollow-core doors will require a few more steps because the door consists of multiple pieces (see page 117).

Tools & Materials ▶

Hammer
Screwdriver
Utility knife
Sawhorses
Circular saw with fine-tooth blade
Straightedge
Clamps
File
Sanding block
Scrap plywood

Changing a floor covering is a great way to update the look of a room, but if the new floor covering is thicker than the old one, you can impede door swing. The solution is to shorten the door.

How to Shorten a Solid Wood Door

1

Set a strip of scrap plywood on the floor against the door, and trace along the plywood to create a reference line for cutting. The thickness of the plywood will set the amount of door gap, and it will help establish an even gap line. Do not press the plywood down into the carpet when drawing the line. If the flooring is uneven, open the door to where it rubs the most and use this spot to mark the gap.

2

Remove the door from the jamb by tapping out the hinge pins with a hammer and flat-blade screwdriver. If the hinge pins are fixed, you'll need to unscrew the hinge leaves from the jamb instead.

3

To prevent the saw from chipping the wood as it cuts, use a sharp utility knife to score along the cutting line. Guide the knife against a metal straightedge. Score both door faces and the edges.

(continued)

Clamp a straightedge to the door so the saw blade will cut about 1/16" on the waste side of your score line. The straightedge provides a guide for the edge of the saw base. Use the saw with a fine-tooth blade installed to check your setup.

Set the blade so the teeth project about 1/4" below the door, and guide the saw along the straightedge to saw off the door bottom. Use steady feed pressure, and slow down your cutting rate at the end to prevent splintering the door edge.

Use a file to soften the sharp edges of the cut and to form a very slight chamfer all around the door bottom. Switch to a sanding block and medium-grit sandpaper to smooth away any blade marks and roughness.

Variation: Hollow-core Doors ▸

With the door in place, measure ⅜" up from the top of the floor covering and mark the door. Remove the door from the hinges by tapping out the hinge pins with a screwdriver and a hammer.

Mark the cutting line. Cut through the door veneer with a sharp utility knife to prevent it from chipping when the door is sawed.

Lay the door on sawhorses and clamp a straightedge to the door as a cutting guide. Saw off the bottom of the door. The hollow core of the door may be exposed.

To reinstall a cutoff frame piece in the bottom of the door, chisel the veneer from both sides of the removed portion.

Apply wood glue to the cutoff piece. Insert the frame piece into the opening of the door and clamp it. Wipe away any excess glue and let the door dry overnight.

Replacing Thresholds

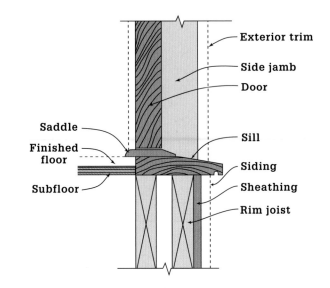

While construction varies from home to home, the part of a door that is generally referred to as the "threshold" is actually made up of two separate components: a sill, which serves as the bottom of the door frame and diverts water and dirt away from the home, and the threshold or saddle, which is attached to the sill and helps to seal the air space under a door. Due to constant traffic and exposure to the elements, sills and saddles may eventually require replacing.

Modern prehung doors often have a cast metal sill with an integrated saddle and are installed directly on top of the subfloor. Older homes often have thick wooden sills that are installed lower than metal sills, flush with the floor framing, with a separate saddle bridging the gap between the sill and the finished floor. Saddles are available in several styles and materials, such as wood, metal, and vinyl. Because the design of entry thresholds can vary, it is important to examine the construction of your door threshold to determine your needs. In this project, we replaced a deteriorating wooden sill and saddle with a new oak sill and a wooden weatherstripped saddle.

Besides replacing a deteriorating threshold, you might also choose to replace an existing threshold for increased accessibility. While standard thresholds are designed to keep mud and dirt out of a home, they deny access to people in wheelchairs and can cause people to trip if they are unsteady on their feet. See page 121 for tips on making thresholds accessible.

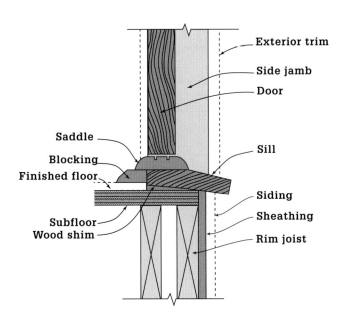

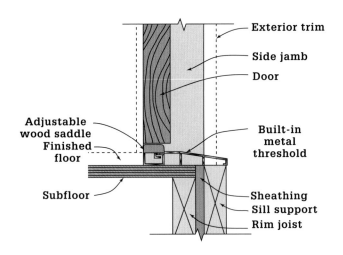

Tools & Materials ▸

Reciprocating saw
Pry bar
Hammer
Drill with
   countersink bit
Pencil
3" galvanized screws
   or 10d galvanized
   casing nails

1½" galvanized
   screws or 8d
   galvanized nails
Shims
Putty
Silicone caulk
Sealer/protectant

How to Replace an Exterior Door Threshold

Remove the old saddle. This may be as easy as unscrewing the saddle and prying it out. If necessary, cut the old saddle in two using a reciprocating saw, then pry out the saddle. Be careful not to damage the flooring or door frame. Note which edge of the saddle is more steeply beveled; the new saddle should be installed the same way.

Examine the sill for damage or deterioration. If it needs replacing, use a reciprocating saw to cut the sill into three pieces, cutting as close to the jambs as possible. Pry out the center piece, then use a hammer and chisel to split out the pieces directly beneath the jambs. Remove any remaining nails from beneath the jambs using a reciprocating saw with a metal cutting blade.

Measure and cut the new sill to size. If possible, use the salvaged end pieces from the old sill as a template to mark the notches on the new sill. Cut the notches using a jigsaw.

Test-fit the new sill, tapping it into place beneath the jambs using a hammer and wood block to protect the sill. Remove the sill and, if necessary, install long wood strips (or tapered shims) beneath the sill so it fits snugly beneath the jambs with a gentle slope away from the home.

(continued)

5

Apply several beads of caulk to the area beneath the sill. Tap the sill back in place. Drill countersunk pilot holes every 4 to 5" and fasten the sill with 10d galvanized casing nails or 3" screws.

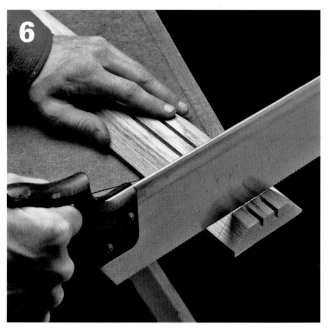

6

Measure the distance between the jambs and cut the new saddle to length. Test-fit the saddle. Mark the ends and cut notches to fit around the door jamb stops using a jigsaw. Apply caulk to the bottom of the saddle and position it so it covers the gap between the sill and the finished floor. Fasten the saddle using 1½" galvanized screws.

Variation ▶

If you are installing a metal saddle, instead of cutting notches in the saddle, use a hammer and chisel to notch the jamb stops to fit.

Waterproofing Tip ▶

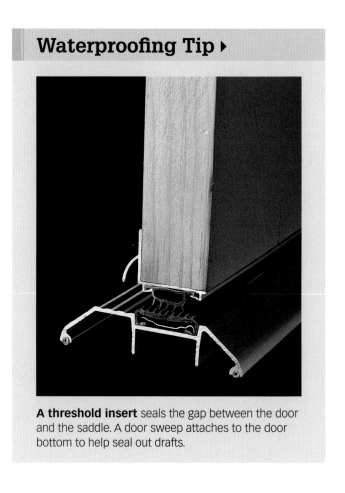

A threshold insert seals the gap between the door and the saddle. A door sweep attaches to the door bottom to help seal out drafts.

Variation: Making Thresholds Accessible ▸

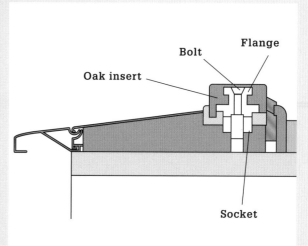

Adjustable sills: Many prehung doors have an aluminum sill with an adjustable wood saddle. Some versions can be made accessible without additional modification by lowering the saddle as far as possible. Other types can be adapted by recessing the sill into the subfloor.

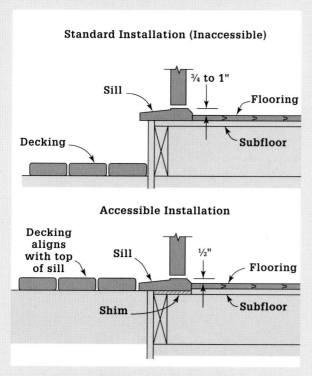

Accessible thresholds: There are many ways to modify standard thresholds for accessibility. Often, the first step is to raise the exterior surface or decking to the same level as the threshold. Entry thresholds should be no higher than ¼" for square-edged sills and ½" high for beveled sills.

Mini-ramps: The slide channels on most sliding glass doors present a major obstacle for wheelchair users. The height difference can be as much as 2" from the bottom to the top of the track. Commercially available mini-ramps can make standard sliding glass door thresholds accessible.

Improving Window Operation

Many of us have experienced difficulty with opening windows due to swelled wood or painted channels. Almost as frequent, windows won't stay open because of a broken sash cord or chain. To avoid difficulties with windows, regular maintenance is crucial. Double-hung windows with spring-loaded sash tracks require cleaning and an occasional adjustment of the springs in (or behind) the tracks. Casement windows are often faulty at the crank mechanisms. If cleaning doesn't fix the problem, the crank mechanism must be replaced. For storm windows, the window track must be clean, and greaseless lubricant must be applied each time the windows and screens are removed.

Tools & Materials ▸

Screwdrivers	Toothbrush
Paint zipper or	Paint solvent
utility knife	Rags
Hammer	Sash cord
Vacuum	Lubricant
Small pry bar	Wax candle
Scissors	String
Stiff brush	All-purpose grease

Windows endure temperature extremes, house setting, and all sorts of wear and tear. Sooner or later you'll need to perform a bit of maintenance to keep them working properly.

How to Adjust Windows

Spring-loaded windows have an adjustment screw on the track insert. Adjust both sides until the window is balanced and opens and closes smoothly.

Spring-lift windows operate with the help of a spring-loaded lift rod inside a metal tube. Adjust them by unscrewing the top end of the tube from the jamb, then twisting the tube to change the spring tension: clockwise for more lifting power; counterclockwise for less. Maintain a tight grip on the tube at all times to keep it from unwinding.

Tips for Freeing Sticking Windows ▸

Cut the paint film if the window is painted shut. Insert a paint zipper or utility knife between the window stop and the sash, and slide it down to break the seal.

Place a block of scrap wood against the window sash. Tap lightly with a hammer to free the window.

Clean the tracks on sliding windows and doors with a hand vacuum and a toothbrush. Dirt buildup is common on storm window tracks.

Clean weatherstrips by spraying with a cleaner and wiping away dirt. Use paint solvent to remove paint that may bind windows. Then apply a small amount of lubricant to prevent sticking.

Lubricate wood window channels by rubbing them with a white candle, then open and close the window a few times. Do not use liquid lubricants on wood windows.

How to Replace Broken Sash Cords

Cut any paint seal between the window frame and stops with a utility knife or paint zipper. Pry the stops away from the frame, or remove the molding screws.

Bend the stops out from the center to remove them from the frame. Remove any weatherstripping that's in the way.

Slide out the lower window sash. Pull knotted or nailed cords from holes in the sides of the sash (see step 9).

Pry out or unscrew the weight pocket cover in the lower end of the window channel. Pull the weight from the pocket, and cut the old sash cord from the weight.

Tie one end of a piece of string to a nail and the other end to the new sash cord. Run the nail over the pulley and let it drop into the weight pocket. Retrieve the nail and string through the pocket.

Pull on the string to run the new sash cord over the pulley and through the weight pocket. Make sure the new cord runs smoothly over the pulley.

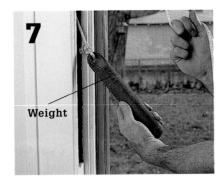

Attach the end of the sash cord to the weight using a tight double knot. Set the weight in the pocket. Pull on the cord until the weight touches the pulley.

Rest the bottom sash on the sill. Hold the sash cord against the side of the sash, and cut enough cord to reach 3" past the hole in the side of the sash.

Knot the sash cord and wedge the knot into the hole in the sash. Replace the pocket cover. Slide the window and any weatherstripping into the frame, then attach the stops in the original positions.

How to Clean & Lubricate a Casement Window Crank

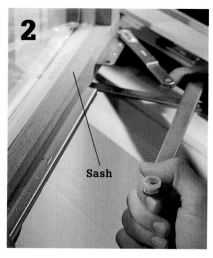

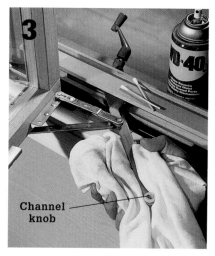

If a casement window is hard to crank, clean the accessible parts. Open the window until the roller at the end of the extension arm is aligned with the access slot in the window track.

Disengage the extension arm by pulling it down and out of the track. Clean the track with a stiff brush, and wipe the pivoting arms and hinges with a rag.

Lubricate the track and hinges with spray lubricant or household oil. Wipe off excess lubricant with a cloth, then reattach the extension arm. If that doesn't solve the problem, repair or replace the crank assembly (below).

How to Repair a Casement Window Crank Assembly

Disengage the extension arm from the window track, then remove the molding or cap concealing the crank mechanism. Unhinge any pivot arms connected to the window.

Remove the screws securing the crank assembly, then remove the assembly and clean it thoroughly. If the gears are badly worn, replace the assembly. Check a home center or call the manufacturer for new parts. Note which way the window opens—to the right or left—when ordering replacement parts.

Apply an all-purpose grease to the gears, and reinstall the assembly. Connect the pivot arms, and attach the extension arm to the window. Test the window operation before installing the cap and molding.

How to Fix a Broken Windowpane

1

Wearing heavy leather gloves, remove the broken pieces of glass. Then, soften the old glazing compound using a heat gun or a hair dryer. Don't hold the heat gun too long in one place because it can be hot enough to scorch the wood or crack adjacent panes of glass.

2

Once a section of compound is soft, remove it using a putty knife. Work carefully to avoid gouging the wood frame. If a section is difficult to scrape clean, reheat it with the heat gun. Soft compound is always easy to remove.

3

Once the wood opening is scraped clean, seal the wood with a coat of linseed oil or primer. If the wood isn't sealed, the dry surface will draw too much moisture from the glazing compound and reduce its effectiveness.

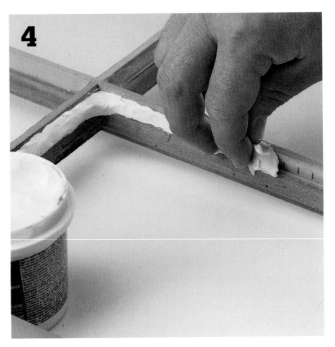

4

Apply a thin bed of glazing compound to the wood frame opening and smooth it in place with your thumb.

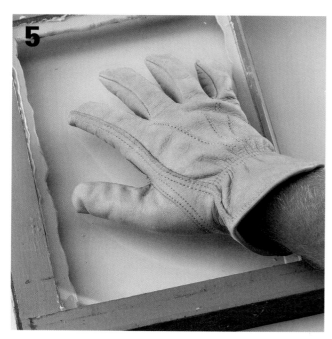

5

Press the new pane into the opening, making sure to achieve a tight seal with the compound on all sides. Wiggle the pane from side to side and up and down until the pane is seated. There will be some squeeze-out, but do not press all the compound out.

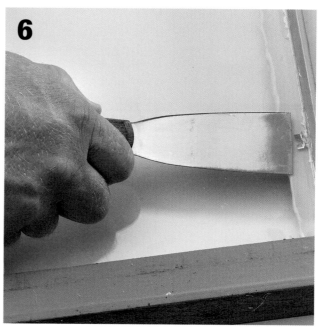

6

Drive glazier's points into the wood frame to hold the pane in place. Use the tip of a putty knife to slide the point against the surface of the glass. Install at least 2 points on each side of the pane.

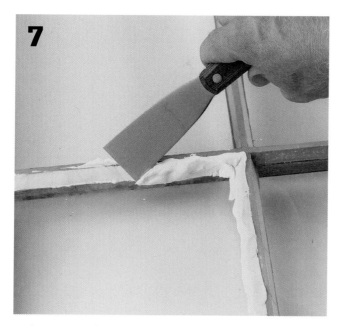

7

Make a rope of compound (about ½" dia.) by rolling it between your hands. Then press it against the pane and the wood frame. Smooth it in place by drawing a putty knife, held at a 45° angle, across its surface. Scrape off excess.

8

Allow the glazing compound at least one week to dry completely. Then prime and paint it to match the rest of the sash. Be sure to spread the paint over the joint between the compound and the glass. This will seal the joint completely. When the paint is dry, scrape off the extra with a razor blade paint scraper.

Repairing & Maintaining Storm Windows & Doors

Compared to removable wood storm windows and screens, repairing combination storm windows is a little more complex. But there are several repairs you can make without too much difficulty, as long as you find the right parts. Take the old corner keys, gaskets, or other original parts to a hardware store that repairs storm windows so the clerk can help you find the correct replacement parts. If you cannot find the right parts, have a new sash built.

Remove the metal storm window sash by pressing in the release hardware in the lower rail then lifting the sash out. Sash hangers on the corners of the top rail should be aligned with the notches in the side channels before removal.

Tools & Materials ▸

Tape measure
Screwdriver
Scissors
Drill
Utility knife
Spline roller

Nail set
Hammer
Spline cord
Screening, glass
Rubber gasket
Replacement hardware

How to Replace Screening in a Metal Storm Window

1

Pry the vinyl spline from the groove around the edge of the frame with a screwdriver. Retain the old spline if it is still flexible, or replace it with a new spline.

2

Stretch the new screen tightly over the frame so that it overlaps the edges of the frame. Keeping the screen taut, use the convex side of a spline roller to press the screen into the retaining grooves.

3

Use the concave side of the spline roller to press the spline into the groove (it helps to have a partner for this). Cut away excess screen using a utility knife.

How to Replace Glass in a Metal Storm Window

Remove the sash frame from the window, then completely remove the broken glass from the sash. Remove the rubber gasket that framed the old glass pane and remove any glass remnants. Find the dimensions for the replacement glass by measuring between the inside edges of the frame opening, then adding twice the thickness of the rubber gasket to each measurement.

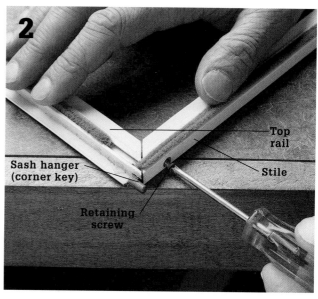

Set the frame on a flat surface, and disconnect the top rail. Remove the retaining screws in the sides of the frame stiles where they join the top rail. After unscrewing the retaining screws, pull the top rail loose, pulling gently in a downward motion to avoid damaging the L-shaped corner keys that join the rail and the stiles. For glass replacement, you need only disconnect the top rail.

Fit the rubber gasket (buy a replacement if the original is in poor condition) around one edge of the replacement glass pane. At the corners, cut the spine of the gasket partway so it will bend around the corner. Continue fitting the gasket around the pane, cutting at the corners, until all four edges are covered. Trim off any excess gasket material.

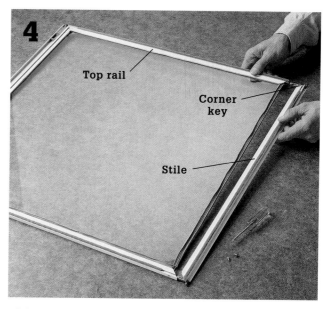

Slide the glass pane into the channels in the stiles and bottom rail of the sash frame. Insert corner keys into the top rail, then slip the other ends of the keys into the frame stiles. Press down on the top rail until the mitered corners are flush with the stiles. Drive the retaining screws back through the stiles and into the top rail to join the frame together. Reinsert the frame into the window.

How to Disassemble & Repair a Metal Sash Frame

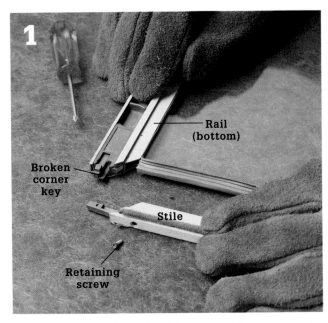

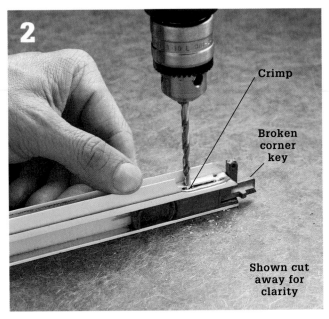

Metal window sash are held together at the corner joints by L-shaped pieces of hardware that fit into grooves in the sash frame pieces. To disassemble a broken joint, start by disconnecting the stile and rail at the broken joint—there is usually a retaining screw driven through the stile that must be removed.

Corner keys are secured in the rail slots with crimps that are punched into the metal over the key. To remove keys, drill through the metal in the crimped area using a drill bit the same diameter as the crimp. Carefully knock the broken key pieces from the frame slots with a screwdriver and hammer.

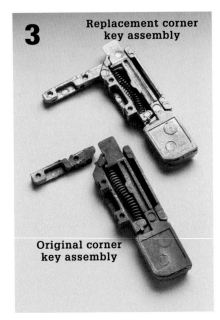

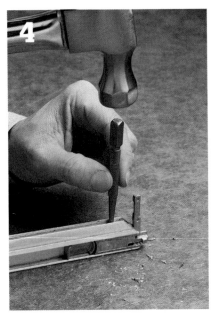

Locate matching replacement parts for the broken corner key, which is usually an assembly of two or three pieces. There are dozens of different types, so it is important that you save the old parts for reference.

Insert the replacement corner key assembly into the slot in the rail. Use a nail set as a punch, and rap it into the metal over the corner key, creating a new crimp to hold the key in place.

Insert the glass and gasket into the frame slots, then reassemble the frame and drive in retainer screws (for screen windows, replace the screening).

Replace turnbuttons and window clips that do not hold storm windows tightly in place. Fill old screw holes with wood dowels and glue before driving the screws.

Lubricate the sliding assemblies on metal-framed combination storm windows or doors once a year using penetrating lubricant.

Replace deteriorated glazing around glass panes in wood-framed windows. Sound glazing makes windows more energy-efficient and more attractive.

Tighten storm door latches by redriving loose screws in the strike plate. If the latch does not catch on the strike plate, loosen the screws on the strike plate, insert thin wood shims between the plate and the jamb, and retighten the screws.

Add a wind chain if your storm door does not have one. Wind chains prevent doors from blowing open too far, causing damage to the door hinges or closer. Set the chain so the door will not open more than 90°.

Adjust the door closer so it has the right amount of tension to close the door securely, without slamming. Most closers have tension-adjustment screws at the end of the cylinder farthest from the hinge side of the door.

Installing New Window Sash

If you're looking to replace or improve old single- or double-hung windows, consider using sash-replacement kits. They can give you energy-efficient, maintenance-free windows without changing the outward appearance of your home or breaking your budget.

Unlike prime window replacement, which changes the entire window and frame, or pocket window replacement, in which a complete window unit is set into the existing frame, sash replacement uses the original window jambs, eliminating the need to alter exterior or interior walls or trim. Installing a sash-replacement kit involves little more than removing the old window stops and sashes and installing new vinyl jamb liners and wood or vinyl sash. And all of the work can be done from inside your home.

Most sash-replacement kits offer tilt features and other contemporary conveniences. Kits are available in vinyl, aluminum, or wood construction with various options for color and glazing, energy efficiency, security features, and noise reduction.

Nearly all major window manufacturers offer sash-replacement kits designed to fit their own windows. You can also order custom kits that are sized to your specific window dimensions. A good fit is essential to the performance of your new windows. Review the tips shown on the next page for measuring your existing windows, and follow the manufacturer's instructions for the best fit.

Tools & Materials ▸

Sill-bevel gauge
Flat pry bar
Scissors
Screwdriver
Nail set
Sash-replacement kit
1" galvanized
    roofing nails
Fiberglass insulation
Finish nails
Wood-finishing
    materials
Torpedo Level

Upgrade old, leaky windows with new, energy-efficient sash-replacement kits. Kits are available in a variety of styles to match your existing windows or to add a new decorative accent to your home. Most kits offer natural or painted interior surfaces and a choice of outdoor surface finishes.

How to Install a New Window Sash

Measure the width of the existing window at the top, middle, and bottom of the frame. Use the smallest measurement, then reduce the figure by ⅜". Measure the height of the existing window from the head jamb to the point where the outside edge of the bottom sash meets the sill. Reduce the figure by ⅜". *Note: Manufacturers' specifications for window sizing may vary.*

Check for a straight, level, and plumb sill, side, and head jambs using a torpedo level. Measure the frame diagonally to check for square (if the diagonal measurements are equal, the frame is square). If the frame is not square, check with the sash-kit manufacturer: Most window kits can accommodate some deviation in frame dimensions.

Carefully remove the interior stops from the side jambs, using a putty knife or pry bar. Save the stops for reinstallation.

With the bottom sash down, cut the cord holding the sash, balancing weight on each side of the sash. Let the weights and cords fall into the weight pockets.

(continued)

Lift out the bottom sash. Remove the parting stops from the head and side jambs. (The parting stops are the strips of wood that separate the top and bottom sash.) Cut the sash cords for the top sash, then lift out the top sash. Remove the sash-cord pulleys. If possible, pull the weights from the weight pockets at the bottom of the side jambs, then fill the weight pockets with fiberglass insulation. Repair any parts of the jambs that are rotted or damaged.

Position the jamb-liner brackets, and fasten them to the jambs with 1" galvanized roofing nails. Place one bracket approximately 4" from the head jamb and one 4" from the sill. Leave 1/16" clearance between the blind stop and the jamb-liner bracket. Install any remaining brackets, spacing them evenly along the jambs.

Position any gaskets or weatherstripping provided for the jamb liners. Carefully position each liner against its brackets and snap it into place. When both liners are installed, set the new parting stop into the groove of the existing head jamb, and fasten it with small finish nails. Install a vinyl sash stop in the interior track at the top of each liner to prevent the bottom sash from being opened too far.

Set the sash control mechanism, using a slotted screwdriver. Gripping the screwdriver firmly, slide down the mechanism until it is about 9" above the sill, then turn the screwdriver to lock the mechanism and prevent it from springing upward. The control mechanisms are spring-loaded—do not let them go until they are locked in place. Set the mechanism in each of the four sash channels.

Install the top sash into the jamb liners. Set the cam pivot on one side of the sash into the outside channel. Tilt the sash, and set the cam pivot on the other side of the sash. Make sure both pivots are set above the sash control mechanisms. Holding the sash level, tilt it up, depress the jamb liners on both sides, and set the sash in the vertical position in the jamb liners. Once the sash is in position, slide it down until the cam pivots contact the locking terminal assemblies.

Install the bottom sash into the jamb liners, setting it into the inside sash channels. When the bottom sash is set in the vertical position, slide it down until it engages the control mechanisms. Open and close both sash to make sure they operate properly.

Reinstall the stops that you removed in step 3. Fasten them with finish nails, using the old nail holes, or drill new pilot holes for the nails.

Check the tilt operation of the bottom sash to make sure the stops do not interfere. Remove the labels, and clean the windows. Paint or varnish the new sash as desired.

Securing Windows & Doors

Securing windows and doors is often simply a matter of having the right hardware pieces. But skimping on strength or quality with any of them will undermine the security of the whole system.

Glass is both the strength and weakness of windows, in terms of security. An intruder can easily break the glass, but may not, since the noise it would make is likely to draw attention. Aside from installing metal bars, there's no way to secure the glass, so make sure your windows can't be opened from the outside.

Entry doors should be metal or solid wood—at least 1¾" thick—and each one in the home should have a deadbolt lock, as doorknob locks provide little security. Lock quality varies widely; just make sure to choose one that has a bolt (or bolt core) of hardened steel and a minimum 1" throw—the distance the bolt protrudes from the door when engaged.

Door hinges are easy to secure. Manufacturers offer a variety of inexpensive devices that hold a door in place even when the hinge pins are removed.

Garage doors are structurally secure, but their locking devices can make them easy targets. When you're away from home, place a padlock in the roller track. If you have an automatic door opener, make sure the remote transmitter uses a rolling code system, which prevents thieves from copying your signal. An electronic keypad can make your garage door as secure and easy to use as your front door.

Tools & Materials ▸

Hammer	Plywood
Drill	Casing nails
Hole saw	Board
Spade bit	Eye bolts
Awl	Hinge
Screwdriver	Screws
Chisel	Dowel
Utility knife	Security devices

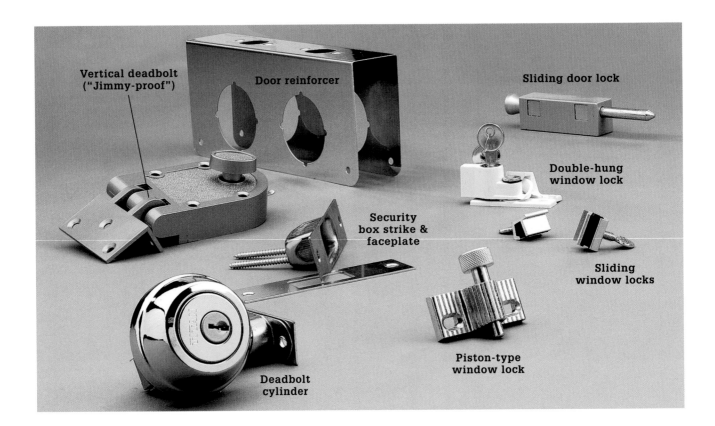

Vertical deadbolt ("Jimmy-proof")

Door reinforcer

Sliding door lock

Double-hung window lock

Security box strike & faceplate

Sliding window locks

Piston-type window lock

Deadbolt cylinder

Tips for Securing Windows

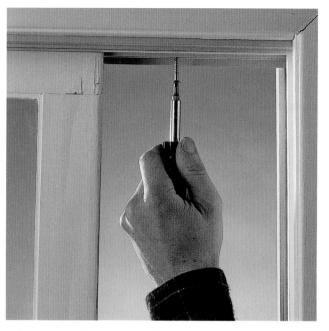

Pin together sashes of single- and double-hung windows with ¼ × 3" eye bolts. With the window closed, drill a ¼"-dia. hole, at a slight downward angle, through the top rail of the bottom sash and into the bottom rail of the top sash. Avoid hitting the glass, and stop the hole about ¾ of the way through the top sash. To lock the window in open positions, drill holes along the sash stiles (vertical pieces) instead.

Drive screws into the top channel of sliding windows to prevent intruders from lifting the window sash out of the lower channel. The screws should just clear the top of the window and not interfere with its operation. Use sturdy screws, and space them about 6" apart.

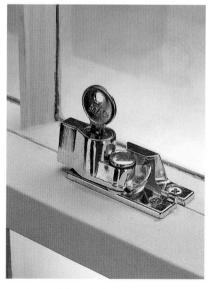

Block sash channels on sliding windows with a narrow board or a thick dowel.

Use auxiliary locks on sliding windows when a dowel or board won't work. Most types can be installed on the upper or lower window track.

Replace old sash locks on double-hung windows with keyed devices. Traditional sash locks can be highly vulnerable—especially on old windows. Be sure to store a key nearby, for emergency exits.

(continued)

Removing the handles from casement and awning windows keeps intruders from cranking the window open after breaking the glass.

Security bars or gates can be installed in ground-floor windows to prevent intruders from gaining entry to your home.

Tips for Securing Sliding Glass Doors

Make a custom lock for your door track, using a thick board and a hinge. Cut the board to fit behind the closed door, then cut it again a few inches from one end. Install a hinge so you can flip up the end and keep the door secure while it's ajar. Attach knobs to facilitate use.

Drive screws into the upper track to keep the sliding panel from being pried up and out of the lower track. Use sturdy pan-head screws, spaced about every 8", and drive them so their heads just clear the top of the door. For metal door frames, use self-tapping screws and a low drill speed.

Attach a sliding-door lock to the frame of the sliding panel. Drill a hole for the deadbolt into the upper track. Then drill an additional hole a few inches away so you can lock the door in an open position.

Tips for Securing Doors

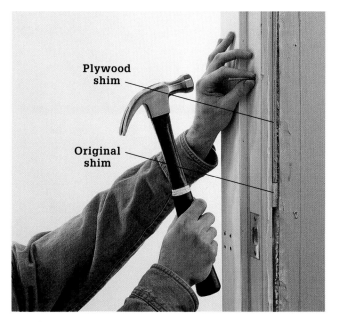

Install plywood shims in the gaps between the door frame and wall studs, to prevent pry-bar attacks. Remove the casing molding on the inside of the frame and inspect the gap; if it's wider than ¼", install new plywood shims in the spaces between the original shims. Be sure to shim directly above, below, and behind the strike plate. Drill pilot holes, and secure the shims with 10d casing nails.

Replace short hinge screws with longer screws (3" or 4") that extend through the door jamb and into the wall studs. This helps resist door kick-ins. Tighten the screws snug, but avoid overtightening them, which can pull the frame out of square.

Add metal door reinforcers to strengthen the areas around locks and prevent kick-ins. Remove the lockset and slip the reinforcer over the door's edge. Be sure to get a reinforcer that is the correct thickness for your door.

Add a heavy-duty latch guard to reinforce the door jamb around the strike plate. For added protection, choose a guard with a flange that resists pry-bar attacks. Install the guard with long screws that reach the wall studs.

(continued)

Have lock cylinders re-keyed to ensure that lost or stolen keys can't be used by unwanted visitors. Remove cylinder, leaving bolt mechanism in door, and take it to a locksmith.

Putting a peephole into an exterior door is a quick and easy security measure. Simply drill a hole at the appropriate height, then screw the two halves of the peephole together.

How to Install a Security Box Strike

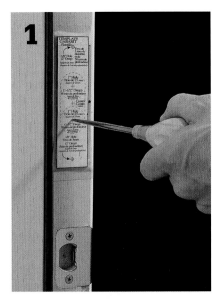

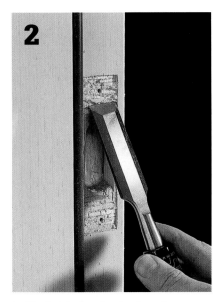

Mark the horizontal center of the deadbolt on the door jamb and tape the box strike template to the jamb, aligning the center marks. Use an awl to mark the drilling points, then use a utility knife to score a ⅛"-deep line around the outside of the template.

Drill pilot holes for the faceplate screws, and bore holes for the box mortise, using the recommended spade bit. To chisel the faceplate mortise, make parallel cuts ⅛" deep, holding the chisel at a 45° angle with the bevel side in. Flip the chisel over, and drive it downward to remove the material.

Insert the box strike into the mortise and install the screws inside the box. Angle the screws slightly toward the center of the wall stud, to increase their holding power. Position the faceplate and install the screws.

How to Install a Deadbolt Lock

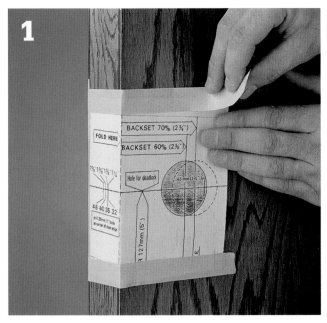

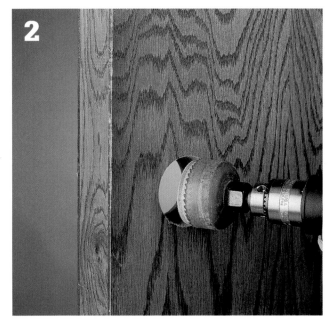

Measure up from the floor or existing lockset to locate the lock. Its center should be at least 3½" from the lockset center. Tape the template (supplied with lock) to the door. Use an awl to mark the center- points of the cylinder and deadbolt holes on the door. Close the door and use the template to mark the centerline for the deadbolt hole in the door jamb.

Bore the cylinder hole with a hole saw and drill. To avoid splintering the door, drill through one side until the hole saw pilot (mandrel) just comes out the other side. Remove the hole saw, then complete the hole from the opposite side of the door.

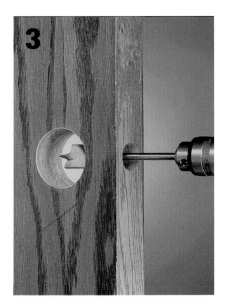

Use a spade bit to bore the deadbolt hole from the edge of the door into the cylinder hole. Be sure to keep the drill perpendicular to the door edge while drilling.

Insert the deadbolt into the edge hole. Fit the two halves of the lock into the door, aligning the cylinder tailpiece and connecting screw fittings with the proper holes in the deadbolt. Secure the two halves together with the connecting screws.

Use the centerline mark on the jamb to locate the hole for the deadbolt. Bore the hole, then chisel a mortise for the strike plate. Install the strike plate. Or, for greater security, install a security box strike, instead of the standard strike plate.

Tuning Up Garage Doors

Imagine this: You're driving home late at night, it's pouring outside, and you're shivering because you've got the flu. Then, you turn into your driveway, punch a little button, and your garage door opens, a light comes on, you pull in, and you're HOME. You didn't have to get drenched, or lift a door that felt like heavy metal, or scream at the heavens for making you so miserable. Thanks to a well-maintained garage door and opener, you escaped all of this, and that is a good thing.

Unfortunately, over time, many good things become bad things, especially if they aren't well-maintained. An overhead garage door is no exception. To keep everything running smoothly requires effort on three fronts: the door, the opener, and the opener's electronic safety sensors. Here's what you need to know to keep all three in tiptop shape.

Tools & Materials ▸

Mineral spirits
Graphite spray lubricant
Garage door weather-stripping
Level
Soft-faced mallet
Penetrating lubricant
Toweling
Socket wrenches
Lightweight oil
Pliers
Open-end wrenches

A bit of routine maintenance now and again will help keep your garage door working exactly as it should, rain or shine.

How to Tune-Up a Garage Door

Begin the tune-up by lubricating the door tracks, pulleys, and rollers. Use a lightweight oil, not grease, for this job. The grease catches too much dust and dirt.

Remove clogged or damaged rollers from the door by loosening the nuts that hold the roller brackets. The roller will come with the bracket when the bracket is pulled free.

Mineral spirits and kerosene are good solvents for cleaning roller bearings. Let the bearing sit for a half-hour in the solvent. Then brush away the grime build-up with an old paintbrush or toothbrush.

(continued)

4

If the rollers are making a lot of noise as they move over the tracks, the tracks are probably out of alignment. To fix this, check the tracks for plumb. If they are out of plumb, the track mounting brackets must be adjusted.

5

To adjust out-of-plumb tracks, loosen all the track mounting brackets (usually 3 or 4 per track) and push the brackets into alignment.

6

It's often easier to adjust the brackets by partially loosening the bolts and tapping the track with a soft-faced mallet. Once the track is plumb, tighten all the bolts.

7

Sometimes the door lock bar opens sluggishly because the return spring has lost its tension. The only way to fix this is to replace the spring. One end is attached to the body of the lock; the other end hooks onto the lock bar.

8

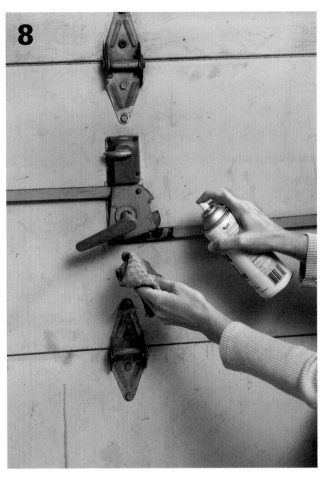

If a latch needs lubrication, use graphite in powder or liquid form. Don't use oil because it attracts dust that will clog the lock even more.

Alternative: Sometimes the lock bar won't lock the door because it won't slide into its opening on the door track. To fix this, loosen the guide bracket that holds the lock bar and move it up or down until the bar hits the opening.

(continued)

10

Worn or broken weather stripping on the bottom edge of the door can let in a lot of cold air and stiff breezes. Check to see if this strip is cracked, broken, or has holes along its edges. If so, remove the old strip and pull any nails left behind.

11

Measure the width of your garage door, then buy a piece of weather stripping to match. These strips are standard lumber-yard and home center items. Sometimes they are sold in kit form, with fasteners included. If not, just nail the stripping in place with galvanized roofing nails.

12

If the chain on your garage door opener is sagging more than ½" below the bottom rail, it can make a lot of noise and cause drive sprocket wear. Tighten the chain according to the directions in the owner's manual.

13

On openers with a chain, lubricate the entire length of the chain with lightweight oil. Do not use grease. Use the same lubricant if your opener has a drive screw instead.

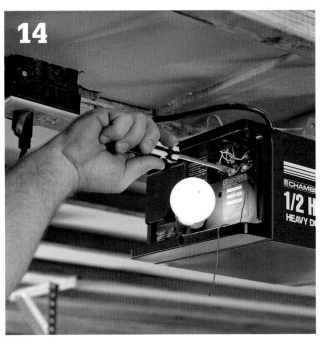

14

Test the door's closing force sensitivity and make adjustments at the opener's motor case if needed. Because both the sensitivity and the adjustment mechanism vary greatly between opener models, you'll have to rely on your owner's manual for guidance. If you don't have the owner's manual, you can usually download one from the manufacturer's website.

15

Check for proper alignment on the safety sensors near the floor. They should be pointing directly at one another and their lenses should be clean of any dirt and grease.

16

Make sure that the sensors are "talking" to the opener properly. Start to close the door, then put your hand down between the two sensors. If the door stops immediately and reverses direction, it's working properly. If it's not, make the adjustment recommended in the owner's manual. If that doesn't do the trick, call a professional door installer and don't use the door until it passes this test.

Removing Windows & Doors

If your remodeling project requires removing old windows and doors, do not start this work until all preparation work is finished and the interior wall surfaces and trim have been removed. You will need to close up the wall openings as soon as possible, so make sure you have all the necessary tools, framing lumber, and new window or door units before starting the final stages of demolition. Be prepared to finish the work as quickly as possible.

Windows and doors are removed using the same basic procedures. In many cases, old units can be salvaged for resale or later use, so use care when removing them.

Tools & Materials ▸

Utility knife
Flat pry bar
Screwdriver
Hammer
Reciprocating saw
Plywood
Masking tape
Screws

Masking tape used to keep windows from shattering

Removing windows or doors is a similar process and often easier with a helper. Use care when removing large windows or patio doors, which can be very heavy.

How to Remove Doors

Using a pry bar and hammer, gently remove the interior door trim. Save the trim to use after the new door is installed.

Cut away the old caulk between the exterior siding and the brick molding on the door frame using a utility knife.

Use a flat pry bar or a cat's paw to remove the casing nails securing the door jambs to the framing. Cut stubborn nails with a reciprocating saw (see step 2, below). Remove the door from the opening.

How to Remove Windows

Carefully pry off the interior trim around the window frame. For double-hung windows with sash weights, remove the weights by cutting the cords and pulling the weights from the weight pockets near the bottom of the side jambs.

Cut through the nails holding the window jambs to the framing members using a reciprocating saw. Place tape over the windowpanes to prevent shattering, then remove the window unit from the opening.

Variation: For windows and doors attached with nailing flanges, cut or pry loose the siding material, then remove the nails holding the unit to the sheathing. See pages 186 to 187 for more information on removing siding.

Installing Prehung Interior Doors

Install prehung interior doors after the framing work is complete and the wallboard has been installed. If the rough opening for the door has been framed accurately, installing the door takes about an hour.

Standard prehung doors have 4½"-wide jambs and are sized to fit walls with 2 × 4 construction and ½" wallboard. If you have 2 × 6 construction or thicker wall surface material, you can special-order a door to match, or you can add jamb extensions to a standard-sized door (see Tip, next page).

Tools & Materials ▸

Level	Prehung interior door
Hammer	Wood shims
Handsaw	8d casing nails

Prehung doors save you time and effort during installation because the jamb is already installed on the door.

How to Install a Prehung Interior Door

Slide the door unit into the framed opening so the edges of the jambs are flush with the wall surface and the hinge-side jamb is plumb.

Insert pairs of wood shims driven from opposite directions into the gap between the framing members and the hinge-side jamb, spaced every 12". Check the hinge-side jamb to make sure it is still plumb and does not bow.

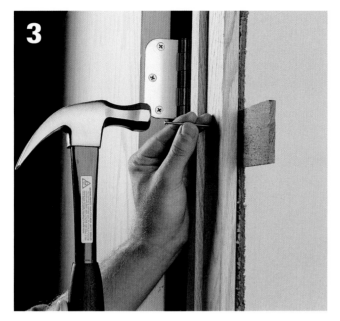

3

Anchor the hinge-side jamb with 8d casing nails driven through the jamb and shims and into the jack stud. You may want to predrill the nail holes to prevent splitting the shims.

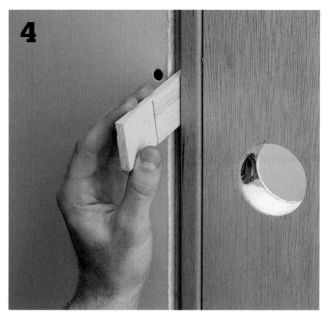

4

Insert pairs of shims in the gap between the framing members and the latch-side jamb and top jamb, spaced every 12". With the door closed, adjust the shims so the gap between the door edge and jamb is ⅛" wide. Drive 8d casing nails through the jambs and shims into the framing members.

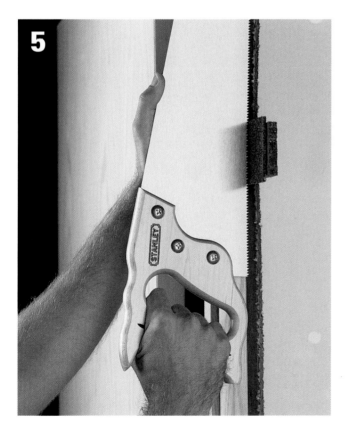

5

Cut the shims flush with the wall surface using a handsaw. Hold the saw vertically to prevent damage to the door jamb or wall. Finish the door and install the lockset as directed by the manufacturer. Install trim.

Tip ▶

1"-thick jamb extension

If your walls are built with 2 × 6 studs, you'll need to extend the jambs by attaching 1"-thick wood strips to the edges of the jamb after the door is installed. Use glue and 4d casing nails when attaching jamb extensions. Make the strips from the same wood as the jamb.

How to Install a Replacement Window with a Nailing Flange

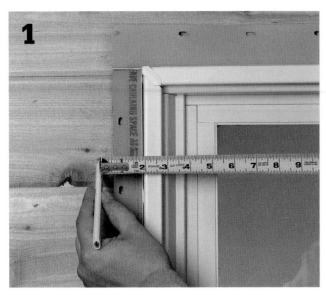

Remove the existing window (see page 149), and set the new window into the rough opening. Center it left to right, and shim beneath the sill to level it. On the exterior side, measure out from the window on all sides, and mark the siding for the width of the brick molding you'll install around the new window. Extend layout lines to mark where you'll cut the siding.

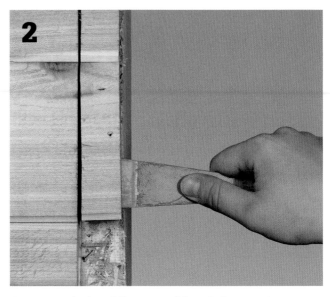

Remove exterior siding around the window area to expose the wall sheathing. Use a zip tool to separate vinyl siding for removal or use a pry bar and hammer to remove wood clapboard. For more on removing exterior surfaces, see page 187.

Cover the sill and rough opening framing members with self-adhesive, rolled flashing. Apply additional strips of flashing behind the siding and up the sill flashing. Finish flashing with a strip along the header. The flashing should cover the front edges and sides of the opening members.

Apply a bead of silicone caulk around the back face of the window flange, then set it into the rough opening, centering it side-to-side in the opening. Tack the window in place by driving one roofing nail partway through the top flange. On the interior side, level and plumb the window, using shims to make any necessary adjustments.

5

Tack the window to the header at one end of the nailing flange, using a 1" galvanized roofing nail. Drive a roofing nail through the other top corner of the flange to hold the window in place, then secure the flange all around the window with more roofing nails. Apply strips of rolled, self-adhesive flashing to cover the window flanges. Start with a strip that covers the bottom flange, then cover the side flanges, overlapping the bottom flashing and extending 8 to 10" above the window. Complete the flashing with a strip along the top, overlapping the side flashing.

6

Install a piece of metal drip edge behind the siding and above the window. Secure it with silicone caulk only.

7

Cut and attach brick molding around the window, leaving a slight gap between the brick molding and the window frame. Use 8d galvanized casing nails driven into pilot holes to secure the brick molding to the rough framing. Miter the corner joints. Reinstall the siding in the window installation area, trimming as needed.

8

Use high-quality caulk to fill the gap between the brick molding and the siding. On the interior side, fill gaps between the window frame and surrounding framing with foam backer rod, low-expansion foam, or fiberglass insulation. Install the interior casing.

Installing Storm Doors

Storm doors are important features for energy efficiency as well as protecting your entry door. In harsh climates, storm doors protect the entry door from driving rain or snow. They create a dead air buffer between the two doors that acts like insulation. When the screen panels are in place, the door provides great ventilation on a hot day. And, they deliver added security, especially when outfitted with a lockset and a deadbolt lock.

If you want to install a new storm door or replace an old one that's seen better days, your first job is to go shopping. Storm doors come in many different styles to suit just about anyone's design needs. And they come in different materials, including aluminum, vinyl, and even fiberglass. (Wood storm doors are still available but they must be trimmed and fit by hand, as they're not sold in prehung kits.) Most units feature a prehung door in a frame that is mounted on the entry door casing boards. Depending on the model you buy, installation instructions can vary. Be sure to check the directions that come with your door before starting the job.

Once purely utilitarian, today's storm doors can be an important design element of your home. Do your research carefully, and choose a door that complements both the entry door and other trim on your home.

Tools & Materials ▶

Drill/driver
Tape measure
Finish nails
Screwdriver
Paintbrush

Masking tape
Hacksaw
Level
Primer
Paint

A quality storm door helps seal out cold drafts, keeps rain and snow off your entry door, and lets a bug-free breeze into your home when you want one.

How to Install a Storm Door

Test-fit the door in the opening. If it is loose, add a shim to the hinge side of the door. Cut the piece with a circular saw and nail it to the side of the jamb, flush with the front of the casing.

Install the drip edge molding at the top of the door opening. The directions for the door you have will explain exactly how to do this. Sometimes it's the first step, like we show here; otherwise it's installed after the door is in place.

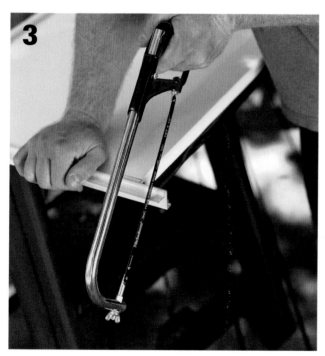

Measure the height of the opening and cut the hinge flange to match this measurement. Use a hacksaw and work slowly so the saw won't hop out of the cut and scratch a visible area of the hinge.

Lift the door and push it tightly into the opening. Partially drive one mounting screw near the bottom and another near the top. Check the door for plumb, and when satisfied, drive all the mounting screws tight to the flange.

Hanging a New Door in an Old Jamb

If you've got an unsightly or damaged door to replace but the jamb and trimwork are in good condition, there's no need to remove the jambs. Instead, buy a slab door and hang it in the existing jamb. It's an excellent way to preserve existing moldings and trim, especially if you live in an old home, and you won't have to color-match a new jamb to its surroundings.

If the hinges are also in good condition, you can reuse them as well. This may be particularly desirable in a historic home with ornate hinges. Most home centers stock six-panel slab doors, or you can order them in a variety of styles and wood types. For aesthetic and practical reasons, choose a door size as close to the original door as possible.

The process for hanging the door involves shimming the door into position in the jamb, scribing the ends and edges, and trimming or planing it to fit the opening. You'll also need to chisel hinge mortises in the door edge to accommodate the jamb hinge positions.

This is a project where patience and careful scribing will pay dividends in the end. Have a helper on hand to hold the door in position as you scribe and fit the door in place.

Tools & Materials ▸

Door shims	Power plane or
Tape measure	hand plane
Compass	Hammer
Combination square	Chisel
Utility knife	Drill/driver
Circular saw	Hole saw
C-clamps	Spade bit
Self-centering	Slab door
drill bit	Hinge screws

Before

After

Installing a new door in an old jamb dramatically updates the curb appeal of your home.

How to Hang a New Door in an Old Jamb

Have a helper hold the new door in place against the jamb from inside the room. Slide a pair of thick shims under the door to raise it up slightly off the floor or threshold. Move the shims in or out until the door's top and side rails are roughly even with the jamb so it looks balanced in the opening, then make a mark along the top edge of the door.

Use pieces of colored masking tape to mark the outside of the door along the hinge edge. This will help keep the door's orientation clear throughout the installation process.

Use a pencil compass, set to an opening of ³⁄₁₆", to scribe layout lines along both long edges of the door and across the top. These lines will create a clear space for the hinges and door swing. If the bottom of the door will close over carpet, set the dividers for ½" and scribe the bottom edge. Remove the door and transfer these scribe lines to the other door face.

Lay the door on a sturdy bench or across a pair of sawhorses with the tape side facing up. Score the top and bottom scribe lines with a utility knife to keep the wood fibers from splintering when you cut across the ends.

(continued)

5

Straightedge

Trim the door ends with a circular saw equipped with a fine-cutting blade. Run the saw base along a clamped straightedge with the blade cutting 1/16" on the waste side of the layout lines. Check to make sure the blade is set square to the saw base before cutting. Use a power planer or hand plane to plane the door ends to the layout lines.

6

Stand the door on edge and use a power planer or hand plane to plane down to the edge of the scribe lines. Set the tool for a fine cut; use a 1/16" cutting depth for power planing and a shallower cutting depth for a hand plane. Try to make each planing pass in long strokes from one end of the door to the other.

7

Shim the door back into position in the jamb with a helper supporting it from behind. Set the door slightly out from the doorstop moldings so you can mark the hinge locations on the door face.

8

Use a combination square or one of the hinge leaves to draw hinge mortise layout lines on the door edge. Score the layout lines with a utility knife.

Cut shallow hinge leaf mortises in the door edge with a sharp chisel and hammer. First score the mortise shape with a straightedge and utility knife or a chisel, then make a series of shallow chisel cuts inside the hinge leaf area. Pare away this waste so the mortise depth is slightly deeper than the hinge leaf thickness.

Set the hinges in the door mortises, and drill pilot holes for the hinge screws. Attach the hinges to the door.

Hang the door in the jamb by tipping it into place so the top hinge leaf rests in the top mortise of the jamb. Drive one screw into this mortise. Then set the other leaves into their mortises and install the remaining hinge screws.

Bore holes for the lockset and bolt using a hole saw and spade bit. If you're reusing the original hardware, measure the old door hole sizes and cut matching holes in the new door, starting with the large lockset hole. For new locksets, use the manufacturer's template and hole sizing recommendations to bore the holes. Install the hardware.

Installing Entry Doors

Few parts of a house have a more dramatic effect on the way your home is perceived than the main entry door. A lovely, well-maintained entryway that is tastefully matched architecturally to the house can utterly transform a home's appearance. In fact, industry studies have suggested that upgrading a plain entry door to a higher-end entry door system can pay back multiple times in the resale of your house. But perhaps more importantly, depending on your priorities, it makes a great improvement in how you feel about your home. Plus, it usually pays benefits in home security and energy efficiency as well.

If you are replacing a single entry door with a double door or a door with a sidelight or sidelights, you will need to enlarge the door opening. Be sure to file your plans with your local building department and obtain a permit. You'll need to provide temporary support from the time you remove the wall studs in the new opening until you've installed and secured a new door header that's approved for the new span distance.

The American Craftsman style door with sidelights installed in this project has the look and texture of a classic wood door, but it is actually created from fiber-glass. Today's fiberglass doors are quite convincing in their ability to replicate wood grain, while still offering the durability and low-maintenance of fiberglass.

Tools & Materials ▸

Tape measure	Shims
Level	Framing nails
Reciprocating saw	Finish nails
Caulk & caulk gun	Nail set
Hammer	Finishing materials

After

Before

Replacing an ordinary entry door with a beautiful new upgrade has an exceptionally high payback in increased curb appeal and in perceived home value, according to industry studies.

How to Replace an Entry Door

Remove the old entry door by cutting through the fasteners driven into the jamb with a reciprocating saw. If the new door or door system is wider, mark the edges of the larger rough opening onto the wall surface. If possible, try to locate the new opening so one edge will be against an existing wall stud. Be sure to include the thickness of the new framing you'll need to add when removing the wall coverings.

Frame in the new rough opening for the replacement door. The instructions that come with the door will recommend a rough opening size, which is usually sized to create a ½" gap between the door and the studs and header. Patch the wall surfaces.

Cut metal door dripcap molding to fit the width of the opening and tuck the back edge up behind the wallcovering at the top of the door opening. Attach the dripcap with caulk only–do not use nails or screws.

Unpack the door unit and set it in the rough opening to make sure it fits correctly. Remove it. Make sure the subfloor is clean and in good repair, and then apply heavy beads of caulk to the underside of the door sill and to the subfloor in the sill installation area. Use plenty of caulk.

(continued)

5

Set the door sill in the threshold and raise the unit up so it fits cleanly in the opening, with the exterior trim flush against the wall sheathing. Press down on the sill to seat it in the caulk and wipe up any squeeze-out with a damp rag

6

Use a 6-ft. level to make sure the unit is plumb and then tack it to the rough opening stud on the hinge side, using pairs of 10d nails driven partway through the casing on the weatherstripped side of the door (or the sidelight). On single, hinged doors, drive the nails just above the hinge locations. *Note: Many door installers prefer deck screws over nails when attaching the jambs. Screws offer more gripping strength and are easier to adjust, but covering the screw heads is more difficult than filling nail holes.*

7

Drive wood shims between the jamb and the wall studs to create an even gap. Locate the shims directly above the pairs of nails you drove. Doublecheck the door with the level to make sure it is still plumb.

8

Drive shims between the jamb on the latch side of the unit and into the wall stud. Only drive the nails part way. Test for plumb again and then add shims at nail locations (you may need to double-up the shims, as this gap is often wider than the one on the hinge side). Check to make sure the door jamb is not bowed.

9

Drive finish nails at all remaining locations, following the nailing schedule in the manufacturer's installation instructions.

10

Use a nail set to drive the nail heads below the wood surface. Fill the nail holes with wood putty (you'll get the best match if you apply putty that's tinted to match the stained wood after the finish is applied). The presence of the wood shims at the nail locations should prevent the jamb from bowing as you nail.

11

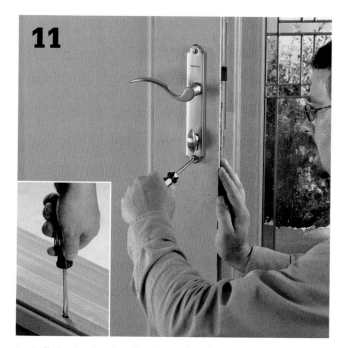

Install the lockset, strikeplates, deadbolts or multipoint locks, and any other door hardware. If the door finish has not been applied, you may want to do so first, but generally it makes more sense to install the hardware right away so the door can be operated and locked. Attach the door sill to the threshold and adjust it as needed, normally using the adjustment screws (inset).

12

Apply your door finish if it has not yet been applied. Read the manufacturer's suggestions for finishing very closely and follow the suggested sequences. Some manufacturers offer finish kits that are designed to be perfectly compatible with their doors. Install interior case molding and caulk all the exterior gaps after the finish dries.

Installing Bifold Doors

Bifold doors provide easy access to a closet without requiring much clearance for opening. Most home centers stock kits that include two pairs of prehinged doors, a head track, and all the necessary hardware and fasteners. Typically, the doors in these kits have predrilled holes for the pivot and guide posts. Hardware kits are also sold separately for custom projects. There are many types of bifold door styles, so be sure to read and follow the manufacturer's instructions for the product you use.

Tools & Materials ▸

Tape measure	Screwdriver
Level	Hacksaw
Circular saw	Prehinged bifold doors
Straightedge	Head track
(optional)	Mounting hardware
Drill	Panhead screws
Plane	Flathead screws

A variety of designer bifold doors are available for installation between rooms and closets. They provide the same attractive appearance as French doors but require much less floor space.

How to Install Bifold Doors

Cut the head track to the width of the opening using a hacksaw. Insert the roller mounts into the track, then position the track in the opening. Fasten it to the header using panhead screws.

Measure and mark each side jamb at the floor for the anchor bracket so the center of the bracket aligns exactly with the center of the head track. Fasten the brackets in place with flathead screws.

Check the height of the doors in the opening, and trim if necessary. Insert pivot posts into predrilled holes at the bottoms and tops of the doors. Insert guide posts at the tops of the leading doors. Make sure all posts fit snugly.

Fold one pair of doors closed and lift into position, inserting the pivot and guide posts into the head track. Slip the bottom pivot post into the anchor bracket. Repeat for the other pair of doors. Close the doors and check alignment along the side jambs and down the center. If necessary, adjust the top and bottom pivots following the manufacturer's instructions.

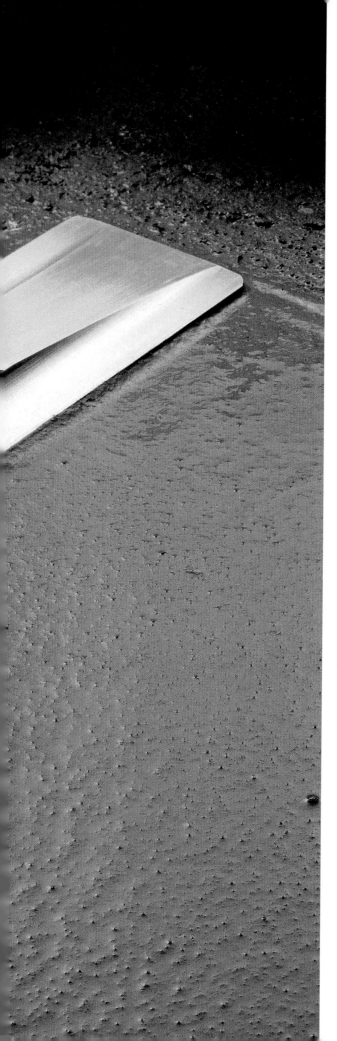

Exterior Repairs

In this chapter:

Inspecting & Repairing a Roof

A roof system is composed of several elements that work together to provide three basic, essential functions for your home: shelter, drainage, and ventilation. The roof covering and flashing are designed to shed water, directing it to gutters and downspouts. Air intake and outtake vents keep fresh air circulating below the roof sheathing, preventing moisture and heat buildup.

When your roof system develops problems that compromise its ability to protect your home—cracked shingles, incomplete ventilation, or damaged flashing—the damage quickly spreads to other parts of your house. Routine inspections are the best way to make sure the roof continues to do its job effectively.

Tools & Materials ▸

Tape measure	Replacement flashing
Wire brush	Replacement shingles
Aviation snips	Roofing cement
Trowel	Roofing nails
Flat pry bar	Double-headed nails
Hammer	Rubber-gasket nails
Utility knife	
Caulk gun	
Plywood	

Ice dams above entries pose a danger to everyone entering and leaving the house. To permanently solve ice damming problems, like the one shown here, improve roof ventilation to reduce attic temperatures.

Tips for Identifying Roofing Problems ▸

Ice dams occur when melting snow refreezes near the eaves, causing ice to back up under the shingles, where it melts onto the sheathing and seeps into the house.

Inspect both the interior and the exterior of the roof to spot problems. From inside the attic, check the rafters and sheathing for signs of water damage. Symptoms will appear in the form of streaking or discoloration. A moist or wet area also signals water damage.

Common Roofing Problems

Wind, weather, and flying debris can damage shingles. The areas along valleys and ridges tend to take the most weather-related abuse. Torn, loose, or cracked shingles are common in these areas.

Buckled and cupped shingles are usually caused by moisture beneath the shingles. Loosened areas create an entry point for moisture and leave shingles vulnerable to wind damage.

A sagging ridge might be caused by the weight of too many roofing layers. It might also be the result of a more significant problem, such as a rotting ridge board or insufficient support for the ridge board.

Dirt and debris attract moisture and decay, which shorten a roof's life. To protect shingles, carefully wash the roof once a year, using a pressure washer. Pay particular attention to areas where moss and mildew may accumulate.

In damp climates, it's a good idea to nail a zinc strip along the center ridge of a roof, under the ridge caps. Minute quantities of zinc wash down the roof each time it rains, killing moss and mildew.

Overhanging tree limbs drop debris and provide shade that encourages moss and mildew. To reduce chances of decay, trim any limbs that overhang the roof.

How to Locate & Evaluate Leaks

If you have an unfinished attic, examine the underside of your roof with a flashlight on a rainy day. If you find wetness, discoloration, or other signs of moisture, trace the trail up to where the water is making its entrance.

Water that flows toward a wall can be temporarily diverted to minimize damage. Nail a small block of wood in the path of the water, and place a bucket underneath to catch the drip. On a dry day, drive a nail through the underside of the roof decking to mark the hole.

If the leak is finding its way to a finished ceiling, take steps to minimize damage until the leak can be repaired. As soon as possible, reduce the accumulation of water behind a ceiling by poking a small hole in the wallboard or plaster and draining the water.

Once you mark the source of a leak from inside, measure from that spot to a point that will be visible and identifiable from outside the house, such as a chimney, vent pipe, or the peak of the roof. Get up on the roof and use that measurement to locate the leak.

How to Make Emergency Repairs

If your roof is severely damaged, the primary goal is to prevent additional damage until permanent repairs are made. Nail a sheet of plywood to the roof to serve as emergency cover to keep out the wind and water.

Cover the damaged area by nailing strips of lath around the edges of a plastic sheet or tarp. *Tip: For temporary repairs, use double-headed nails, which can be easily removed. Fill nail holes with roofing cement when the repair is complete.*

How to Make Spot Repairs with Roofing Cement

To reattach a loose shingle, wipe down the felt paper and the underside of the shingle. Let each dry, then apply a liberal coat of roofing cement. Press the shingle down to seat it in the bed of cement.

Tack down buckled shingles by cleaning below the buckled area. Fill the area with roofing cement, then press the shingle into the cement. Patch cracks and splits in shingles with roofing cement.

Check the joints around flashing, which are common places for roof leaks to occur. Seal any gaps by cleaning out and replacing any failed roofing cement. *Tip: Heat softens the roof's surface, and cold makes it brittle. If needed, warm shingles slightly with a hair dryer to make them easier to work with and less likely to crack.*

How to Replace Asphalt Shingles

Pull out damaged shingles, starting with the uppermost shingle in the damaged area. Be careful not to damage surrounding shingles that still are in good condition.

Remove old nails in and above the repair area, using a flat pry bar. Patch damaged felt paper with roofing cement.

Install the replacement shingles, beginning with the lowest shingle in the repair area. Nail above the tab slots, using ⅞" or 1" roofing nails.

Install all but the top shingle with nails, then apply roofing cement to the underside of the top shingle, above the seal line.

Slip the last shingle into place, under the overlapping shingle. Lift the shingles immediately above the repair area, and nail the top replacement shingle.

How to Replace Wood Shakes & Shingles

To age new shakes and shingles so they match existing ones, dissolve 1 pound of baking soda in 1 gallon of water. Brush the solution onto the shakes or shingles, then place them in direct sunlight for four to five hours. Rinse them thoroughly and let dry. Repeat this process until the color closely matches the originals.

Split the damaged shakes or shingles, using a hammer and chisel. Remove the pieces. Slide a hacksaw blade under the overlapping shingles and cut the nail heads. Pry out the remaining pieces of the shakes or shingles.

Gently pry up, but don't remove, the shakes or shingles above the repair area. Cut new pieces for the lowest course, leaving a ⅜" gap between pieces. Nail replacements in place with ring-shank siding nails. Fill in all but the top course in the repair area.

Cut the shakes or shingles for the top course. Because the top course can't be nailed, use roofing cement to fasten the pieces in place. Apply a coat of roofing cement where the shakes or shingles will sit, then slip them beneath the overlapping pieces. Press down to seat them in the roofing cement.

How to Patch Valley Flashing

  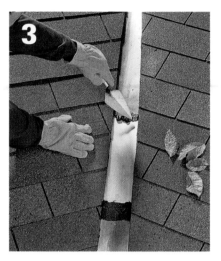

Measure the damaged area and mark an outline for the patch. Cut a patch wide enough to fit under shingles on both sides of the repair area, and tapered to a point at one end. Using a trowel or flat pry bar, carefully break the seal between the damaged flashing and surrounding shingles.

Scrub the damaged flashing with a wire brush, and wipe it clean. Apply a heavy bead of roofing cement to the back of the patch. Cut a slit in the old flashing. Insert the tapered end of the patch into the slit, and slip the side edges under the shingles. *Tip: Use the same material for your patch as the original flashing. When dissimilar materials are joined, corrosion accelerates.*

Rest the square end of the patch on top of the old flashing, and press it firmly to seal the roofing cement joint. Add roofing cement to the exposed seams. Using a trowel, feather out the cement to create a smooth path for water flow.

How to Replace Vent Flashing

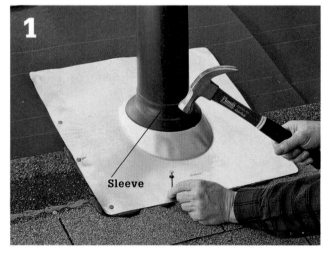 

Sleeve

Remove the shingles above and on the sides of the vent pipe. Remove the old vent flashing, using a flat pry bar. Apply a heavy, double bead of roofing cement along the bottom edge of the flange of the new flashing. Set the new flashing in place so it covers at least one course of shingles. Nail around the perimeter of the flange, using rubber-gasket nails.

Cut the shingles to fit around the neck of the flashing so they lie flat against the flange. Apply roofing cement to the shingle and flashing joints, and cover any exposed nail heads.

How to Replace Step Flashing

Carefully bend up the counterflashing or the siding covering the damaged flashing. Cut any roofing cement seals, and pull back the shingles. Use a flat pry bar to remove the damaged flashing. *Tip: When replacing flashing around masonry, such as a chimney, use copper or galvanized steel. Lime from mortar can corrode aluminum.*

Cut the new flashing to fit, and apply roofing cement to all unexposed edges. Slip the flashing in place, making sure it's overlapped by the flashing above and overlaps the flashing and shingle below.

Drive one roofing nail through the flashing, at the bottom corner, and into the roof deck. Do not fasten the flashing to the vertical roof element, such as the chimney.

Reposition the shingles and counterflashing, and seal all joints with roofing cement.

Repairing Wood Fascia & Soffits

Fascia and soffits add a finished look to your roof and promote a healthy roof system. A well-ventilated soffit system prevents moisture from building up under the roof and in the attic.

Most fascia and soffit problems can be corrected by cutting out sections of damaged material and replacing them. Joints between fascia boards are lock-nailed at rafter locations, so you should remove whole sections of fascia to make accurate bevel cuts for patches. Soffits can often be left in place for repairs.

Tools & Materials ▸

Circular saw
Jigsaw
Drill
Putty knife
Hammer
Flat pry bar
Nail set
Chisel
Caulk gun

Paint-brush
Replacement materials
Nailing strips
2" and 2½" galvanized
    deck screws
4d galvanized casing nails
Acrylic caulk
Primer
Paint

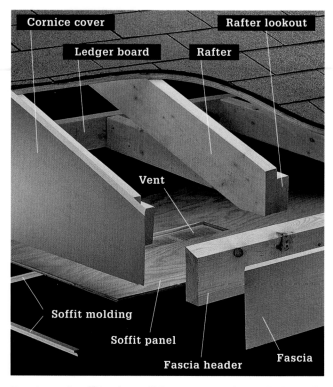

Fascia and soffits close off the eaves area beneath the roof overhang. The fascia covers the ends of rafters and rafter lookouts, and provides a surface for attaching gutters. Soffits are protective panels that span the area between the fascia and the side of the house.

How to Repair Wood Fascia

Remove gutters, shingle moldings, and any other items mounted on the fascia. Carefully pry off the damaged fascia board, using a pry bar. Remove the entire board and all old nails.

Set your circular saw for a 45° bevel, and cut off the damaged portion of the fascia board. Reattach the undamaged original fascia to the rafters or rafter lookouts, using 2" deck screws. Bevel-cut a patch board to replace the damaged section.

Set the patch board in place. Drill pilot holes through both fascia boards into the rafter. Drive nails in the holes to create a lock-nail joint (inset). Replace shingle moldings and trim pieces, using 4d casing nails. Set the nail heads. Prime and paint the new board.

How to Repair Wood Panel Soffits

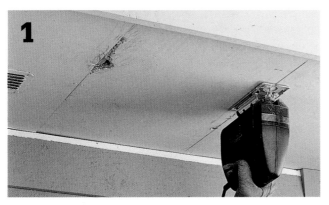

1

In the area where soffits are damaged, remove the support moldings that hold the soffits in place along the fascia and exterior wall. Drill entry holes, then use a jigsaw to cut out the damaged soffit area. *Tip: Cut soffits as close as possible to the rafters or rafter lookouts. Finish cuts with a chisel, if necessary.*

2

Remove the damaged soffit section, using a pry bar. Cut nailing strips the same length as the exposed area of the rafters, and fasten them to the rafters or rafter lookouts at the edges of the openings, using 2½" deck screws.

3

Using soffit material similar to the original panel, cut a replacement piece ⅛" smaller than the opening. If the new panel will be vented, cut the vent openings.

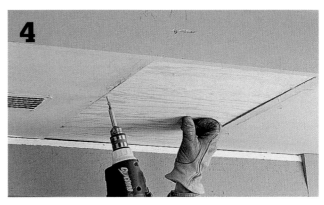

4

Attach the replacement panel to the nailing strips, using 2" deck screws. If you are not going to paint the entire soffit after the repair, prime and paint the replacement piece before installing it.

5

Reattach the soffit molding, using 4d casing nails. Set the nail heads.

6

Using siliconized acrylic caulk, fill all nail holes, screw holes, and gaps. Smooth out the caulk with a putty knife until the caulk is even with the surface. Prime and paint the soffit panels.

Repairing Gutters

Gutters perform the important task of channeling water away from your house. A good gutter system prevents damage to your siding, foundation, and landscaping, and it helps prevent water from leaking into your basement. When gutters fail, evaluate the type and extent of damage to select the best repair method. Clean your gutters and downspouts as often as necessary to keep the system working efficiently.

Tools & Materials ▸

Flat pry bar	Chalk line
Hacksaw	Wood scraps
Caulk gun	Replacement
Pop rivet gun	gutter materials
Drill	Siliconized
Hammer	acrylic caulk
Stiff-bristled brush	Roofing cement
Putty knife	Metal flashing
Steel wool	Sheet-metal screws
Aviation snips	or pop rivets
Level	Gutter hangers
Paintbrush	Primer and paint
Trowel	Gutter patching kit
Garden hose	Gutter guards

Use a trowel to clean leaves, twigs, and other debris out of the gutters before starting the repairs.

Keep gutters and downspouts clean so rain falling on the roof is directed well away from the foundation. Nearly all wet basement problems are caused by water collecting near the foundation, a situation that can frequently be traced to clogged and overflowing gutters and downspouts.

How to Unclog Gutters

Flush clogged downspouts with water. Wrap a large rag around a garden hose and insert it in the downspout opening. Arrange the rag so it fills the opening, then turn on the water full force.

Check the slope of the gutters, using a level. Gutters should slope slightly toward the downspouts. Adjust the hangers, if necessary.

Place gutter guards over the gutters to prevent future clogs.

How to Rehang Sagging Gutters & Patch Leaks

For sagging gutters, snap a chalk line on the fascia that follows the correct slope. Remove hangers in and near the sag. Lift the gutter until it's flush with the chalk line. *Tip: A good slope for gutters is a ¼" drop every 10 ft. toward the downspouts.*

Reattach hangers every 24", and within 12" of seams. Use new hangers, if necessary. Avoid using the original nail holes. Fill small holes and seal minor leaks, using gutter caulk.

Use a gutter patching kit to make temporary repairs to a gutter with minor damage. Follow manufacturer's directions. For permanent repairs, see page 181.

How to Repair Leaky Joints

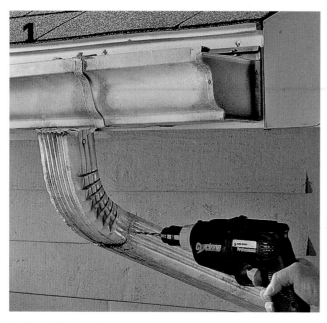

Drill out the rivets or unfasten the metal screws to disassemble the leaky joint. Scrub both parts of the joint with a stiff-bristled brush. Clean the damaged area with water, and allow to dry completely.

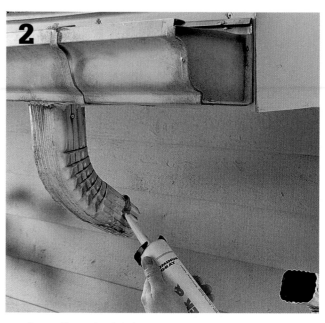

Apply caulk to the joining parts, then reassemble the joint. Secure the connection with pop rivets or sheet-metal screws.

How to Patch Metal Gutters

Clean the area around the damage with a stiff-bristled brush. Scrub it with steel wool or an abrasive pad to loosen residue, then rinse it with water.

Apply a ⅛"-thick layer of roofing cement evenly over the damage. Spread the roofing cement a few inches past the damaged area on all sides.

Cut and bend a piece of flashing to fit inside the gutter. Bed the patch in the roofing cement. Feather out the cement to reduce ridges so it won't cause significant damming. *Tip: To prevent corrosion, make sure the patch is the same type of metal as the gutter.*

How to Replace a Section of Metal Gutter

Remove gutter hangers in and near the damaged area. Insert wood spacers in the gutter, near each hanger, before prying. *Tip: If the damaged area is more than 2 ft. long, replace the entire section with new material.*

Slip spacers between the gutter and fascia, near each end of the damaged area, so you won't damage the roof when cutting the gutter. Cut out the damaged section, using a hacksaw.

Cut a new gutter section at least 4" longer than the damaged section.

Clean the cut ends of the old gutter, using a wire brush. Caulk the ends, then center the gutter patch over the cutout area and press into the caulk.

Secure the gutter patch with pop rivets or sheet-metal screws. Use at least three fasteners at each joint. On the inside surfaces of the gutter, caulk over the heads of the fasteners.

Reinstall gutter hangers. If necessary, use new hangers, but don't use old holes. Prime and paint the patch to match the existing gutter.

Repairing & Replacing Chimney Caps

Chimney caps undergo stress because the temperatures of the cap and chimney flue fluctuate dramatically. Use fire-rated silicone caulk to patch minor cracks. For more extensive repairs, reapply fresh mortar over the cap, or replace the old cap for a permanent solution.

Tools & Materials ▸

Hammer	½" and ¾" plywood
Stone chisel	¼" dowel
Wire brush	1½" wood screws
Drill	Vegetable oil
Float	or a commercial
Pointing trowel	release agent
Tape measure	Fire-rated
Caulk gun	silicone caulk
Mortar	Fire-rated rope
Concrete fortifier	or mineral wool

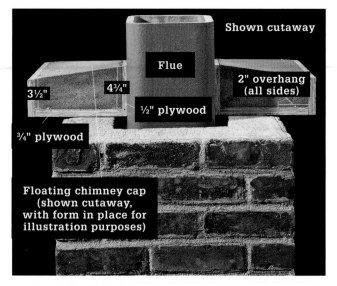

A chimney cap expands and shrinks as temperatures change inside and outside the chimney. This often results in cracking and annual treks up to the roof for repairs. A floating chimney cap (above) is cast in a form, using mortar or sand-mix concrete, then placed on the top of the chimney (opposite page). You can repair a damaged cap by chipping off the deteriorated sections and adding fresh mortar (below).

How to Repair a Chimney

Carefully break apart and remove the deteriorated sections of the chimney cap, using a stone chisel and hammer. Be very careful when chiseling around the flue.

Mix a batch of latex-fortified mortar. Trowel an even layer of mortar all the way around the chimney cap, following the slope of the existing cap. Mortar should cover the chimney from the outside edges of the chimney bricks to the flue. Smooth out the mortar with a wood float, trying to recreate the original slope of the chimney cap. Inspect mortar annually.

How to Cast & Install a Replacement Chimney Cap

Measure the chimney and the chimney flue and build a form from ½" and ¾" plywood (form dimensions on opposite page, top). Attach the form to a plywood base, using 1½" wood screws to connect all form parts. Glue ⅜" dowels to the base, 1" inside the form. The dowels will cast a drip edge into the cap. Coat the inside of the form with vegetable oil or a commercial release agent.

Prepare a stiff (dry) mixture of mortar to cast the cap—for average-sized chimneys, two 60-lb. bags of dry mix should yield enough mortar. Fill the form with mortar. Rest a wood float across the edges of the form, and smooth the mortar. Keep angles sharp at the corners. Let the cap cure for at least a week, then carefully disassemble the form.

Chip off the old mortar cap completely, and clean the top of the chimney with a wire brush. With a helper, transport the chimney cap onto the roof and set it directly onto the chimney, centered so the overhang is equal on all sides. For the new cap to function properly, do not bond it to the chimney or the flue.

Shift the cap so the gap next to the flue is even on all sides, then fill in the gap with fire-rated rope or mineral wool. Caulk over the fill material with a very heavy bead of fire-rated silicone caulk. Also caulk the joint at the underside of the cap. Inspect caulk every other year, and refresh as needed.

Evaluating Siding & Trim

The first step in inspecting and evaluating siding and trim is to identify the type of material used on the house. Is it natural wood? Aluminum or vinyl? Once you determine the material, take a close look at the problem area and determine the best method to fix it. If your siding is still under warranty, read through the warranty document before starting any repairs. Making repairs yourself could invalidate the product warranty. If the siding was professionally installed, you may want to talk to your contractor about the repairs.

In addition to looking unsightly, small siding problems can escalate into larger and more costly problems. As soon as you spot any siding damage, take steps to fix it immediately, especially if there's a possibility of water infiltration. Manufacturers change siding styles frequently, so you may have trouble buying replacement siding. A bit of legwork may be necessary, or you may find it necessary to settle for replacement materials that are a close, but not exact, match.

Check window and door trim for rot, especially on horizontal surfaces and at joints. Try to make repairs without removing the trim.

Tips for Inspecting Trim ▶

Inspect decorative trim, like the gingerbread trim shown here. If you suspect damage, remove the trim and make repairs in a workshop.

Evaluate broad trim pieces, such as the end cap trim shown above, and make repairs, using the same techniques as for siding.

Common Siding Problems

Separated joints can occur in any type of lap siding, but they're most common in wood lap. Gaps between ⅛" and ¼" thick can be filled with caulk. Gaps ⅜" or wider could mean that your house has a serious moisture or shifting problem. Consult a building inspector.

Buckling occurs most frequently in manufactured siding, when expansion gaps are too small at the points where the siding fits into trim and channels. If possible, move the channels slightly to give the siding more room. If not, remove the siding, trim the length slightly, then reinstall.

Minor surface damage to metal siding is best left alone in most cases—unless the damage has penetrated the surface. With metal products, cosmetic surface repairs often look worse than the damage.

Missing siding, such as cedar shakes that have been blown away from the wall, should be replaced immediately. Check the surrounding siding to make sure it's secure.

Removing Exterior Siding

Although it's sometimes possible to install new siding over old if the old siding is solid and firmly attached to the house, it's often better to remove the siding, especially if it's damaged. Taking off the old siding allows you to start with a flat, smooth surface. And because the overall thickness of the siding will remain unchanged, you won't have to add extensions to your window and door jambs.

There's no "right" way to remove siding. Each type of siding material is installed differently, and consequently, they have different removal techniques. A couple of universal rules do apply, however. Start by removing trim that's placed over the siding, and work from the top down. Siding is usually installed from the bottom up, and working in the opposite direction makes removal much easier. Determine the best removal method for your project based on your type of siding.

Strip one side of the house at a time, then re-side that wall before ripping the siding off another section. This minimizes the amount of time your bare walls are exposed to the elements. Take care not to damage the sheathing. If you can't avoid tearing the housewrap, it can easily be replaced, but the sheathing is another story.

While the goal is to remove the siding as quickly as possible, it's also important to work safely. Take care when working around windows so the siding doesn't crack or break the glass. Invest the necessary time to protect the flowers and shrubs before starting the tear-off.

Renting a dumpster will expedite the cleanup process. It's much easier to dispose of the siding as soon as it's removed rather than stacking it up in an unsightly pile in your yard, then throwing it away later. When you're finished with your cleanup, use a release magnet to collect the nails on the ground.

Tools & Materials ▶

Cat's paw	Hammer
Flat pry bar	Masonry-cutting blade
Zip tool	Masonry bit
Drill	Aviation snips
Circular saw	Roofing shovel
Masonry chisel	Release magnet

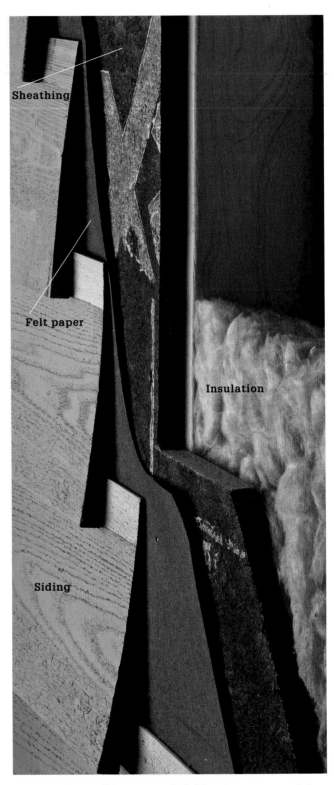

The exterior wall is composed of siding, housewrap or felt paper, and sheathing. Remove the siding without disturbing or damaging the sheathing.

Tips for Removing Siding ▸

Brick molding comes preattached to most wood-frame window and door units. To remove the molding, pry along the outside of the frame to avoid marring the exposed parts of the jambs and molding.

Lap siding is nailed at the top, then covered by the next course. Pry off the trim at the top of the wall to expose the nails in top row. Remove the nails using a cat's paw, and work your way down the wall.

Shakes and shingles are best removed with a roofing shovel. Use the shovel to pry the siding away from the wall. Once the siding is removed, use the shovel or a hammer to pull out remaining nails.

Board and batten siding is removed by prying off the battens from over the boards. Use a pry bar or cat's paw to remove the nails from the boards.

Siding shown cutaway for clarity

Vinyl siding has a locking channel that fits over the nailing strip of the underlying piece. To remove, use a zip tool to separate the panels, and use a flat pry bar or hammer to remove the nails.

Building paper

Sheathing

Metal lath

Stucco

Stucco siding is difficult to remove. It's usually much easier to apply the new siding over the stucco than to remove it. If you're determined to take it off, use a cold chisel and hammer to break it into pieces, and aviation snips to cut the lath.

Replacing Wall Sheathing

After removing the old siding, inspect the sheathing to make sure it's still in good condition. If water penetrated behind the siding, there's a good chance the sheathing is warped, rotted, or otherwise damaged, and will need to be replaced. You'll only need to replace the section of sheathing that's damaged. Before cutting into the wall, make sure there are no wires, cables, or pipes under the sheathing.

Older homes typically have planks or plywood sheathing, while new homes may have a nonstructural sheathing. The replacement material doesn't have to be the same material as the original sheathing, but it does have to be the same thickness.

Tools & Materials ▸

Hammer	Sheathing
Circular saw	2 × 4
Tape measure	3" deck screws
Chalk line	2¼" deck screws
Pry bar	Drill

Although the sheathing isn't visible, a smooth, solid sheathing installation is essential to a professional looking siding finish.

How to Replace Wall Sheathing

Snap chalk lines around the area of damaged sheathing, making sure the vertical lines are next to wall studs. Remove any nails or staples in your path. Set the depth of the circular saw blade to cut through the sheathing, but not cut the studs.

Pry off the damaged sheathing. Remove any remaining nails or staples in the studs. Measure the opening, subtract ⅛" from each side, then cut a piece of sheathing to size.

Align 2 × 4 nailing strips with the edges of the wall studs. Fasten the strips in place, using 3" deck screws.

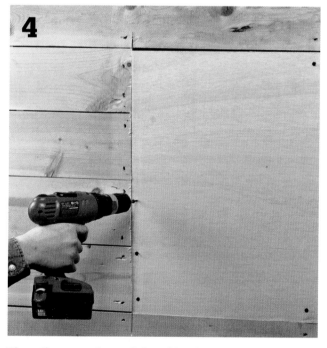

Place the new piece of sheathing in the opening, keeping a ⅛" gap on each side to allow for expansion. Attach the sheathing to the nailing strips and studs, using 2¼" deck screws driven every 12".

Repairing Siding

Damage to siding is fairly common, but fortunately, it's also easy to fix. Small to medium holes, cracks, and rotted areas can be repaired with filler or by replacing the damaged sections with matching siding.

If you cannot find matching siding for repairs at building centers, check with salvage yards or siding contractors. When repairing aluminum or vinyl siding, contact the manufacturer or the contractor who installed the siding to help you locate matching materials and parts. If you're unable to find an exact match, remove a section of original siding from a less visible area of the house, such as the back of the garage, and use it for the patch. Cover the gap in the less visible area with a close matching siding, where the mismatch will be less noticeable.

Tools & Materials ▸

Aviation snips	Chisel	Stud finder	30# felt paper
Caulk gun	Trowel	Paintbrush	Sheathing
Drill	Screwdrivers	Epoxy wood filler	Trim
Flat pry bar	Hacksaw	Epoxy glue	Replacement siding
Hammer	Circular saw	Galvanized ring-shank	End caps
Straightedge	Jigsaw	siding nails	Wood preservative
Tape measure	Key hole saw	Siliconized	Primer
Utility knife	Flat pry bar	acrylic caulk	Paint or stain
Zip-lock tool	Nail set	Roofing cement	Metal sandpaper

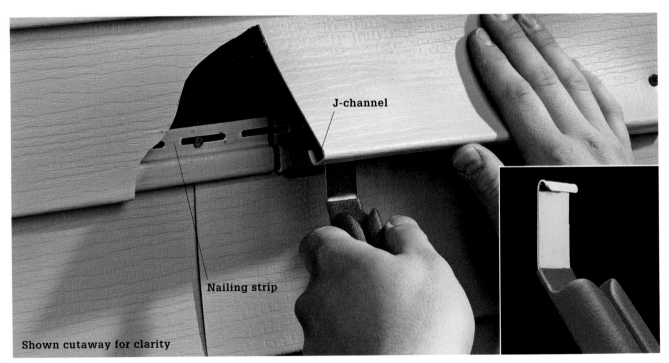

J-channel

Nailing strip

Shown cutaway for clarity

Vinyl and metal siding panels have a locking J-channel that fits over the bottom of the nailing strip on the underlying piece. Use a zip-lock tool (inset) to separate panels. Insert the tool at the seam nearest the repair area. Slide it over the J-channel, pulling outward slightly, to unlock the joint from the siding below.

How to Repair Vinyl Siding

Starting at the seam nearest the damaged area, unlock interlocking joints, using a ziplock tool. Insert spacers between the panels, then remove the fasteners in the damaged siding, using a flat pry bar. Cut out the damaged area, using aviation snips. Cut a replacement piece 4" longer than the open area, and trim 2" off the nailing strip from each end. Slide the piece into position.

Insert siding nails in the nailing strip, then position the end of a flat pry bar over each nail head. Drive the nails by tapping on the neck of the pry bar with a hammer. Place a scrap piece of wood between the pry bar and siding to avoid damaging the siding. Slip the locking channel on the overlapping piece over the nailing strip of the replacement piece. *Tip: If the damaged panel is near a corner, door, or window, replace the entire panel. This eliminates an extra seam.*

How to Patch Aluminum Siding

Cut out the damaged area, using aviation snips. Leave an exposed area on top of the uppermost piece to act as a bonding surface. Cut a patch 4" larger than the repair area. Remove the nailing strip. Smooth the edges with metal sandpaper.

Nail the lower patch in place by driving siding nails through the nailing flange. Apply roofing cement to the back of the top piece, then press it into place, slipping the locking channel over the nailing strip of the underlying piece. Caulk the seams.

How to Replace Aluminum End Caps

Remove the damaged end cap. If necessary, pry the bottom loose, then cut along the top with a hacksaw blade. Starting at the bottom, attach the replacement end caps by driving siding nails through the nailing tabs and into the framing members.

Trim the nailing tabs off the top replacement cap. Apply roofing cement to its back. Slide the cap over the locking channels of the siding panels. Press the top cap securely in place.

How to Replace Board & Batten Siding

Remove the battens over the damaged boards. Pry out the damaged boards in their entirety. Inspect the underlying housewrap, and patch if necessary.

Cut replacement boards from the same type of lumber, allowing a ⅛" gap at the side seams. Prime or seal the edges and the back side of the replacement boards. Let them dry.

Nail the new boards in place, using ring-shank siding nails. Replace the battens and any other trim. Prime and paint or stain the new boards to blend with the surrounding siding.

How to Replace Wood Shakes & Shingles

Split damaged shakes or shingles with a hammer and chisel, and remove them. Insert wood spacers under the shakes or shingles above the repair area, then slip a hacksaw blade under the top board to cut off any remaining nail heads.

Cut replacement shakes or shingles to fit, leaving a ⅛"- to ¼"-wide gap at each side. Coat all sides and edges with wood preservative. Slip the patch pieces under the siding above the repair area. Drive siding nails near the top of the exposed area on the patches. Cover nail heads with caulk. Remove the spacers.

How to Replace Lap Siding

If the damage is caused by water, locate and repair the leak or other source of the water damage.

Mark the area of siding that needs to be replaced. Make the cutout lines over the center of the framing members on each side of the repair area, staggering the cuts to offset the joints. *Tip: Use an electronic studfinder to locate framing members, or look for the nail heads.*

Insert spacers beneath the board above the repair area. Make entry cuts at the top of the cutting lines with a keyhole saw, then saw through the boards and remove them. Pry out any nails or cut off the nail heads, using a hacksaw blade. Patch or replace the sheathing and building paper, if necessary.

Measure and cut replacement boards to fit, leaving an expansion gap of ⅛" at each end. Use the old boards as templates to trace cutouts for fixtures and openings. Use a jigsaw to make the cutouts. Apply wood sealer or primer to the ends and backs of the boards. Let them dry.

Nail the new boards in place with siding nails, starting with the lowest board in the repair area. At each framing member, drive nails through the bottom of the new board and the top of the board below. *Tip: If you removed the bottom row of siding, nail a 1 × 2 starter strip along the bottom of the patch area.*

Fill expansion joints with caulk (use paintable caulk for painted wood or tinted caulk for stained wood). Prime and paint or stain the replacement boards to match the surrounding siding.

Repairing Trim

Some exterior trim serves as decoration, like gingerbread and ornate cornice moldings. Other trim, such as brick molding and end caps, works with siding to seal your house from the elements. Damaged brick molding and corner boards should be patched with stock material similar to the original.

If you cannot find matching replacement parts for decorative trim at home improvement stores, check salvage shops or contact a custom millworker.

Repair delicate or ornamental trim molding in your workshop, whenever possible. You'll get better results than if you try repairing it while it's still attached.

Tools & Materials ▶

Hammer
Chisel
Circular saw
Nail set
Putty knife
Utility knife
Paintbrush
Flat pry bar
Caulk gun
Epoxy wood filler
Epoxy glue

Caulk
10d galvanized
  casing nails
Galvanized
  ring-shank
  siding nails
Sandpaper
Paint
Building paper
Drip edge
Replacement trim

Tips for Repairing & Replacing Trim ▶

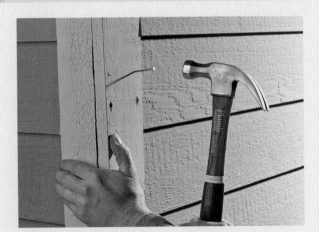

Reattach loose trim with new ring-shank siding nails driven near old nail locations. Fill old nail holes with paintable caulk, and touch up caulk and new nail heads with paint to match the surrounding surface.

Repair decorative trim molding with epoxy glue or wood filler. For major repairs, make your own replacement parts, or take the trim to a custom millwork shop.

How to Replace Brick Molding

1

Pry off old brick molding around windows and doors, using a flat pry bar. Remove any old drip edge. Inspect and repair the building paper.

2

Brick molding

Hold a replacement piece of brick molding, slightly longer than the original piece, across the opening. Mark cutting lines to fit the opening. Cut the replacement molding at the marks, matching any miter cuts.

3

Drip edge

Cut a 3"-wide piece of flashing to fit between the jambs, then bend it in half lengthwise to form the new drip edge (preformed drip edge is also available). Slip it between the siding and building paper, above the door or window. Do not nail the drip edge in place.

4

Test-fit the replacement piece of brick molding, then apply exterior-grade panel adhesive to the back side. Follow the manufacturer's directions for allowing the adhesive to set.

5

Nail the brick molding to the door header, using 10d galvanized casing nails. Lock-nail the miter joints, and set all nail heads. Seal joints, and cover nail holes with caulk. Prime and paint when the caulk dries.

Identifying Exterior Paint Problems

Two enemies work against painted surfaces—moisture and age. A simple leak or a failed vapor barrier inside the house can ruin even the finest paint job. If you notice signs of paint failure, such as blistering or peeling, take action to correct the problem right away. If the surface damage is discovered in time, you may be able to correct it with just a little bit of touch-up painting.

Evaluating the painted surfaces of your house can help you identify problems with siding, trim, roofs, and moisture barriers. The pictures on these two pages show the most common forms of paint failure, and how to fix them. Be sure to fix any moisture problems before repainting.

Evaluate exterior painted surfaces every year, starting with areas sheltered from the sun. Paint failure will appear first in areas that receive little or no direct sunlight and is a warning sign that similar problems are developing in neighboring areas.

Common Forms of Paint Failure

Blistering appears as a bubbled surface. It results from poor preparation or hurried application of primer or paint. The blisters indicate trapped moisture is trying to force its way through the surface. To fix isolated spots, scrape and touch up. For widespread damage, remove paint down to bare wood, then apply primer and paint.

Peeling occurs when paint falls away in large flakes. It's a sign of persistent moisture problems, generally from a leak or a failed vapor barrier. If the peeling is localized, scrape and sand the damaged areas, then touch up with primer and paint. If it's widespread, remove the old paint down to bare wood, then apply primer and paint.

Alligatoring is widespread flaking and cracking, typically seen on surfaces that have many built-up paint layers. It can also be caused by inadequate surface preparation or by allowing too little drying time between coats of primer and paint. Remove the old paint, then prime and repaint.

Localized blistering and peeling indicates that moisture, usually from a leaky roof, gutter system, or interior pipe, is trapped under the paint. Find and eliminate the leak, then scrape, prime, and repaint the area.

Clearly defined blistering and peeling occurs when a humid room has an insufficient vapor barrier. If there's a clear line where an interior wall ends, remove the siding and replace the vapor barrier.

Mildew forms in cracks and in humid areas that receive little direct sunlight. Wash mildewed areas with a 1:1 solution of household chlorine bleach and water, or with trisodium phosphate (TSP).

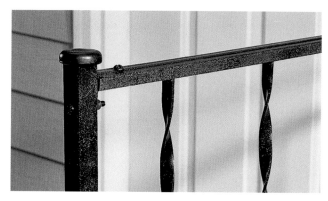

Rust occurs when moisture penetrates paint on iron or steel. Remove the rust and loose paint with a drill and wire brush attachment, then prime and repaint.

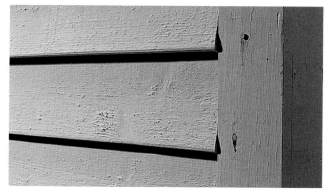

Bleeding spots occur when nails in siding begin to rust. Remove the nails, sand out the rust, then drive in galvanized ring-shank nails. Apply metal primer, then paint to blend in with the siding.

Efflorescence occurs in masonry when minerals leech through the surface, forming a crystalline or powdery layer. Use a scrub brush and a muriatic acid solution to remove efflorescence before priming and painting.

Preparing to Paint

The key to an even paint job is to work on a smooth, clean, dry surface—so preparing the surface is essential. Generally, the more preparation work you do, the smoother the final finish will be and the longer it will last.

For the smoothest finish, sand all the way down to the bare wood with a power sander. For a less time-consuming (but rougher) finish, scrape off any loose paint, then spot-sand rough areas. You can use pressure washing to remove some of the flaking paint, but by itself, pressure washing won't create a smooth surface for painting.

Tools & Materials ▸

Pressure washer
Scraper
Sander
Sanding block
Putty knife
Stiff-bristled brush
Wire brush
Steel wool
Coarse abrasive pad
Drill
Wire-wheel attachment
Caulk gun
Heat gun
80-, 120-, and 150-grit
   sandpaper
Putty
Paintable
   siliconized caulk
Muriatic acid
Sealant

The amount of surface preparation you do will largely determine the final appearance of your paint job. Decide how much sanding and scraping you're willing to do to obtain a finish you'll be happy with.

How to Remove Paint

Use a heat gun to loosen thick layers of old paint. Aim the gun at the surface, warm the paint until it starts to bubble, then scrape the paint as soon as it releases.

To remove large areas of paint on wood lap siding, use a siding sander with a disk that's as wide as the reveal on your siding.

How to Prepare Surfaces for Paint

Clean the surface and remove loose paint by pressure washing the house. As you work, direct the water stream downward, and don't get too close to the surface with the sprayer head. Allow all surfaces to dry thoroughly before continuing.

Scrape off loose paint, using a paint scraper. Be careful not to damage the surface by scraping too hard.

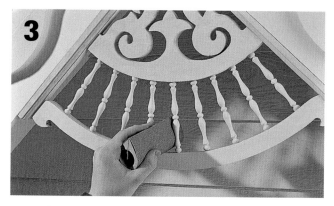

Smooth out rough paint with a finishing sander and 80-grit sandpaper. Use sanding blocks and 80- to 120-grit sandpaper to sand hard-to-reach areas of trim. *Tip: You can make sanding blocks from dowels, wood scraps, or garden hoses.*

Use detail scrapers to remove loose paint in hard-to-reach areas. Some of these scrapers have interchangeable heads that match common trim profiles.

Inspect all surfaces for cracks, rot, and other damage. Mark affected areas with colored push pins or tape. Fill the holes and cracks with epoxy wood filler.

Use a finishing sander with 120-grit sandpaper to sand down repaired areas, ridges, and hard edges left from the scraping process, creating a smooth surface.

How to Prepare Trim Surfaces for Paint

Scuff-sand glossy surfaces on doors, window casings, and all surfaces painted with enamel paint. Use a coarse abrasive pad or 150-grit sandpaper.

Fill cracks in siding and gaps around window and door trim with paintable siliconized acrylic caulk.

How to Remove Clear Finishes

Pressure-wash stained or unpainted surfaces that have been treated with a wood preservative or protectant before recoating them with fresh sealant.

Use a stiff-bristled brush to dislodge any flakes of loosened surface coating that weren't removed by pressure washing. Don't use a wire brush on wood surfaces.

How to Prepare Metal & Masonry for Paint

Remove rust and loose paint from metal hardware, such as railings and ornate trim, using a wire brush. Cover the surface with metal primer immediately after brushing to prevent the formation of new rust.

Scuff-sand metal siding and trim with medium-coarse steel wool or a coarse abrasive pad. Wash the surface and let dry before priming and painting.

Remove loose mortar, mineral deposits, or paint from mortar lines in masonry surfaces with a drill and wire-wheel attachment. Clean broad, flat masonry surfaces with a wire brush. Correct any minor damage before repainting.

Dissolve rust on metal hardware with diluted muriatic acid solution. When working with muriatic acid, it's important to wear safety equipment, work in a well-ventilated area, and follow all manufacturer's directions and precautions.

Applying Primer & Paint

Schedule priming and painting tasks so that you can paint within two weeks of priming surfaces. If more than two weeks pass, wash the surface with soap and water before applying the next coat.

Check the weather forecast and keep an eye on the sky while you work. Damp weather or rain within two hours of application will ruin a paint job. Don't paint when the temperature is below 50° or above 90°F. Avoid painting on windy days—it's dangerous to be on a ladder in high winds, and wind blows dirt onto the fresh paint.

Plan each day's work so you can follow the shade. Prepare, prime, and paint one face of the house at a time, and follow a logical painting order. Work from the top of the house down to the foundation, covering an entire section before you move the ladder or scaffolding.

Tools & Materials ▸

4" paintbrush	Primer
2½" or 3" paintbrush	House paint
Sash brush	Trim paint
Scaffolding	Cleanup materials
Ladders	

Paint in a logical order, starting from the top and working your way down. Cover as much surface as you can reach comfortably without moving your ladder or scaffolding. After the paint or primer dries, touch up any unpainted areas that were covered by the ladder or ladder stabilizer.

Tips for Applying Primer & Paint ▸

Use the right primer and paint for each job. Always read the manufacturer's recommendations.

Plan your painting sequence so you paint the walls, doors, and trim before painting stairs and porch floors. This prevents the need to touch up spills.

Apply primer and paint in the shade or indirect sunlight. Direct sun can dry primers and paints too quickly and trap moisture below the surface, which leads to blistering and peeling.

Tips for Selecting Brushes & Rollers ▸

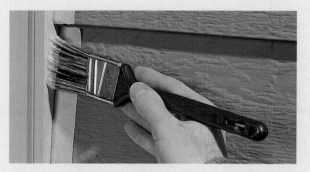

Wall brushes, which are thick, square brushes 3" to 5" wide, are designed to carry a lot of paint and distribute it widely. *Tip: It's good to keep a variety of clean brushes on hand, including 2½", 3", and 4" flat brushes, 2" and 3" trim brushes, and tapered sash brushes.*

Trim and tapered sash brushes, which are 2" to 3" wide, are good for painting doors and trim, and for cutting-in small areas.

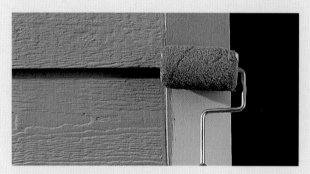

Paint rollers work best for quickly painting smooth surfaces. Use an 8" or 9" roller sleeve for broad surfaces.

Use a 3" roller to paint flat-surfaced trim, such as end caps and corner trim.

Tips for Loading & Distributing Paint ▸

Load your brush with the right amount of paint for the area you're covering. Use a full load of paint for broad areas, a moderate load for smaller areas and feathering strokes, and a light load when painting or working around trim.

Hold the brush at a 45° angle and apply just enough downward pressure to flex the bristles and squeeze the paint from the brush.

How to Use a Paintbrush

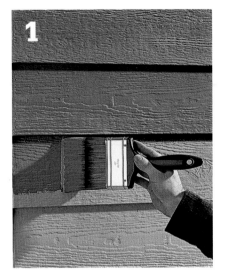

1

Load the brush with a full load of paint. Starting at one end of the surface, make a long, smooth stroke until the paint begins to feather out. *Tip: Paint color can vary from one can to the next. To avoid problems, pour all of your paint into one large container and mix it thoroughly. Pour the mixed paint back into the individual cans and seal them carefully. Stir each can before use.*

2

At the end of the stroke, lift the brush without leaving a definite ending point. If the paint appears uneven or contains heavy brush marks, smooth it out without overbrushing.

3

Reload the brush and make a stroke from the opposite direction, painting over the feathered end of the first stroke to create a smooth, even surface. If the junction of the two strokes is visible, rebrush with a light coat of paint. Feather out the starting point of the second stroke.

Tips for Using Paint Rollers ▸

Wet the roller nap, then squeeze out the excess water. Position a roller screen inside a five-gallon bucket. Dip the roller into the paint, then roll it back and forth across the roller screen. The roller sleeve should be full, but not dripping, when lifted from the bucket.

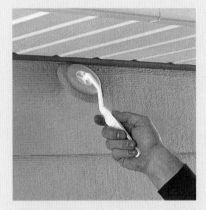

Cone-shaped rollers work well for painting the joints between intersecting surfaces.

Doughnut-shaped rollers work well for painting the edges of lap siding and moldings.

Tips for Cleaning Painting Tools ▸

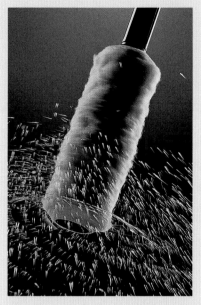

Scrape paint from roller covers with the curved side of a cleaner tool.

Use a spinner tool to remove paint and solvent from brushes and roller covers.

Comb brushes with the spiked side of a cleaner tool to properly align bristles for drying.

How to Paint Fascia, Soffits & Trim

Prime all surfaces to be painted, and allow ample drying time. Paint the face of the fascia first, then cut in paint at the bottom edges of the soffit panels. *Tip: Fascia and soffits are usually painted the same color as the trim.*

Paint the soffit panels and trim with a 4" brush. Start by cutting in around the edges of the panels, using the narrow edge of the brush, then feather in the broad surfaces of the soffit panels with full loads of paint. Be sure to get good coverage in the grooves.

Paint any decorative trim near the top of the house at the same time you paint the soffits and fascia. Use a 2½" or 3" paintbrush for broader surfaces, and a sash brush for more intricate trim areas.

How to Paint Siding

Paint the bottom edges of lap siding by holding the paintbrush flat against the wall. Paint the bottom edges of several siding pieces before returning to paint the faces of the same boards.

Paint the broad faces of the siding boards with a 4" brush, using the painting technique shown on page 204. Working down from the top of the house, paint as much surface as you can reach without leaning beyond the sides of the ladder.

Paint the siding all the way down to the foundation, working from top to bottom. Shift the ladder or scaffolding, then paint the next section. *Tip: Paint up to the edges of end caps and window or door trim that will be painted later. If you're not planning to paint the trim, mask it off or use a paint shield.*

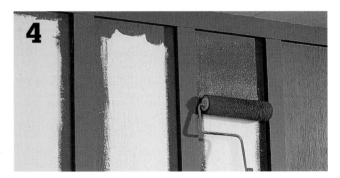

On board and batten or vertical panel siding, paint the edges of the battens, or top boards, first. Paint the faces of the battens before the sides dry, then use a roller with a ⅝"-nap sleeve to paint the large, broad surfaces between the battens.

How to Paint Stucco Walls

Using a large paintbrush, paint the foundation with anti-chalking masonry primer, and let it dry. Using concrete paint and a 4" brush, cut in the areas around basement windows and doors.

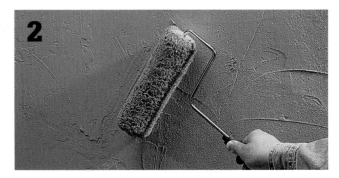

Apply concrete paint to board surfaces with a paint roller and a ⅝"-nap sleeve. Use a 3" trim roller or a 3" paintbrush for trim.

How to Paint Doors, Windows & Trim

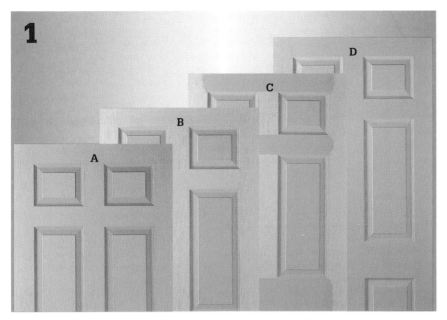

1 Using a sash brush, paint doors in this sequence: beveled edges of raised door panels (A), panel faces (B), horizontal rails (C), and vertical stiles (D).

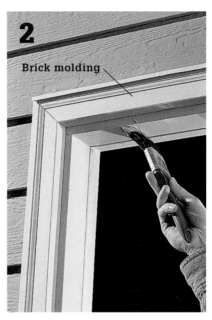

2 For trim, use a trim brush or sash brush and a moderate load of paint to paint the inside edges of door and window jambs, casings, and brick molding. *Tip: Paint surfaces on the interior side of the door-stop to match the interior trim.*

3 Mask off the siding—if freshly painted, make sure it's completely dry first. Paint the outside edges of casings and brick molding. Work paint all the way into the corners created by the siding's profile.

4 Paint the faces of door jambs, casings, and brick molding, feathering fresh paint around the previously painted edges.

5 Paint wood door thresholds and porch floors with specially formulated enamel floor paint.

Using Paint-spraying Equipment

Spray equipment can make quick work of painting, but it still requires the same careful preparation work as traditional brush and roller methods. Part of that prep work involves using plastic to completely cover doors, windows, and other areas that you don't want painted, rather than just taping them off.

Spray equipment can be purchased or rented at hardware and home improvement stores. There are several types and sizes of spray equipment, including high-volume low-pressure (HVLP), airless, air-assisted airless, and electrostatic enhanced. They all work the same way—by atomizing paint and directing it to a worksurface in a spray or fan pattern. For our project, we used an HVLP sprayer, which we recommend because it produces less overspray and more efficient paint application than other sprayers.

Be sure to read and follow all safety precautions for the spray equipment. Since the paint is under a lot of pressure, it can not only tear the skin, but it can inject toxins into the blood stream if used incorrectly. Wear the proper safety protection, such as safety glasses and a respirator, when spray painting the house.

As with other paint applications, pay close attention to the weather. Don't spray if rain is likely, and don't spray on windy days, since the wind can carry the paint particles away from the siding.

Tools & Materials ▸

Utility knife	Masking tape
Spray equipment	Plastic
Paint	Cardboard
Safety glasses	Cheese-cloth
Respirator	5-gallon bucket

Paint sprayers allow you to cover large areas of siding and trim in a short amount of time. They also make it easier to paint areas that are hard to reach with a brush or roller.

How to Paint Using a Paint Sprayer

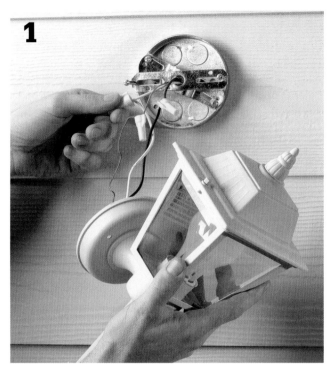

Remove outside light fixtures, window and door screens, and other detachable items that you don't want painted.

Cover doors, windows, and any other areas you don't want painted, using plastic and masking tape.

Strain the paint through cheese cloth to remove particles and debris. Mix the paint together in a 5-gallon bucket. Fill the sprayer container.

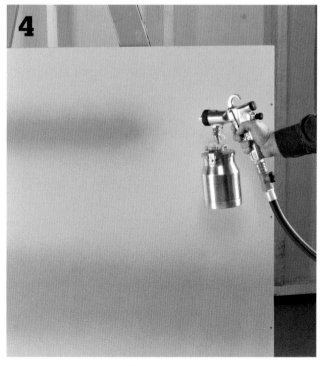

Spray a test pattern of paint on a scrap piece of cardboard. Adjust the pressure until you reach an even "fan" without any thick lines along the edge of the spray pattern.

(continued)

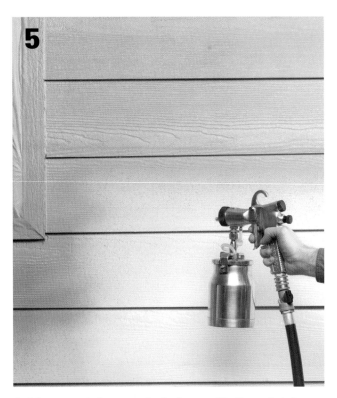

Cut-in around doors and windows with the paint. Spray the paint along each side of the doors and windows, applying the paint evenly.

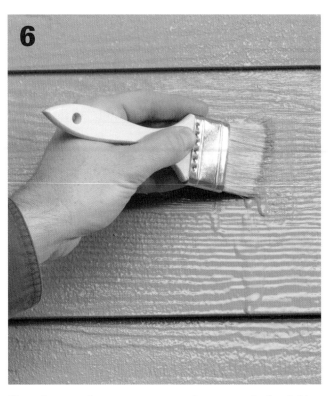

If you happen to spray an excessive amount of paint in an area and it starts to run, stop the sprayer. Use a paintbrush to spread out the paint and eliminate the runs.

Hold the spray gun perpendicular to the house, approximately 12" from the wall. Start painting near the top of the wall, close to a corner. Move your entire arm, rather than just the wrist, in a steady, side-to-side motion. Do not wave your arm in an arc. Start your arm movement, then start the gun.

Spray the paint in an even motion, being careful not to tilt the gun. As you sweep your arm back and forth, overlap each coat of paint by 20 to 30 percent, working your way down the wall. When stopping, release the trigger before discontinuing your motion.

How to Paint Doors Using a Paint Sprayer

Remove the door by taking off the hinges. Remove all hardware from the door, such as handles and locks. If the door contains glass, you can either tape it off, or allow paint to get on the glass and then scrape it off with a razor after it's dry.

Prop up the door so it stands vertically. Starting at the top of the door, spray on the paint. As you make passes across the door, slightly go past the edges before sweeping back in the opposite direction. Wait until the paint is completely dry, then turn the door around and paint the other side.

Staining Siding

Stain lends color to wood siding, but because it is partially transparent, it also allows the natural beauty of the wood grain to show through. Water-based stains are applied with an acrylic or synthetic brush. Oil-based stains are usually applied with a natural-bristle brush.

Work in small sections at a time. Complete an entire length of board without stopping in the middle. Unlike paint, stain can darken or leave streaks if you go back over an area after it dries. Save the trim until the end, then stain it separately to get an even coverage.

Staining requires the same careful preparation work as painting. The surface must be clean and dry. Avoid working in direct sunlight so the stain doesn't dry too quickly. Check manufacturer's recommendations before staining. Some stains cannot be applied in temperatures below 50°F.

Tools & Materials ▸

Paintbrush
    or foam brush

Cloths
Stain

How to Stain Log Cabin Siding

Load the brush with stain. Starting at a corner, move the brush across the siding with a long, smooth stroke. Cover the entire width of the log with stain, reloading the brush as needed, applying stain in the same direction. *Tip: Mix the stain thoroughly and often as it's being applied.*

Wipe away excess stain with a clean cloth. Keep applying stain until you reach the opposite corner or an edge. Once the top course is stained, go back to the corner and start on the next row of siding, using the same technique. If the run of siding is short, such as between windows, apply stain to two rows at a time. Stain remaining courses the same way.

How to Stain Shingle Siding

Load the brush with stain. Starting at the top of a wall by a corner, apply stain to the shingles, using smooth, downward strokes. Wipe off excess stain with a cloth. Cover the face of the shingle and stain the bottom edge before moving on to the next one. Apply stain to one or two courses at a time, moving across the wall as you go. Never stop in the middle of a shingle. When you reach the opposite corner, start over on the next set of shingles. Stain remaining rows the same way.

Once all of the shingles are stained, apply stain to the trim. Move the brush in the same direction as the wood grain, then wipe away excess with a cloth.

Repairing Stucco

Although stucco siding is very durable, it can be damaged, and over time it can crumble or crack. The directions given below work well for patching small areas less than two sq. ft. For more extensive damage, the repair is done in layers, as shown on the opposite page.

Tools & Materials ▸

Caulk gun	Stucco patching
Disposable paintbrush	compound
Putty knife	Bonding adhesive
Mason's trowel	Denatured alcohol
Square-end trowel	Metal primer
Hammer	Stucco mix
Whisk broom	Masonry paint
Wire brush	1½" roofing nails
Masonry chisel	15# building paper
Aviation snips	Self-furring
Pry bar	metal lath
Drill with masonry bit	Masonry caulk
Scratching tool	Tint
Metal primer	Metal stop bead

Fill thin cracks in stucco walls with masonry caulk.
Overfill the crack with caulk, and feather until it's flush with the stucco. Allow the caulk to set, then paint it to match the stucco. Masonry caulk stays semiflexible, preventing further cracking.

How to Patch Small Areas

Remove loose material from the repair area, using a wire brush. Use the brush to clean away rust from any exposed metal lath, then apply a coat of metal primer to the lath.

Apply premixed stucco repair compound to the repair area, slightly overfilling the hole, using a putty knife or trowel. Read manufacturer's directions, as drying times vary.

Smooth the repair with a putty knife or trowel, feathering the edges to blend into the surrounding surface. Use a whisk broom or trowel to duplicate the original texture. Let the patch dry for several days, then touch it up with masonry paint.

How to Repair Large Areas

Make a starter hole with a drill and masonry bit, then use a masonry chisel and hammer to chip away stucco in the repair area. *Note: Wear safety glasses and a particle mask or respirator when cutting stucco. Cut self-furring metal lath to size and attach it to the sheathing, using roofing nails. Overlap pieces by 2". If the patch extends to the base of the wall, attach a metal stop bead at the bottom.*

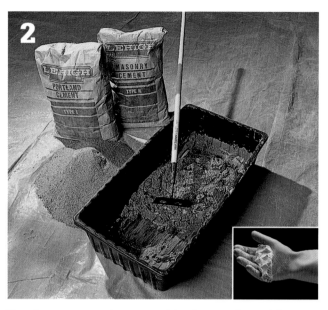

To mix your own stucco, combine three parts sand, two parts portland cement, and one part masonry cement. Add just enough water so the mixture holds its shape when squeezed (inset). Mix only as much as you can use in one hour. *Tip: Premixed stucco works well for small jobs, but for large ones, it's more economical to mix your own.*

Apply a ⅜"-thick layer of stucco directly to the metal lath. Push the stucco into the mesh until it fills the gap between the mesh and the sheathing. Score horizontal grooves into the wet surface, using a scratching tool. Let the stucco dry for two days, misting it with water every two to four hours.

Apply a second, smooth layer of stucco. Build up the stucco to within ¼" of the original surface. Let the patch dry for two days, misting every two to four hours.

Combine finish-coat stucco mix with just enough water for the mixture to hold its shape. Dampen the patch area, then apply the finish coat to match the original surface. Dampen the patch periodically for a week. Let it dry for several more days before painting.

Maintaining & Repairing Concrete

Concrete is one of the most durable building materials, but it still requires occasional repair and maintenance. Freezing and thawing, improper finishing techniques, a poor subbase, or lack of reinforcement all can cause problems with concrete. By addressing problems as soon as you discover them, you can prevent further damage that may be difficult or impossible to fix.

Concrete repairs fall into a wide range, from simple cleaning and sealing, to removing and replacing whole sections. Filling cracks and repairing surface damage are the most common concrete repairs.

Another effective repair is resurfacing—covering an old concrete surface with a layer of fresh concrete. It's a good solution to spalling, crazing, or popouts—minor problems that affect the appearance more than the structure. These problems often result from inadequate preparation or incorrect finishing techniques.

As with any kind of repair, the success of the project depends largely on good preparation and the use of the best repair products for the job. Specially formulated repair products are manufactured for just about every type of concrete repair. Be sure to read the product-use information before purchasing any products; some products need to be used in combination with others.

A good repair can outlast the rest of the structure in some cases, but if structural damage has occurred, repairing the concrete is only a temporary solution. By using the right products and techniques, however, you can make cosmetic repairs that improve the appearance of the surface and keep damage from becoming worse.

Probably the most important point to remember when repairing concrete is that curing makes repairs last longer. That means covering repaired surfaces with plastic sheeting and keeping them damp for at least a week. In dry, hot weather, lift the plastic occasionally, and mist with water.

Before

After

Good repairs restore both the appearance and the function to failing concrete structures and surfaces. Careful work can produce a well-blended, successful repair like the one shown above.

Concrete Repair Products

Concrete repair products include: vinyl-reinforced concrete patch (A) for filling holes, popouts, and larger cracks; hydraulic cement (B) for repairing foundations, retaining walls, and other damp areas; quick-setting cement (C) for repairing vertical surfaces and unusual shapes; anchoring cement (D) for setting hardware in concrete; concrete sealing products (E); masonry paint (F) concrete recoating product (G) for creating a fresh surface on old concrete; joint-filler caulk (H); pour-in crack sealer (I); concrete cleaner (J); concrete fortifier (K) to strengthen concrete; bonding adhesive (L) to prepare the repair area; and concrete sand mix (M) for general repairs and resurfacing.

Tips for Disguising Repairs ▸

Add concrete pigment or liquid cement color to concrete patching compound to create a color that matches the original concrete. Experiment with different mixtures until you find a matching color. Samples should be dry to show the actual colors.

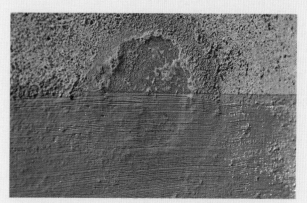

Use masonry paint to cover concrete repairs. Paint can be used on vertical or horizontal surfaces, but high-traffic surfaces will require more frequent touch-up or repainting.

Identifying Problems with Concrete

There are two general types of concrete failure: structural failure, usually resulting from outside forces like freezing water; and surface damage, most often caused by improper finishing techniques or concrete mixtures that do not have the right ratio of water to cement. Surface problems sometimes can be permanently repaired if the correct products and techniques are used. More significant damage can be patched for cosmetic purposes and to resist further damage, but the structure will eventually need to be replaced.

Common Concrete Problems

Sunken concrete is usually caused by erosion of the subbase. Some structures, like sidewalks, can be raised to repair the subbase, then relaid. A more common (and more reliable) solution is to hire a mudjacking contractor to raise the surface by injecting fresh concrete below the surface.

Frost heave is common in colder climates. Frozen ground forces concrete slabs upward, and sections of the slab can pop up. The best solution is to break off and remove the affected section or sections, repair the subbase, and pour new sections that are set off by isolation joints.

Moisture buildup occurs in concrete structures, like foundations and retaining walls, that are in constant ground contact. To identify the moisture source, tape a piece of foil to the wall. If moisture collects on the outer surface of the foil, the source likely is condensation, which can be corrected by installing a dehumidifier. If moisture is not visible on the foil, it is likely seeping through the wall. Consult a professional mason.

Staining can ruin the appearance of a concrete surface or structure. Stains can be removed with commercial-grade concrete cleaner or a variety of other chemicals. For protection against staining, seal masonry surfaces with clear sealant.

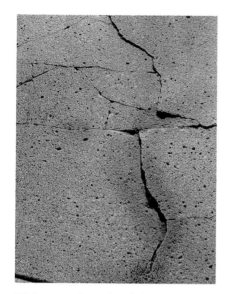

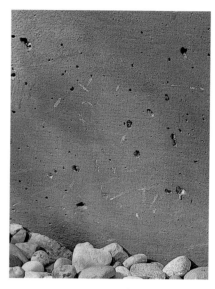

Widespread cracks all the way through the surface, and other forms of substantial damage, are very difficult to repair effectively. If the damage to the concrete is extensive, remove and replace the structure.

Isolated cracks occur on many concrete building projects. Fill small cracks with concrete caulk or crack-filler, and patch large cracks with vinyl-reinforced patching material.

Popouts can be caused by freezing moisture or stress, but very often they occur because the concrete surface was improperly floated or cured, causing the aggregate near the surface of the concrete to loosen. A few scattered popouts do not require attention, but if they are very large or widespread, you can repair them as you would repair holes.

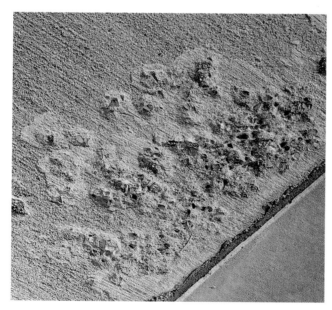

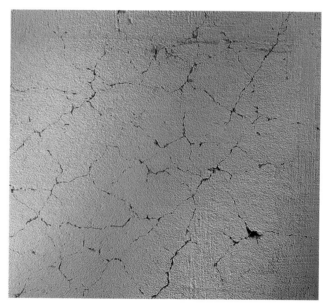

Spalling is surface deterioration of concrete. Spalling is caused by overfloating, which draws too much water to the surface, causing it to weaken and peel off over time. When spalling occurs, it is usually widespread, and the structure may need resurfacing.

Crazing is widespread hairline cracks, usually caused by overfloating or too much portland cement in the concrete. Clean and seal the surface to help prevent further crazing. For a long-term solution, resurface.

Patching Holes

Large and small holes are treated differently when repairing concrete. The best product for filling in smaller holes (less than ½" deep) is vinyl-reinforced concrete patcher, which is often sold in convenient quart of gallon containers of dry powder. Reinforced repair products should be applied only in layers that are ½" thick or less.

For deeper holes, use sand-mix concrete with an acrylic or latex fortifier, which can be applied in layers up to 2" thick. This material is sold in 60- or 80-pound bags of dry mix.

Patches in concrete will be more effective if you create clean, backward-angled cuts (page 221) around the damaged area, to create a stronger bond. For extensive cutting of damaged concrete, it's best to score the concrete first with a circular saw equipped with a masonry blade. Use a chisel and maul to complete the job.

Tools & Materials ▸

Trowels
Drill with masonry-
    grinding disc
Circular saw
    with masonry-
    cutting blade
Cold chisel
Hand maul
Paint brush
Screed board
Float
Scrap lumber

Vegetable oil
    or commercial
    release agent
Hydraulic cement
Latex bonding agent
Vinyl-reinforced
    patching
    compound
Sand-mix
Concrete fortifier
Plastic sheeting

Use hydraulic cement or quick-setting cement for repairing holes and chip-outs in vertical surfaces. Because they set up in just a few minutes, these products can be shaped to fill holes without the need for forms. If the structure is exposed constantly to moisture, use hydraulic cement.

How to Patch Large Areas

Mark straight cutting lines around the damaged area, then cut with a circular saw equipped with a masonry-cutting blade. Set the foot of the saw so the cut bevels away from the damage at a 15° angle. Chisel out any remaining concrete within the repair area. *Tip: Set the foot of the saw on a thin board to protect it from the concrete.*

Tip ▶

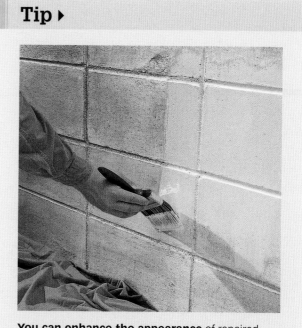

You can enhance the appearance of repaired vertical surfaces by painting with waterproof concrete paint once the surface has cured for at least a week. Concrete paint is formulated to resist chalking and efflorescence.

Mix sand-mix concrete with concrete acrylic fortifier, and fill the damaged area slightly above the surrounding surface.

Smooth and feather the repair with a float until the repair is even with the surrounding surface. Re-create any surface finish, like brooming, used on the original surface. Cover the repair with plastic and protect from traffic for at least one week.

How to Caulk Gaps around Masonry

Cracks between a concrete walk and foundation may result in seepage, leading to a wet basement. Repair cracks with caulk-type concrete patcher.

Caulk around the mud sill, the horizontal wooden plate where the house rests on the foundation. This area should be recaulked periodically to prevent heat loss.

How to Patch Small Holes

Cut out around the damaged area with a masonry-grinding disc mounted on a portable drill (or use a hammer and stone chisel). The cuts should bevel about 15° away from the center of the damaged area. Chisel out any loose concrete within the repair area. Always wear gloves and eye protection.

Apply a thin layer of latex bonding agent. The adhesive will bond with the damaged surface and create a strong bonding surface for the patching compound. Wait until the latex bonding agent is tacky (no more than 30 minutes) before proceeding to the next step.

Fill the damaged area with vinyl-reinforced patching compound, applied in ¼ to ½" layers. Wait about 30 minutes between applications. Add layers of the mixture until the compound is packed to just above surface level. Feather the edges smooth, cover the repair with plastic, and protect from traffic for at least one week.

How to Patch Concrete Floors

Clean the floor with a vacuum, and remove any loose or flaking concrete with a masonry chisel and hammer. Mix a batch of vinyl floor patching compound following manufacturer's directions. Apply the compound using a smooth trowel, slightly overfilling the cavity. Smooth the patch flush with the surface.

After the compound has cured fully, use a floor scraper to scrape the patched areas smooth.

How to Apply Floor Leveler

Remove any loose material and clean the concrete thoroughly; the surface must be free of dust, dirt, oils, and paint. Apply an even layer of concrete primer to the entire surface, using a long-nap paint roller. Let the primer dry completely.

Following the manufacturer's instructions, mix the floor leveler with water. The batch should be large enough to cover the entire floor area to the desired thickness (up to 1"). Pour the leveler over the floor.

Distribute the leveler evenly using a gage rake or spreader. Work quickly: the leveler begins to harden in 15 minutes. You can use a trowel to feather the edges and create a smooth transition with an uncovered area. Let the leveler dry for 24 hours.

Filling Cracks

The materials and methods you should use for repairing cracks in concrete depend on the location and size of the crack. For small cracks (less than ¼" wide), you can use gray-tinted concrete caulk for a quick fix. For more permanent solutions, use pourable crack filler or fortified patching cements. The patching cements are polymer compounds that significantly increase the bonding properties of cement, and also allow some flexibility. For larger cracks on horizontal surfaces, use fortified sand-mix concrete; for cracks on vertical surfaces, use hydraulic or quick-setting cement. Thorough preparation of the cracked surface is essential for creating a good bonding surface.

Tools & Materials ▶

Wire brush
Drill with wire wheel attachment
Stone chisel
Hand maul
Paint brush
Trowel
Latex bonding agent
Vinyl-reinforced patching compound
Concrete caulk
Sand-mix concrete
Plastic sheeting

Use concrete repair caulk for quick-fix repairs to minor cracks. Although convenient, repair caulk should be viewed only as a short-term solution to improve appearance and help prevent further damage from water penetration.

Tips for Preparing Cracked Concrete for Repair ▶

Clean loose material from the crack using a wire brush, or a portable drill with a wire wheel attachment. Loose material or debris left in the crack will result in a poor bond and an ineffective repair.

Chisel out the crack to create a backward-angled cut (wider at the base than at the surface), using a stone chisel and hammer. The angled cutout shape prevents the repair material from pushing out of the crack.

How to Repair Small Cracks

Prepare the crack for the repair (opposite page), then apply a thin layer of latex bonding agent to the entire repair area, using a paint brush. The latex bonding agent helps keep the repair material from loosening or popping out of the crack.

Mix vinyl-reinforced patching compound, and trowel it into the crack. Feather the repair with a trowel, so it is even with the surrounding surface. Cover the surface with plastic and protect it from traffic for at least a week.

Variations for Repairing Large Cracks ▸

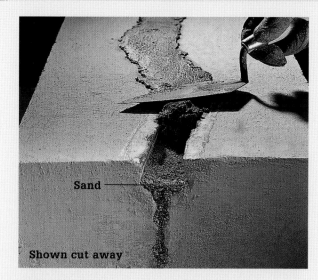

Horizontal surfaces: Prepare the crack (opposite page), then pour sand into the crack to within ½" of the surface. Prepare sand-mix concrete, adding a concrete fortifier, then trowel the mixture into the crack. Feather until even with the surface, using a trowel.

Vertical surfaces: Prepare the crack (opposite page). Mix vinyl-reinforced concrete or hydraulic cement, then trowel a ¼"- to ½"-thick layer into the crack until the crack is slightly overfilled. Feather the material even with the surrounding surface, then let it dry. If the crack is over ½" deep, trowel in consecutive layers. Let each layer dry before applying another.

How to Seal Cracks in Concrete Foundation Walls

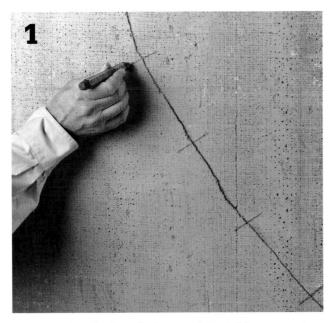

To determine if a foundation crack is stable, you need to monitor it over the course of several months, particularly over the fall and spring seasons. Draw marks across the crack at various points, noting the length as well as its width at the widest gaps. If the crack moves more than 1/16", consult a building engineer or foundation specialist.

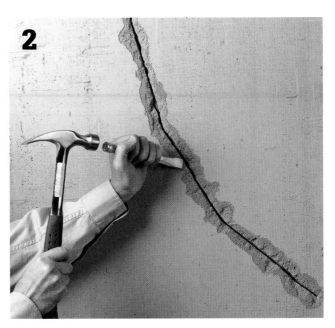

To repair a stable crack, use a chisel to cut a keyhole cut that's wider at the base then at the surface, and no more than 1/2" deep. Clean out the crack with a wire brush.

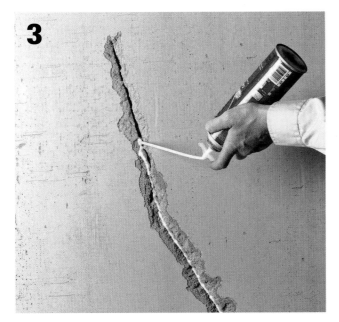

To help seal against moisture, fill the crack with expanding insulating foam, working from bottom to top.

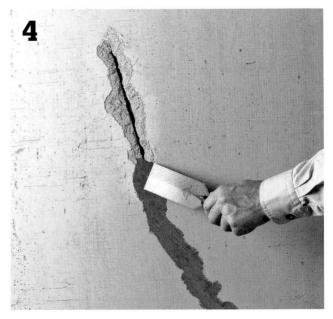

Mix hydraulic cement according to the manufacturer's instructions, then trowel it into the crack, working from the bottom to top. Apply cement in layers no more than 1/2" thick, until the patch is slightly higher than the surrounding area. Feather cement with the trowel until it's even with the surface and allow to dry thoroughly.

Repairing Steps

Steps require more maintenance and repair than other concrete structures around the house because heavy use makes them more susceptible to damage. Horizontal surfaces on steps can be treated using the same products and techniques used on other masonry surfaces. For vertical surfaces, use quick-setting cement, and shape it to fit.

Tools & Materials ▸

Trowel
Wire brush
Paint brush
Circular saw with masonry-cutting blade
Chisel
Float
Edger
Scrap lumber

Vegetable oil or commercial release agent
Latex bonding agent
Vinyl-reinforced patching compound
Quick-setting cement
Plastic sheeting

Isolated damage to step surfaces, like the deep popout being repaired above, can be fixed to renew your steps. If damage is extensive, you may need to replace the steps.

Damaged concrete steps are an unsightly and unsafe way to welcome visitors to your home. Repairing cracks as they develop not only keeps the steps in a safer and better looking condition, it prolongs their life.

How to Replace a Step Corner

Retrieve the broken corner, then clean it and the mating surface with a wire brush. Apply latex bonding agent to both surfaces. If you do not have the broken piece, you can rebuild the corner with patching compound (below).

Spread a heavy layer of fortified patching compound on the surfaces to be joined, then press the broken piece into position. Lean a heavy brick or block against the repair until the patching compound sets (about 30 minutes). Cover the repair with plastic and protect it from traffic for at least one week.

How to Patch a Step Corner

Clean chipped concrete with a wire brush. Brush the patch area with latex bonding agent.

Mix patching compound with latex bonding agent, as directed by the manufacturer. Apply the mixture to the patch area, then smooth the surfaces and round the edges, as necessary, using a flexible knife or trowel.

Tape scrap lumber pieces around the patch as a form. Coat the insides with vegetable oil or commercial release agent so the patch won't adhere to the wood. Remove the wood when the patch is firm. Cover with plastic and protect from traffic for at least one week.

How to Patch Step Treads

Make a cut in the stair tread just outside the damaged area, using a circular saw with a masonry-cutting blade. Make the cut so it angles toward the back of the step. Make a horizontal cut on the riser below the damaged area, then chisel out the area in between the two cuts.

Cut a form board the same height as the step riser. Coat one side of the board with vegetable oil or commercial release agent to prevent it from bonding with the repair, then press it against the riser of the damaged step, and brace it in position with heavy blocks. Make sure the top of the form is flush with the top of the step tread.

Apply latex bonding agent to the repair area with a clean paint brush, wait until the bonding agent is tacky (no more than 30 minutes), then press a stiff mixture of quick-setting cement into the damaged area with a trowel.

Smooth the concrete with a float, and let it set for a few minutes. Round over the front edge of the nose with an edger. Use a trowel to slice off the sides of the patch, so it is flush with the side of the steps. Cover the repair with plastic and wait a week before allowing traffic on the repaired section.

Miscellaneous Concrete Repairs

There are plenty of concrete problems you may encounter around your house that are not specifically addressed in many repair manuals. These miscellaneous repairs include such tasks as patching contoured objects that have been damaged and repairing masonry veneer around the foundation of your house. You can adapt basic techniques to make just about any type of concrete repair. Remember to dampen concrete surfaces before patching so that the moisture from concrete and other patching compounds is not absorbed into the existing surface. Be sure to follow the manufacturer's directions for the repair products you use.

Tools & Materials ▸

Putty knife	Soft-bristle brush
Trowel	Quick-setting cement
Hand maul	Emery paper
Chisel	Wire lath
Wire brush	Masonry anchors
Aviation snips	Concrete acrylic fortifier
Drill	Sand-mix

Concrete slabs that slant toward the house can lead to foundation damage and a wet basement. Even a level slab near the foundation can cause problems. Consider asking a concrete contractor to fix it by mud-jacking, forcing wet concrete underneath the slab to lift the edge near the foundation.

How to Repair Shaped Concrete

Scrape all loose material and debris from the damaged area, then wipe down with water. Mix quick-setting cement and trowel it into the area. Work quickly—you only have a few minutes before concrete sets up.

Use the trowel or a putty knife to mold the concrete to follow the form of the object being repaired. Smooth the concrete as soon as it sets up. Buff with emery paper to smooth out any ridges after the repair dries.

How to Repair Masonry Veneer

Chip off the crumbled, loose, or deteriorated veneer from the wall, using a cold chisel and maul. Chisel away damaged veneer until you have only good, solid surface remaining. Use care to avoid damaging the wall behind the veneer. Clean the repair area with a wire brush.

Old metal lath

New metal lath

Clean up any metal lath in the repair area if it is in good condition. If not, cut it out with aviation snips. Add new lath where needed, using masonry anchors to hold it to the wall.

Mix fortified sand-mix concrete (or specialty concrete blends for wall repair), and trowel it over the lath until it is even with the surrounding surfaces.

Recreate the surface texture to match the surrounding area. For our project, we used a soft-bristled brush to stipple the surface. To blend in the repair, add pigment to the sand mixture or paint the repair area after it dries.

Resurfacing a Concrete Walkway

Concrete that has surface damage but is still structurally sound can be preserved by resurfacing—applying a thin layer of new concrete over the old surface. If the old surface has deep cracks or extensive damage, resurfacing will only solve the problem temporarily. Because new concrete will bond better if it is packed down, use a dry, stiff concrete mixture that can be compacted with a shovel.

Tools & Materials ▸

Shovel	Rubber mallet
Wood float	Level
Broom	Mortar bag
Circular saw	Stakes
Maul	2 × 4 lumber
Drill	Vegetable oil
Paint brush	or commercial
Paint roller and tray	release agent
Wheelbarrow	4" wall-board screws
Screed board	Sand-mix concrete
Groover	Bonding adhesive
Edger	Plastic sheets
Hose	Brick pavers
Bricklayer's trowel	Type N mortar
Jointer	

New surface

Old surface

Shown cutaway

Resurface concrete that has surface damage, such as spalling or popouts. Because the new surface will be thin (1" to 2"), use sand-mix concrete. If you are having ready-mix concrete delivered by a concrete contractor, make sure they do not use aggregate larger than ½" in the mixture.

How to Resurface Using Fresh Concrete

Clean the surface thoroughly. If the surface is flaking or spalled, scrape it with a spade to dislodge as much loose concrete as you can, then sweep the surface clean.

Dig a 6"-wide trench around the surface on all sides to create room for 2 × 4 forms.

Stake 2 × 4 forms flush against the sides of the concrete slabs, 1" to 2" above the surface (make sure height is even). Drive stakes every 3 ft. and at every joint in forms. Mark control joint locations onto the outside of the forms directly above existing control joints. Coat the inside edges of the forms with vegetable oil or commercial release agent.

Apply a thin layer of bonding adhesive over the entire surface. Follow the directions on the bonding adhesive product carefully. Instructions for similar products may differ slightly.

Mix concrete, using sand-mix concrete. Make the mixture slightly stiffer (drier) than normal concrete. Spread the concrete, then press down on the concrete with a shovel or 2 × 4 to pack the mixture into the forms. Smooth the surface with a screed board.

Float the concrete with a wood float, then tool with an edger, and cut control joints in the original locations. Recreate any surface treatment, such as brooming, used on the original surface. Let the surface cure for one week, covered with plastic. Seal the concrete.

Rebuilding Concrete Steps

Designing steps requires some calculations and some trial and error. As long as the design meets safety guidelines, you can adjust elements such as the landing depth and the dimensions of the steps. Sketching your plan on paper will make the job easier.

Before demolishing your old steps, measure them to see if they meet safety guidelines. If so, you can use them as a reference for your new steps. If not, start from scratch so your new steps do not repeat any design errors.

For steps with more than two risers, you'll need to install a handrail. Ask a building inspector about other requirements.

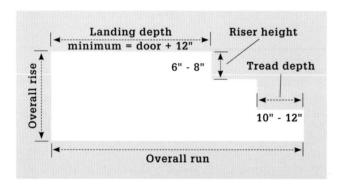

Tools & Materials ▸

Tape measure	2 × 4 lumber
Sledge hammer	Steel rebar grid
Shovel	Wire
Drill	Bolsters
Reciprocating saw	Construction
Level	adhesive
Mason's string	Compactible gravel
Hand tamper	Fill material
Mallet	Exterior-grade
Concrete	¾" plywood
mixing tools	2" deck screws
Jigsaw	Isolation board
Clamps	#3 rebar
Ruler or	Stakes
framing square	Latex caulk
Float	Vegetable oil
Step edger	or commercial
Broom	release agent

New concrete steps give a fresh, clean appearance to your house. And if your old steps are unstable, replacing them with concrete steps that have a non-skid surface will create a safer living environment.

How to Design Steps

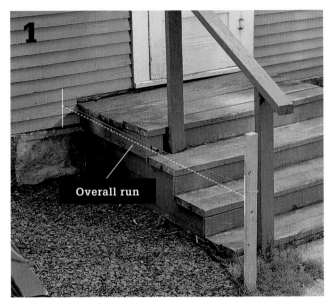

Overall run

Attach a mason's string to the house foundation, 1" below the bottom of the door threshold. Drive a stake where you want the base of the bottom step to fall. Attach the other end of the string to the stake and use a line level to level it. Measure the length of the string—this distance is the overall depth, or run, of the steps.

Overall rise

Measure down from the string to the bottom of the stake to determine the overall height, or rise, of the steps. Divide the overall rise by the estimated number of steps. The rise of each step should be between 6" and 8". For example, if the overall rise is 21" and you plan to build three steps, the rise of each step would be 7" (21 divided by 3), which falls within the recommended safety range for riser height.

Minimum landing depth   12"

Measure the width of your door and add at least 12"; this number is the minimum depth you should plan for the landing area of the steps. The landing depth plus the depth of each step should fit within the overall run of the steps. If necessary, you can increase the overall run by moving the stake at the planned base of the steps away from the house, or by increasing the depth of the landing.

Sketch a detailed plan for the steps, keeping these guidelines in mind: each step should be 10" to 12" deep, with a riser height between 6" and 8", and the landing should be at least 12" deeper than the swing radius (width) of your door. Adjust the parts of the steps as needed, but stay within the given ranges. Creating a final sketch will take time, but it is worth doing carefully.

How to Build Concrete Steps

Remove or demolish existing steps; if the old steps are concrete, set aside the rubble to use as fill material for the new steps. Wear protective gear, including eye protection and gloves, when demolishing concrete.

Dig 12"-wide trenches to the required depth for footings. Locate the trenches perpendicular to the foundation, spaced so the footings will extend 3" beyond the outside edges of the steps. Install steel rebar grids for reinforcement. Affix isolation boards to the foundation wall inside each trench, using a few dabs of construction adhesive.

Mix the concrete and pour the footings. Level and smooth the concrete with a screed board. You do not need to float the surface afterwards.

When bleed water disappears, insert 12" sections of rebar 6" into the concrete, spaced at 12" intervals and centered side to side. Leave 1 ft. of clear space at each end.

Let the footings cure for two days, then excavate the area between them to 4" deep. Pour in a 5"-thick layer of compactible gravel subbase and tamp until it is level with the footings.

Transfer the measurements for the side forms from your working sketch onto ¾" exterior-grade plywood. Cut out the forms along the cutting lines, using a jigsaw. Save time by clamping two pieces of plywood together and cutting both side forms at the same time. Add a ⅛" per foot back-to-front slope to the landing part of the form.

Make slopes ⅛" per foot

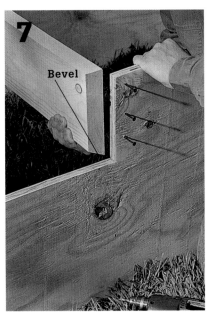

Bevel

Cut form boards for the risers to fit between the side forms. Bevel the bottom edges of the boards when cutting to create clearance for the float at the back edges of the steps. Attach the riser forms to the side forms with 2" deck screws.

Cleats

Riser support

Cut a 2 × 4 to make a center support for the riser forms. Use 2" deck screws to attach 2 × 4 cleats to the riser forms, then attach the support to the cleats. Check to make sure all corners are square.

Cut an isolation board and glue it to the house foundation at the back of the project area. Set the form onto the footings, flush against the isolation board. Add 2 × 4 bracing arms to the sides of the form, attaching them to cleats on the sides and to stakes driven into the ground.

(continued)

10

Fill the form with clean fill (broken concrete or rubble). Stack the fill carefully, keeping it 6" away from the sides, back, and top edges of the form. Shovel smaller fragments onto the pile to fill the void areas.

11

Lay pieces of #3 metal rebar on top of the fill at 12" intervals, and attach them to bolsters with wire to keep them from moving when the concrete is poured. Keep rebar at least 2" below the top of the forms. Mist the forms and the rubble with water.

12

Coat the forms with vegetable oil or a commercial release agent, then mist them with water so concrete won't stick to the forms. Mix concrete and pour steps one at a time, beginning at the bottom. Settle and smooth the concrete with a screed board. Press a piece of #3 rebar 1" down into the "nose" of each tread for reinforcement.

13

Float the steps, working the front edge of the float underneath the beveled edge at the bottom of each riser form.

14

Pour concrete into the forms for the remaining steps and the landing. Press rebar into the nose of each step. Keep an eye on the poured concrete as you work, and stop to float any concrete as soon as the bleed water disappears.

Shown cut away for clarity

Option: For railings with mounting plates that attach to sunken J-bolts, install the bolts before the concrete sets. Otherwise, choose railings with surface-mounted hardware (see step 16) that can be attached after the steps are completed.

15

Once the concrete sets, shape the steps and landing with a step edger. Float the surface. Sweep with a stiff-bristled broom for maximum traction.

16

Mounting plate

Remove the forms as soon as the surface is firm to the touch, usually within several hours. Smooth rough edges with a float. Add concrete to fill any holes. If forms are removed later, more patching may be required. Backfill the area around the base of the steps, and seal the concrete. Install a grippable hand railing that is securely anchored to the steps and the wall.

Resurfacing a Patio Slab

Patio tile is most frequently applied over a concrete subbase—either an existing concrete patio, or a new concrete slab. A third option, which we show you on the following pages, is to pour a new tile subbase over an existing concrete patio. This option involves far less work and expense than removing an old patio and pouring a new slab. And it ensures that your new tiled patio will not develop the same problems that may be present in the existing concrete surface.

See the following photographs to help you determine the best method for preparing your existing concrete patio slab. To resurface a concrete sidewalk, see pages 232 to 233.

Tools & Materials ▸

Basic hand tools	Concrete edger
Shovel	Utility knife
Maul	Margin trowel
Straightedge	30# building paper
Aviation snips	Plastic sheeting
Masonry hoe	2 × 4 and 2 × 2 lumber
Mortar box	2½" and 3" deck screws
Hand tamper	⅜" stucco lath
Magnesium float	Roofing cement

New subbase

Old patio

How to Install a Subbase for Patio Tile

1

Form braces

2 × 4 form boards

Dig a trench at least 6" wide, and no more than 4" deep, around the patio to create room for 2 × 4 forms. Clean dirt and debris from the exposed sides of the patio. Cut and fit 2 × 4 frames around the patio, joining the ends with 3" deck screws. Cut wood stakes from 2 × 4s and drive them next to the forms, at 2-ft. intervals.

2

2 × 2 spacer

Stucco lath

Adjust the form height: set stucco lath on the surface, then set a 2 × 2 spacer on top of the lath (their combined thickness equals the thickness of the subbase). Adjust the form boards so the tops are level with the 2 × 2, and screw the stakes to the forms with 2½" deck screws.

3

Building paper "bond-breaker"

Remove the 2 × 2 spacers and stucco lath, then lay strips of 30# building paper over the patio surface, overlapping seams by 6", to create a bond-breaker for the new surface. Crease the building paper at the edges and corners, making sure the paper extends past the tops of the forms. Make a small cut in the paper at each corner for easier folding.

4

Lay strips of stucco lath over the building-paper bond-breaker, overlapping seams by 1". Keep the lath 1" away from forms and the wall. Use aviation snips to cut the stucco lath (wear heavy gloves when handling metal).

5

Screed board

Build temporary 2 × 2 forms to divide the project into working sections and provide rests for the screed board used to level and smooth the fresh concrete. Make the sections narrow enough that you can reach across the entire section (3-ft. to 4-ft. sections are comfortable for most people). Screw the ends of the 2 × 2s to the form boards so the tops are level.

6

Mix dry floor-mix concrete with water in a mortar box, blending with a masonry hoe, according to the manufacturer's directions, or use a power mixer.

(continued)

7

Note: The mixture should be very dry when prepared so it can be pressed down into the voids in the stucco lath with a tamper.

Fill one working section with floor-mix concrete, up to the tops of the forms. Tamp the concrete thoroughly with a lightweight tamper to help force it into the voids in the lath and into corners. The lightweight tamper shown above is made from a 12" × 12" piece of ¾" plywood, with a 2 × 4 handle attached.

8

9

Level off the surface of the concrete by dragging a straight 2 × 4 screed board across the top, with the ends riding on the forms. Move the 2 × 4 in a sawing motion as you progress, creating a level surface and filling any voids in the concrete. If voids or hollows remain, add more concrete and smooth it off.

Use a magnesium float to smooth the surface of the concrete. Applying very light pressure, move the float back and forth in an arching motion, tipping the lead edge up slightly to avoid gouging the surface.

Pour and smooth out the next working section, repeating steps 7 to 9. After floating this section, remove the 2 × 2 temporary form between the two sections. Fill the void left behind with fresh concrete. Float the fresh concrete with the magnesium float until the concrete is smooth and level and blends into the working section on each side. Pour and finish the remaining working sections one at a time, using the same techniques.

Let the concrete dry until pressing the surface with your finger does not leave a mark. Cut contours around all edges of the subbase with a concrete edger. Tip the lead edge of the edger up slightly to avoid gouging the surface. Smooth out any marks left by the edger using a float.

Cover the concrete with sheets of plastic, and cure for at least three days (see manufacturer's directions for recommended curing time). Weight down the edges of the sheeting. After curing is compete, remove the plastic and disassemble and remove the forms.

Trim off the building paper around the sides of the patio using a utility knife. Apply roofing cement to the exposed sides of the patio, using a trowel or putty knife to fill and seal the seam between the old and new surfaces. After the roofing cement dries, shovel dirt or ground cover back into the trench around the patio.

Sealing Concrete Floors

Most people are accustomed to thinking of concrete primarily as a utilitarian substance, but it can also mimic a variety of flooring types and be a colorful and beautiful addition to any room. Whether your concrete floor is a practical surface for the garage or an artistic statement of personal style in your dining room, it should be sealed.

Concrete is a hard and durable building material, but it is also porous—so it is susceptible to staining. Many stains can be removed with the proper cleaner, but sealing and painting prevents oil, grease, and other stains from penetrating the surface in the first place; and cleanup is a whole lot easier.

Even after degreasing a concrete floor, residual grease or oils can create serious adhesion problems for coatings of sealant or paint. To check to see whether your floor has been adequately cleaned, pour a glass of water on the concrete floor. If it is ready for sealing, the water will soak into the surface quickly and evenly. If the water beads, you may have to clean it again. Detergent used in combination with a steam cleaner can remove stubborn stains better than a cleaner alone.

There are four important reasons to seal your concrete floor: to protect the floor from dirt, oil, grease, chemicals, and stains; to dust-proof the surface; to protect the floor from abrasion and sunlight exposure; and to repel water and protect the floor from freeze-thaw damage.

Tools & Materials ▸

Acid-tolerant pump sprayer
Alkaline-base neutralizer
Sealant
Rubber Boots
Garden hose with nozzle
Acid-tolerant bucket
Eye protection
Paint roller frame

Soft-woven roller cover
Paint
Roller tray
Wet vacuum
High-pressure washer
Paintbrush
Respirator
Stiff bristle broom
Extension handle
Rubber gloves

How to Seal Concrete Floors

Clean and prepare the surface by first sweeping up all debris. Next, remove all surface muck: mud, wax, and grease. Finally, remove existing paints or coatings. See the chapter on cleaning concrete for tips on what to use to remove a variety of common stains.

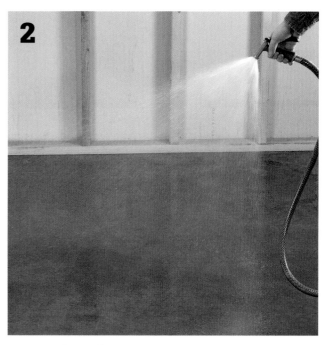

Saturate the surface with clean water. The surface needs to be wet before acid etching. Use this opportunity to check for any areas where water beads up. If water beads on the surface, contaminants still need to be cleaned off with a suitable cleaner or chemical stripper.

Test your acid-tolerant pump sprayer with water to make sure it releases a wide, even mist. Once you have the spray nozzle set, check the manufacturer's instructions for the etching solution and fill the pump sprayer with the recommended amount of water.

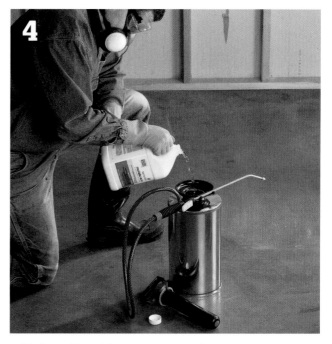

Add the acid etching contents to the water in the acid-tolerant pump sprayer (or sprinkling can). Follow the directions (and mixing proportions) specified by the manufacturer. Use caution.

(continued)

Apply the acid solution. Using the sprinkling can or acid-tolerant pump spray unit, evenly apply the diluted acid solution over the concrete floor. Do not allow acid solution to dry at any time during the etching and cleaning process. Etch small areas at a time, 10 × 10 ft. or smaller. If there is a slope, begin on the low side of the slope and work upward.

Use a stiff bristle broom or scrubber to work the acid solution into the concrete. Let the acid sit for 5 to 10 minutes, or as indicated by the manufacturer's directions. A mild foaming action indicates that the product is working. If no bubbling or fizzing occurs, it means there is still grease, oil, or a concrete treatment on the surface that is interfering. If this occurs, follow steps 7 to 12 and then clean again.

Once the fizzing has stopped, the acid has finished reacting with the alkaline concrete surface and formed pH-neutral salts. Neutralize any remaining acid with an alkaline-base solution. Put a gallon of water in a 5-gallon bucket and then stir in an alkaline-base neutralizer. Using a stiff bristle broom, make sure the concrete surface is completely covered with the solution. Continue to sweep until the fizzing stops.

Use a garden hose with a pressure nozzle or, ideally, a pressure washer in conjunction with a stiff bristle broom to thoroughly rinse the concrete surface. Rinse the surface 2 to 3 times. Re-apply the acid (repeat Steps 5, 6, 7, and 8).

If you have any leftover acid you can make it safe for your septic system by mixing more alkaline solution in the 5-gallon bucket and carefully pouring the acid from the spray unit into the bucket until all of the fizzing stops.

Use a wet vacuum to clean up the mess. Some sitting acids and cleaning solutions can harm local vegetation, damage your drainage system, and are just plain environmentally unfriendly. Check your local disposal regulations for proper disposal of the neutralized spent acid.

To check for residue, rub a dark cloth over a small area of concrete. If any white residue appears, continue the rinsing process. Check for residue again.

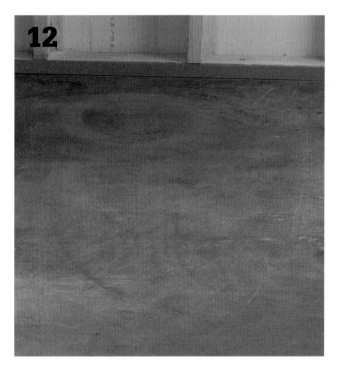

Let the concrete dry for at least 24 hours and sweep up dust, dirt, and particles leftover from the acid etching process. Your concrete should now have the consistency of 120-grit sandpaper and be able to accept concrete sealants.

(continued)

13

Once etched, clean, and dry, your concrete is ready for clear sealer or liquid repellent. Mix the sealer in a bucket with a stir stick. Lay painter's tape down for a testing patch. Apply sealer to this area and allow to dry to ensure desired appearance. Concrete sealers tend to make the surface slick when wet. Add an anti-skid additive to aid with traction, especially on stairs.

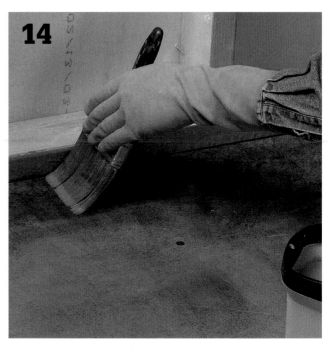

14

Use wide painter's tape to protect walls and then, using a good quality 4"-wide synthetic bristle paintbrush, coat the perimeter with sealer.

15

Use a long-handled paint roller with at least ½" nap to apply an even coat to the rest of the surface. Do small sections at a time (about 2' × 3'). Work in one orientation (e.g., north to south). Avoid lap marks by always maintaining a wet edge. Do not work the area once the coating has partially dried; this could cause it to lift from the surface.

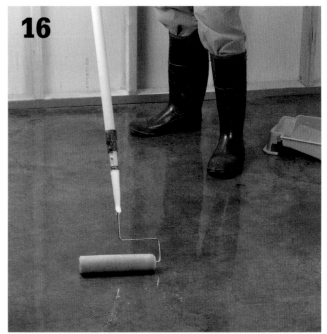

16

Allow surface to dry according to the manufacturer's instructions, usually 8 to 12 hours minimum. Then apply a second coat in the opposite direction to the first coat, so if the first coat was north to south, the second coat should be east to west.

Painting Concrete Floors

This book includes two ways of building new floors on top of concrete. But sometimes it just isn't practical to add a new layer. Maybe your basement ceiling is already low, and you need to preserve as much headroom as possible. Or maybe you don't use the space often enough to justify a full makeover.

To give concrete flooring a facelift, nothing is simpler than paint. You can protect the surface from dirt and stains with a clear sealer, give it a translucent color wash, or cover it with an opaque floor paint. Just make sure the surface is clean, dry, level, smooth, and free of any grease or wax.

Before you choose a surface treatment for your concrete floor, do some browsing. Try your local library, the Web, and building supply and paint stores.

Once you find the look you're after, the directions here will help you create it.

Basements seldom have adequate ventilation for working with paint. Set up fans to keep the air moving. If your concrete floor is on a porch or garage, just leave the doors open.

Tools & Materials ▸

Bleach solution	Nylon-bristle brush
Cleaning supplies	Paint roller and tray
Electric fan(s)	Patching compound
Eye protection	Roller extension handle
Nylon paint brush	Rubber gloves

How to Paint Concrete Floors

Concrete floors can hold paint made for them, but first the concrete must be clean and dry. Sweep, vacuum, and mop the floor thoroughly. To remove any stains, scrub the floor with solution of 1 part bleach to 3 parts water. Wear eye protection and rubber gloves.

Rinse the surface well with clean water and let it dry.

Following the manufacturer's directions, use a concrete patching compound to repair any cracks. Make sure the floor surface does not flake or crumble anywhere.

Test the absorption of the concrete by sprinkling some water on the floor. If the water is absorbed quickly, paint will probably bond well. If it beads up, you should probably use the acid etching method shown on pages 245 to 247. After etching, let the floor dry at least overnight.

If you expect to use more than one container of paint, open them all and mix them together for a uniform color. You do not need to thin a paint for use on a floor. One exception is if you use a sprayer that requires thinned paint.

Using a nylon brush, such as a 2½-inch sash brush, cut in the sides and corners with primer. This creates a sharp, clean edge. Start this way for the top coat as well.

Using a roller pad with the nap length recommended by the manufacturer, apply a primer coat to the surface. Start at the corner farthest away from the door, and back up as you work. Allow the primer to dry for at least 8 hours.

With a clean roller pad, apply the first top coat. Make the top coat even but not too thick, then let it dry for 24 hours. If you choose to add another top coat, work the roller in another direction to cover any thin spots. Let the final coat dry another day before you walk on it.

Identifying Brick & Block Problems

Inspect damaged brick and block structures closely before you begin any repair work. Accurately identifying the nature and cause of the damage is an important step before choosing the best solution for the problem and preventing the problems from recurring in the future.

Look for obvious clues, like overgrown tree roots, or damaged gutters that let water drain onto masonry surfaces. Also check the slope of the adjacent landscape; it may need to be regraded to direct water away from a brick or block wall. Water is the most common cause of problems, but major cracks that recur can be a sign of serious structural problems that should be examined by an engineer.

Repairs fail when the original source of the problem is not eliminated prior to making the repair. When a concrete patch separates, for example, it means that the opposing stresses causing the crack are still at work on the structure. Find and correct the cause (often a failing subbase or stress from water or freezing and thawing), then redo the repair.

Types of Brick & Block Problems

Deteriorated mortar joints are common problems in brick and block structures—mortar is softer than most bricks or blocks and is more prone to damage. Deterioration is not always visible, so probe surrounding joints with a screwdriver to see if they are sound.

Major structural damage, like the damage to this brick porch, usually requires removal of the existing structure, improvements to the subbase, and reconstruction of the structure. Projects of this nature should only be attempted by professional masons.

Damage to concrete blocks often results from repeated freezing and thawing of moisture trapped in the wall or in the blocks themselves. Instead of replacing the whole block, chip out the face of the block and replacing it with a concrete paver with the same dimensions as the face of the block (pages 258 to 259).

Spalling occurs when freezing water or other forces cause enough directional pressure to fracture a brick. The best solution is to replace the entire brick (pages 256 to 257) while eliminating the source of the pressure, if possible. *Tip: Chip off a piece of the damaged brick to use as a color reference when looking for a replacement.*

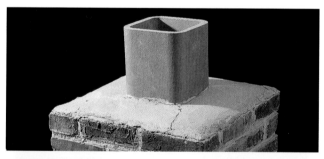

Damaged mortar caps on chimneys allow water into the flue area, where it can damage the chimney and even the roof or interior walls. Small-scale damage (top photo) can be patched with fire-rated silicone caulk. If damage is extensive (bottom photo), repair or replace the mortar cap.

Stains and discoloration can be caused by external sources or by minerals leeching to the surface from within the brick or block (called efflorescence). If the stain does not wash away easily with water, use a cleaning solution.

Repairing Brick & Block Walls

The most common brick and block wall repair is tuck-pointing, the process of replacing failed mortar joints with fresh mortar. Tuck-pointing is a highly useful repair technique for any homeowner. It can be used to repair walls, chimneys, brick veneer, or any other structure where the bricks or blocks are bonded with mortar.

Minor cosmetic repairs can be attempted on any type of wall, from free-standing garden walls to block foundations. Filling minor cracks with caulk or repair compound, and patching popouts or chips are good examples of minor repairs. Consult a professional before attempting any major repairs, like replacing brick or blocks, or rebuilding a structure—especially if you are dealing with a load-bearing structure.

Basement walls are a frequent trouble area for homeowners. Constant moisture and stress created by ground contact can cause leaks, bowing, and paint failure. Small leaks and cracks can be patched with hydraulic cement. Masonry-based waterproofing products can be applied to give deteriorated walls a fresh appearance. Persistent moisture problems are most often caused by improper grading of soil around the foundation or a malfunctioning downspout and gutter system.

Note: The repairs shown in this section feature brick and block walls. The same techniques may be used for other brick and block structures.

Tools & Materials ▸

Raking tool	Drill with masonry
Mortar hawk	disc and bit
Tuck-pointer	Stiff-bristle brush
Jointing tool	Mortar
Bricklayer's hammer	Gravel
Mason's trowel	Scrap of metal flashing
Mason's or	Concrete fortifier
stone chisel	Replacement bricks
Pointing trowel	or blocks

Make timely repairs to brick and block structures. Tuck-pointing deteriorated mortar joints is a common repair that, like other types of repair, improves the appearance of the structure or surface and helps prevent further damage.

How to Tuck-point Mortar Joints

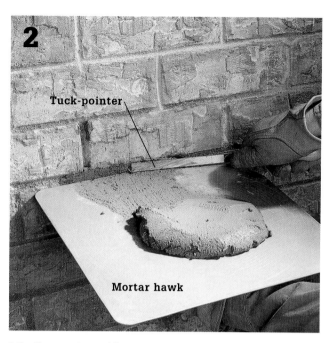

Clean out loose or deteriorated mortar to a depth of ¼" to ¾". Use a mortar raking tool (top) first, then switch to a masonry chisel and a hammer (bottom) if the mortar is stubborn. Clear away all loose debris, and dampen the surface with water before applying fresh mortar.

Mix the mortar, adding concrete fortifier; add tint if necessary. Load mortar onto a mortar hawk, then push it into the horizontal joints with a tuck-pointer. Apply mortar in ¼"-thick layers, and let each layer dry for 30 minutes before applying another. Fill the joints until the mortar is flush with the face of the brick or block.

Apply the first layer of mortar into the vertical joints by scooping mortar onto the back of a tuck-pointer, and pressing it into the joint. Work from the top downward.

After the final layer of mortar is applied, smooth the joints with a jointing tool that matches the profile of the old mortar joints. Tool the horizontal joints first. Let the mortar dry until it is crumbly, then brush off the excess mortar with a stiff-bristle brush.

How to Replace a Damaged Brick

Score the damaged brick so it will break apart more easily for removal: use a drill with a masonry-cutting disc to score lines along the surface of the brick and in the mortar joints surrounding the brick.

Use a mason's chisel and hammer to break apart the damaged brick along the scored lines. Rap sharply on the chisel with the hammer, being careful not to damage surrounding bricks. *Tip: Save fragments to use as a color reference when you shop for replacement bricks.*

Chisel out any remaining mortar in the cavity, then brush out debris with a stiff-bristle or wire brush to create a clean surface for the new mortar. Rinse the surface of the repair area with water.

Mix the mortar for the repair, adding concrete fortifier to the mixture, and tint if needed to match old mortar. Use a pointing trowel to apply a 1"-thick layer of mortar at the bottom and sides of the cavity.

5

Dampen the replacement brick slightly, then apply mortar to the ends and top of the brick. Fit the brick into the cavity and rap it with the handle of the trowel until the face is flush with the surrounding bricks. If needed, press additional mortar into the joints with a pointing trowel.

6

Scrape away excess mortar with a masonry trowel, then smooth the joints with a jointing tool that matches the profile of the surrounding mortar joints. Let the mortar set until crumbly, then brush the joints to remove excess mortar.

Tips for Removing & Replacing Several Bricks ▸

For walls with extensive damage, remove bricks from the top down, one row at a time, until the entire damaged area is removed. Replace bricks using the techniques shown above and in the section on building with brick and block. Caution: Do not dismantle load-bearing brick structures like foundation walls—consult a professional mason for these repairs.

For walls with internal damaged areas, remove only the damaged section, keeping the upper layers intact if they are in good condition. Do not remove more than four adjacent bricks in one area—if the damaged area is larger, it will require temporary support, which is a job for a professional mason.

How to Reface a Damaged Concrete Block

Cores (hollow)

Drill several holes into the face of the deteriorated block at the cores (hollow spots) of the block using a drill and masonry bit. Wear protective eye covering when drilling or breaking apart concrete.

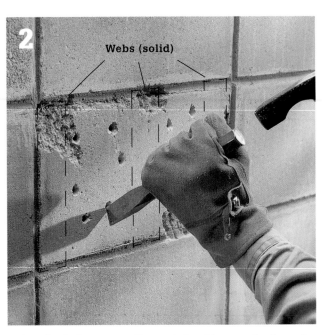

Webs (solid)

Using the holes as starting points, chip away the face of the block over the core areas, using a chisel and hammer. Be careful not to damage surrounding blocks and try to leave the block face intact in front of the solid web areas.

2"

Use a stone chisel to carefully chip out a 2"-deep recess in the web areas. Mark and score cutting lines 2" back from the block face, then chisel away the block in the recess area. Avoid deepening the recess more than 2" because the remaining web sections provide a bonding surface for the concrete paver that will be installed to replace the face of the concrete block.

Mix mortar, then apply a 1"-thick layer to the sides and bottom of the opening, to the webs, and to the top edge and web locations on the paver (use an 8 × 16" paver to fit standard blocks). Press the paver into the cavity, flush with the surrounding blocks. Add mortar to the joints if needed, then prop a 2 × 4 against the paver until the mortar sets. Finish the joints with a jointing tool.

How to Reinforce a Section of Refaced Blocks

Reinforce repair areas spanning two or more adjacent block faces. Start by drilling a few holes in a small area over a core in the block located directly above the repair area. Chip out the block face between the holes with a cold chisel.

Prepare a thin mortar mix made from 1 part gravel and 2 parts dry mortar, then add water. The mixture should be thin enough to pour easily, but not soupy. *Note: Adding small amounts of gravel increases the strength of the mortar and increases the yield of the batch.*

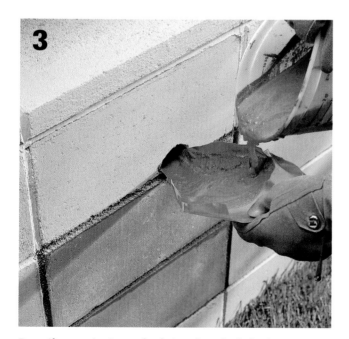

Pour the mortar/gravel mixture into the hole above the repair area, using a piece of metal flashing as a funnel. Continue mixing and filling the hole until it will not accept any more mortar. The mortar will dry to form a reinforcing column that is bonded to the backs of the pavers used to reface the blocks.

Patch the hole above the repair area by using a pointing trowel to fill the hole with plain mortar mix. Smooth the surface with the pointing trowel. When the mortar resists finger pressure, finish the joint below the patch with a jointing tool.

Cleaning & Painting Brick & Block

Check brick and block surfaces annually and remove stains or discoloration. Most problems are easy to correct if they are treated in a timely fashion. Regular maintenance will help brick and block structures remain attractive and durable for a long time. Refer to the information below for cleaning tips that address specific staining problems.

Painted brick and block structures can be spruced up by applying a fresh coat of paint. As with any other painting job, thorough surface preparation and a quality primer are critical to a successful outcome.

Many stains can be removed easily, using a commercial brick and block detergent, available at home centers, but remember:

- Always test cleaning solutions on a small inconspicuous part of the surface and evaluate the results.
- Some chemicals and their fumes may be harmful. Be sure to follow manufacturer's safety and use recommendations. Wear protective clothing.
- Soak the surface to be cleaned with water before you apply any solutions. This keeps solutions from soaking in too quickly. Rinse the surface thoroughly after cleaning to wash off any remaining cleaning solution.

Use a pressure washer to clean large brick and block structures. Pressure washers can be rented from most rental centers. Be sure to obtain detailed operating and safety instructions from the rental agent.

Solvent Solutions for Common Brick & Block Blemishes ▶

- Egg splatter: Dissolve oxalic acid crystals in water, following manufacturer's instructions, in a nonmetallic container. Brush onto the surface.
- Efflorescence: Scrub surface with a stiff-bristled brush. Use a household cleaning solution for surfaces with heavy accumulation.
- Iron stains: Spray or brush a solution of oxalic acid crystals dissolved in water, following manufacturer's instructions. Apply directly to the stain.
- Ivy: Cut vines away from the surface (do not pull them off). Let remaining stems dry up, then scrub them off with a stiff-bristled brush and household cleaning solution.
- Oil: Apply a paste made of mineral spirits and an inert material like sawdust.
- Paint stains: Remove new paint with a solution of trisodium phosphate (TSP) and water, following manufacturer's mixing instructions. Old paint can usually be removed with heavy scrubbing or sandblasting.
- Plant growth: Use weed killer according to manufacturer's directions.
- Smoke stains: Scrub surface with household cleanser containing bleach, or use a mixture of ammonia and water.

Tips for Cleaning Brick & Block Surfaces ▸

Mix a paste made from cleaning solvents (chart, opposite page) and talcum or flour. Apply paste directly to stain, let it dry, then scrape it off with a vinyl or plastic scraper.

Use a nylon scraper or a thin block of wood to remove spilled mortar that has hardened. Avoid using metal scrapers, which can damage masonry surfaces.

Mask off windows, siding, decorative millwork, and other exposed nonmasonry surfaces before cleaning brick and block. Careful masking is essential if you are using harsh cleaning chemicals, such as muriatic acid.

Tips for Painting Masonry ▸

Clean mortar joints, using a drill with a wire wheel attachment before applying paint. Scrub off loose paint, dirt, mildew, and mineral deposits so the paint will bond better.

Apply masonry primer before repainting brick or block walls. Primer helps eliminate stains and prevent problems such as efflorescence.

Repairing a Firebox

Masonry fireplaces are built according to strict specifications designed to maximize heating efficiency, smoke exhaustion, and above all, safety. The internal chamber where the fire burns, known as the firebox, is made with heat-resistant firebrick and a special mortar that can withstand extremely high temperatures. For added heat resistance, mortar joints in firebrick construction are smaller than with other types of brick, usually 1/16" to 1/4" thick.

The firebox reflects the fire's heat into the room, and it insulates the surrounding structure from the high temperatures that can cause damage. Therefore, in addition to having your fireplace and chimney inspected and cleaned regularly, it's a good idea to check the firebox for crumbling mortar joints and loose, cracked, or chipped bricks.

Signs of severe damage or wear in the firebox may indicate serious problems elsewhere in the fireplace or chimney and should be reported to a professional. But you can fix most minor problems yourself, provided you use only materials rated for fireplaces. Some refractory mortars are sold premixed so it is not necessary to add water. Whichever product you select, make sure it is rated for use with fire brick.

Tools & Materials ▸

Shop light	Masonry or stone chisel
Mirror	Mason's trowel
Flashlight	Jointing tool
Stiff-bristle brush	Fireplace cleaner
Sponge	Firebrick
Screwdriver	Refractory mortar

A masonry fireplace is a treasured feature in many homes. Most fireplaces are constructed with several different materials, including two or more types of brick and mortar, concrete, concrete block, metal, and fireclay. Routine maintenance is essential to the efficiency and longevity of your fireplace, as well as to the safety of your home.

How to Inspect & Repair a Firebox

Begin your inspection by cleaning the fireplace thoroughly. If the bricks and mortar joints are not clearly visible, use a fireplace cleaner and a stiff-bristle brush to remove the soot and creosote buildup. Use a shop light and mirror to view the upper areas of the firebox and the damper opening.

Using a flashlight, inspect the bricks and mortar in the firebox. Check for loose mortar by lightly scraping the joints with a screwdriver. Look for cracks and feel around for any loose bricks.

Remove any loose or damaged bricks, and scrape off the old mortar, using a masonry or stone chisel. Clean the edges of the surrounding brick with a stiff-bristle brush. If you need replacement bricks, bring an original one to a fireplace or brick supplier to be sure you get a perfect match.

Apply refractory mortar to the new bricks, following the mortar manufacturer's directions. Gently slide the bricks into place until they are flush with the surrounding bricks. Scrape off excess mortar with a trowel. Use a jointing tool to tool the mortar joints.

Repairing Stonework

Damage to stonework is typically caused by frost heave, erosion or deterioration of mortar, or by stones that have worked out of place. Dry-stone walls are more susceptible to erosion and popping, while mortared walls develop cracks that admit water, which can freeze and cause further damage.

Inspect stone structures once a year for signs of damage and deterioration. Replacing a stone or repointing crumbling mortar now will save you work in the long run.

A leaning stone column or wall probably suffers from erosion or foundation problems, and can be dangerous if neglected. If you have the time, you can tear down and rebuild dry-laid structures, but mortared structures with excessive lean need professional help.

Tools & Materials ▸

Maul	Mortar bag
Chisel	Masonry chisels
Camera	Wood shims
Shovel	Carpet-covered 2 × 4
Hand tamper	Chalk
Level	Compactible gravel
Batter gauge	Replacement stones
Stiff-bristle brush	Type M mortar
Trowels for mixing	Mortar tint
and pointing	

Stones in a wall can become dislodged due to soil settling, erosion, or seasonal freeze-thaw cycles. Make the necessary repairs before the problem migrates to other areas.

Tips for Replacing Popped Stones ▸

Return a popped stone to its original position. If other stones have settled in its place, drive shims between neighboring stones to make room for the popped stone. Be careful not to wedge too far.

Use a 2 × 4 covered with carpet to avoid damaging the stone when hammering it into place. After hammering, make sure a replacement stone hasn't damaged or dislodged the adjoining stones.

How to Rebuild a Dry-stone Wall Section

Before you start, study the wall and determine how much of it needs to be rebuilt. Plan to dismantle the wall in a "V" shape, centered on the damaged section. Number each stone and mark its orientation with chalk so you can rebuild it following the original design. *Tip: Photograph the wall, making sure the markings are visible.*

Capstones are often set in a mortar bed atop the last course of stone. You may need to chip out the mortar with a maul and chisel to remove the capstones. Remove the marked stones, taking care to check the overall stability of the wall as you work.

Rebuild the wall, one course at a time, using replacement stones only when necessary. Start each course at the ends and work toward the center. On thick walls, set the face stones first, then fill in the center with smaller stones. Check your work with a level, and use a batter gauge to maintain the batter of the wall. If your capstones were mortared, re-lay them in fresh mortar. Wash off the chalk with water and a stiff-bristle brush.

Tip ▶

If you're rebuilding because of erosion, dig a trench at least 6" deep under the damaged area, and fill it with compactible gravel. Tamp the gravel with a hand tamper. This will improve drainage and prevent water from washing soil out from beneath the wall.

Tips for Repairing Mortared Stone Walls ▸

Tint mortar for repair work so it blends with the existing mortar. Mix several samples of mortar, adding a different amount of tint to each, and allow them to dry thoroughly. Compare each sample to the old mortar, and choose the closest match.

Use a mortar bag to restore weathered and damaged mortar joints over an entire structure. Remove loose mortar (see below) and clean all surfaces with a stiff-bristle brush and water. Dampen the joints before tuck-pointing, and cover all of the joints, smoothing and brushing as necessary.

How to Repoint Mortar Joints

Carefully rake out cracked and crumbling mortar, stopping when you reach solid mortar. Remove loose mortar and debris with a stiff-bristle brush. *Tip: Rake the joints with a chisel and maul, or make your own raking tool by placing an old screwdriver in a vice and bending the shaft about 45°.*

Mix type M mortar, then dampen the repair surfaces with clean water. Working from the top down, pack mortar into the crevices, using a pointing trowel. Smooth the mortar when it has set up enough to resist light finger pressure. Remove excess mortar with a stiff-bristle brush.

How to Replace a Stone in a Mortared Wall

Remove the damaged stone by chiseling out the surrounding mortar, using a masonry chisel or a modified screwdriver (opposite page). Drive the chisel toward the damaged stone to avoid harming neighboring stones. Once the stone is out, chisel the surfaces inside the cavity as smooth as possible.

Brush out the cavity to remove loose mortar and debris. Test the surrounding mortar, and chisel or scrape out any mortar that isn't firmly bonded.

Dry-fit the replacement stone. The stone should be stable in the cavity and blend with the rest of the wall. You can mark the stone with chalk and cut it to fit, but excessive cutting will result in a conspicuous repair.

Mist the stone and cavity lightly, then apply type M mortar around the inside of the cavity, using a trowel. Butter all mating sides of the replacement stone. Insert the stone and wiggle it forcefully to remove any air pockets. Use a pointing trowel to pack the mortar solidly around the stone. Smooth the mortar when it has set up.

Replacing Flagstone

General maintenance on stone floors can be a little trickier than with other patio surfaces. Because stone is a natural material, and often porous, it can be difficult to clean and can also react adversely to many common cleaning agents.

Replacing a damaged stone presents the challenges of finding a new piece that matches the look of the patio, as well as cutting the replacement to fit. Extra care taken when working with stone is always well rewarded by the uncommon beauty of the material.

When it comes to cleaning stone, start with the gentlest treatment—water and a natural or synthetic fiber brush (never metal). If that won't do the job, consult your stone supplier for cleaning recommendations. All stone is different, and the people who work with your particular varieties should know it best. Be warned that some cleaners can stain some stones. Never use acid-based solutions on any stone. After your patio has been thoroughly cleaned, consider sealing the surface to protect against stains and water intrusion, using a sealer recommended by your supplier.

Replacing a damaged flagstone in a sandset patio is an easy project that just takes some patience. If you're replacing a large stone that has split in two, you may be able to reuse it by shaping the edges of the broken pieces to look like individual stones. To keep a mortared stone floor in top condition, replace any loose, cracked, or deteriorated mortar joints. To replace a damaged mortared stone, complete all of the steps shown here.

Tools & Materials ▸

Cold chisels
Stone chisel
Hammer
Shop vacuum
Replacement stone

Supplies for
  mixing mortar
Mason's trowel
Straightedge or level
Grout bag

Replace a sandset flagstone by lifting out the damaged stone, leveling and tamping the sand bed, and setting in a new stone and repacking the sand joints. Trim and dress the new stone as needed.

How to Replace a Mortared Flagstone

STEP 1: REMOVE THE MORTAR

1. Using a cold chisel or stone chisel and hammer, carefully chip out the mortar surrounding the damaged stone. Point the chisel away from neighboring stones to prevent damaging them.

Note: If you're simply removing damaged mortar, direct the chisel into the mortar only. Stop chiseling once all loose mortar is removed.

Chisel out the mortar around the damaged stone, being careful not to strike surrounding stones.

STEP 2: REMOVE THE DAMAGED STONE

1. Working carefully to avoid cracking neighboring stones or mortar, break up the damaged stone with a hammer and chisel. Direct the chisel into the damaged stone and away from healthy areas. Strike sharply, but avoid heavy blows that shake the general patio surface.
2. Once the stone is removed, chisel out the remaining mortar bed, using the same care to prevent further damage.

Break up and remove the damaged stone in pieces, then clean out the old mortar bed.

STEP 3: FIT THE NEW STONE

1. Position the replacement stone over the cavity, and mark any cuts needed to fit it. When the new stone is installed, the size of the mortar joints should roughly match the surrounding joints for an inconspicuous repair.
2. Trim and/or dress the new stone as needed.
3. Test-fit the new stone in the cavity. Make sure the cavity is deep enough to accommodate a new ½"-thick mortar bed so the replacement stone will sit level with the surrounding stones.

STEP 4: SET THE NEW STONE

1. Vacuum the cavity thoroughly with a shop vacuum to remove all dust and debris.
2. Mix a batch of mortar, using the same type used on the original installation. Mist the cavity with water, then spread an even layer of mortar, about ½" thick, using a small mason's trowel.
3. Set the replacement stone and press down firmly to bed it into the mortar. Check with a straightedge to make sure the stone is roughly level with the neighboring surfaces. Make any necessary adjustments to level the stone. Let the mortar dry for at least 24 hours.
4. Mix a batch of mortar for the new mortar joints. If desired, add tint to match the old mortar. (Experiment with small sample batches of mortar and tint and let them dry to determine the best formula.) Mist the empty joints around the replacement stone, then fill and shape the joints.

Mark the replacement stone so it will fit into the cavity with the proper spacing for mortar joints.

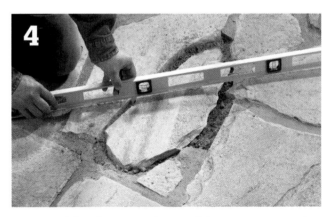

Set a straightedge across the top of the new stone to make sure it is even with the neighboring stones.

Pressure Washing Masonry & Stonework

To clean the masonry and stonework surfaces around the outside of your home, there is nothing that works faster or more effectively than a pressure washer. A typical residential-grade unit can be as much as 50 times more powerful than a standard garden hose, while using up to 80% less water.

A pressure washer comprises an engine to generate power, a pump to force water supplied from a garden hose through a high-pressure hose, and a nozzle to accelerate the water stream leaving the system. This results in a high-pressure water jet ranging from 500 to 4000 PSI (pounds per square inch).

But PSI only does not account for a pressure washers cleaning power. Gallons per minute (GPM) dictates the spray's ability to rinse away loosened dirt and grime from the area; a pressure washer with a higher GPM cleans faster than a lower-flow unit. For general cleaning around your outdoor home, a pressure washer around 2500 PSI and 2.5 GPM is more than sufficient.

Pressure washing is quite simple: firmly grasp the spray wand with both hands, depress the trigger and move the nozzle across the surface to be cleaned. Although different surfaces require different spray patterns and pressure settings, it is not difficult to determine the appropriate cleaning approach for each project. The nozzle is adjustable—from a low-pressure, wide-fan spray for general cleaning and rinsing, to a narrow, intense stream for stubborn stains. But the easiest way to control the cleaning is to simply adjust the distance between the nozzle and the surface—move the nozzle back to reduce the pressure; move the nozzle closer to intensify it.

To successfully clean any masonry or stone surface using a pressure washer, follow these tips:

- When cleaning a new surface, start in an inconspicuous area, with a wide spray pattern and the nozzle 4- to 5-ft. from the surface. Move closer to the surface until the desired effect is achieved.
- Keep the nozzle in constant motion, spraying at a steady speed with long, even strokes to ensure consistent results.
- Maintain a consistent distance between the nozzle and the cleaning surface.
- When cleaning heavily soiled or stained surfaces, use cleaning detergents formulated for pressure washers. Always rinse the surface before applying the detergent. On vertical surfaces, apply detergent from bottom to top, and rinse from top to bottom. Always follow the detergent manufacturer's directions.
- After pressure washing, always seal the surface with an appropriate surface sealer (e.g., concrete sealer for cement driveways), following the product manufacturer's instructions.

Pressure Washer Safety ▶

- Always wear eye protection.
- Do not wear open-toed shoes.
- Make sure the unit is on a stable surface and the cleaning area has adequate slopes and drainage to prevent puddles.
- Assume a solid stance, and firmly grasp the spray gun with both hands to avoid injury if the gun kicks back.
- Always keep the high-pressure hose connected to both the pump and the spray gun while the system is pressurized.
- Never aim the nozzle at people or animals—the high-pressure stream of water can cause serious injury.

Tips for Pressure Washing Masonry & Stonework ▸

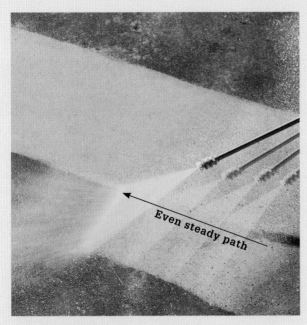

Always keep the nozzle in motion, spraying at a steady speed and using long, even strokes. Take multiple passes over heavily soiled areas. Take care not to dwell on one spot for too long, especially when using narrow, high-pressure spray patterns.

Hold the spray wand so that the nozzle distributes the spray pattern across the surface evenly. Holding the nozzle at too low an angle can cause an uneven spray pattern, resulting in "zebra striping." Also, maintain a consistent distance between the nozzle and the cleaning surface to ensure consistent results and help flush dirt and debris from the area.

Work in identifiable sections, such as the area between the expansion joints in concrete. If there is a slope, work downhill to promote drainage and help flush away dirt and debris. Wet entire surface to prevent streaking.

To prevent streaks on vertical surfaces, always begin pressure washing or applying cleaning detergent at the bottom of the surface, then work upward. When rinsing, start at the top and work downward—gravity will help the clean water flush away dirt, debris, and detergent residue.

Repairing an Asphalt Driveway

The two most popular hard surface driveway materials are asphalt and concrete. Both are used, almost interchangeably, throughout the country in cold and hot climates. But there are some basic differences. Concrete generally costs more to install and asphalt generally costs more to maintain as the years go by. And, concrete doesn't always perform well in cold areas. It's susceptible to damage from the freeze-and-thaw cycle and it can be damaged by exposure to road salt. Asphalt, on the other hand, doesn't always perform well in hot climates. It absorbs a lot of heat from the sun and tends to stay soft during very hot periods. And, of course, when the surface is soft, it can wear more quickly.

A typical asphalt driveway is formed by pouring and compressing a layer of hot asphalt over a subbase of compacted gravel.

How to Repair an Asphalt Driveway

Carefully inspect the asphalt surface for any oil and grease stains. Then remove them with driveway cleaner or household detergent. Scrub the cleaner into the surface with a soft brush and rinse the area clean with a garden hose. Repeat until the stain is gone. If using driveway cleaner, wear the recommended safety equipment.

Once the stains are removed, thoroughly rinse the entire driveway with a garden hose and nozzle. The goal is to wash away any debris and to remove the dust and dirt from the surface cracks.

Repair the small cracks first. Chip out any loose debris with a cold chisel and hammer. Then clean out all debris with a wire brush. Remove all the dust with a shop vacuum. A crevice tool on the end of the hose will do the best job.

Place asphalt patching compound in the holes with a small trowel. Overfill the hole so the patch material is about ½" higher than the surrounding asphalt surface.

Compact the patch material with a small piece of 2 × 4. Tamp the board up and down with your hand, or strike the board with a hammer. Keep working until you can't compress the patch any more.

Finish the patch by covering it with a piece of 2 × 6 and striking it with a hammer or mallet. Work back and forth across the board to smooth out the entire patch and make it flush to the surrounding surface.

(continued)

On narrower patches, the compound can be smoothed with a small trowel. Just move the tool across the surrounding surface and then over the patch. This should flatten the patch. Finish up by compressing the compound by pushing it down with the trowel.

Prepare larger potholes by undercutting the edges with a cold chisel and a hammer. Then, remove all the debris and fill the hole with cold-patch asphalt mix. Working directly from the bag, fill the hole about 1 in. higher than the surrounding surface. Then compact it with a 2 × 4, as before.

One great way to compress cold-patch asphalt is to cover the patch with a piece of plywood. Then, drive your car onto the plywood and stop when one tire is centered on the panel. Wait a few minutes, then move the car back and forth a few times.

Once the hole patching is done, fill the routine cracks (less than ¼" wide) with asphalt crack filler. This material comes in a caulk tube, which makes it very easy to apply. Just clean the crack with a wire brush and a vacuum, then squeeze the filler into the crack.

After the crack filler has cured for about 10 or 15 minutes, smooth it out with a putty knife as you force the filler down into the crack. If this creates small depressions, fill these with a second application of filler.

Driveway sealer should always be mixed thoroughly before use. Take a 2× stir stick that's about 30 in. long and stir the sealer until it has a uniform consistency. Pour out enough to cover a strip across the driveway that's about 3-ft. or 4-ft. wide.

Spread the sealer with the squeegee side of the application brush. Try to keep this coat as uniform as possible. Work the sealer into the small cracks and pull it gently over the big patches.

Flip the squeegee over to the brush side and smooth out the lap marks and other irregularities that were left from the application coat. Work at right angles to the first pass.

Maintaining a Deck

Inspect your deck once each year. Replace loose or rusting hardware or fasteners, and apply fresh finish to prevent water damage.

Look carefully for areas that show signs of damage. Replace or reinforce damaged wood as soon as possible (pages 278 to 279).

Restore an older, weathered deck to the original wood color with a deck-brightening solution. Brighteners are available at any home improvement store.

Tools & Materials ▸

Flashlight
Awl or screwdriver
Screwgun
Putty knife
Scrub brush
Rubber gloves

Eye protection
Pressure sprayer
2½" corrosion-
   resistant
   deck screws
Deck brightener

Inspect hidden areas regularly for signs of rotted or damaged wood. Apply a fresh coat of finish yearly.

Tips for Maintaining an Older Deck ▸

Use an awl or screwdriver to check deck for soft, rotted wood. Replace or reinforce damaged wood.

Clean debris from cracks between decking boards with a putty knife. Debris traps moisture, and can cause wood to rot.

How to Renew a Deck

Drive new fasteners to secure loose decking to joists. If using the old nail or screw holes, new fasteners should be slightly longer than the originals.

Mix deck-brightening solution as directed by manufacturer. Apply solution with pressure sprayer. Let solution set for 10 minutes.

Scrub deck thoroughly with a stiff scrub brush. Wear rubber gloves and eye protection.

Rinse deck with clear water. If necessary, apply a second coat of brightener to extremely dirty or stained areas. Rinse and let dry. Apply a fresh coat of sealer or stain.

Repairing a Deck

Replace or reinforce damaged deck wood as soon as possible. Wood rot can spread and weaken solid wood.

After replacing or reinforcing the rotted wood, clean the entire deck and apply a fresh coat of clear sealer-preservative or staining sealer. Apply a fresh coat of finish each year to prevent future water damage. If you need to repair more than a few small areas, it is probably time to replace the entire deck.

Tools & Materials ▶

Cat's paw or flat pry bar	Circular saw	Ratchet wrench	⅝" masonry
Screwgun	Scrub brush	Sealer-preservative or staining	anchor
Awl or screwdriver	Paint brush	sealer	⅜" lag screw
Hammer	Hydraulic jack	Galvanized nails (6d, 10d)	Rubber gloves
Chisel	Drill or hammer drill	Deck lumber	Bucket
Eye protection	⅝" masonry bit	Baking soda	Concrete block
Pressure-sprayer	Level	Corrosion-resistant deck screws	Scrap plywood

How to Repair Damaged Decking & Joists

Remove nails or screws from the damaged decking board, using a cat's paw or screwgun. Remove the damaged board.

Inspect the underlying joists for signs of rotted wood. Joists with discolored, soft areas should be repaired and reinforced.

Use a hammer and chisel to remove any rotted portions of joist.

Apply a thick coat of sealer-preservative to damaged joist. Let dry, then apply a second coat of sealer. Cut a reinforcing joist (sister joist) from pressure-treated lumber.

Treat all sides of sister joist with clear sealer-preservative, and let dry. Position sister joist tightly against the damaged joist, and attach with 10d nails driven every 2 feet.

Attach sister joist to ledger and header joist by toenailing with 10d nails. Cut replacement decking boards from matching lumber, using a circular saw.

If the existing decking is gray, "weather" the new decking by scrubbing with a solution made from 1 cup baking soda and 1 gallon warm water. Rinse and let dry.

(continued)

Apply a coat of sealer-preservative or staining sealer to all sides of the new decking boards.

Position the new decking and attach to joists with galvanized deck screws or nails. Make sure space between boards matches that of existing decking.

How to Replace a Post on an Older Deck

Build a support, using plywood scraps, a concrete block, and a hydraulic jack. Place 1½" layer of plywood between head of jack and beam. Apply just enough pressure to lift the beam slightly.

Anchor pad

Remove the nails or lag screws holding the damaged post to the anchor pad and to the beam. Remove the damaged post and the wood anchor pad on the concrete pier.

Drill a hole in the middle of the concrete pier, using a hammer drill and a ⅝" masonry bit. Insert ⅝" masonry anchor into hole.

Position galvanized post anchor on pier block, and thread a ⅜" lag screw with washer through the hole in the anchor and into the masonry anchor. Tighten the screw with a ratchet wrench.

Cut new post from pressure-treated lumber, and treat cut ends with sealer-preservative. Position post and make sure it is plumb.

Attach the bottom of the post to the post anchor, using 10d or 16d joist hanger nails. Attach the post to the beam by redriving the lag screws, using a ratchet wrench. Release the pressure on the jack and remove the support.

Plumbing & Wiring

The Home Plumbing System

Because most of a plumbing system is hidden inside walls and floors, it may seem to be a complex maze of pipes and fittings. In fact, home plumbing is simple and straightforward. Understanding how home plumbing works is an important first step toward doing routine maintenance and money-saving repairs.

A typical home plumbing system includes three basic parts: a water supply system, a fixture and appliance set, and a drain system. These three parts can be seen clearly in the photograph of the cut-away house on the opposite page.

Fresh water enters a home through a main supply line (1). This fresh water source is provided by either a municipal water company or a private underground well. If the source is a municipal supplier, the water passes through a meter (2) that registers the amount of water used. A family of four uses about 400 gallons of water each day.

Immediately after the main supply enters the house, a branch line splits off (3) and is joined to a water heater (4). From the water heater, a hot water line runs parallel to the cold water line to bring the water supply to fixtures and appliances throughout the house. Fixtures include sinks, bathtubs, showers, and laundry tubs. Appliances include water heaters, dishwashers, clothes washers, and water softeners.

Toilets and exterior sillcocks are examples of fixtures that require only a cold water line.

The water supply to fixtures and appliances is controlled with faucets and valves. Faucets and valves have moving parts and seals that eventually may wear out or break, but they are easily repaired or replaced.

Waste water then enters the drain system. It first must flow past a trap (5), a U-shaped piece of pipe that holds standing water and prevents sewer gases from entering the home. Every fixture must have a drain trap.

The drain system works entirely by gravity, allowing waste water to flow downhill through a series of large-diameter pipes. These drain pipes are attached to a system of vent pipes. Vent pipes (6) bring fresh air to the drain system, preventing suction that would slow or stop drain water from flowing freely. Vent pipes usually exit the house at a roof vent (7).

All waste water eventually reaches a main waste and vent stack (8). The main stack curves to become a sewer line (9) that exits the house near the foundation. In a municipal system, this sewer line joins a main sewer line located near the street. Where sewer service is not available, waste water empties into a septic system.

Water meter and main shutoff valves are located where the main water supply pipe enters the house. The water meter is the property of your local municipal water company. If the water meter leaks, or if you suspect it is not functioning properly, call your water company for repairs.

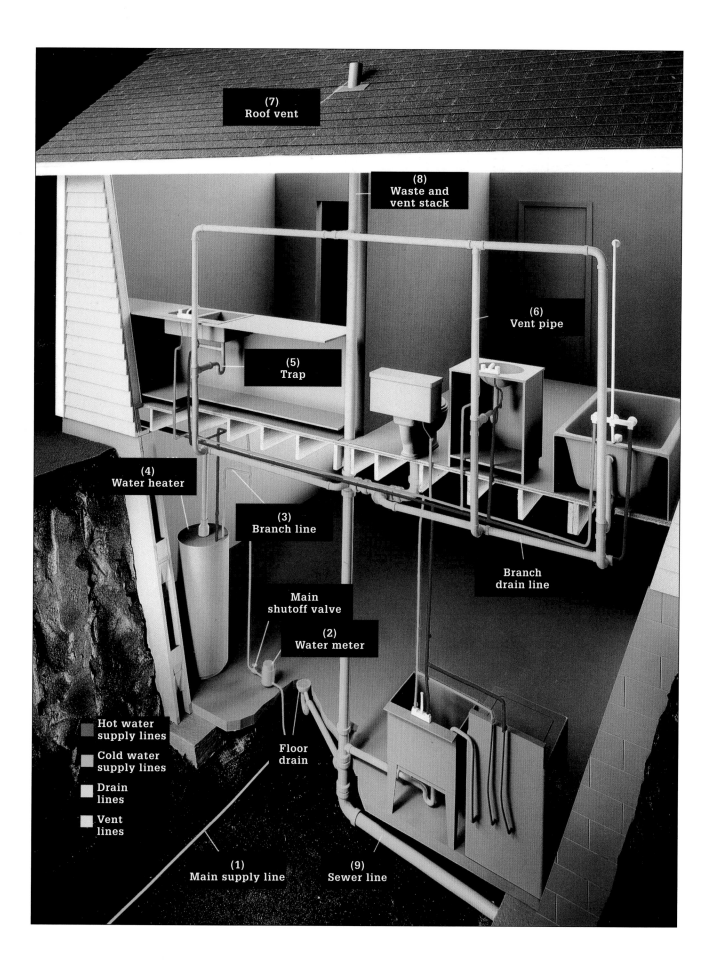

(7)
Roof vent

(8)
Waste and
vent stack

(6)
Vent pipe

(5)
Trap

(4)
Water heater

(3)
Branch line

Branch
drain line

Main
shutoff valve

(2)
Water meter

Hot water
supply lines

Cold water
supply lines

Drain
lines

Vent
lines

Floor
drain

(1)
Main supply line

(9)
Sewer line

Working with Plastic Pipes

Plastic pipes and fittings are popular with do-it-yourselfers because they are lightweight, inexpensive, and easy to use. Most local plumbing codes now allow the use of plastics for home plumbing.

Plastic pipes are available in rigid and flexible forms. Rigid plastics include ABS (acrylonitrile butadiene styrene), PVC (polyvinyl chloride), and CPVC (chlorinated polyvinyl chloride). The most commonly used flexible plastics are PE (polyethylene) and PEX (cross-linked polyethylene).

ABS and PVC are used in drain systems. ABS is no longer approved for new installations. PVC resists chemical damage and heat better than ABS. It is approved for above-ground use by all plumbing codes. However, some codes still require cast-iron pipe for main drains that run under concrete slabs. CPVC is used in water supply systems.

PE is used in outdoor plumbing. PEX is approved for all indoor supply applications.

Plastic pipes can be joined to existing iron or copper pipes using transition fittings, but different types of plastics should not be joined. For example, if your drain pipes are PVC plastic, use only PVC pipes and fittings when making repairs and replacements.

Prolonged exposure to sunlight eventually can weaken plastic plumbing pipe, so plastics should not be installed or stored in areas that receive constant direct sunlight.

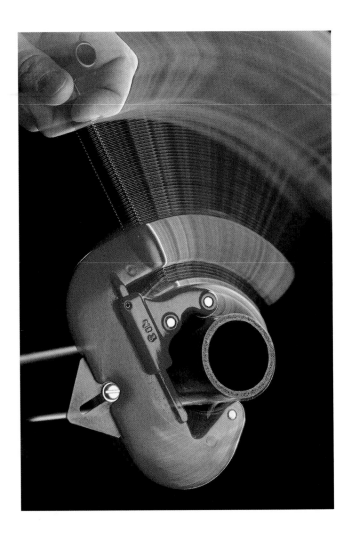

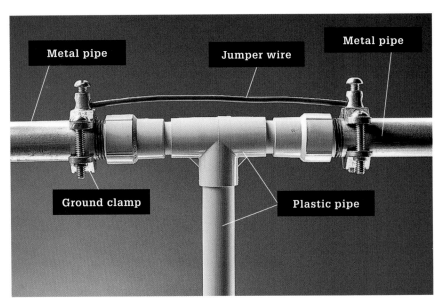

Metal pipe · Jumper wire · Metal pipe · Ground clamp · Plastic pipe

Caution: Your home electrical system could be grounded through metal water pipes. When adding plastic pipes to a metal plumbing system, make sure the electrical ground circuit is not broken. Use ground clamps and jumper wires, available at any hardware store, to bypass the plastic transition and complete the electrical ground circuit. Clamps must be firmly attached to bare metal on both sides of the plastic pipe.

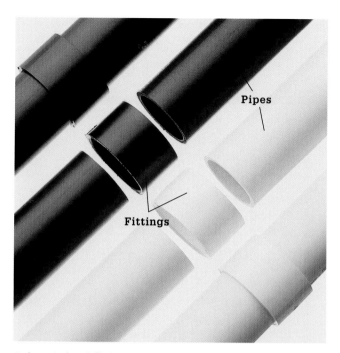

Pipes

Fittings

Solvent-glued fittings are used on rigid plastic pipes. Solvent dissolves a thin layer of plastic and bonds the pipe and fitting together.

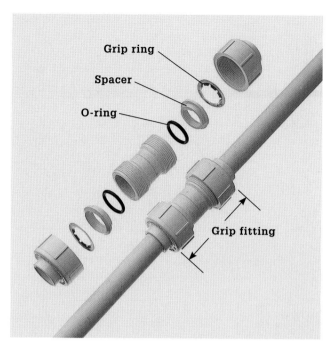

Grip ring

Spacer

O-ring

Grip fitting

Grip fittings are used to join CPVC pipe. Each fitting has a metal grip ring, plastic compression ring, and rubber O-ring.

▮ Plastic Pipe Grade Stamps

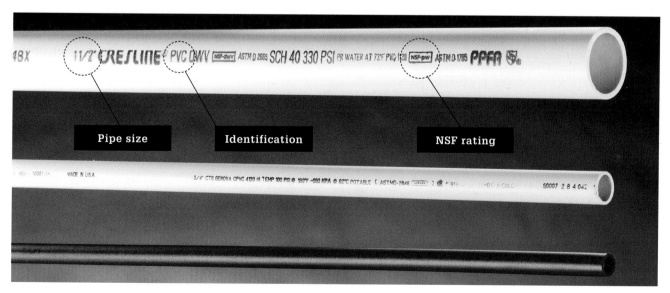

Pipe size

Identification

NSF rating

Plastic pipe comes with three important labels. Material identification shows the type of plastic. For sink traps and drain pipes, use PVC pipe. For water supply pipes, use CPVC pipe or PEX. PE is used for outdoor cold water supply. The NSF rating indicates the pipe's proper application. For sink traps and drains, choose PVC pipe that has a "DWV" rating. For water supply pipes, choose CPVC or PEX pipe that has a "PW" (pressurized water) rating. Pipe size is also specified. PVC pipe for drains usually has an inside diameter of 1¼" to 4". CPVC and PEX pipes for water supply usually have an inside diameter of ½" or ¾".

Cutting & Fitting Rigid Plastic Pipe

Cut rigid ABS, PVC, or CPVC plastic pipes with a tubing cutter or with any saw. Cuts must be straight to ensure watertight joints.

Rigid plastics are joined with plastic fittings and solvent glue. Use a solvent glue that is made for the type of plastic pipe you are installing. For example, do not use ABS solvent on PVC pipe. Some solvent glues, called "all-purpose" or "universal" solvents, may be used on all types of plastic pipe.

Solvent glue hardens in about 30 seconds, so test-fit all plastic pipes and fittings before gluing the first joint. For best results, the surfaces of plastic pipes and fittings should be dulled with emery cloth and liquid primer before they are joined.

Liquid solvent glues and primers are toxic and flammable. Provide adequate ventilation when fitting plastics, and store the products away from any source of heat.

Plastic grip fittings can be used to join rigid or flexible plastic pipes to copper plumbing pipes.

Tools & Materials ▸

Tape measure
Felt-tipped pen
Tubing cutter (or miter box or hacksaw)

Utility knife
Channel-type pliers
Gloves
Plastic pipe

Fittings
Emery cloth
Plastic pipe primer

Solvent glue
Rag
Petroleum jelly

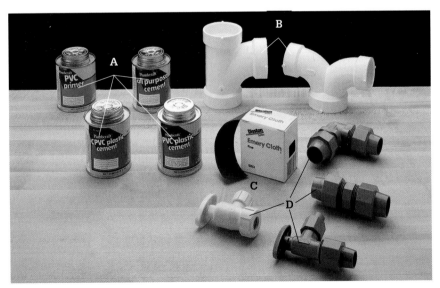

Specialty materials for plastics include: solvent glues and primer (A), solvent-glue fittings (B), emery cloth (C), and plastic grip fittings (D).

Measuring Plastic Pipe

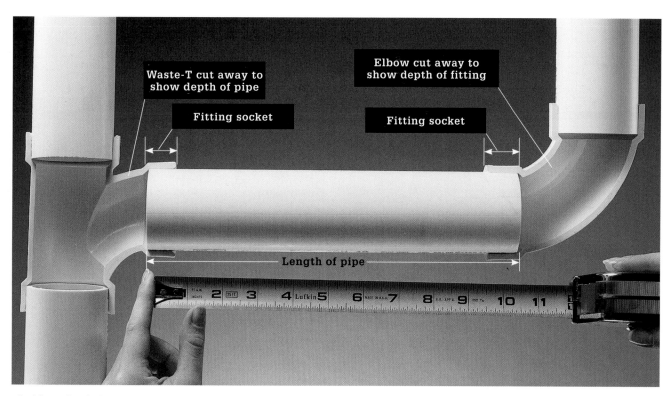

Find length of plastic pipe needed by measuring between the bottoms of the fitting sockets (fittings shown in cutaway). Mark the length on the pipe with a felt-tipped pen.

How to Cut Rigid Plastic Pipe

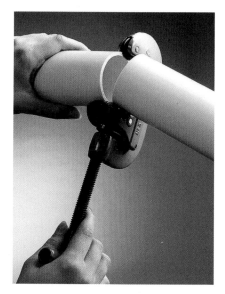

Tubing cutter: Tighten tool around pipe so cutting wheel is on marked line. Rotate tool around pipe, tightening screw every two rotations, until pipe snaps.

Miter box: Make straight cuts on all types of plastic pipe with a power or hand miter box.

Hacksaw: Clamp plastic pipe in a portable gripping bench or a vise, and keep the hacksaw blade straight while sawing.

How to Solvent-glue Rigid Plastic Pipe

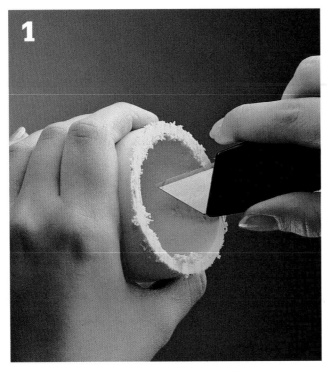

1

Remove rough burrs on cut ends of plastic pipe, using a utility knife.

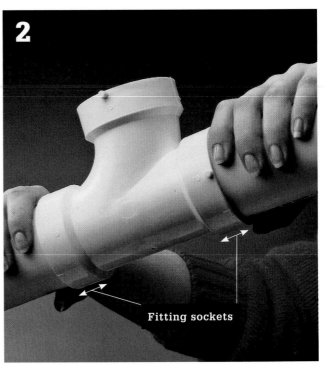

2

Fitting sockets

Test-fit all pipes and fittings. Pipes should fit tightly against the bottom of the fitting sockets.

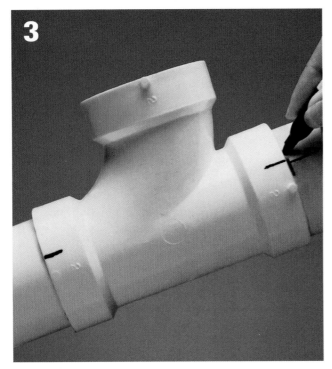

3

Mark depth of the fitting sockets on pipes. Take pipes apart. Clean ends of pipes and fitting sockets with emery cloth.

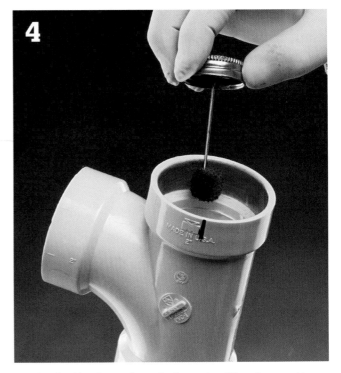

4

Apply plastic pipe primer to the ends of the pipes and to the insides of the fitting sockets. Primer dulls glossy surfaces and ensures a good seal.

Solvent-glue each joint by applying a thick coat of solvent glue to end of pipe. Apply a thin coat of solvent glue to inside surface of fitting socket. Work quickly: solvent glue hardens in about 30 seconds.

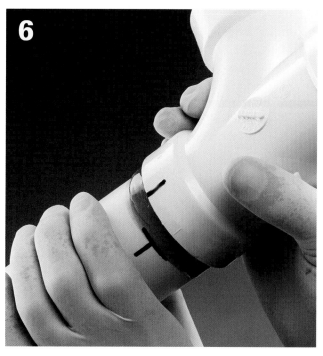

Quickly position pipe and fitting so that alignment marks are offset by about 2 inches. Force pipe into fitting until the end fits flush against the bottom of the socket.

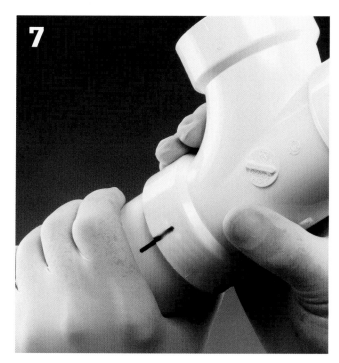

Spread solvent by twisting the pipe until marks are aligned. Hold pipe in place for about 20 seconds to prevent joint from slipping.

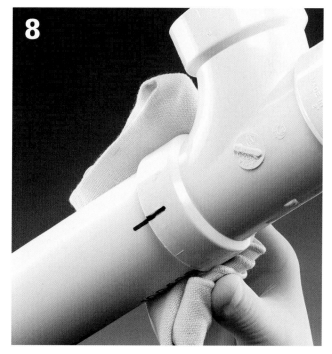

Wipe away excess solvent glue with a rag. Do not disturb the joint for 30 minutes after gluing.

Working with Copper Pipe

Copper is the ideal material for water supply pipes. It resists corrosion and has smooth surfaces that provide good water flow. Copper pipes are available in several diameters, but most home water supply systems use ½" or ¾" pipe. Copper pipe is manufactured in rigid and flexible forms.

Rigid copper, sometimes called hard copper, is approved for home water supply systems by all local codes. It comes in three wall-thickness grades: Types M, L, and K. Type M is the thinnest, the least expensive, and a good choice for do-it-yourself home plumbing.

Rigid Type L usually is required by code for commercial plumbing systems. Because it is strong and solders easily, Type L may be preferred by some professional plumbers and do-it-yourselfers for home use. Type K has the heaviest wall thickness and is used most often for underground water service lines.

Flexible copper, also called soft copper, comes in two wall-thickness grades: Types L and K. Both are approved for most home water supply systems, although flexible Type L copper is used primarily for gas service lines. Because it is bendable and will resist a mild frost, Type L may be installed as part of a water supply system in unheated indoor areas, like crawl spaces. Type K is used for underground water service lines.

A third form of copper, called DWV, is used for drain systems. Because most codes now allow low-cost plastic pipes for drain systems, DWV copper is seldom used.

Copper pipes are connected with soldered, compression, or flare fittings (see chart below). Always follow your local code for the correct types of pipes and fittings allowed in your area.

Soldered fittings, also called sweat fittings, often are used to join copper pipes. Correctly soldered fittings (pages 296 to 299) are strong and trouble-free. Copper pipe can also be joined with compression fittings (pages 300 to 301) or flare fittings (pages 302 to 303). See chart below.

Copper Pipe & Fitting Chart ▶

Fitting Method	Type M	Rigid Copper Type L	Type K	Flexible Copper Type L	Type K	General Comments
Soldered	yes	yes	yes	yes	yes	Inexpensive, strong, and trouble-free fitting method. Requires some skill.
Compression	yes	not recommended		yes	yes	Easy to use. Allows pipes or fixtures to be repaired or replaced readily. More expensive than solder. Best used on flexible copper.
Flare	no	no	no	yes	yes	Use only with flexible copper pipes. Usually used as a gas-line fitting. Requires some skill.

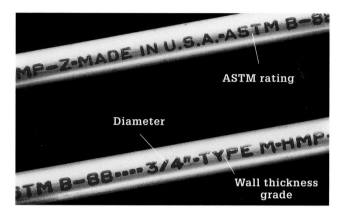

Grade stamp information includes the pipe diameter, the wall-thickness grade, and a stamp of approval from the ASTM (American Society for Testing and Materials). Type M pipe is identified by red lettering, Type L by blue lettering.

Bend flexible copper pipe with a coil-spring tubing bender to avoid kinks. Select a bender that matches the outside diameter of the pipe. Slip bender over pipe using a twisting motion. Bend pipe slowly until it reaches the correct angle, but not more than 90º.

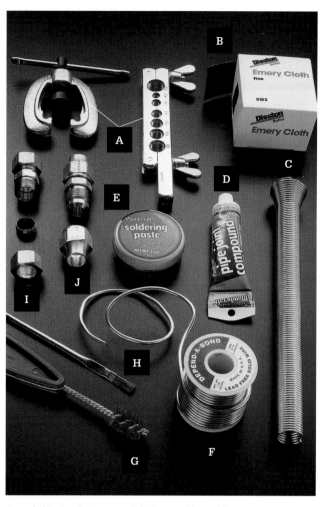

Specialty tools & materials for working with copper include: flaring tools (A), emery cloth (B), coil-spring tubing bender (C), pipe joint compound (D), self-cleaning soldering paste (flux) (E), lead-free solder (F), wire brush (G), flux brush (H), compression fitting (I), flare fitting (J).

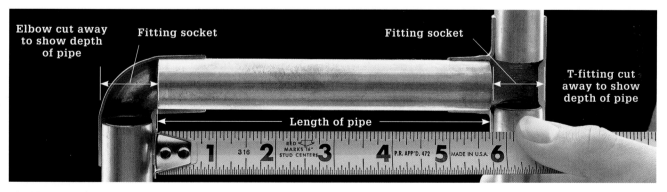

Find length of copper pipe needed by measuring between the bottom of the copper fitting sockets (fittings shown in cutaway). Mark length on the pipe with a felt-tipped pen.

Cutting & Soldering Copper

The best way to cut rigid and flexible copper pipe is with a tubing cutter. A tubing cutter makes a smooth, straight cut, an important first step toward making a watertight joint. Remove any metal burrs on the cut edges with a reaming tool or round file.

Copper can be cut with a hacksaw. A hacksaw is useful in tight areas where a tubing cutter will not fit. Take care to make a smooth, straight cut when cutting with a hacksaw.

A soldered pipe joint, also called a sweated joint, is made by heating a copper or brass fitting with a propane torch until the fitting is just hot enough to melt metal solder. The heat draws the solder into the gap between the fitting and pipe to form a watertight seal. A fitting that is overheated or unevenly heated will not draw in solder. Copper pipes and fittings must be clean and dry to form a watertight seal.

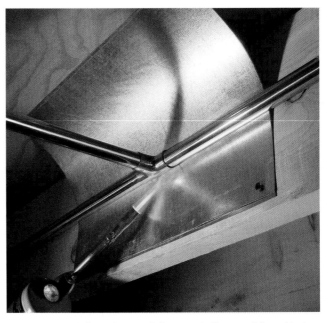

Protect wood from heat of the torch flame while soldering, using a double layer (two 18" × 18" pieces) of 26-gauge sheet metal. Buy sheet metal at hardware stores or building supply centers and keep it to use with all soldering projects.

Tools & Materials ▸

Tubing cutter with reaming tip (or hacksaw and round file)	Adjustable wrench
	Channel-type pliers
	Copper pipe
	Copper fittings
Wire brush	Emery cloth
Flux brush	Soldering paste (flux)
Propane torch	Sheet metal
Spark lighter (or matches)	Lead-free solder
	Rag

Soldering Tips ▸

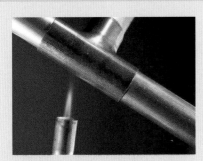

Use caution when soldering copper. Pipes and fittings become very hot and must be allowed to cool before handling.

Keep joint dry when soldering existing water pipes by plugging the pipe with bread. Bread absorbs moisture that may ruin the soldering process and cause pinhole leaks. The bread dissolves when water is turned back on.

Torch valve

Prevent accidents by shutting off propane torch immediately after use. Make sure valve is closed completely.

How to Cut Rigid & Flexible Copper Pipe

Place tubing cutter over the pipe and tighten the handle so that pipe rests on both rollers, and cutting wheel is on marked line.

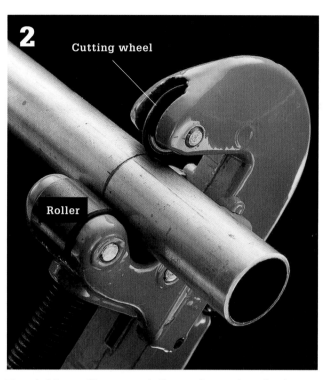

Turn tubing cutter one rotation so that cutting wheel scores a continuous straight line around the pipe.

Rotate the cutter in the opposite direction, tightening the handle slightly after every two rotations, until cut is complete.

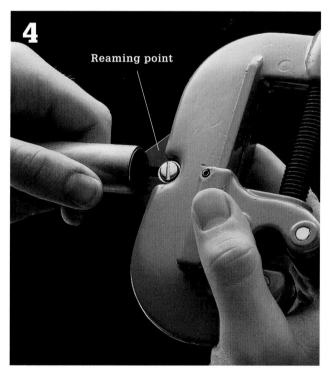

Remove sharp metal burrs from inside edge of the cut pipe, using the reaming point on the tubing cutter, or a round file.

How to Solder Copper Pipes & Fittings

1

Emery cloth

Clean end of each pipe by sanding with emery cloth. Ends must be free of dirt and grease to ensure that the solder forms a good seal.

2

Clean inside of each fitting by scouring with a wire brush or emery cloth.

3

Flux brush

Plumbcraft®
soldering
paste

NON CORROSIV

Apply a thin layer of soldering paste (flux) to end of each pipe, using a flux brush. Soldering paste should cover about 1" of pipe end.

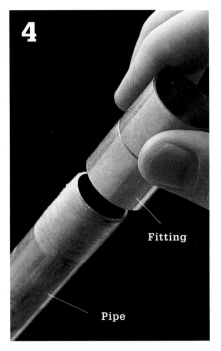

4

Fitting

Pipe

Assemble each joint by inserting the pipe into the fitting so it is tight against the bottom of the fitting sockets. Twist each fitting slightly to spread soldering paste.

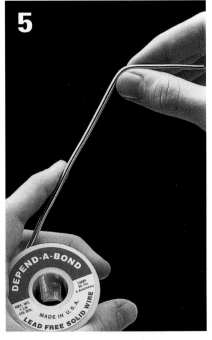

5

DEPEND-A-BOND
NET. WT.
1 LB.
.125 DIA.
13898
95 Tin
5 Antimony
MADE IN U.S.A.
LEAD FREE SOLID WIRE

Prepare the wire solder by unwinding 8" to 10" of wire from spool. Bend the first 2" of the wire to a 90° angle.

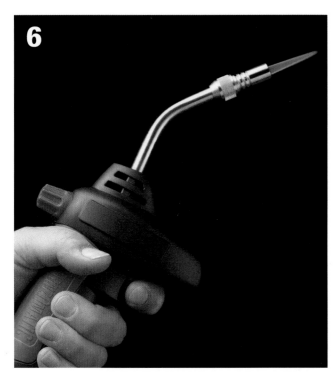

6

Open the gas valve and trigger the spark lighter to ignite the torch.

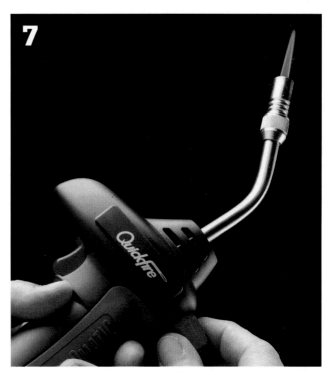

7

Adjust the torch valve until the inner portion of the flame is 1" to 2" long.

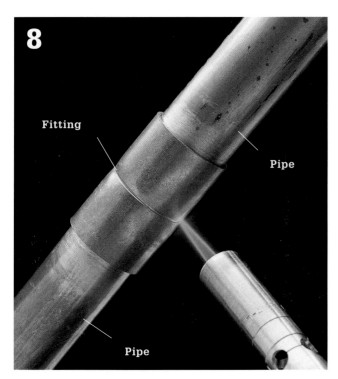

8

Fitting

Pipe

Pipe

Hold flame tip against middle of fitting for 4 to 5 seconds, until soldering paste begins to sizzle.

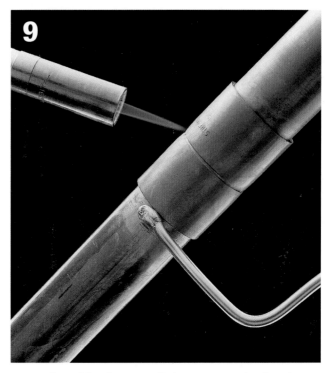

9

Heat other side of copper fitting to ensure that heat is distributed evenly. Touch solder to pipe. If solder melts, pipe is ready to be soldered.

(continued)

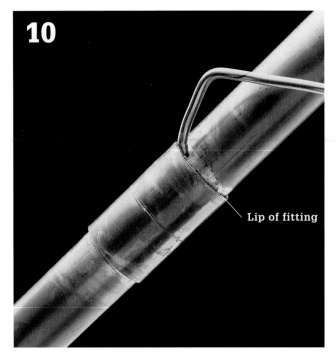

10

Lip of fitting

When pipe is hot enough to melt solder, remove torch and quickly push ½" to ¾" of solder into each joint. Capillary action fills joint with liquid solder. A correctly soldered joint should show a thin bead of solder around the lip of the fitting.

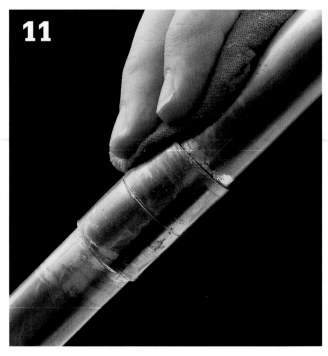

11

Allow the joint to cool briefly, then wipe away excess solder with a dry rag. Caution: Pipes will be hot. If joints leak after water is turned on, disassemble and resolder.

How to Solder Brass Valves

1

Remove the valve stem with an adjustable wrench. Removing the stem prevents heat damage to rubber or plastic stem parts while soldering. Prepare the copper pipes and assemble joints.

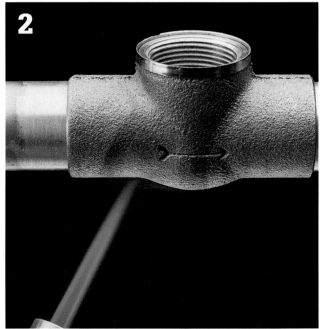

2

Light propane torch. Heat body of valve, moving flame to distribute heat evenly. Brass is denser than copper, so it requires more heating time before joints will draw solder. Apply solder. Let metal cool, then reassemble valve.

How to Take Apart Soldered Joints

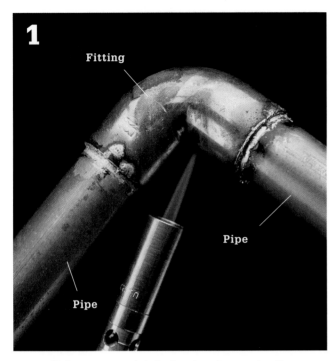

Fitting

Pipe

Pipe

Turn off the water and drain the pipes by opening the highest and lowest faucets in the house. Light propane torch. Hold flame tip to the fitting until the solder becomes shiny and begins to melt.

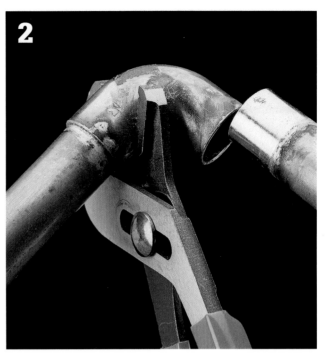

Use channel-type pliers to separate the pipes from the fitting.

Remove old solder by heating ends of pipe with propane torch. Use dry rag to wipe away melted solder quickly. Caution: Pipes will be hot.

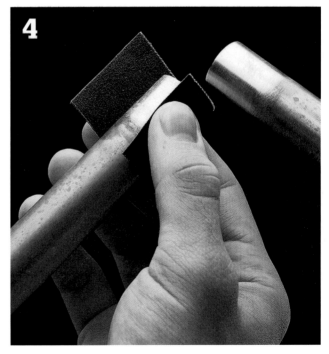

Use emery cloth to polish ends of pipe down to bare metal. Never reuse old fittings.

Using Compression Fittings

Compression fittings are used to make connections that may need to be taken apart. Compression fittings are easy to disconnect and often are used to install supply tubes and fixture shutoff valves. Use compression fittings in places where it is unsafe or difficult to solder, such as in crawl spaces.

Compression fittings are used most often with flexible copper pipe. Flexible copper is soft enough to allow the compression ring to seat snugly, creating a watertight seal. Compression fittings also may be used to make connections with Type M rigid copper pipe. See the chart on page 292.

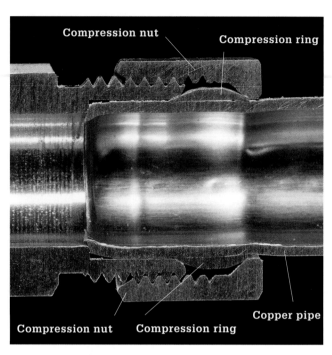

Compression fitting (shown in cutaway) shows how threaded compression nut forms seal by forcing the compression ring against the copper pipe. Compression ring is covered with pipe joint compound before assembling to ensure a perfect seal.

Tools & Materials ▸

Felt-tipped pen
Tubing cutter
  or hacksaw
Adjustable wrenches

Brass compression
  fittings
Pipe joint compound
  or Teflon tape

How to Attach Supply Tubes to Fixture Shutoff Valves with Compression Fittings

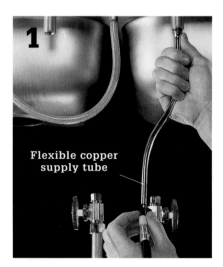

1

Flexible copper supply tube

Bend flexible copper supply tube and mark to length. Include ½" for portion that will fit inside valve. Cut tube.

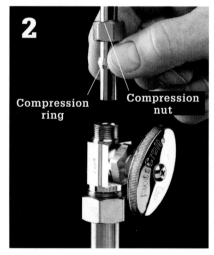

2

Compression ring

Compression nut

Slide the compression nut and then the compression ring over end of the pipe. The threads of the nut should face the valve.

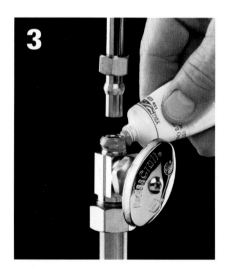

3

Apply a layer of pipe joint compound or Teflon tape over the threads on the valve. This helps ensure a watertight seal.

4

Socket

Insert the end of the pipe into the fitting so it fits flush against the bottom of the fitting socket.

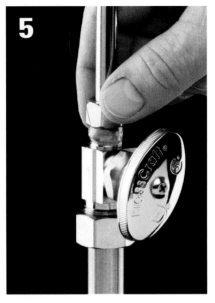

5

Slide the compression ring and nut against the threads of the valve. Hand-tighten the nut onto the valve.

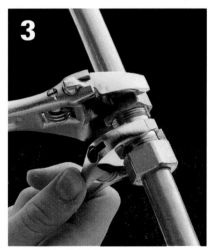

6

Tighten the compression nut with adjustable wrenches. Do not overtighten. Turn on the water and watch for leaks. If the fitting leaks, tighten the nut gently.

How to Join Two Copper Pipes with a Compression Union Fitting

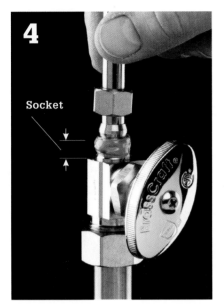

1

Compression nut

Compression ring

Union

Slide compression nuts and rings over the ends of pipes. Place a threaded union between the pipes.

2

Apply a layer of pipe joint compound or Teflon tape to the union's threads, then screw compression nuts onto the union.

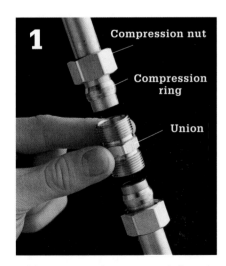

3

Hold the center of the union fitting with an adjustable wrench and use another wrench to tighten each compression nut one complete turn. Turn on the water. If the fitting leaks, tighten the nuts gently.

Using Flare Fittings

Flare fittings are used more often for flexible copper gas lines. Flare fittings may be used with flexible copper water supply pipes, but they cannot be used where the connections will be concealed inside walls. Always check your local code regarding the use of flare fittings.

Flare fittings are easy to disconnect. Use flare fittings in places where it is unsafe or difficult to solder, such as in crawl spaces.

Tools & Materials ▸

Two-piece flaring tool
Adjustable wrenches
Brass flare fittings

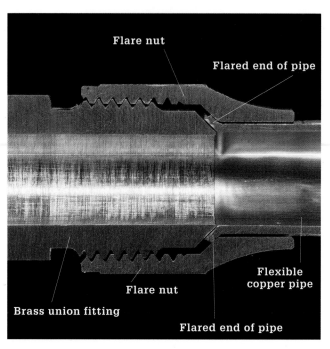

Flare fitting (shown in cutaway) shows how flared end of flexible copper pipe forms seal against the head of a brass union fitting.

How to Join Two Copper Pipes with a Flare Union Fitting

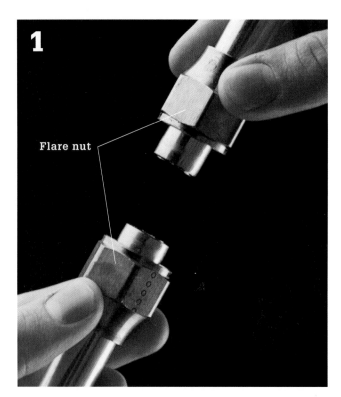

Slide flare nuts onto ends of pipes. Nuts must be placed on pipes before ends can be flared. Ream inside of pipe to create smooth edge.

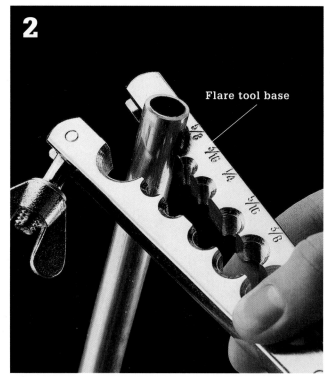

Select hole in flaring tool base that matches outside diameter of pipe. Open base, and place end of pipe inside hole.

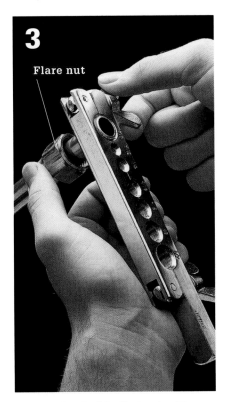

3

Flare nut

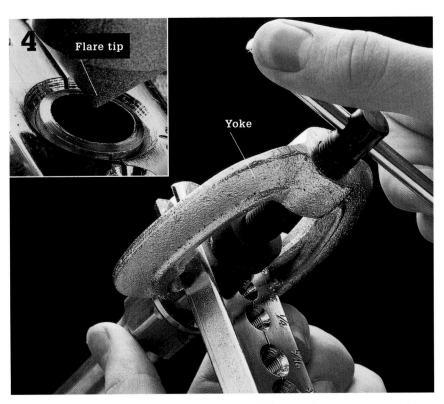

4

Flare tip

Yoke

Clamp pipe inside flaring tool base.
End of pipe must be flush with flat
surface of base.

Slip yoke of flaring tool around base. Center flaring tip of yoke over end of pipe
(inset photo above). Tighten handle of yoke to shape the end of the pipe. Flare is
completed when handle cannot be turned farther.

5

6

7

Remove yoke and remove pipe from
base. Repeat flaring for other pipe.

Place flare union between flared ends
of pipe and screw flare nuts onto union.

Hold center of flare union with
adjustable wrench and use another
wrench to tighten flare nuts one
complete turn. Turn on water. If fitting
leaks, tighten nuts.

Working with Galvanized Iron

Galvanized iron pipe often is found in older homes, where it is used for water supply and small drain lines. It can be identified by the zinc coating that gives it a silver color and by the threaded fittings used to connect pipes.

Galvanized iron pipes and fittings will corrode with age and eventually must be replaced. Low water pressure may be a sign that the insides of galvanized pipes have a buildup of rust. Blockage usually occurs in elbow fittings. Never try to clean the insides of galvanized iron pipes. Instead, remove and replace them as soon as possible.

Galvanized iron pipe and fittings are available at hardware stores and home improvement centers. Always specify the interior diameter (I.D.) when purchasing galvanized pipes and fittings. Pre-threaded pipes, called nipples, are available in lengths from 1" to 1 ft. If you need a longer length, have the store cut and thread the pipe to your dimensions.

Old galvanized iron can be difficult to repair. Fittings often are rusted in place, and what seems like a small job may become a large project. For example, cutting apart a section of pipe to replace a leaky fitting may reveal that adjacent pipes are also in need of replacement. If your job takes an unexpected amount of time, you can cap off any open lines and restore water to the rest of your house. Before you begin a repair, have on hand nipples and end caps that match your pipes.

Taking apart a system of galvanized iron pipes and fittings is time-consuming. Disassembly must start at the end of a pipe run, and each piece must be unscrewed before the next piece can be removed. Reaching the middle of a run to replace a section of pipe can be a long and tedious job. Instead, use a special three-piece fitting called a union. A union makes it possible to remove a section of pipe or a fitting without having to take the entire system apart.

Note: Galvanized iron is sometimes confused with "black iron." Both types have similar sizes and fittings. Black iron is used only for gas lines.

Tools & Materials ▸

Tape measure	Wire brush
Reciprocating saw	Nipples
with metal-	End caps
cutting blade	Union fitting
or a hacksaw	Pipe joint compound
Pipe wrenches	Replacement fittings
Propane torch	(if needed)

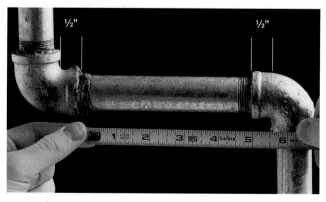

Measure old pipe. Include ½" at each end for the threaded portion of the pipe inside fitting. Bring overall measurement to the store when shopping for replacement parts.

How to Remove & Replace a Galvanized Iron Pipe

Cut through galvanized iron pipe with a reciprocating saw and a metal-cutting blade or with a hacksaw.

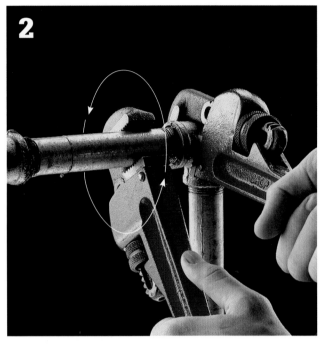

Hold fitting with one pipe wrench, and use another wrench to remove old pipe. Jaws of wrenches should face opposite directions. Always move wrench handle toward jaw opening.

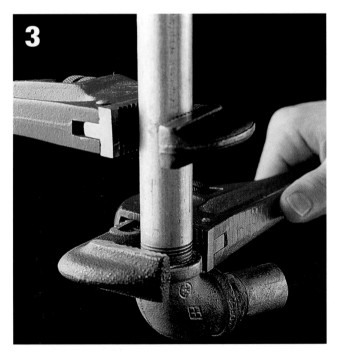

Remove any corroded fittings using two pipe wrenches. With jaws facing in opposite directions, use one wrench to turn fitting and the other to hold the pipe. Clean pipe threads with a wire brush.

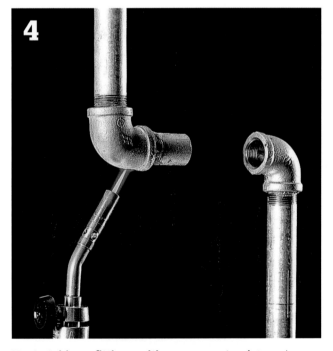

Heat stubborn fittings with a propane torch to make them easier to remove. Apply flame for 5 to 10 seconds. Protect wood and other flammable materials from heat, using a double layer of sheet metal.

(continued)

5

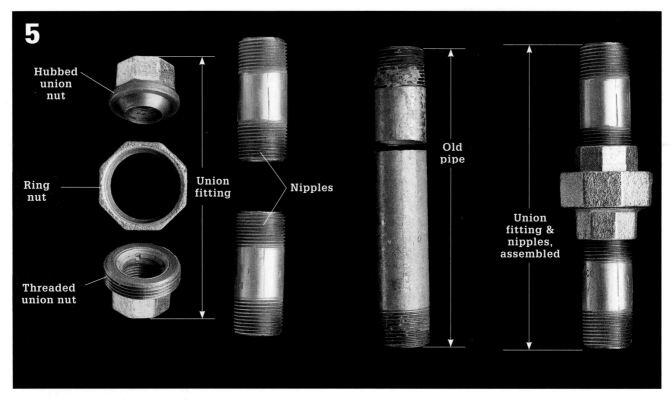

Hubbed
union
nut

Ring
nut

Threaded
union nut

Union
fitting

Nipples

Old
pipe

Union
fitting &
nipples,
assembled

Replace a section of galvanized iron pipe with a union fitting and two threaded pipes (nipples). When assembled, the union and nipples must equal the length of the pipe that is being replaced.

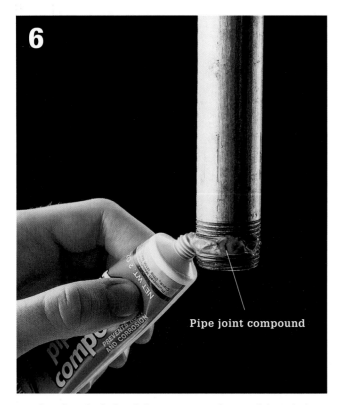

Pipe joint compound

Apply a bead of pipe joint compound around threaded ends of all pipes and nipples. Spread compound evenly over threads with fingertip.

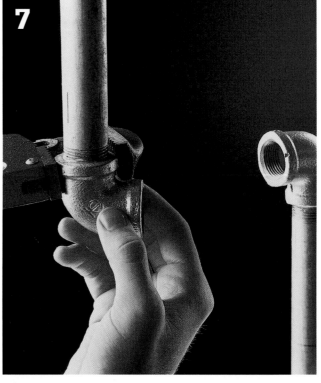

Screw new fittings onto pipe threads. Tighten fittings with two pipe wrenches, leaving them about ⅛ turn out of alignment to allow assembly of union.

Screw first nipple into fitting, and tighten with pipe wrench.

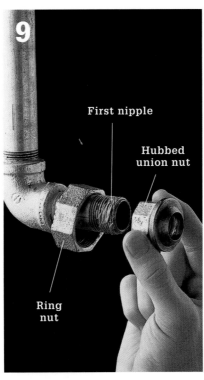

Slide ring nut onto the installed nipple, then screw the hubbed union nut onto the nipple and tighten with a pipe wrench.

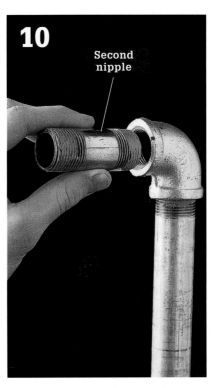

Screw second nipple onto other fitting. Tighten with a pipe wrench.

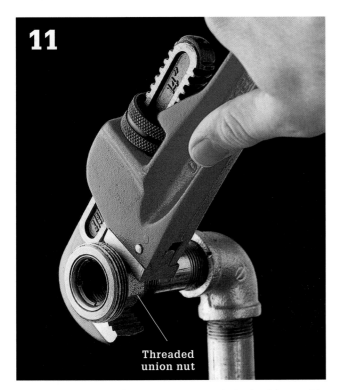

Screw threaded union nut onto second nipple. Tighten with a pipe wrench. Turn pipes into alignment, so that lip of hubbed union nut fits inside threaded union nut.

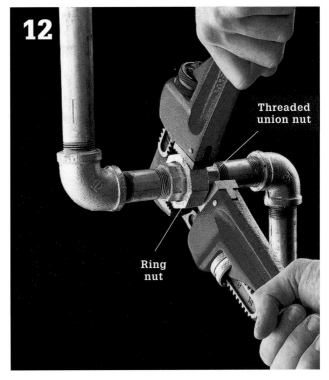

Complete the connection by screwing the ring nut onto the threaded union nut. Tighten ring nut with pipe wrenches.

Working with Cast Iron

Cast iron pipe often is found in older homes, where it is used for large DWV pipes, especially the main stack and sewer service lines. It can be identified by its dark color, rough surface, and large size. Cast iron pipes in home drains usually are 3" or more in diameter.

Cast iron pipes may rust through or hubbed fittings (below) may leak. If your house is more than 30 years old, you may find it necessary to replace a cast iron pipe or joint.

Cast iron is heavy and difficult to cut and fit. For this reason, leaky cast iron pipe usually is replaced with PVC of the same diameter. PVC can be joined to cast iron easily, using a banded coupling (below).

Snap cutters are the traditional tool of choice for cutting cast iron (see page 310), but today's variable-speed reciprocating saws do the job easily and safely. Use a long metal-cutting blade and set the saw at low speed. Wear eye and ear protection when cutting cast iron pipe.

Tools & Materials ▸

Tape measure
Chalk
Adjustable wrenches
Reciprocating
    saw (or rented
    snap cutter)
Ratchet wrench

Screwdriver
Riser clamps or
    strap hangers
Two wood blocks
2½" wallboard screws
Banded couplings
Plastic replacement pipe

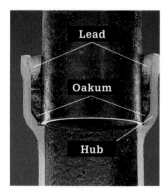

Hubbed fittings (shown cutaway, left) may be used to join old cast iron pipe. Hubbed pipe has a straight end and a flared end. The straight end of one pipe fits inside the hub of the next pipe. Joints are sealed with packing material (oakum) and lead. Repair leaky joints by cutting out the entire hubbed fitting and replacing with plastic pipe.

Banded couplings may be used to replace leaky cast iron with a PVC or ABS plastic pipe. The new plastic pipe is connected to the remaining cast iron pipe with banded coupling. Banded coupling has a neoprene sleeve that seals the joint. Pipes are held together with stainless steel bands and screw clamps.

Before cutting a horizontal run of cast iron drain pipe, make sure it is supported with strap hangers every 5 ft. and at every joint connection.

Before cutting a vertical run of cast iron pipe, make sure it is supported at every floor level with a riser clamp. Never cut apart pipe that is not supported.

How to Remove & Replace a Section of Cast Iron Pipe

Use chalk to mark cut lines on the cast iron pipe. If replacing a leaky hub, mark at least 6" on each side of hub.

Support lower section of pipe by installing a riser clamp flush against bottom plate or floor.

Support upper section of pipe by installing a riser clamp 6" above pipe section to be replaced. Attach wood blocks to the studs with 2½" wallboard screws, so that the riser clamp rests on tops of blocks.

(continued)

4

Wrap chain of the snap cutter around the pipe, so that the cutting wheels are against the chalk line.

5

Tighten the chain and snap the pipe according to the tool manufacturer's directions.

6

Repeat cutting at the other chalk line. Remove cut section of pipe.

7

Cut a length of PVC plastic pipe to be ½" shorter than the section of cast iron pipe that has been cut away.

8

Screw clamp

Banded coupling

Neoprene sleeve

Slip a banded coupling and a neoprene sleeve onto each end of the cast iron pipe.

9

Make sure the cast iron pipe is seated snugly against the rubber separator ring molded into the interior of the sleeve.

Fold back the end of each neoprene sleeve, until the molded separator ring on the inside of the sleeve is visible.

Separator ring

Position the new plastic pipe so it is aligned with the cast iron pipes.

Roll the ends of the neoprene sleeves over the ends of the new plastic pipe.

Slide stainless steel bands and clamps over the neoprene sleeves.

Tighten the screw clamps with a ratchet wrench or screwdriver.

Repairing Valves & Hose Bibs

Valves make it possible to shut off water at any point in the supply system. If a pipe breaks or a plumbing fixture begins to leak, you can shut off water to the damaged area so that it can be repaired. A hose bib is a faucet with a threaded spout, often used to connect rubber utility or appliance hoses.

Valves and hose bibs leak when washers or seals wear out. Replacement parts can be found in the same universal washer kits used to repair compression faucets. Coat replacement washers with heatproof grease to keep them soft and prevent cracking.

Remember to turn off the water before beginning work.

Tools & Materials ▸

Screwdriver
Adjustable wrench
Universal washer kit
Heatproof grease

How to Fix a Leaky Hose Bib

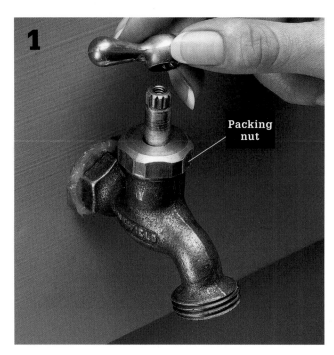

Remove the handle screw, and lift off the handle. Unscrew the packing nut with an adjustable wrench.

Unscrew the spindle from the valve body. Remove the stem screw and replace the stem washer. Replace the packing washer, and reassemble the valve.

Common Types of Valves

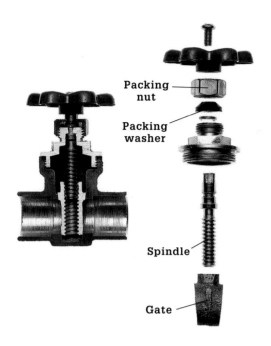

Gate valve has a movable brass wedge, or "gate," that screws up and down to control water flow. Gate valves may develop leaks around the handle. Repair leaks by replacing the packing washer or packing string found underneath the packing nut.

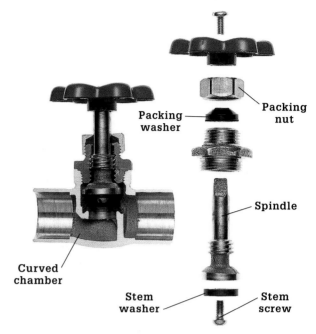

Globe valve has a curved chamber. Repair leaks around the handle by replacing the packing washer. If valve does not fully stop water flow when closed, replace the stem washer.

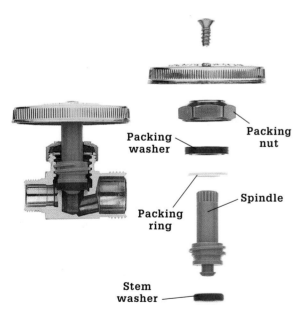

Shutoff valve controls water supply to one or more fixtures. A shutoff valve has a plastic spindle with a packing washer and a snap-on stem washer. Repair leaks around the handle by replacing the packing washer. If a valve does not fully stop water flow when closed, replace the stem washer. Shutoff valves with multiple outlets are available to supply several fixtures from a single supply.

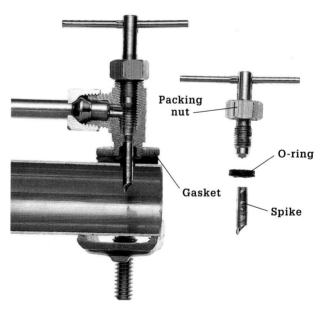

Saddle valve is a small fitting often specified to connect a refrigerator icemaker or sink-mounted water filter to copper pipe. A saddle valve contains a hollow spike that punctures the water pipe when valve is first closed. The fitting is sealed with a rubber gasket. Some codes prohibit their use. A dual-outlet shutoff valve or a T-fitting are better substitutes.

Installing & Repairing Sillcocks

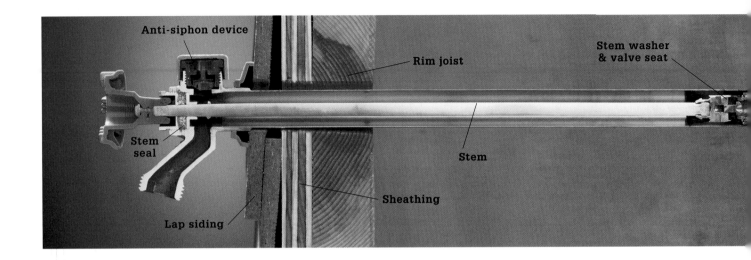

Anti-siphon device

Rim joist

Stem washer & valve seat

Stem seal

Stem

Sheathing

Lap siding

A sillcock is a compression faucet attached to the outside of the house. Repair a leaky sillcock by replacing the stem washer and the O-ring.

Sillcocks can be damaged by frost. To repair a ruptured pipe, see pages 404 to 405. To prevent pipes from rupturing, close the indoor shutoff valve at the start of the cold weather season, disconnect all garden hoses, and open the sillcock to let trapped water drain out.

A special frost-proof sillcock has a long stem that reaches at least 6" inside the house to protect it from cold. Install a sillcock so the pipe angles downward from the shutoff valve. This allows water to drain away each time the faucet is turned off.

Remember to turn off the water before beginning work.

Tools & Materials ▶

Screwdriver	Silicone caulk
Channel-type pliers	2" corrosion-
Pencil	resistant screws
Right-angle drill	Copper pipe
or standard drill	T-fitting
1" spade bit	Teflon tape
Caulk gun	Threaded adapter
Hacksaw or	Shutoff valve
tubing cutter	Emery cloth
Propane torch	Soldering paste
Universal washer kit	(flux)
Sillcock	Solder

How to Repair a Sillcock

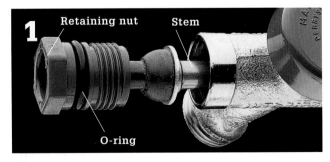

1

Retaining nut   Stem

O-ring

Remove sillcock handle, and loosen retaining nut with channel-type pliers. Remove stem. Replace O-ring found on retaining nut or stem.

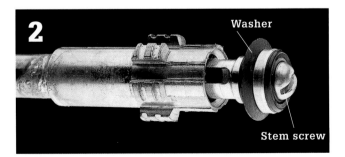

2

Washer

Stem screw

Remove the brass stem screw at the end of the stem, and replace the washer. Reassemble the sillcock.

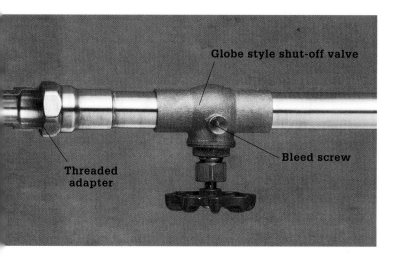

Globe style shut-off valve

Threaded adapter

Bleed screw

Frost-proof sillcock is mounted against the rim joist (sill) and has a long stem that reaches 6" to 30" inside the house to protect the valve from cold. A sillcock should angle downward slightly from the main toward the sill to provide drainage. The stem washer and O-ring (or packing string) can be replaced if the sillcock begins to leak. In a copper plumbing system, the sillcock is connected to a nearby cold water supply pipe with a threaded adapter, two lengths of soldered copper pipe, and a shutoff valve. A T-fitting (not shown) is used to tap into an existing cold water pipe.

How to Install a Frost-proof Sillcock

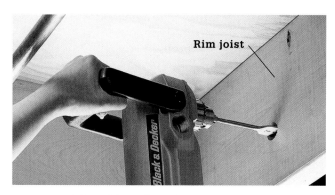

Rim joist

Locate position of hole for sillcock. From nearest cold water pipe, mark a point on rim joist that is slightly lower than water pipe. Drill a hole through the joist, sheathing, and siding, using a 1" spade bit.

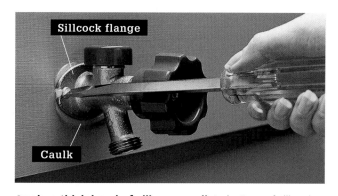

Sillcock flange

Caulk

Apply a thick bead of silicone caulk to bottom of sillcock flange, then insert sillcock into hole, and attach to siding with 2" corrosion-resistant screws. Turn handle to ON position. Wipe away excess caulk.

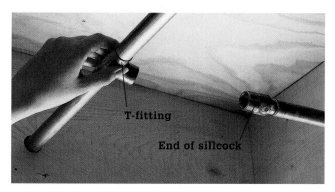

T-fitting

End of sillcock

Mark cold water pipe, then cut pipe and install a T-fitting. Wrap Teflon tape around threads of sillcock.

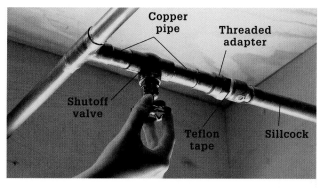

Copper pipe

Threaded adapter

Shutoff valve

Teflon tape

Sillcock

Join T-fitting to sillcock with threaded adapter, a shutoff valve, and two lengths of copper pipe. Prepare pipes and solder the joints. Turn on water, and close sillcock when water runs steadily.

Installing Pedestal Sinks

Pedestal sinks move in and out of popularity more frequently than other sink types, but even during times they aren't particularly trendy they retain fairly stable demand. You'll find them most frequently in small half baths, where their small footprint makes them an efficient choice. Designers are also discovering the appeal of tandem pedestal sinks of late, where the smaller profiles allow for his-and-hers sinks that don't dominate visually.

The primary drawback to pedestal sinks is that they don't offer any storage. Their chief practical benefit is that they conceal plumbing some homeowners would prefer not to see.

Pedestal sinks are mounted in two ways. Most of the more inexpensive ones you'll find at home stores are hung in the manner of wall–hung sinks. The pedestal is actually installed after the sink is hung and its purpose is only decorative. But other pedestal sinks (typically on the higher end of the design scale) have structurally important pedestals that do most or all of the bearing for the sink.

Pedestal sinks are available in a variety of styles and are a perfect fit for small half baths. They keep plumbing hidden, lending a neat, contained look to the bathroom.

How to Install a Pedestal Sink

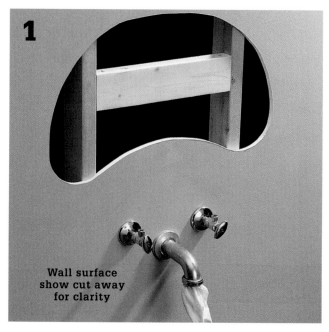

Install 2 × 4 blocking between the wall studs, behind the planned sink location. Cover the wall with water-resistant drywall.

Set the basin and pedestal in position and brace it with 2 × 4s. Outline the top of the basin on the wall, and mark the base of the pedestal on the floor. Mark reference points on the wall and floor through the mounting holes found on the back of the sink and the bottom of the pedestal.

Set aside the basin and pedestal. Drill pilot holes in the wall and floor at the reference points, then reposition the pedestal. Anchor the pedestal to the floor with lag screws.

Attach the faucet, then set the sink on the pedestal. Align the holes in the back of the sink with the pilot holes drilled in the wall, then drive lag screws and washers into the wall brace using a ratchet wrench. Do not overtighten the screws.

Hook up the drain and supply fittings. Caulk between the back of the sink and the wall when installation is finished.

Installing Integral Vanity Tops

Most bathroom countertops installed today are integral (one-piece) sink-countertop units made from cultured marble or other solid materials, like solid surfacing. Integral sink/countertops are convenient, and many are inexpensive, but style and color options are limited.

Some remodelers and designers still prefer the distinctive look of a custom-built countertop with a self-rimming sink basin, which gives you a much greater selection of styles and colors. Installing a self-rimming sink is very simple.

Integral sink-countertops are made in standard sizes to fit common vanity widths. Because the sink and countertop are cast from the same material, integral sink-countertops do not leak, and do not require extensive caulking and sealing.

Tools & Materials ▸

Pencil
Scissors
Carpenter's level
Screwdriver
Channel-type pliers
Ratchet wrench

Basin wrench
Cardboard
Masking tape
Plumber's putty
Lag screws
Tub & tile caulk

How to Install a Vanity Cabinet

1

Pop-up drain lever

Drain flange

Set the sink-countertop unit onto sawhorses. Attach the faucet and slip the drain lever through the faucet body. Place a ring of plumber's putty around the drain flange, then insert the flange in the drain opening.

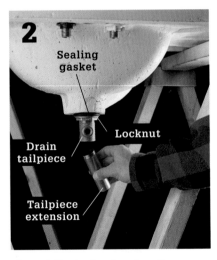

2

Sealing gasket

Locknut

Drain tailpiece

Tailpiece extension

Thread the locknut and sealing gasket onto the drain tailpiece, then insert the tailpiece into the drain opening and screw it onto the drain flange. Tighten the locknut securely. Attach the tailpiece extension. Insert the pop-up stopper linkage.

3

Apply a layer of tub & tile caulk (or adhesive, if specified by the countertop manufacturer) to the top edges of the cabinet vanity, and to any corner braces.

Center the sink-countertop unit over the vanity, so the overhang is equal on both sides and the backsplash of the countertop is flush with the wall. Press the countertop evenly into the caulk.

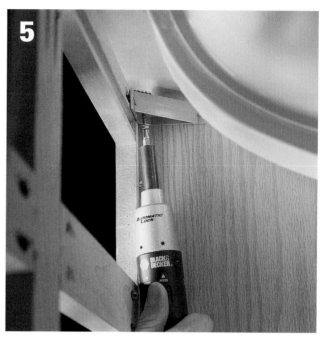

Cabinets with corner braces: Secure the counter-top to the cabinet by driving a mounting screw through each corner brace and up into the countertop. *Note: Cultured marble and other hard countertops require predrilling and a plastic screw sleeve.*

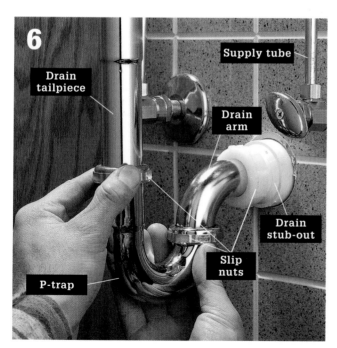

Supply tube

Drain tailpiece

Drain arm

Drain stub-out

Slip nuts

P-trap

Attach the drain arm to the drain stub-out in the wall, using a slip nut. Attach one end of the P-trap to the drain arm, and the other to the tailpiece of the sink drain, using slip nuts. Connect supply tubes to the faucet tailpieces.

Seal the gap between the backsplash and the wall with tub & tile caulk.

Installing a Drop-In Kitchen Sink

Most drop-in, self-rimming kitchen sinks are easily installed.

Drop-in sinks for do-it-yourself installation are made from cast iron coated with enamel, stainless steel, enameled steel, acrylic, fiberglass or resin composites. Because cast-iron sinks are heavy, their weight holds them in place and they require no mounting hardware. Except for the heavy lifting, they are easy to install. Stainless steel and enameled-steel sinks weigh less than cast-iron and most require mounting brackets on the underside of the countertop. Some acrylic and resin sinks rely on silicone caulk to hold them in place.

If you are replacing a sink, but not the countertop, make sure the new sink is the same size or larger. All old silicone caulk residue must be removed with acetone or denatured alcohol, or else the new caulk will not stick.

Tools & Materials ▸

Caulk gun
Spud wrench
Screwdriver
Sink
Sink frame

Plumber's putty or
    silicone caulk
Mounting clips
Jigsaw
Pen or pencil

Shopping Tips ▸

- When purchasing a sink you also need to buy strainer bodies and baskets, sink clips and a drain trap kit.
- Look for basin dividers that are lower than the sink rim—this reduces splashing.
- Drain holes in the back or to the side make for more usable space under the sink.
- When choosing a sink, make sure the predrilled openings will fit your faucet.

Drop-in sinks, also known as self-rimming sinks, have a wide sink flange that extends beyond the edges of the sink cutout. They also have a wide back flange to which the faucet is mounted directly.

How to Install a Self-rimming Sink

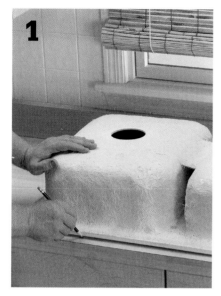

Invert the sink and trace around the edges as a reference for making the sink cutout cutting lines, which should be parallel to the outlines, but about 1" inside of them to create a 1" ledge. If your sink comes with a template for the cutout, use it.

Drill a starter hole and cut out the sink opening with a jigsaw. Cut right up to the line. Because the sink flange fits over the edges of the cutout, the opening doesn't need to be perfect, but as always you should try to do a nice, neat job.

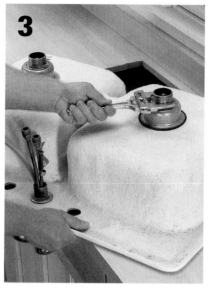

Attach as much of the plumbing as makes sense to install prior to setting the sink into the opening. Having access to the underside of the flange is a great help when it comes to attaching the faucet body, sprayer and strainer, in particular.

Apply a bead of silicone caulk around the edges of the sink opening. The sink flange most likely is not flat, so try and apply the caulk in the area that will make contact with the flange.

Place the sink in the opening. Try and get the sink centered right away so you don't need to move it around and disturb the caulk, which can break the seal. If you are installing a heavy cast-iron sink, it's best to leave the strainers off so you can grab onto the sink at the drain openings.

For sinks with mounting clips, tighten the clips from below using a screwdriver or wrench (depending on the type of clip your sink has). There should be at least three clips on every side. Don't overtighten the clips—this can cause the sink flange to flatten or become warped.

Fixing Leaky Faucets

A leaky faucet is the most common home plumbing problem. Leaks occur when washers, O-rings, or seals inside the faucet are dirty or worn. Fixing leaks is easy, but the techniques for making repairs will vary, depending on the design of the faucet. Before beginning work, you must first identify your faucet design and determine what replacement parts are needed.

There are four basic faucet designs: ball-type, cartridge, disc, and compression. Many faucets can be identified easily by outer appearance, but others must be taken apart before the design can be recognized.

The compression design is used in many double-handle faucets. Compression faucets all have washers or seals that must be replaced from time to time. These repairs are easy to make, and replacement parts are inexpensive.

Ball-type, cartridge, and disc faucets are all known as washerless faucets. Many washerless faucets are controlled with a single handle, although some cartridge models use two handles. Washerless faucets are more trouble-free than compression faucets and are designed for quick repair.

When installing new faucet parts, make sure the replacements match the original parts. Replacement parts for popular washerless faucets are identified by brand name and model number. To ensure a correct selection, you may want to bring the worn parts to the store for comparison.

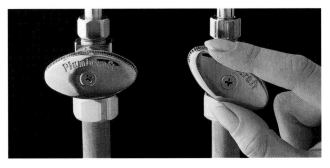

Turn off water before starting any faucet repair, using shutoff valves underneath faucet, or main service valve found near the water meter. When opening shutoff valves after finishing repairs, keep faucet handle in open position to release trapped air. When water runs steadily, close faucet.

Typical faucet has a single handle attached to a hollow cartridge. The cartridge controls hot and cold water flowing from the supply tubes into the mixing chamber. Water is forced out the spout and through the aerator. When repairs are needed, replace the entire cartridge.

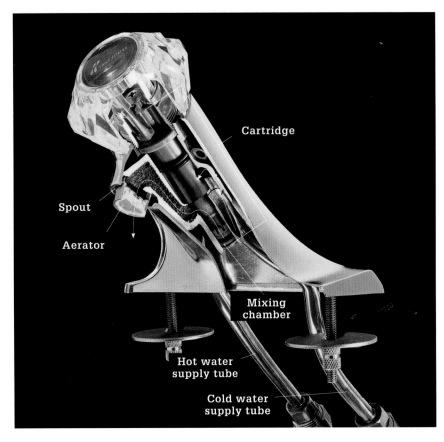

Cartridge

Spout

Aerator

Mixing chamber

Hot water supply tube

Cold water supply tube

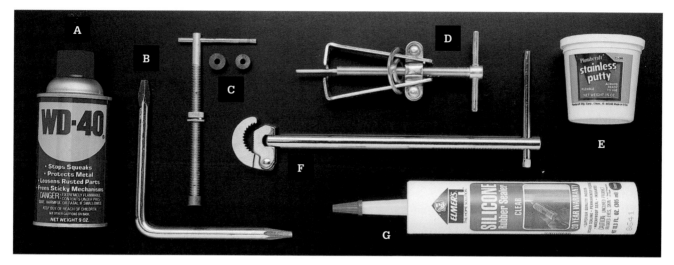

Specialty tools and materials for faucet repairs include penetrating oil (A), seat wrench (B), seat-dressing (reamer) tool (C), handle puller (D), plumber's putty (E), basin wrench (F), silicone caulk (G).

How to Identify Faucet Designs

Ball-type faucet has a single handle over a dome-shaped cap. If your single-handle faucet is made by Delta or Peerless, it is probably a ball-type faucet. See pages 324 to 325 to fix a ball-type faucet.

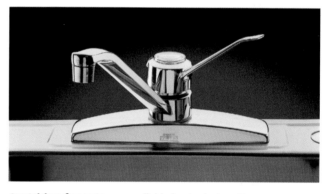

Cartridge faucets are available in single-handle or double-handle models. Popular cartridge faucet brands include Price Pfister, Moen, Valley, and Aqualine. See pages 326 to 327 to fix a cartridge faucet.

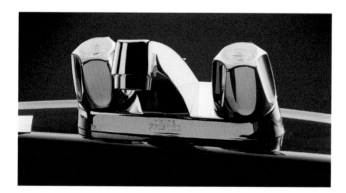

Compression faucet has two handles. When shutting the faucet off, you usually can feel a rubber washer being squeezed inside the faucet. Compression faucets are sold under many brand names. See pages 328 to 329 to fix a compression faucet.

Disc faucet has a single handle and a solid, chromed-brass body. If your faucet is made by American Standard or Reliant, it may be a disc faucet. See pages 332 to 333 to fix a disc faucet.

Fixing Ball-type Faucets

A ball-type faucet has a single handle and is identified by the hollow metal or plastic ball inside the faucet body. Many ball-type faucets have a rounded cap with knurled edges located under the handle. If your faucet leaks from the spout and has this type of cap, first try tightening the cap with channel-type pliers. If tightening does not fix the leak, disassemble the faucet and install replacement parts.

Faucet manufacturers offer several types of replacement kits for ball-type faucets. Some kits contain only the springs and neoprene valve seats, while better kits also include the cam and cam washer.

Replace the rotating ball only if it is obviously worn or scratched. Replacement balls are either metal or plastic. Metal balls are slightly more expensive than plastic but are more durable.

Remember to turn off the water before beginning work.

Tools & Materials ▸

Channel-type pliers
Allen wrench
Screwdriver
Utility knife
Ball-type faucet
  repair kit
New rotating ball
  (if needed)
Masking tape
O-rings
Heatproof grease

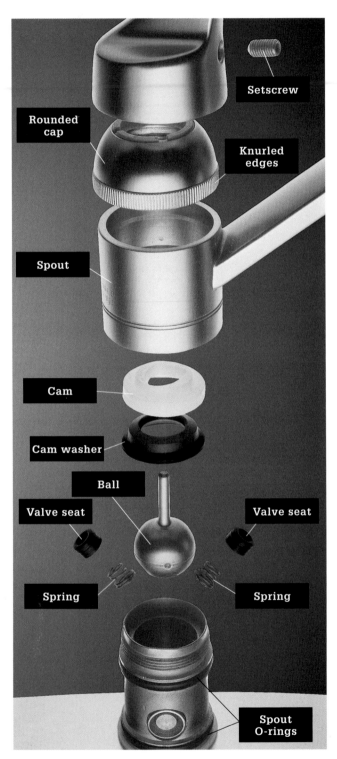

Repair kit for a ball-type faucet includes rubber valve seats, springs, cam, cam washer, and spout O-rings. Kit may also include small Allen wrench tool used to remove faucet handle. Make sure kit is made for your faucet model. Replacement ball can be purchased separately but is not needed unless old ball is obviously worn.

Ball-type faucet has a hollow ball that controls the temperature and flow of water. Dripping at the faucet spout is caused by worn-out valve seats, springs, or a damaged ball. Leaks around the base of the faucet are caused by worn O-rings.

How to Fix a Ball-type Faucet

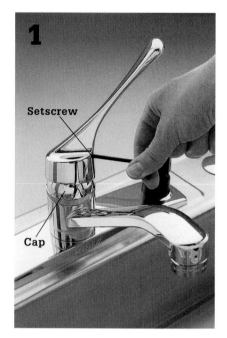

Loosen handle setscrew with an Allen wrench. Remove handle to expose faucet cap.

Remove the cap with channel-type pliers. To prevent scratches to the shiny chromed finish, wrap masking tape around the jaws of the pliers.

Lift out the faucet cam, cam washer, and the rotating ball. Check the ball for signs of wear.

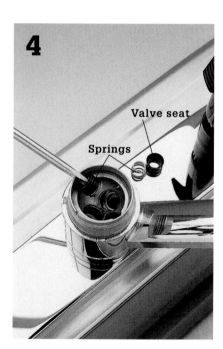

Reach into the faucet with a screwdriver and remove the old springs and neoprene valve seats.

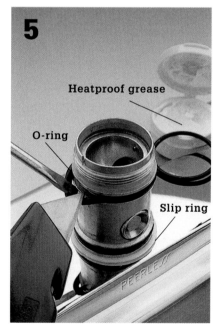

Remove spout by twisting it upward, then cut off old O-rings. Coat new O-rings with heatproof grease and install. Reattach spout, pressing downward until the collar rests on plastic slip ring. Install new springs and valve seats.

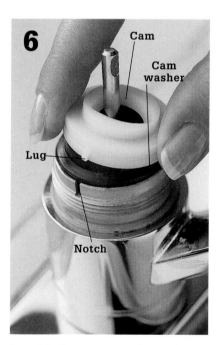

Insert ball, new cam washer, and cam. Small lug on cam should fit into notch on faucet body. Screw cap onto faucet and attach handle.

Fixing Cartridge Faucets

A cartridge faucet is identified by the narrow metal or plastic cartridge inside the faucet body. Many single-handed faucets and some double-handle models use cartridge designs.

Replacing a cartridge is an easy repair that will fix most faucet leaks. Faucet cartridges come in many styles, so you may want to bring the old cartridge along for comparison when shopping for a replacement.

Make sure to insert the new cartridge so it is aligned in the same way as the old cartridge. If the hot and cold water controls are reversed, take the faucet apart and rotate the cartridge 180°.

Remember to turn off the water before beginning work.

Tools & Materials ▸

Screwdriver
Channel-type pliers
Utility knife

Replacement cartridge
O-rings
Heat-proof grease

Replacement cartridges come in dozens of styles.
Cartridges are available for popular faucet brands, including (from left) Price-Pfister, Moen, and Kohler. O-ring kits may be sold separately.

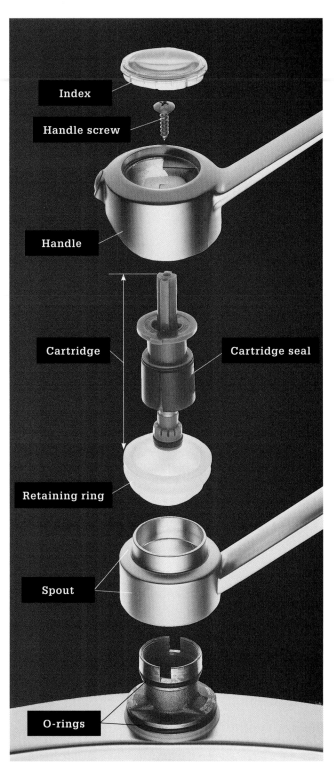

Cartridge faucet has a hollow cartridge insert that lifts and rotates to control the flow and temperature of water. Dripping at the spout occurs when the cartridge seals become worn. Leaks around the base of the faucet are caused by worn O-rings.

How to Fix a Cartridge Faucet

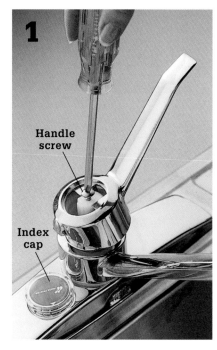

Pry off the index cap on top of faucet, and remove the handle screw underneath the cap.

Remove faucet handle by lifting it up and tilting it backwards.

Remove the threaded retaining ring with channel-type pliers. Remove any retaining clip holding cartridge in place.

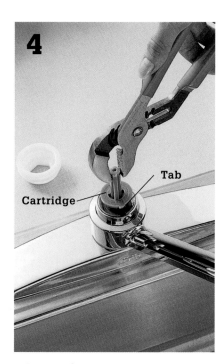

Grip top of the cartridge with channel-type pliers. Pull straight up to remove cartridge. Install replacement cartridge so that tab on cartridge faces forward.

Remove the spout by pulling up and twisting, then cut off old O-rings with a utility knife. Coat new O-rings with heatproof grease, and install.

Reattach the spout. Screw the retaining ring onto the faucet, and tighten with channel-type pliers. Attach the handle, handle screw, and index cap.

Fixing Compression Faucets

Compression faucets have separate controls for hot and cold water and are identified by the threaded stem assemblies inside the faucet body. Compression stems come in many different styles, but all have some type of neoprene washer or seal to control water flow. Compression faucets leak when stem washers and seals become worn.

Older compression faucets often have corroded handles that are difficult to remove. A specialty tool called a handle puller makes this job easier. Handle pullers may be available at rental centers.

When replacing washers, also check the condition of the metal valve seats inside the faucet body. If the valve seats feel rough, they should be replaced or resurfaced.

Remember to turn off the water before beginning work.

Tools & Materials ▸

Screwdriver
Handle puller
    (if needed)
Channel-type
    pliers
Utility knife

Seat wrench or seat-
    dressing tool (if needed)
Universal washer kit
Packing string
Heatproof grease
Replacement valve seats
    (if needed)

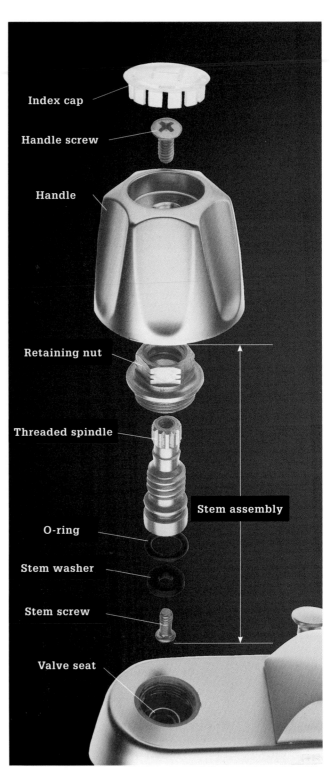

A **compression faucet** has a stem assembly that includes a retaining nut, threaded spindle, O-ring, stem washer, and stem screw. Dripping at the spout occurs when the washer becomes worn. Leaks around the handle are caused by a worn O-ring.

Labels: Index cap, Handle screw, Handle, Retaining nut, Threaded spindle, Stem assembly, O-ring, Stem washer, Stem screw, Valve seat

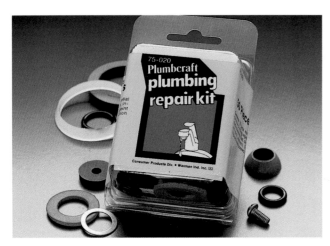

Universal washer kit contains parts needed to fix most types of compression faucets. Choose a kit that has an assortment of neoprene washers, O-rings, packing washers, and brass stem screws.

Tips for Fixing a Compression Faucet ▸

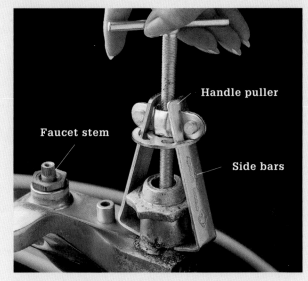

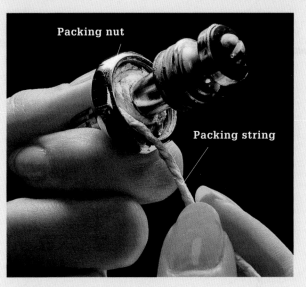

Remove stubborn handles with a handle puller. Remove the faucet index cap and handle screw, and clamp the side bars of the puller under the handle. Thread the puller into the faucet stem, and tighten until the handle comes free.

Packing string is used instead of an O-ring on some faucets. To fix leaks around the faucet handle, wrap new packing string around the stem, just underneath the packing nut or retaining nut.

Three Common Types of Compression Stems

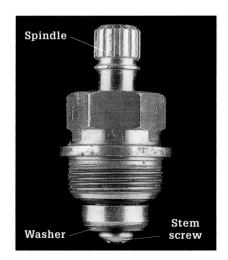

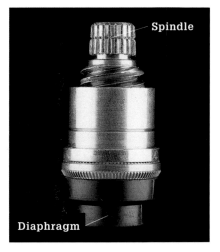

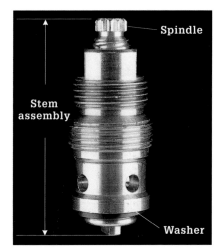

Standard stem has a brass stem screw that holds either a flat or beveled neoprene washer to the end of the spindle. If stem screw is worn, it should be replaced.

Tophat stem has a snap-on neoprene diaphragm instead of a standard washer. Fix leaks by replacing the diaphragm.

Reverse-pressure stem has a beveled washer at the end of the spindle. To replace washer, unscrew spindle from rest of the stem assembly. Some stems have a small nut that holds washer.

How to Fix a Compression Faucet

Remove index cap from top of faucet handle, and remove handle screw. Remove handle by pulling straight up. If necessary, use a handle puller to remove handle (page 329).

Unscrew the stem assembly from body of faucet, using channel-type pliers. Inspect valve seat for wear, and replace or resurface as needed (page opposite). If faucet body or stems are badly worn, it usually is best to replace the faucet.

Remove the brass stem screw from the stem assembly. Remove worn stem washer.

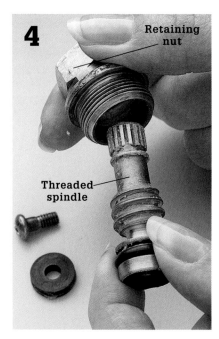

Unscrew the threaded spindle from the retaining nut.

Cut off O-ring and replace with an exact duplicate. Install new washer and stem screw. Coat all parts with heatproof grease, then reassemble the faucet.

How to Replace Worn Valve Seats

Check valve seat for damage by running a fingertip around the rim of the seat. If the valve seat feels rough, replace the seat, or resurface it with a seat-dressing (reamer) tool (below).

Seat wrench

Remove valve seat, using a seat wrench. Select end of wrench that fits seat, and insert into faucet. Turn counterclockwise to remove seat, then install an exact duplicate. If seat cannot be removed, resurface with a seat-dressing tool (below).

How to Resurface Valve Seats

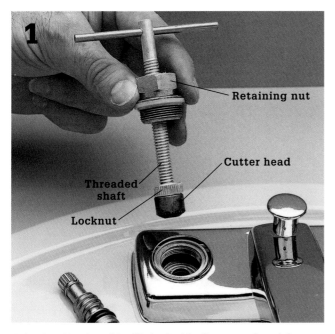

Retaining nut

Cutter head

Threaded shaft

Locknut

Select cutter head to fit the inside diameter of retaining nut. Slide retaining nut over threaded shaft of seat-dressing tool, then attach the locknut and cutter head to the shaft.

Retaining nut

Screw retaining nut loosely into faucet body. Press the tool down lightly and turn tool handle clockwise two or three rotations. Reassemble faucet.

Fixing Disc Faucets

A disc faucet has a single handle and is identified by the wide cylinder inside the faucet body. The cylinder contains a pair of closely fitting ceramic discs that control the flow of water.

A ceramic disc faucet is a top-quality fixture that is easy to repair. Leaks usually can be fixed by lifting out the cylinder and cleaning the neoprene seals and the cylinder openings. Install a new cylinder only if the faucet continues to leak after cleaning.

After making repairs to a disc faucet, make sure handle is in the ON position, then open the shutoff valves slowly. Otherwise, ceramic discs can be cracked by the sudden release of air from the faucet. When water runs steadily, close the faucet.

Remember to turn off the water before beginning work.

Tools & Materials ▸

Screwdriver
Fiber abrasive pad

Replacement cylinder (if needed).

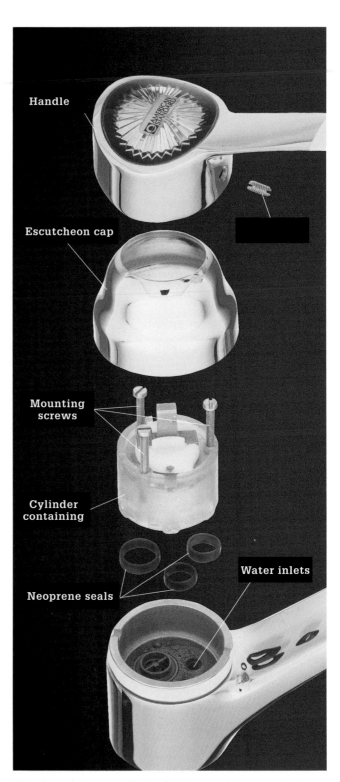

Disc faucet has a sealed cylinder containing two closely fitting ceramic discs. Faucet handle controls water by sliding the discs into alignment. Dripping at the spout occurs when the neoprene seals or cylinder openings are dirty.

Labels: Handle, Escutcheon cap, Mounting screws, Cylinder containing, Neoprene seals, Water inlets

Replacement cylinder for disc faucet is necessary only if faucet continues to leak after cleaning. Continuous leaking is caused by cracked or scratched ceramic discs. Replacement cylinders come with neoprene seals and mounting screws.

How to Fix a Ceramic Disc Faucet

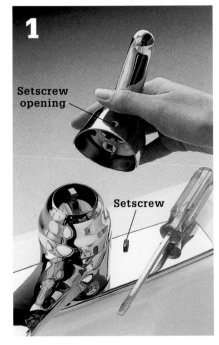

Rotate faucet spout to the side, and raise the handle. Remove the setscrew and lift off the handle.

Remove the escutcheon cap. Remove cartridge mounting screws, and lift out the cylinder.

Remove the neoprene seals from the cylinder openings.

Clean the cylinder openings and the neoprene seals with an abrasive pad. Rinse cylinder with clear water.

Return seals to the cylinder openings, and reassemble faucet. Move handle to ON position, then slowly open shutoff valves. When water runs steadily, close faucet.

Install a new cylinder only if the faucet continues to leak after cleaning.

Replacing a Sink Faucet

Installing a new faucet is an easy project that takes about one hour. Before buying a new faucet, first find the diameter of the sink openings, and then measure the distance between the tailpieces (measured on-center). Make sure the tailpieces of the new faucet match the sink openings.

When shopping for a new faucet, choose a model made by a reputable manufacturer. Replacement parts for a well-known brand will be easy to find if the faucet ever needs repairs. Better faucets have solid brass bodies. They are easy to install and provide years of trouble-free service. Some washerless models have lifetime warranties.

Always install new supply tubes when replacing a faucet. Old supply tubes should not be reused. Most codes accept the use of manufactured PB plastic supply tubes for exposed, undersink supply tubes.

If water pipes underneath the sink do not have shutoff valves, you may choose to install the valves while replacing the faucet.

Remember to turn off the water before beginning work.

Tools & Materials ▸

Basin wrench or channel-type pliers
Putty knife
Caulk gun
Adjustable wrenches
Penetrating oil
Silicone caulk or plumber's putty
Two flexible supply tubes

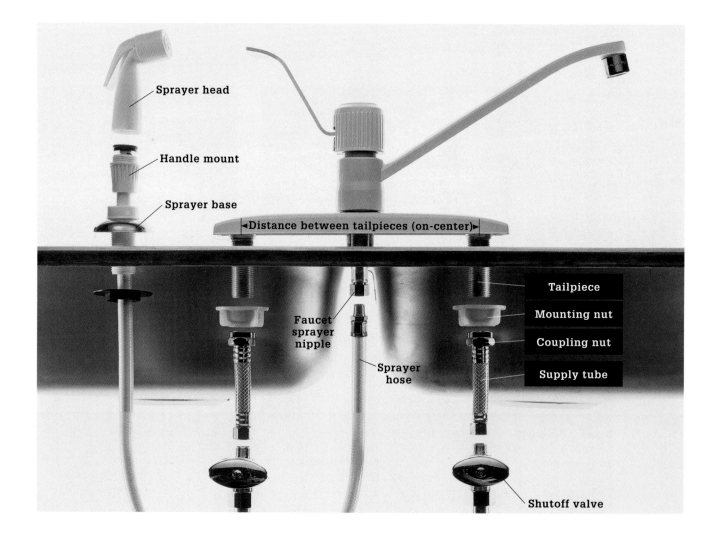

Sprayer head
Handle mount
Sprayer base
◂Distance between tailpieces (on-center)▸
Faucet sprayer nipple
Sprayer hose
Tailpiece
Mounting nut
Coupling nut
Supply tube
Shutoff valve

How to Remove an Old Sink Faucet

Spray penetrating oil on tailpiece mounting nuts and supply tube coupling nuts. Remove the coupling nuts with a basin wrench or channel-type pliers.

Remove the tailpiece mounting nuts with a basin wrench or channel-type pliers. Basin wrench has a long handle that makes it easy to work in tight areas.

Remove faucet. Use a putty knife to clean away old putty from surface of sink.

Faucet Hookup Variations

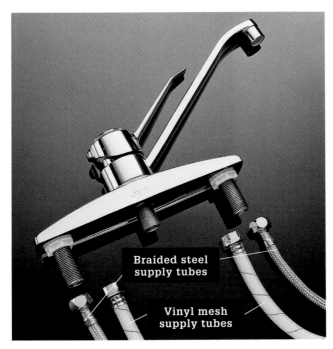

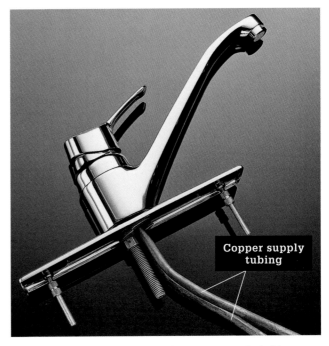

New faucet without supply tubes: Buy two supply tubes. Supply tubes are available in braided steel or vinyl mesh (shown above), PB plastic (acceptable by most codes for exposed supply lines), or chromed copper.

New faucet with preattached copper supply tubing: Make water connections by attaching the supply tubing directly to the shutoff valves with compression fittings.

How to Install a New Sink Faucet

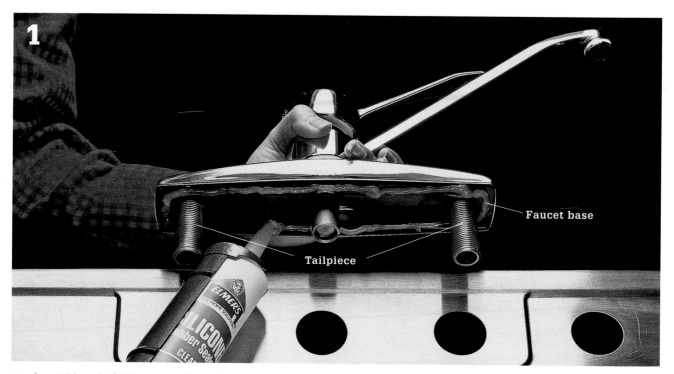

1

Faucet base

Tailpiece

Apply a ¼" bead of silicone caulk or plumber's putty around the base of the faucet. Insert the faucet tailpieces into the sink openings. Position the faucet so base is parallel to back of sink, and press the faucet down to make sure caulk forms a good seal.

2

Friction washer

Mounting nut

Screw the metal friction washers and the mounting nuts onto the tailpieces, then tighten with a basin wrench or channel-type pliers. Wipe away excess caulk around base of faucet.

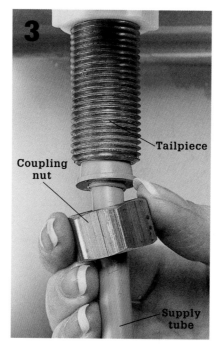

3

Tailpiece

Coupling nut

Supply tube

Connect flexible supply tubes to faucet tailpieces. Tighten coupling nuts with a basin wrench or channel-type pliers.

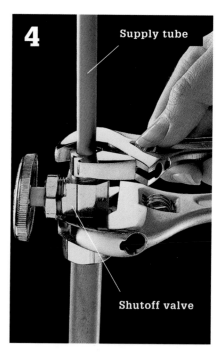

4

Supply tube

Shutoff valve

Attach supply tubes to shut-off valves, using compression fittings (pages 300 to 301). Hand-tighten nuts, then use an adjustable wrench to tighten nuts ¼ turn. If necessary, hold valve with another wrench while tightening.

How to Connect a Faucet with Preattached Supply Tubing

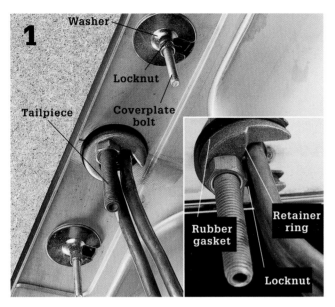

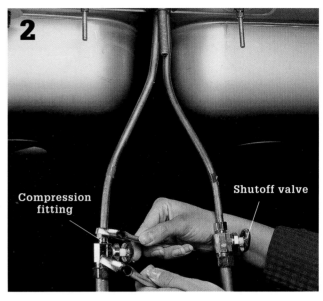

Attach faucet to sink by placing rubber gasket, retainer ring, and locknut onto threaded tailpiece. Tighten locknut with a basin wrench or channel-type pliers. Some center-mounted faucets have a decorative coverplate. Secure coverplate from underneath with washers and locknuts screwed onto coverplate bolts.

Connect preattached supply tubing to shutoff valves with compression fittings (pages 300 to 301). Red-coded tube should be attached to the hot water pipe, blue-coded tube to the cold water pipe.

How to Attach a Sink Sprayer

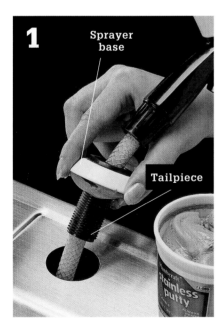

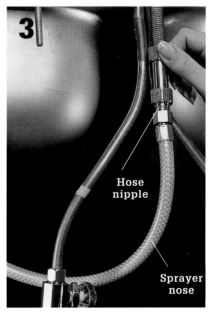

Apply a ¼" bead of plumber's putty or silicone caulk to bottom edge of sprayer base. Insert tailpiece of sprayer base into sink opening.

Place friction washer over tailpiece. Screw the mounting nut onto tailpiece and tighten with a basin wrench or channel-type pliers. Wipe away excess putty around base of sprayer.

Screw sprayer hose onto the hose nipple on the bottom of the faucet. Tighten ¼ turn, using a basin wrench or channel-type pliers.

Installing Shutoff Valves & Supply Tubes

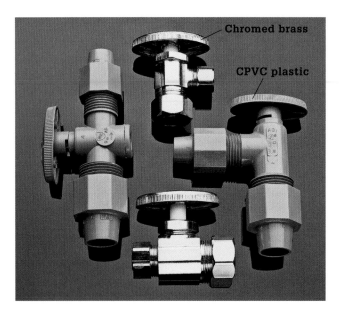

Shutoff valves allow you to shut off the water to an individual fixture so it can be repaired. They can be made from durable chromed brass or lightweight plastic. Shutoff valves come in ½" and ¾" diameters to match common water pipe sizes.

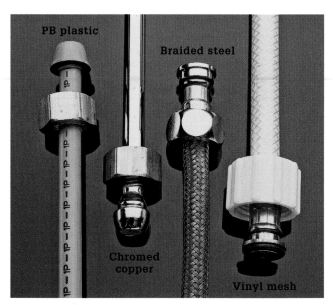

Supply tubes are used to connect water pipes to faucets, toilets, and other fixtures. They come in 12", 20", and 30" lengths. PB plastic and chromed copper tubes are inexpensive. Braided steel and vinyl mesh supply tubes are easy to install.

Worn-out shutoff valves or supply tubes can cause water to leak underneath a sink or other fixture. First, try tightening the fittings with an adjustable wrench. If this does not fix the leak, replace the shutoff valves and supply tubes.

Shutoff valves are available in several fitting types. For copper pipes, valves with compression-type fittings are easiest to install. For plastic pipes, use grip-type valves. For galvanized iron pipes, use valves with female threads.

Older plumbing systems often were installed without fixture shutoff valves. When repairing or replacing plumbing fixtures, you may want to install shutoff valves if they are not already present.

Tools & Materials ▸

Hacksaw
Tubing cutter
Adjustable wrench
Tubing bender
Felt-tipped pen
Shutoff valves
Supply tubes
Pipe joint compound

How to Install Shutoff Valves & Supply Tubes

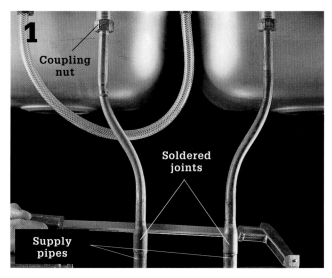

Turn off water at the main shutoff valve. Remove old supply pipes. If pipes are soldered copper, cut them off just below the soldered joint, using a hacksaw or tubing cutter. Make sure the cuts are straight. Unscrew the coupling nuts and discard the old pipes.

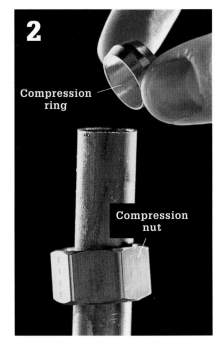

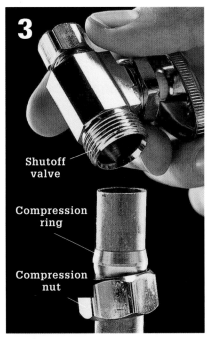

Slide a compression nut and compression ring over copper water pipe. Threads of nut should face end of pipe.

Apply pipe joint compound to the threads of the shutoff valve or compression nut. Screw the compression nut onto the shutoff valve and tighten with an adjustable wrench.

Bend chromed copper supply tube to reach from the tailpiece of the fixture to the shutoff valve, using a tubing bender. Bend the tube slowly to avoid kinking the metal.

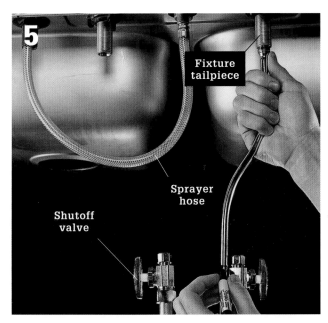

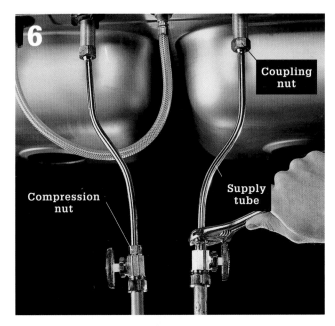

Position the supply tube between fixture tailpiece and shutoff valve, and mark tube to length. Cut supply tube with a tubing cutter.

Attach bell-shaped end of supply tube to fixture tailpiece with coupling nut, then attach other end to shutoff valve with compression ring and nut (pages 300 to 301). Tighten all fittings with adjustable wrench.

Fixing Sprayers & Aerators

If water pressure from a sink sprayer seems low, or if water leaks from the handle, it is usually because lime buildup and sediment have blocked small openings inside the sprayer head. To fix the problem, first take the sprayer head apart and clean the parts. If cleaning the sprayer head does not help, the problem may be caused by a faulty diverter valve. The diverter valve inside the faucet body shifts water flow from the faucet spout to the sprayer when the sprayer handle is pressed. Cleaning or replacing the diverter valve may fix water pressure problems.

Whenever making repairs to a sink sprayer, check the sprayer hose for kinks or cracks. A damaged hose should be replaced.

If water pressure from a faucet spout seems low, or if the flow is partially blocked, take the spout aerator apart and clean the parts. The aerator is a screw-on attachment with a small wire screen that mixes tiny air bubbles into the water flow. Make sure the wire screen is not clogged with sediment and lime buildup. If water pressure is low throughout the house, it may be because galvanized iron water pipes are corroded. Corroded pipes should be replaced with copper.

Clean faucet aerators and sink sprayers to fix most low water-pressure problems. Take aerator or sprayer head apart, then use a small brush dipped in vinegar to remove sediment.

How to Fix a Diverter Valve

Shut off the water. Remove the faucet handle and the spout (see directions for your faucet type, pages 322 to 333).

Pull diverter valve from faucet body with needlenose pliers. Use a small brush dipped in vinegar to clean lime buildup and debris from valve.

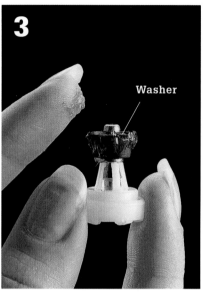

Replace any worn O-rings or washers if possible. Coat the new parts with heatproof grease, then reinstall the diverter valve and reassemble the faucet.

How to Replace a Sprayer Hose

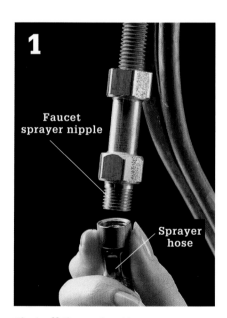

Shut off the water. Unscrew sprayer hose from faucet sprayer nipple, using channel-type pliers. Pull sprayer hose through sink opening.

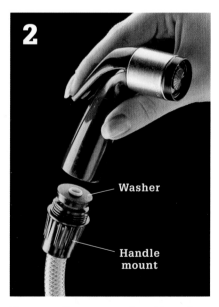

Unscrew the sprayer head from the handle mount. Remove washer.

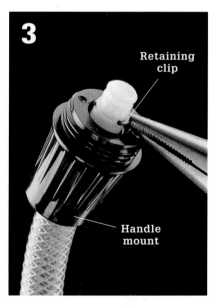

Remove retaining clip with needle-nose pliers; discard old hose. Attach handle mount, retaining clip, washer, and sprayer head to new hose. Attach sprayer hose to faucet sprayer nipple on faucet.

Tub & Shower Plumbing

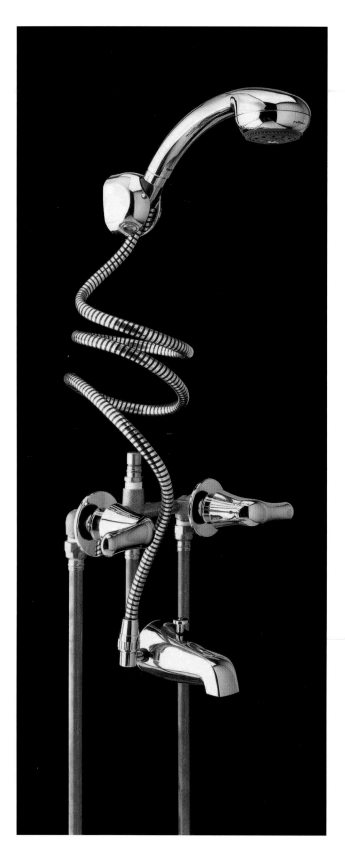

Tub and shower faucets have the same basic designs as sink faucets, and the techniques for repairing leaks are the same as described in the faucet repair section of this book (pages 322 to 333). To identify your faucet design, you may have to take off the handle and disassemble the faucet.

When a tub and shower are combined, the showerhead and the tub spout share the same hot and cold water supply lines and handles. Combination faucets are available as three-handle, two-handle, or single-handle types (below). The number of handles gives clues as to the design of the faucets and the kinds of repairs that may be necessary.

Tub & Shower Combination Faucets

Three-handle faucet (pages 344 to 345) has valves that are either compression or cartridge design.

With combination faucets, a diverter valve or gate diverter is used to direct water flow to the tub spout or the showerhead. On three-handle faucet types, the middle handle controls a diverter valve. If water does not shift easily from tub to showerhead, or if water continues to run out the spout when the shower is on, the diverter valve probably needs to be cleaned and repaired (page 345).

Two-handle and single-handle types use a gate diverter that is operated by a pull lever or knob on the tub spout. Although gate diverters rarely need repair, the lever occasionally may break, come loose, or refuse to stay in the UP position. To repair a gate

diverter set in a tub spout, replace the entire spout (page 347).

Tub and shower faucets and diverter valves may be set inside wall cavities. Removing them may require a deep-set ratchet wrench (page 347).

If spray from the showerhead is uneven, clean the spray holes. If the showerhead does not stay in an upright position, remove the head and replace the O-ring (page 350).

To add a shower to an existing tub, install a flexible shower adapter (page 351). Several manufacturers make complete conversion kits that allow a shower to be installed in less than one hour.

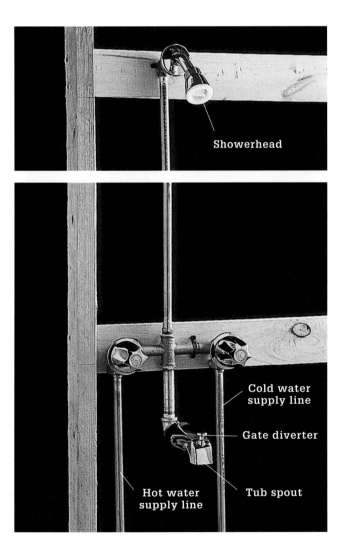

Two-handle faucet has valves that are either compression or cartridge design.

Single-handle faucet has valves that are cartridge, ball-type, or disc design.

Fixing Three-handle Tub & Shower Faucets

A three-handle faucet type has two handles to control hot and cold water, and a third handle to control the diverter valve and direct water to either a tub spout or a shower head. The separate hot and cold handles indicate cartridge or compression faucet designs. To repair them, see pages 332 to 333 for cartridge, and 330 to 331 for compression.

If a diverter valve sticks, if water flow is weak, or if water runs out of the tub spout when the flow is directed to the showerhead, the diverter needs to be repaired or replaced. Most diverter valves are similar to either compression or cartridge faucet valves. Compression-type diverters can be repaired, but cartridge types should be replaced.

Remember to turn off the water before beginning work.

Tools & Materials ▸

Screwdriver
Adjustable wrench or channel-type pliers
Deep-set ratchet wrench
Small wire brush
Replacement diverter cartridge or universal
    washer kit
Heatproof grease
Vinegar

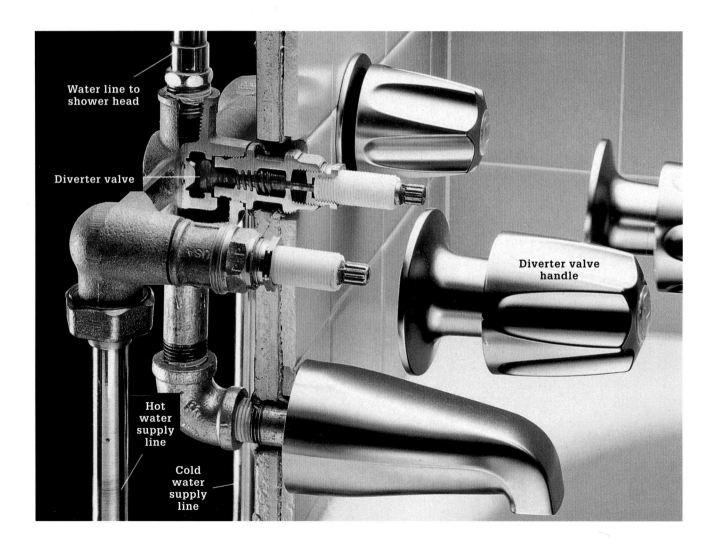

Water line to shower head

Diverter valve

Hot water supply line

Cold water supply line

Diverter valve handle

How to Repair a Compression Diverter Valve

1

Escutcheon

Diverter handle

Remove the diverter valve handle with a screwdriver. Unscrew or pry off the escutcheon.

2

Bonnet nut

Remove bonnet nut with an adjustable wrench or channel-type pliers.

3

Unscrew the stem assembly, using a deep-set ratchet wrench. If necessary, chip away any mortar surrounding the bonnet nut (page 347, step 2).

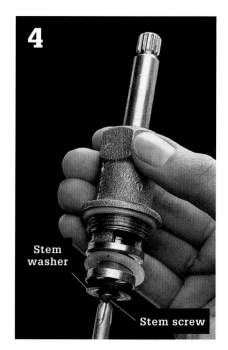

4

Stem washer

Stem screw

Remove brass stem screw. Replace stem washer with an exact duplicate. If stem screw is worn, replace it.

5

Retaining nut

Threaded spindle

Unscrew threaded spindle from retaining nut.

6

Clean sediment and lime build-up from nut, using a small wire brush dipped in vinegar. Coat all parts with heatproof grease, and reassemble diverter valve.

Fixing Two-handle Tub & Shower Faucets

Two-handle tub and shower faucets are either cartridge or compression design. They may be repaired following the directions on pages 332 to 333 for cartridge, or pages 330 to 331 for compression. Because the valves of two-handle tub and shower faucets may be set inside the wall cavity, a deep-set socket wrench may be required to remove the valve stem.

Two-handle tub and shower designs have a gate diverter. A gate diverter is a simple mechanism located in the tub spout. A gate diverter closes the supply of water to the tub spout and redirects the flow to the shower head. Gate diverters seldom need repair. Occasionally, the lever may break, come loose, or refuse to stay in the UP position.

If the diverter fails to work properly, replace the tub spout. Tub spouts are inexpensive and easy to replace.

Remember to turn off the water before beginning work.

Tools & Materials ▸

Screwdriver
Allen wrench
Pipe wrench
Channel-type pliers
Small cold chisel
Ball-peen hammer

Deep-set
   ratchet wrench
Masking tape or cloth
Pipe joint compound
Replacement faucet
   parts, as needed

Water line to shower head

Bonnet nut

Valve stem

Diverter lever

Cold water supply line

Hot water supply line

Gate diverter

Tips on Replacing a Tub Spout ▸

Spout nipple

Check underneath tub spout for a small access slot. The slot indicates the spout is held in place with an Allen screw. Remove the screw, using an Allen wrench. Spout will slide off.

Allen wrench

Unscrew faucet spout. Use a pipe wrench, or insert a large screwdriver or hammer handle into the spout opening and turn spout counterclockwise.

Spread pipe joint compound on threads of spout nipple before replacing spout.

How to Remove a Deep-set Faucet Valve

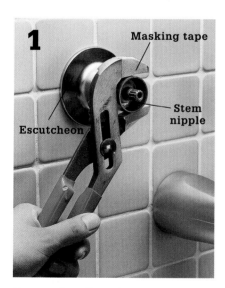

1

Masking tape

Stem nipple

Escutcheon

2

Bonnet nut

3

Remove handle and unscrew the escutcheon with channel-type pliers. Pad the jaws of the pliers with masking tape to prevent scratching the escutcheon.

Chip away any mortar surrounding the bonnet nut, using a ball-peen hammer and a small cold chisel.

Unscrew the bonnet nut with a deep-set ratchet wrench. Remove the bonnet nut and stem from the faucet body.

Fixing Single-handle Tub & Shower Faucets

A single-handle tub and shower faucet has one valve that controls both water flow and temperature. Single-handle faucets may be ball-type, cartridge, or disc designs.

If a single-handle control valve leaks or does not function properly, disassemble the faucet, clean the valve, and replace any worn parts. Use the repair techniques described on pages 324 to 325 for ball-type, or pages 332 to 333 for ceramic disc. Repairing a single-handle cartridge faucet is shown on the opposite page.

Direction of the water flow to either the tub spout or the showerhead is controlled by a gate diverter.

Gate diverters seldom need repair. Occasionally, the lever may break, come loose, or refuse to stay in the UP position. If the diverter fails to work properly, replace the tub spout (page 347).

Tools & Materials ▸

Screwdriver
Adjustable wrench
Channel-type pliers

Replacement faucet parts, as needed

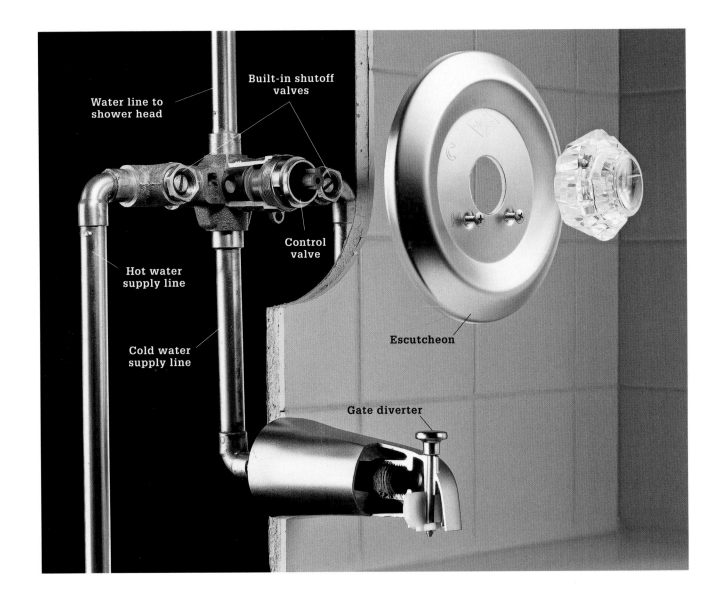

Water line to shower head

Built-in shutoff valves

Hot water supply line

Control valve

Cold water supply line

Escutcheon

Gate diverter

How to Repair a Single-handle Cartridge Tub & Shower Faucet

1 Handle

Escutcheon

Use a screwdriver to remove the handle and escutcheon.

2 Built-in shutoff valves

Turn off water supply at built-in shutoff valves or main shutoff valve.

3 Bonnet nut

Unscrew and remove retaining ring or bonnet nut, using an adjustable wrench.

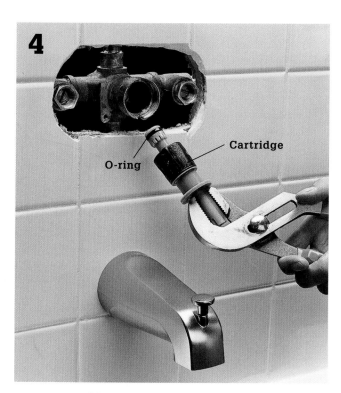

4 O-ring   Cartridge

Remove cartridge assembly by grasping end of valve with channel-type pliers and pulling gently.

5

Flush valve body with clean water to remove sediment. Replace any worn O-rings. Reinstall cartridge and test valve. If faucet fails to work properly, replace the cartridge.

Fixing & Replacing Showerheads

If spray from the showerhead is uneven, clean the spray holes. The outlet or inlet holes of the showerhead may get clogged with mineral deposits. Showerheads pivot into different positions. If a showerhead does not stay in position, or if it leaks, replace the O-ring that seals against the swivel ball.

A tub can be equipped with a shower by installing a flexible shower adapter kit. Complete kits are available at hardware stores and home centers.

Tools & Materials ▸

Adjustable wrench
  or channel-type
  pliers
Pipe wrench
Drill
Glass & tile bit
  (if needed)
Mallet
Screwdriver
Masking tape

Thin wire
  (paper clip)
Heatproof grease
Rag
Replacement O-rings
  (if needed)
Masonry anchors
Flexible shower
  adapter kit
  (optional)

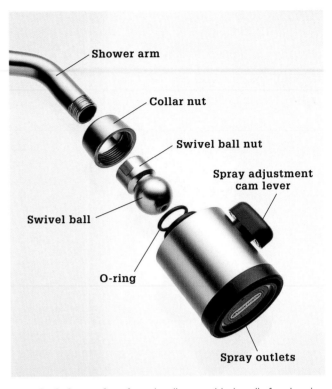

A typical showerhead can be disassembled easily for cleaning and repair. Some showerheads include a spray adjustment cam lever that is used to change the force of the spray.

How to Clean & Repair a Showerhead

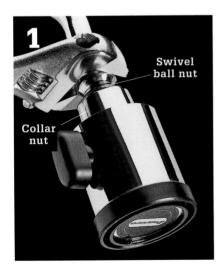

Unscrew the swivel ball nut, using an adjustable wrench or channel-type pliers. Wrap jaws of the tool with masking tape to prevent marring the finish. Unscrew collar nut from the showerhead.

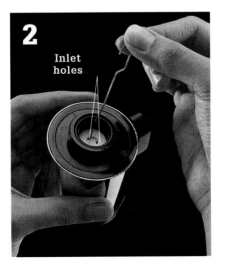

Clean outlet and inlet holes of showerhead with a thin wire. Flush the head with clean water.

Replace the O-ring, if necessary. Lubricate the O-ring with heatproof grease before installing.

How to Install a Flexible Shower Adapter

1

Adapter hose outlet

Remove old tub spout (page 347). Install new tub spout from kit, using a pipe wrench. New spout will have an adapter hose outlet. Wrap the tub spout with a rag to prevent damage to the chrome finish.

2

Adapter hose outlet

Flexible shower hose

Attach flexible shower hose to the adaptor hose outlet. Tighten with an adjustable wrench or channel-type pliers.

3

Flexible shower hose

Determine location of showerhead hanger. Use hose length as a guide, and make sure shower-head can be easily lifted off hanger.

4

Mark hole locations. Use a glass and tile bit to drill holes in ceramic tile for masonry anchors.

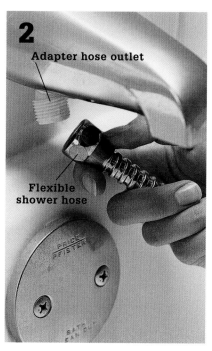

5

Insert anchors into holes, and tap into place with a wooden or rubber mallet.

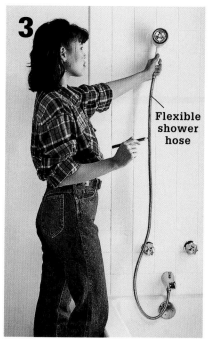

6

Fasten showerhead holder to the wall, and hang showerhead.

Common Toilet Problems

A clogged toilet is one of the most common plumbing problems. If a toilet overflows or flushes sluggishly, clear the clog with a plunger or closet auger (page 374). If the problem persists, the clog may be in the main waste-vent stack (page 380).

Most other toilet problems are fixed easily with minor adjustments that require no disassembly or replacement parts. You can make these adjustments in a few minutes, using simple tools (page 356).

If minor adjustments do not fix the problem, further repairs will be needed. The parts of a standard toilet are not difficult to take apart, and most repair projects can be completed in less than an hour.

A recurring puddle of water on the floor around a toilet may be caused by a crack in the toilet base or in the tank. A damaged toilet should be replaced. Installing a new toilet is an easy project that can be finished in three or four hours.

A standard two-piece toilet has an upper tank that is bolted to a base. This type of toilet uses a simple gravity-operated flush system and can be repaired easily using the directions on the following pages. Some one-piece toilets use a complicated, high-pressure flush valve. High-pressure toilets can be adjusted, but replacing valves should be done by a professional.

Problems	Repairs
Toilet handle sticks or is hard to push.	1. Adjust lift wires (page 354). 2. Clean & adjust handle (page 354).
Handle is loose.	1. Adjust handle (page 354). 2. Reattach lift chain or lift wires to lever (page 354).
Toilet will not flush at all.	1. Make sure water is turned on. 2. Adjust lift chain or lift wires (354).
Toilet does not flush completely.	1. Adjust lift chain (page 354). 2. Adjust water level in tank (page 356). 3. Increase pressure on pressure-assisted toilet (page 362).
Toilet overflows or flushes sluggishly.	1. Clear clogged toilet (page 374). 2. Clear clogged main waste-vent stack (page 380).
Toilet runs continuously.	1. Adjust lift wires or lift chain (page 354). 2. Replace leaky float ball. 3. Adjust water level in tank (page 356). 4. Adjust and clean flush valve (page 359). 5. Replace flush valve (page 359). 6. Repair or replace ballcock (page 358). 7. Service pressure-assist valve (page 362).
Water on floor around toilet.	1. Tighten tank bolts and water connections (page 360). 2. Insulate tank to prevent condensation (page 360). 3. Replace wax ring (page 361). 4. Replace cracked tank or bowl (pages 364 to 366).

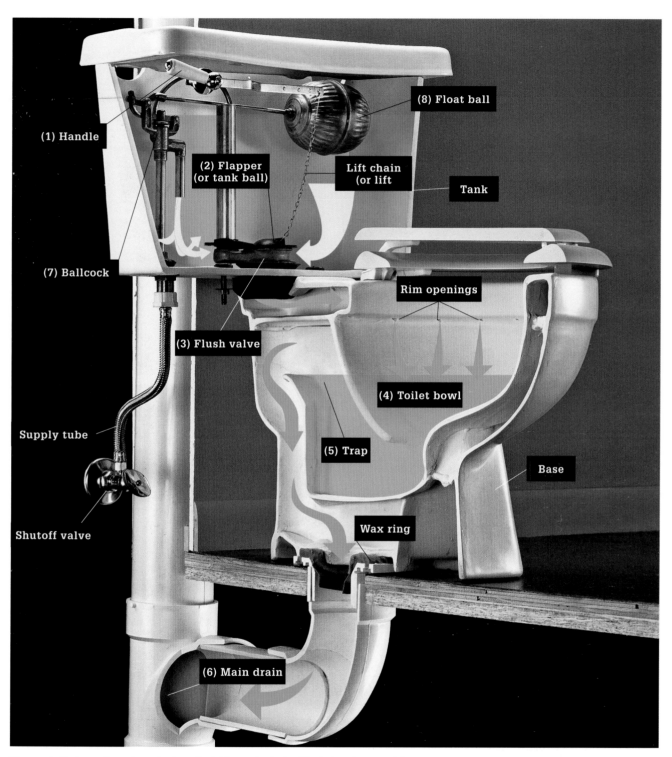

(1) Handle

(8) Float ball

(2) Flapper (or tank ball)

Lift chain (or lift

Tank

(7) Ballcock

Rim openings

(3) Flush valve

(4) Toilet bowl

Supply tube

(5) Trap

Base

Wax ring

Shutoff valve

(6) Main drain

How a toilet works: When the handle (1) is pushed, the lift chain raises a rubber seal, called a flapper, or tank ball (2). Water in the tank rushes down through the flush valve opening (3) in the bottom of the tank, into the toilet bowl (4). Waste water in the bowl is forced through the trap (5) into the main drain (6). When the toilet tank is empty, the flapper seals the tank, and a water supply valve, called a ballcock (7), refills the toilet tank. The ballcock is controlled by a float ball (8) that rides on the surface of the water. When the tank is full, the float ball automatically shuts off the ballcock.

Making Minor Adjustments

Many common toilet problems can be fixed by making minor adjustments to the handle and the attached lift chain (or lift wires).

If the handle sticks or is hard to push, remove the tank cover and clean the handle mounting nut. Make sure the lift wires are straight.

If the toilet will not flush completely unless the handle is held down, you may have to remove excess slack in the lift chain.

If the toilet will not flush at all, the lift chain may be broken or may have to be reattached to the handle lever.

A continuously running toilet (page opposite) can be caused by bent lift wires, kinks in a lift chain, or lime buildup on the handle mounting nut. Clean and adjust the handle and the lift wires or chain to fix the problem.

Tools & Materials ›

Adjustable wrench
Needlenose pliers
Screwdriver

Small wire brush
Vinegar

How to Adjust a Toilet Handle & Lift Chain (or Lift Wires)

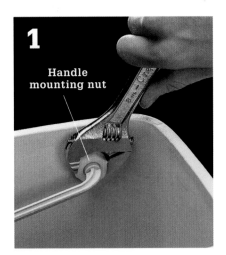

1 Handle mounting nut

Clean and adjust handle mounting nut so handle operates smoothly. Mounting nut has reversed threads. Loosen nut by turning clockwise; tighten by turning counterclockwise. Remove lime buildup with a brush dipped in vinegar.

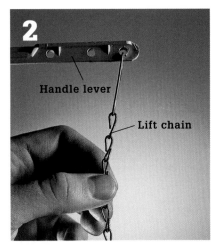

2 Handle lever

Lift chain

Adjust lift chain so it hangs straight from handle lever, with about ½" of slack. Remove excess slack in chain by hooking the chain in a different hole in the handle lever or by removing links with needlenose pliers. A broken lift chain must be replaced.

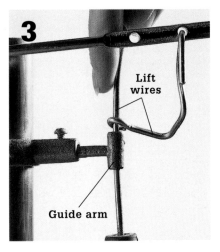

3 Lift wires

Guide arm

Adjust lift wires (found on toilets without lift chains) so that wires are straight and operate smoothly when handle is pushed. A sticky handle often can be fixed by straightening bent lift wires.

Fixing a Running Toilet

The sound of continuously running water occurs if fresh water continues to enter the toilet tank after the flush cycle is complete. A running toilet can waste 20 or more gallons of fresh water each day.

To fix a running toilet, first jiggle the toilet handle. If the sound of running water stops, then either the handle or the lift wires (or lift chain) need to be adjusted (page opposite).

If the sound of running water does not stop when the handle is jiggled, then remove the tank cover and check to see if the float ball is touching the side of the tank. If necessary, bend the float arm to reposition the float ball away from the side of the tank. Make sure the float ball is not leaking. To check for leaks, unscrew the float ball and shake it gently. If there is water inside the ball, replace it.

If these minor adjustments do not fix the problem, then you will have to adjust or repair the ballcock or the flush valve (photo, right). Follow the directions on the following pages.

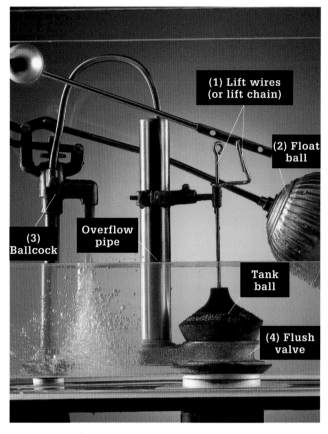

The sound of continuously running water can be caused by several different problems: the lift wire (1) (or lift chain) is bent or kinked; the float ball (2) leaks or rubs against the side of the tank; a faulty ballcock (3) does not shut off the fresh water supply; or the flush valve (4) allows water to leak down into the toilet bowl. First, check the lift wires and float ball. If making simple adjustments and repairs to these parts does not fix the problem, then you will have to repair the ballcock or flush valve (photo, below).

Tools & Materials ▸

Screwdriver	Ballcock (if needed)
Small wire brush	Ballcock seals
Sponge	Emery cloth
Adjustable wrenches	Fiber abrasive pad
Spud wrench or	Flapper or tank ball
channel-type pliers	Flush valve
Universal washer kit	(if needed)

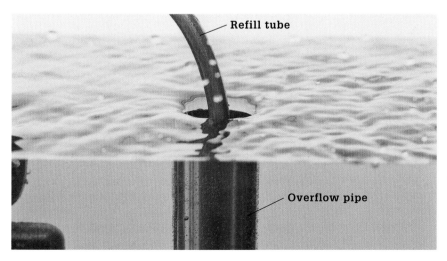

Check the overflow pipe if the sound of running water continues after the float ball and lift wires are adjusted. If you see water flowing into the overflow pipe, the ballcock must be repaired. First adjust ballcock to lower the water level in the tank (page 356). If problem continues, repair or replace the ballcock (page 358). If water is not flowing into the overflow pipe, then the flush valve must be repaired (page 359). First check the tank ball (or flapper) for wear, and replace if necessary. If problem continues, replace the flush valve.

How to Adjust a Ballcock to Set Water Level

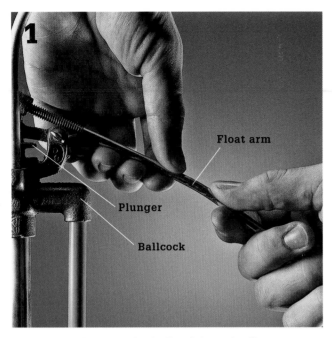

Traditional plunger-valve ballcock is made of brass. Water flow is controlled by a plunger attached to the float arm and ball. Lower the water level by bending the float arm downward slightly. Raise the water level by bending float arm upward.

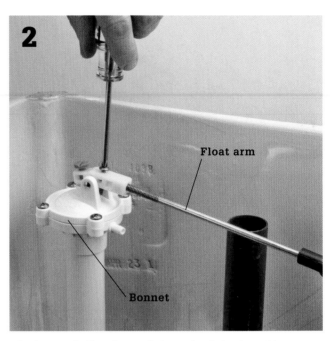

Diaphragm ballcock usually is made of plastic and has a wide bonnet that contains a rubber diaphragm. Turn the adjustment screw clockwise to raise the water level. Turn it counterclockwise to lower the water level. Bend the float arm to make larger adjustments, if necessary.

Float cup ballcock is made of plastic and is easy to adjust. Lower the water level by pinching spring clip on pull rod and moving float cup downward on the ballcock shank. Raise the water level by moving the cup upward.

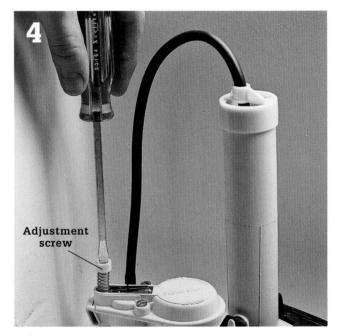

Floatless ballcock controls water level with a pressure-sensing device. Turn the adjustment screw clockwise, ½ turn at a time, to raise the water level; counterclockwise to lower it. *Note: Floatless ballcocks are no longer allowed by code and should be replaced.*

How to Repair a Plunger-valve Ballcock

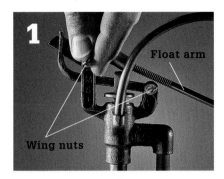

Shut off the water, and flush to empty the tank. Remove the wing nuts on the ballcock. Slip out the float arm.

Pull up on the plunger to remove it. Pry out packing washer or O-ring. Pry out plunger washer. (Remove stem screw, if necessary.)

Install replacement washers. Clean sediment from inside of ballcock with a wire brush. Reassemble ballcock.

How to Repair a Diaphragm Ballcock

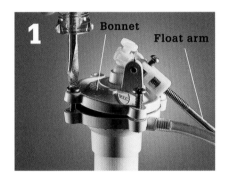

Shut off the water, and flush to empty the tank. Remove the screws from the bonnet.

Lift off float arm with bonnet attached. Check diaphragm and plunger for wear.

Replace any stiff or cracked parts. If assembly is badly worn, replace the entire ballcock.

How to Repair a Float Cup Ballcock

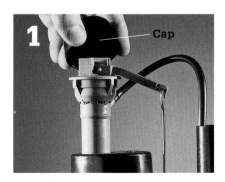

Shut off the water, and flush to empty the tank. Remove the ballcock cap.

Remove bonnet by pushing down on shaft and turning counterclockwise. Clean out sediment inside ballcock with wire brush.

Replace the seal. If assembly is badly worn, replace the entire ballcock.

How to Install a New Ballcock

1

Shut off water, and flush toilet to empty tank. Use a sponge to remove remaining water. Disconnect supply tube coupling nut and ballcock mounting nut with adjustable wrench. Remove old ballcock.

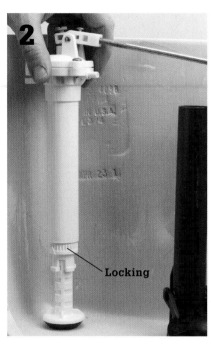

2

Locking

Loosen the shank locking on the new ballcock. Adjust the shank until the top of the ballcock is 1" from the top of the tank. Tighten the locking.

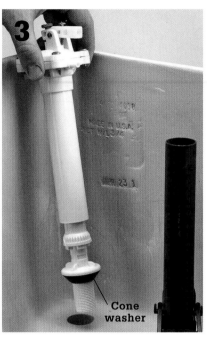

3

Cone washer

Attach a cone washer to the new ballcock, and insert the tailpiece into the tank opening.

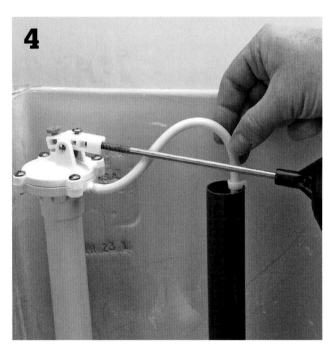

4

Screw in the float arm and align it so it passes in front of the overflow pipe. Screw on the float ball. Position the refill tube so it fits inside the overflow pipe.

5

Screw the mounting nut and the supply tube coupling nut onto ballcock tailpiece. Tighten them. Turn on the water and check for leaks.

How to Adjust & Clean a Flush Valve

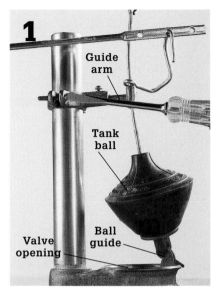

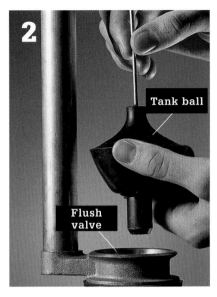

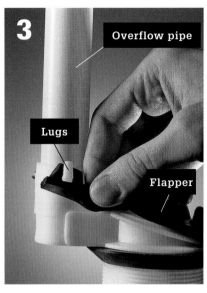

Adjust tank ball (or flapper) so it is directly over flush valve. Tank ball has a guide arm that can be loosened so that tank ball can be repositioned. (Some tank balls have a ball guide that helps seat the tank ball into the flush valve.)

Replace the tank ball if it is cracked or worn. Tank balls have a threaded fitting that screws onto the lift wire. Clean opening of the flush valve, using emery cloth (for brass valves) or a fiber abrasive pad (for plastic valves).

Replace flapper if it is worn. Flappers are attached to small lugs on the sides of overflow pipe.

How to Install a New Flush Valve

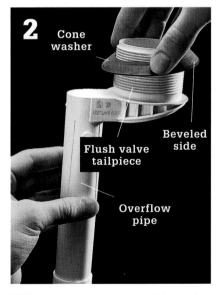

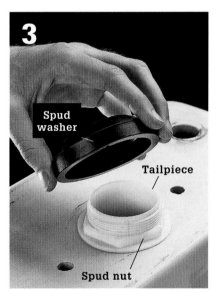

Shut off water, disconnect ballcock (page opposite, step 1), and remove toilet tank (page 361, steps 1 and 2). Remove old flush valve by unscrewing spud nut with spud wrench or channel-type pliers.

Slide cone washer onto tailpiece of new flush valve. Beveled side of cone washer should face end of tailpiece. Insert flush valve into tank opening so that overflow pipe faces ballcock.

Screw spud nut onto tailpiece of flush valve, and tighten with a spud wrench or channel-type pliers. Place soft spud washer over tailpiece, and reinstall toilet tank.

Fixing a Leaking Toilet

Water leaking onto the floor around a toilet may be caused by several different problems. The leaking must be fixed as soon as possible to prevent moisture from damaging the subfloor.

First, make sure all connections are tight. If moisture drips from the tank during humid weather, it is probably condensation. Fix this "sweating" problem by insulating the inside of the tank with foam panels. A crack in a toilet tank also can cause leaks. A cracked tank must be replaced.

Water seeping around the base of a toilet can be caused by an old wax ring that no longer seals against the drain (photo, above), or by a cracked toilet base. If leaking occurs during or just after a flush, replace the wax ring. If leaking is constant, the toilet base is cracked and must be replaced. New toilets usually are sold with flush valves and ballcocks already installed.

If these parts are not included, you will have to purchase them.

Building codes require the installation of 1.6-gallon low-flow toilets in all new construction and bathroom remodeling projects. Refer to page 364 to 367 for toilet installation.

Tools & Materials ▸

Sponge	Tank liner kit
Adjustable wrench	Abrasive cleanser
Putty knife	Rag
Ratchet wrench	Wax ring
Screwdriver	Plumber's putty

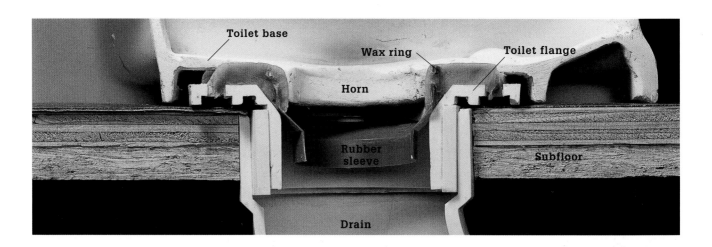

Toilet base · Wax ring · Toilet flange · Horn · Rubber sleeve · Subfloor · Drain

Ballcock mounting nut · Supply tube · Tank bolt

Tighten all connections slightly. Tighten nuts on tank bolts with a ratchet wrench. Tighten ballcock mounting nut and supply tube coupling nut with an adjustable wrench. *Caution: overtightening tank bolts may crack the toilet tank.*

Insulate toilet tank to prevent "sweating," using a toilet liner kit. First, shut off water, drain tank, and clean inside of tank with abrasive cleanser. Cut plastic foam panels to fit bottom, sides, front, and back of tank. Attach panels to tank with adhesive (included in kit). Let adhesive cure as directed.

How to Remove a Toilet & Wax Ring

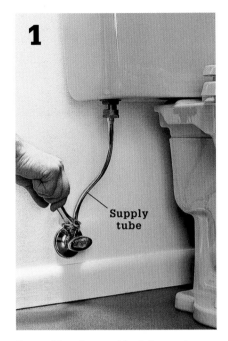

1

Turn off water, and flush to empty toilet tank. Use a sponge to remove remaining water in tank and bowl. Disconnect supply tube with an adjustable wrench.

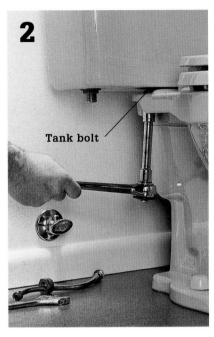

2

Remove the nuts from the tank bolts with a ratchet wrench. Carefully remove the tank and set it aside.

3

Pry off the floor bolt trim caps at the base of the toilet. Remove the floor nuts with an adjustable wrench.

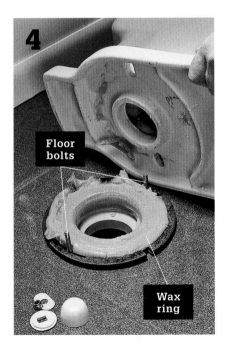

4

Straddle the toilet and rock the bowl from side to side until the seal breaks. Carefully lift the toilet off the floor bolts and set it on its side. Small amount of water may spill from the toilet trap.

5

Remove old wax from the toilet flange in the floor. Plug the drain opening with a damp rag to prevent sewer gases from rising into the house.

6

If old toilet will be reused, clean old wax and putty from the horn and the base of the toilet. *Note: Refer to pages 364 to 366 for toilet installation.*

Fixing a Pressure-assisted Toilet

Pressure-assisted toilets develop problems similar to those of conventional toilets, such as continuously running water and a weak flush. And while the causes may be different, the repairs are just as easy.

Pressure-assisted toilets require a certain level of water-pressure—between 20 and 80 psi—to work properly. Pressure below that level can cause a variety of problems; if you're having trouble with a pressure-assisted toilet, the first thing to check is your home's water pressure.

If the system's pressure is sufficient, clean the water intake screen to ensure maximum flow into the tank. If the pressure is weak, call a plumber or your water utility for advice.

Before making any repairs to your pressure-assisted toilet, turn off the water at the fixture shut-off valve and flush the toilet to relieve the pressure in the tank.

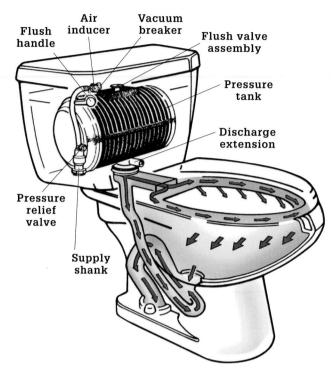

Pressure-assisted toilets rely on pressure rather than water volume to create an adequate flush. The handle is connected to a flush rod that pushes an actuator on the flush valve cartridge to start the flush.

Tools & Materials ▸

Adjustable wrench   Channel-type pliers
Soft brush   5-gallon bucket

How to Test & Improve Water Pressure

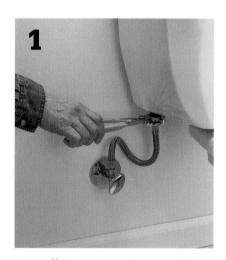

Turn off the water at the shutoff valve and flush the toilet. Use an adjustable wrench or channel-type pliers to loosen the coupling nut connecting the water supply tube to the supply shank at the bottom of the tank.

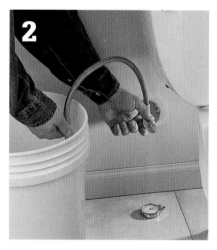

Place the free end of the supply tube into a 5-gallon bucket. Mark the time, then open the shut-off valve all the way for 30 seconds. Close the valve and measure the amount of water: there should be more than a gallon.

Place a bucket under the supply shank. Remove the shank mounting nut, and pull the supply assembly from the tank hole. Inspect the screen inside the shank, and clean it with a soft brush. Reconnect the shank and supply tube.

How to Stop Continuously Running Water

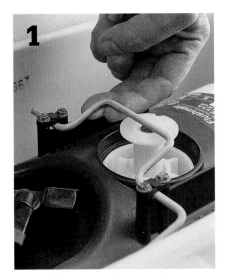

Turn off water at the shutoff valve, and flush the toilet. Lift up on the flush rod: there should be a ⅛" gap between the rod and the top of the actuator. To adjust, loosen the setscrew and rotate the actuator up or down.

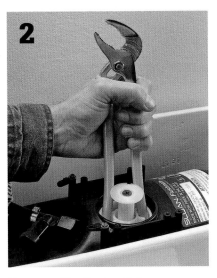

Unscrew the flush valve cartridge, using the handle ends of channel-type pliers.

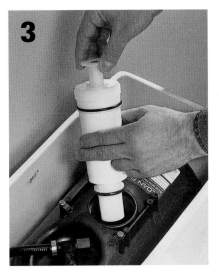

Inspect the O-rings. If they are worn, replace the cartridge. Reinstall the cartridge, and tighten it. Restore the water supply and let the tank refill. If water runs after refill, depress the actuator. If the flow stops, tighten the cartridge in quarter-turns until the water stops; if flow continues, loosen the cartridge until the water stops.

How to Correct a Weak Flow

With the water supply on, flush the toilet by depressing the actuator. Once the unit begins the flush cycle, carefully raise the actuator. This flushes the system with water to remove debris.

Test the air inducer. Remove the inducer cap, and flush the toilet. Look inside the inducer to make sure that the plastic poppet retracts, and listen for air flow. If there is no flow, unscrew the inducer, and clean the inducer, poppet, spring, and cap.

Test for a leaking flush valve cartridge. Turn off the water at the shutoff valve, and flush the toilet. Pour a cup of water into the top of the cartridge, then restore the water supply. If you see a stream of bubbles rising from the cartridge, replace it.

Installing a Toilet

Most toilets in the low-to-moderate price range are two-piece units, with a separate tank and bowl, made of vitreous china. One-piece toilets with integral tank and bowl also are available, but the cost is usually two or three times that of two-piece units.

Code regulations requiring low-flow (1.6 gallons per flush) toilets have been on the books for years. After some initial problems with inadequate flush force, manufacturers have re-engineered the toilet traps and flush mechanisms to maximize efficiency. These new models work considerably better than first-generation low-flow toilets from the 1980s to mid '90s. Most are reasonably priced and well worth the cost for eliminating aggravation (and double flushing).

Tools & Materials ▸

Adjustable wrench	Floor bolts
Ratchet wrench or basin wrench	Tank bolts with rubber washers
Screwdriver	Seat bolts and mounting nuts
Wax ring & sleeve	
Plumber's putty	

Install a toilet by anchoring the bowl to the floor first, then mounting the tank onto the bowl. China fixtures crack easily, so use care when handling them.

How to Replace a Toilet

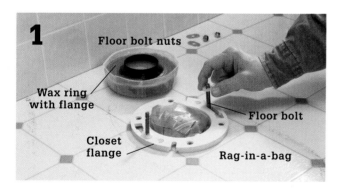

1

Floor bolt nuts

Wax ring with flange

Closet flange

Floor bolt

Rag-in-a-bag

Place a rag in a plastic sack. Slide new brass bolts into the slots on the closet flange, and rotate the bolts a ¼ turn so they cannot be removed. Put the plastic keepers or extra washers and nuts on the bolts to secure the bolts to the flange. Unwrap the wax ring and position it over the closet flange.

2

Lower the new toilet down over the wax ring so the bolts go through the holes on the bottom of the stool. Press down on the toilet to seat it in the wax ring and check for level. If the bowl is not quite level, you can shim the low side with a few pennies. Thread washers and nuts onto the floor bolts and tighten them a little at a time, alternating. Do not overtighten. Cut the bolts off above the nuts with a hacksaw and add the caps. Lay a bead of tub and tile caulk around the base of the toilet.

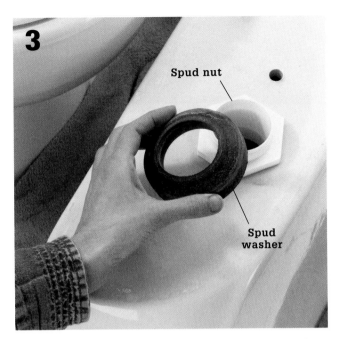

3

Spud nut

Spud washer

Attach the toilet tank. Some tanks come with a flush valve and a fill valve preinstalled, but if yours does not, insert the flush valve through the tank opening and tighten a spud nut over the threaded end of the valve. Place a foam spud washer on top of the spud nut.

4

If necessary, adjust the fill valve as noted in the directions. Fill valves can be adjusted to fit various tank sizes.

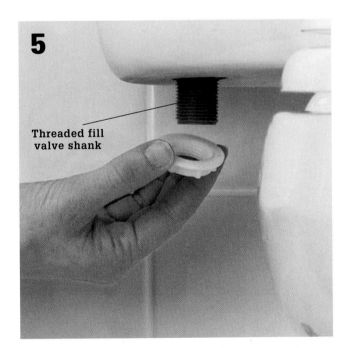

5

Threaded fill valve shank

Position the valve in the tank. Push down on the valve shank (not the top) while hand-tightening the lock nut onto the threaded valve shank (thread the nut on the exterior side of tank). Hand-tighten only.

6

Intermediate nut goes between tank and bowl

With the tank lying on its back, thread a rubber washer onto each tank bolt and insert it into the bolt holes from inside the tank. Then, thread a brass washer and hex nut onto the tank bolts from below and tighten them to a quarter turn past hand tight. Do not overtighten.

(continued)

7

Position the tank on the bowl, spud washer on opening, bolts through bolt holes. Put a rubber washer followed by a brass washer and a wing nut on each bolt and tighten these up evenly.

8

You may stabilize the bolts with a large slotted screwdriver from inside the tank, but tighten the nuts, not the bolts. You may press down a little on a side, the front, or the rear of the tank to level it as you tighten the nuts by hand. Do not overtighten and crack the tank. The tank should be level and stable when you're done.

9

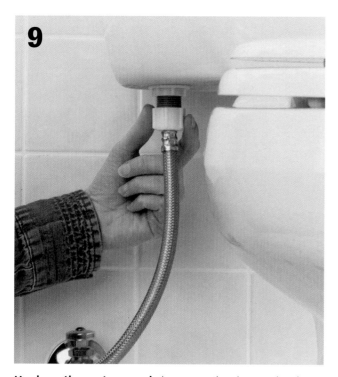

Hook up the water supply by connecting the supply tube to the threaded fill valve with the coupling nut provided. Turn on the water and test for leaks.

10

Attach the toilet seat by threading the plastic or brass bolts provided with the seat through the openings on the back of the rim and attaching nuts.

Macerating Toilets ▸

When a toilet with conventional plumbing is not an option, a macerating toilet may allow you to add a bathroom in a basement. Macerators grind and then eject waste through a ¾" pipe into an existing drain pipe. Most units will also handle waste water from a sink and a shower.

Place the macerating unit in the desired location and make the connections to the 1½" diameter drain lines from the sink and tub or shower to the inlets on the macerating unit. Also connect the ¾" drain line from the soil stack or a branch drain to the discharge port on the unit (you can use either copper or PVC pipe). The drain line may span up to 12 ft. vertically with some models, and it can be run as far as 150 ft. horizontally if a ¼" per-foot drop is maintained. Read the instructions carefully to learn the limits for your fixture, as well as how to factor in pressure drops that occur when the line makes a bend.

Once all connections are made at the macerating unit, place the toilet bowl in front of the unit so that the toilet spigot lines up with the accordion connector on the macerating unit. Mark the location of the toilet bowl's mounting-screw holes. Remove the toilet and drill appropriately sized holes for the toilet's mounting lag screws. Join the toilet to the macerating unit as directed by the manufacturer, and secure the toilet to the floor. The toilet tank connects to the bowl like a standard two-piece toilet. The water supply connection to the fill valve is also standard. Venting should be provided in accordance with local codes and the manufacturer's instructions.

The macerating unit must be plugged in to a 120-volt GFCI-protected outlet (the outlet should be 40" away from the unit). The unit will not function during a power outage. Do not dispose of paper products (other than toilet paper) in the macerating toilet system. Do not use bleach cakes or other submerged tank-and-bowl cleaning products.

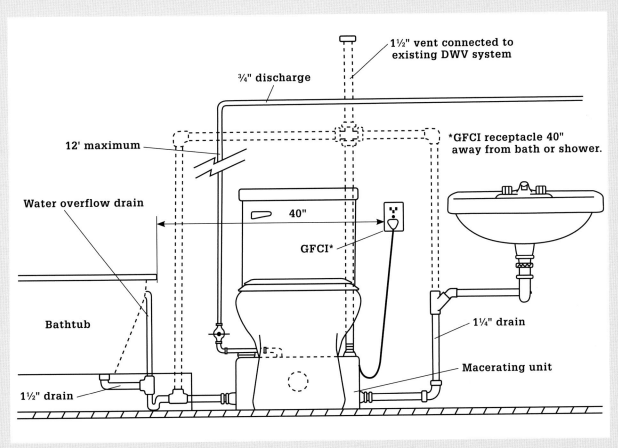

A typical macerating unit will support a toilet, a sink, a tub, and shower. This diagram shows pipe routes for a typical installation. Check local codes before installing.

Clearing Clogs & Fixing Drains

Clear a clogged drain with a plunger, hand auger, or blow bag. A plunger breaks up clogs by forcing air pressure into the drain line. Because a plunger is effective and simple to use, it should be the first choice for clearing a clog.

A hand auger has a flexible steel cable that is pushed into the drain line to break up or remove obstructions. An auger is easy to use, but for best results the user must know the "feel" of the cable in the drain line. A little experience often is necessary to tell the difference between a soap clog and a bend in the drain line (pages 372 to 373).

A blow bag hooks to a garden hose and uses water pressure to clear clogs. Blow bags are most effective on clogs in floor drains (page 379).

Use caustic, acid-based chemical drain cleaners only as a last resort. These drain cleaners, usually available at hardware stores and supermarkets, will dissolve clogs, but they also may damage pipes and must be handled with caution. Always read the manufacturer's directions completely.

Regular maintenance helps keep drains working properly. Flush drains once each week with hot tap water to keep them free of soap, grease, and debris. Or, treat drains once every six months with a non-caustic (copper sulfide- or sodium hydroxide-based) drain cleaner. A non-caustic cleaner will not harm pipes.

Occasionally, leaks may occur in the drain lines or around the drain opening. Most leaks in drain lines are fixed easily by gently tightening all pipe connections. If the leak is at the sink drain opening, fix or replace the strainer body assembly (page 371).

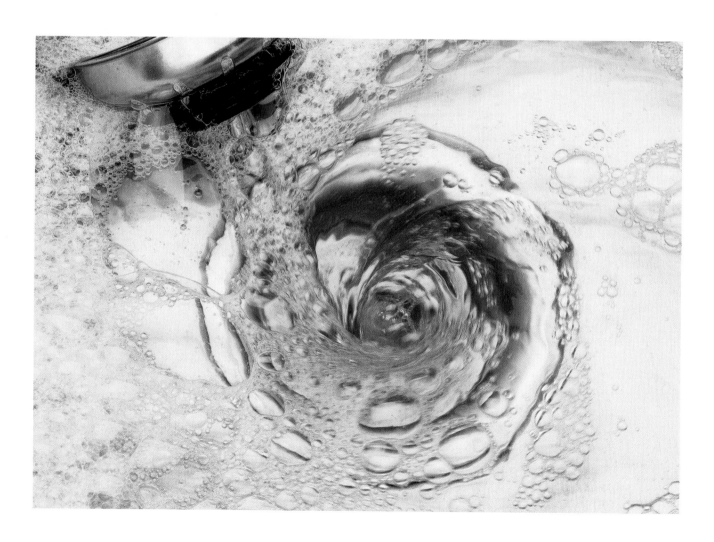

Clearing Clogged Sinks

Every sink has a drain trap and a fixture drain line. Sink clogs usually are caused by a buildup of soap and hair in the trap or fixture drain line. Remove clogs by using a plunger, disconnecting and cleaning the trap (page 370), or using a hand auger (pages 372 to 373).

Many sinks hold water with a mechanical plug called a pop-up stopper. If the sink will not hold standing water, or if water in the sink drains too slowly, the pop-up stopper must be cleaned and adjusted (page 370).

Tools & Materials ▸

Plunger
Channel-type pliers
Small wire brush
Screwdriver
Rag
Bucket
Replacement gaskets

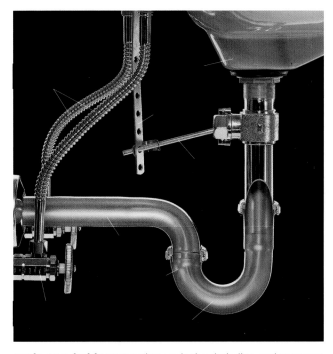

Drain trap holds water that seals the drain line and prevents sewer gases from entering the home. Each time a drain is used, the standing trap water is flushed away and replaced by new water. The shape of the trap and fixture drain line may resemble the letter P, and sink traps sometimes are called P-traps.

How to Clear Sink Drains with a Plunger

Remove drain stopper. Some pop-up stoppers lift out directly; others turn counterclockwise. On some older types of stoppers, the pivot rod must be removed to free the stopper.

Stuff a wet rag in sink overflow opening; rag prevents air from breaking the suction of the plunger. Place plunger cup over drain and run enough water to cover the rubber cup. Move plunger handle up and down rapidly to break up the clog.

How to Clean & Adjust a Pop-up Sink Drain Stopper

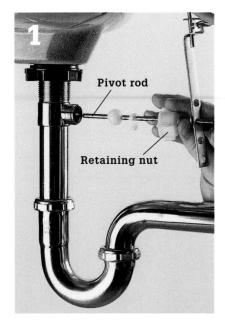

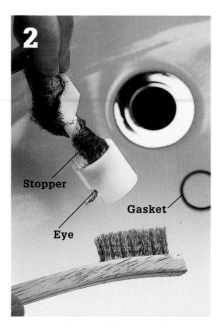

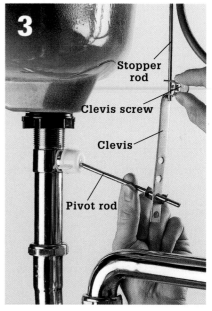

Raise stopper lever to full upright (closed) position. Unscrew the retaining nut that holds pivot rod in position. Pull pivot rod out of drain pipe to release stopper.

Remove stopper. Clean debris from stopper, using a small wire brush. Inspect gasket for wear or damage, and replace if necessary. Reinstall stopper.

If sink does not drain properly, adjust clevis. Loosen clevis screw. Slide clevis up or down on stopper rod to adjust position of stopper. Tighten clevis screw.

How to Remove & Clean a Sink Drain Trap

Place bucket under trap to catch water and debris. Loosen slip nuts on trap bend with channel-type pliers. Unscrew nuts by hand and slide away from connections. Pull off trap bend.

Dump out debris. Clean trap bend with a small wire brush. Inspect slip nut washers for wear, and replace if necessary. Reinstall trap bend, and tighten slip nuts.

Fixing Leaky Sink Strainers

A leak under a sink may be caused by a strainer body that is not properly sealed to the sink drain opening. To check for leaks, close the drain stopper and fill sink with water. From underneath sink, inspect the strainer assembly for leaks.

Remove the strainer body, clean it, and replace the gaskets and plumber's putty. Or, replace the strainer with a new one, available at home centers.

Tools & Materials ▶

Channel-type pliers
Spud wrench
Hammer
Putty knife

Plumber's putty
Replacement parts
(if needed)

Sink strainer assembly connects the sink to the drain line. Leaks may occur where the strainer body seals against the lip of the drain opening.

How to Fix a Leaky Strainer

Unscrew slip nuts from both ends of tailpiece, using channel-type pliers. Disconnect tailpiece from strainer body and trap bend. Remove tailpiece.

Remove the locknut, using a spud wrench. Unscrew the locknut completely, and remove the strainer assembly. If necessary, cut the locknut.

Remove old putty from the drain opening, using a putty knife. If reusing the old strainer body, clean off old putty from under the flange. Old gaskets and washers should be replaced.

Apply a bead of plumber's putty to the lip of the drain opening. Press strainer body into drain opening. From under the sink, place rubber gasket, then metal or fiber friction ring, over strainer. Reinstall locknut and tighten. Reinstall tailpiece.

How to Clear a Fixture Drain Line with a Hand Auger

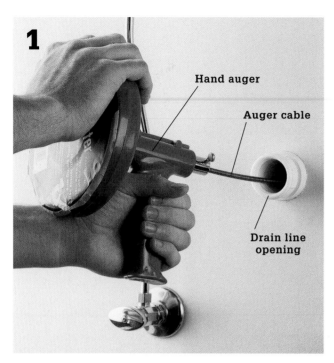

Remove trap bend (page 370). Push the end of the auger cable into the drain line opening until resistance is met. This resistance usually indicates end of cable has reached a bend in the drain pipe.

Set the auger lock so that at least 6" of cable extends out of the opening. Crank the auger handle in a clockwise direction to move the end of the cable past bend in drain line.

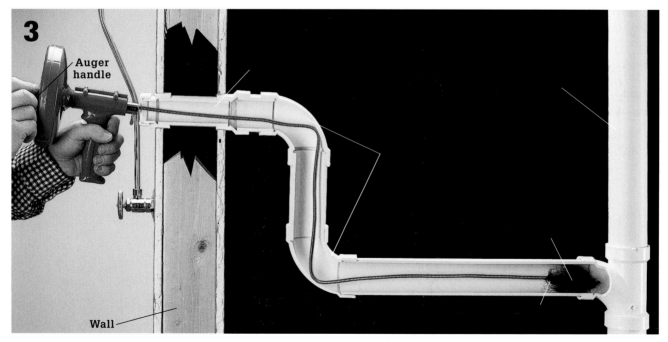

Release the lock and continue pushing the cable into the opening until firm resistance is felt. Set the auger lock and crank the handle in a clockwise direction. Solid resistance that prevents the cable from advancing indicates a clog. Some clogs, such as a sponge or an accumulation of hair, can be snagged and retrieved (step 4). Continuous resistance that allows the cable to advance slowly is probably a soap clog (step 5).

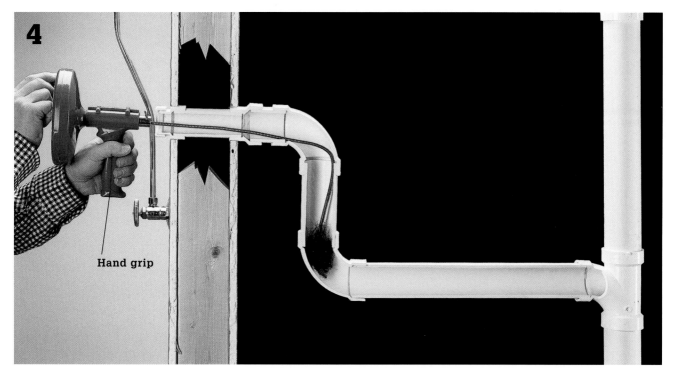

4

Hand grip

Pull an obstruction out of the line by releasing the auger lock and cranking the handle clockwise. If no object can be retrieved, reconnect the trap bend and use the auger to clear the nearest branch drain line or main waste and vent stack (pages 380 to 381).

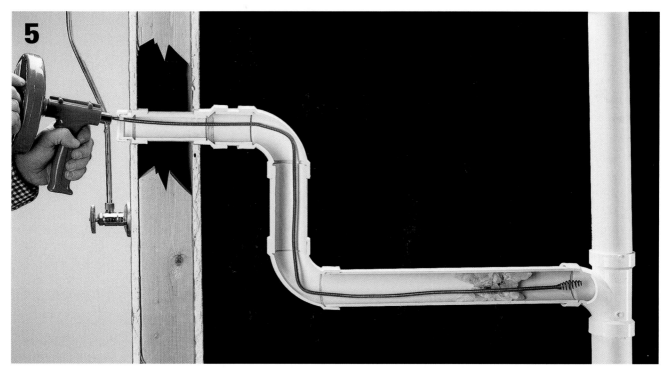

5

Continuous resistance indicates a soap clog. Bore through the clog by cranking the auger handle clockwise, while applying steady pressure on the hand grip of the auger. Repeat the procedure two or three times, then retrieve the cable. Reconnect the trap bend and flush the system with hot tap water to remove debris.

Clearing Clogged Toilets

Most toilet clogs occur because an object is stuck inside the toilet trap. Use a flanged plunger or a closet auger to remove the clog.

A toilet that is sluggish during the flush cycle may be partially blocked. Clear the blockage with a plunger or closet auger. Occasionally, a sluggish toilet flush indicates a blocked waste-vent stack. Clear the stack as shown on page 381.

Tools & Materials ▸

Flanged plunger
Closet auger
Bucket

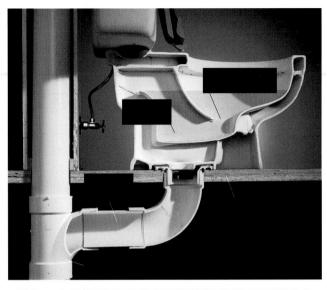

Toilet drain system has a drain outlet at the bottom of the bowl and a built-in trap. The toilet drain is connected to a drain line and a main waste-vent stack.

How to Clear a Toilet with a Plunger

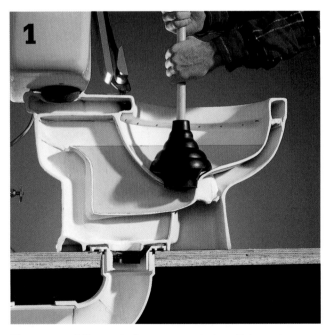

Place cup of flanged plunger over drain outlet opening. Plunge up and down rapidly. Slowly pour a bucket of water into bowl to flush debris through drain. If toilet does not drain, repeat plunging, or clear clog with a closet auger.

How to Clear a Toilet with a Closet Auger

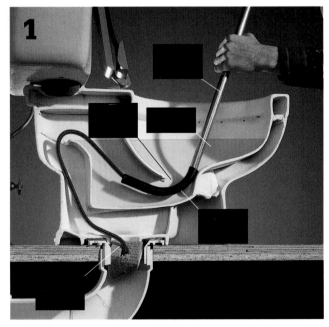

Place the auger bend in the bottom of the drain opening, and push the auger cable into the trap. Crank the auger handle in a clockwise direction to snag obstruction. Continue cranking while retrieving the cable to pull the obstruction out of the trap.

Clearing Clogged Shower Drains

Shower drain clogs usually are caused by an accumulation of hair in the drain line. Remove the strainer cover and look for clogs in the drain opening (below). Some clogs are removed easily with a piece of stiff wire.

Stubborn clogs should be removed with a plunger or hand auger.

Tools & Materials ▸

Screwdriver
Flashlight
Plunger
Hand auger
Stiff wire

Shower drain system has a sloped floor, a drain opening, a trap, and a drain line that connects to a branch drain line or waste-vent stack.

How to Clear a Shower Drain

1

Check for clogs by removing strainer cover, using a screwdriver. Use a flashlight to look for hair clogs in the drain opening. Use a stiff wire to clear shower drain of hair or to snag any obstructions.

2

Use a plunger to clear most shower drain clogs. Place the rubber cup over the drain opening. Pour enough water into the shower stall to cover the lip of the cup. Move plunger handle up and down rapidly.

3

Clear stubborn clogs in the shower drain with a hand auger. Use the auger as shown on pages 372 to 373.

Fixing Tub Drains

When water in the tub drains slowly or not at all, remove and inspect the drain assembly. Both plunger and pop-up type drain mechanisms catch hair and other debris that cause clogs.

If cleaning the drain assembly does not fix the problem, the tub drain line is clogged. Clear the line with a plunger or a hand auger. Always stuff a wet rag in the overflow drain opening before plunging the tub drain. The rag prevents air from breaking the suction of the plunger. When using an auger, always insert the cable down through the overflow drain opening.

If the tub will not hold water with the drain closed, or if the tub continues to drain slowly after the assembly has been cleaned, then the drain assembly needs adjustment. Remove the assembly, and follow the instructions on the opposite page.

Tools & Materials ▸

Plunger
Screwdriver
Small wire brush
Needlenose pliers

Hand auger
Vinegar
Heatproof grease
Rag

Plunger-type tub drain has a hollow brass plug, called a plunger, that slides up and down inside the overflow drain to seal off the water flow. The plunger is moved by a trip lever and linkage that runs through the overflow drain.

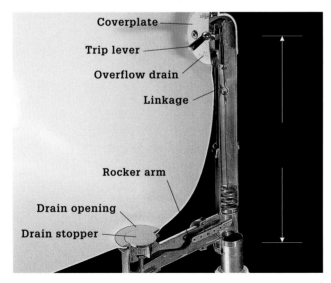

Pop-up tub drain has a rocker arm that pivots to open or close a metal drain stopper. The rocker arm is moved by a trip lever and linkage that runs through the overflow drain.

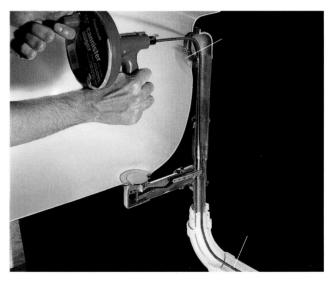

Clear a tub drain by running the auger cable through the overflow opening. First, remove the coverplate and carefully lift out the drain linkage (page opposite). Push auger cable into the opening until resistance is felt (page 372). After using the auger, replace drain linkage. Open drain and run hot water through drain to flush out any debris.

How to Clean & Adjust a Plunger-type Tub Drain

Remove screws on coverplate. Carefully pull coverplate, linkage, and plunger from the overflow drain opening.

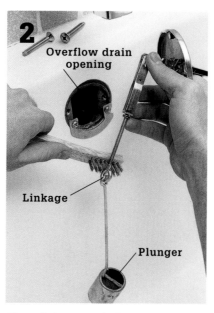

Clean linkage and plunger with a small wire brush dipped in vinegar. Lubricate assembly with heatproof grease.

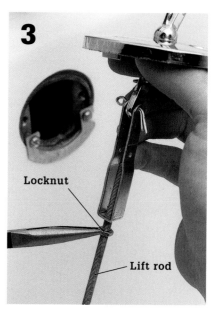

Adjust drain flow and fix leaks by adjusting linkage. Unscrew locknut on threaded lift rod, using needlenose pliers. Screw rod down about ⅛". Tighten locknut and reinstall entire assembly.

How to Clean & Adjust a Pop-up Tub Drain

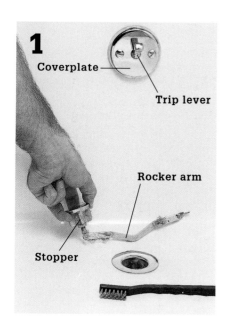

Raise trip lever to the full open position. Carefully pull stopper and rocker arm assembly from drain opening. Clean hair or debris from rocker arm with a small wire brush.

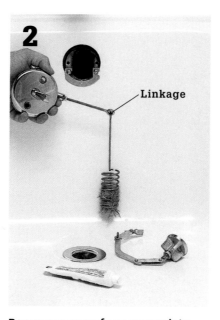

Remove screws from coverplate. Pull coverplate, trip lever, and linkage from overflow drain. Remove hair and debris. Remove corrosion with a small wire brush dipped in vinegar. Lubricate linkage with heatproof grease.

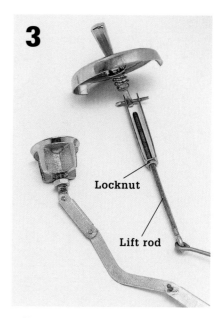

Adjust drain flow and fix leaks by adjusting the linkage. Loosen locknut on threaded lift rod and screw lift rod up about ⅛". Tighten locknut and reinstall entire assembly.

Clearing Clogged Drum Traps

In older homes, clogs in bathroom sinks or bathtubs may be caused by blockage in the drain lines connected to a drum trap. Remove the drum trap cover and use a hand auger to clear each drain line.

Drum traps usually are located in the floor next to the bathtub. They are identified by a flat, screw-in type cover or plug that is flush with the floor. Occasionally, a drum trap will be positioned upside down so that the plug is accessible from below.

Tools & Materials ▸

Adjustable wrench
Hand auger
Rags or towels
Penetrating oil
Teflon tape

A drum trap is a canister made of lead or cast iron. Usually, more than one fixture drain line is connected to the drum. Drum traps are not vented, and they are no longer approved for new plumbing installations.

How to Clear a Clogged Drum Trap

Place rags or towels around the opening of the drum trap to absorb water that may be backed up in the lines.

Remove the trap cover, using an adjustable wrench. Work carefully: older drum traps may be made of lead, which gets brittle with age. If cover does not unscrew easily, apply penetrating oil to lubricate the threads.

Use a hand auger (pages 372 to 373) to clear each drain line. Then wrap the threads of the cover with Teflon tape and install. Flush all drains with hot water for five minutes.

Clearing Clogged Floor Drains

When water backs up onto a basement floor, there is a clog in either the floor drain line, drain trap, or the sewer service line. Clogs in the drain line or trap may be cleared with a hand auger or a blow bag. To clear a sewer service line, see pages 382 to 385.

Blow bags are especially useful for clearing clogs in floor drain lines. A blow bag attaches to a garden hose and is inserted directly into the floor drain line. The bag fills with water and then releases a powerful spurt that dislodges clogs.

Tools & Materials ▶

Adjustable wrench
Screwdriver
Hand auger
Blow bag
Garden hose

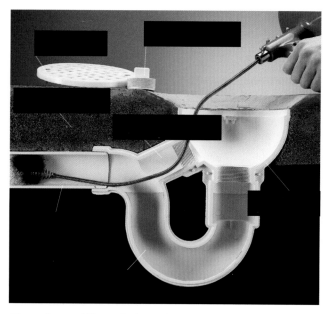

Clear clogged floor drains using a hand auger. Remove the drain cover, then use a wrench to unscrew the cleanout plug in the drain bowl. Push the auger cable through the cleanout opening directly into the drain line.

How to Use a Blow Bag to Clear a Floor Drain

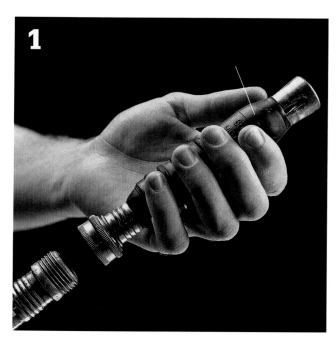

1

Attach blow bag to garden hose, then attach hose to a hose bib or utility faucet.

2

Cleanout opening

Drain cover

Cleanout plug

Remove drain cover and cleanout plug. Insert the blow bag completely into the cleanout opening and turn on water. Allow several minutes for the blow bag to work properly.

Clearing Clogs in Branch & Main Drain Lines

If using a plunger or a hand auger does not clear a clog in a fixture drain line, it means that the blockage may be in a branch line, the main waste-vent stack, or the sewer service line.

First, use an auger to clear the branch drain line closest to any stopped-up fixtures. Branch drain lines may be serviced through the cleanout fittings located at the end of the branch. Because waste water may be backed up in the drain lines, always open a cleanout with caution. Place a bucket and rags under the opening to catch waste water. Never position yourself directly under a cleanout opening while unscrewing the plug or cover.

If using an auger on the branch line does not solve the problem, then the clog may be located in a main waste-vent stack. To clear the stack, run an auger cable down through the roof vent. Make sure that the cable of your auger is long enough to reach down the entire length of the stack. If it is not, you may want to rent or borrow another auger. Always use extreme caution when working on a ladder or on a roof.

If no clog is present in the main stack, the problem may be located in the sewer service line. Locate the main cleanout, usually a Y-shaped fitting at the bottom of the main waste-vent stack. Remove the plug and push the cable of a hand auger into the opening.

Some sewer service lines in older homes have a house trap. The house trap is a U-shaped fitting located at the point where the sewer line exits the house. Most of the fitting will be beneath the floor surface, but it can be identified by its two openings. Use a hand auger to clean a house trap.

If the auger meets solid resistance in the sewer line, retrieve the cable and inspect the bit. Fine, hair-like roots on the bit indicate the line is clogged with tree roots. Dirt on the bit indicates a collapsed line.

Use a power auger to clear sewer service lines that are clogged with tree roots. Power augers (page 382) are available at rental centers. However, a power auger is a large, heavy piece of equipment. Before renting, consider the cost of rental and the level of your do-it-yourself skills versus the price of a professional sewer cleaning service. If you rent a power auger, ask the rental dealer for complete instructions on how to operate the equipment.

Always consult a professional sewer cleaning service if you suspect a collapsed line.

Tools & Materials ▸

Adjustable wrench or pipe wrench	Rags
Hand auger	Penetrating oil
Cold chisel	Cleanout plug (if needed)
Ball-peen hammer	Pipe joint compound
Bucket	

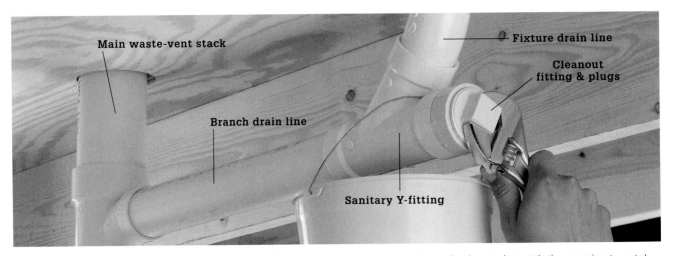

Main waste-vent stack

Branch drain line

Sanitary Y-fitting

Fixture drain line

Cleanout fitting & plugs

Clear a branch drain line by locating the cleanout fitting at the end of the line. Place a bucket underneath the opening to catch waste water, then slowly unscrew the cleanout plug with an adjustable wrench. Clear clogs in the branch drain line with a hand auger (pages 372 to 373).

Clear the main waste and vent stack by running the cable of a hand auger down through the roof vent. Always use extreme caution while working on a ladder or roof.

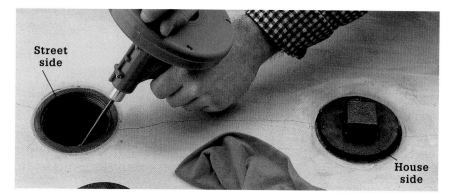

Street side

House side

Clear the house trap in a sewer service line using a hand auger. Slowly remove only the plug on the "street side" of the trap. If water seeps out the opening as the plug is removed, the clog is in the sewer line beyond the trap. If no water seeps out, auger the trap. If no clog is present in the trap, replace the street-side plug and remove the house-side plug. Use the auger to clear clogs located between the house trap and main stack.

How to Remove & Replace a Main Drain Cleanout Plug

1

Cleanout plug

Remove the cleanout plug, using a large wrench. If plug does not turn out, apply penetrating oil around edge of plug, wait 10 minutes, and try again. Place rags and a bucket under fitting opening to catch any water that may be backed up in the line.

2

Remove stubborn plugs by placing the cutting edge of chisel on edge of plug. Strike chisel with a ball-peen hammer to move plug counterclockwise. If plug does not turn out, break it into pieces with the chisel and hammer. Remove all broken pieces.

3

Cleanout fitting

Replace old plug with new plastic plug. Apply pipe joint compound to the threads of the replacement plug and screw into cleanout fitting.

Wing nut

Metal plates

Alternate: Replace old plug with an expandable rubber plug. A wing nut squeezes the rubber core between two metal plates. The rubber bulges slightly to create a watertight seal.

Advanced Clog Clearing

When plungers and hand augers meet a clog they can't dislodge, you have one more DIY option before you call a professional drain cleaning service. Most rental centers stock power augers in several sizes. These electric tools work in much the same manner as a hand auger, but with much more tenacity. With spear tools, cutting tools, and spring tools, they can push or cut through a clog, or snag an object and drag it out from your floor or branch drainline.

Always read the instructions carefully and be sure to get through operating instructions at the rental center. If used improperly, power augers can cause major damage to your plumbing system. They are designed to be inserted beyond the trap or through cleanouts in the drainline, so they do not need to be forced through the drain trap. Never run a power auger through a toilet—it could scratch the porcelain or even break the fixture.

Tools & Materials ▸

Auger with 50-ft. ½" cable
Eye protection
Grounded extension cord
Channel-type pliers
Tool wrench
Heavy leather gloves
Penetrating oil
Teflon tape
Screwdriver

When the going gets tough, the tough rent power tools. The medium duty auger shown here is perfect for augering the 2-inch-diameter floor drainlines and branch drainlines.

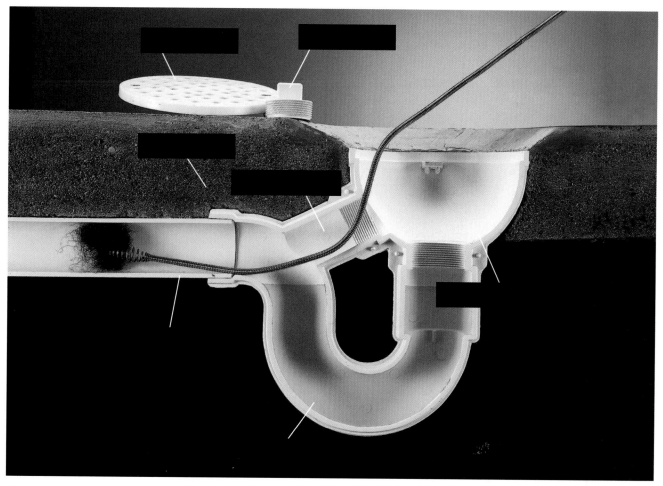

Floor drains can develop extremely robust clogs, especially if the drain cover is absent. A power auger that's inserted through the cleanout opening can travel 50 feet or more to hunt down and remove stubborn clogs. These rental tools come in several sizes and may also be used to clear tub/shower drainlines, branch drainlines and even a 3- to 4-inch diameter soil stack or house drain.

Tool Tip ▶

Power augers can be fitted with three different head styles. The spring tool is affixed to the cable end to snag and retrieve an obstruction. The spear tool is used to penetrate a clog and puncture it to create a starter hole for the cutting tool, which can cut apart very resistant clogs (often tree roots).

Spring tool

Spear tool

Cutter tool

How to Power-auger a Floor Drain

Remove the cover from the floor drain using a screwdriver. On one wall of the drain bowl you'll see a cleanout plug. Remove the plug from the drain bowl with your largest channel-type pliers. This cleanout allows you to bypass the trap. If it's stuck, apply penetrating oil to the threads and let it sit a half an hour before trying to free it again. If the wrench won't free it, rent a large pipe wrench. You can also auger through the trap if you have to.

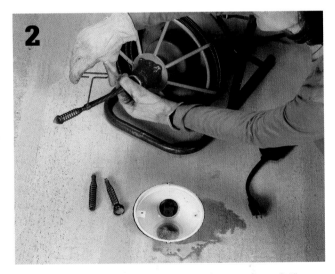

Rent an electric drum auger with at least 50 feet of ½" cable. The rental company should provide a properly sized, grounded extension cord, heavy leather gloves, and eye protection. The auger should come with a spear tool, cutter tool, and possibly a spring-tool suitable for a 2" drainline. Attach the spearhead first (with the machine unplugged).

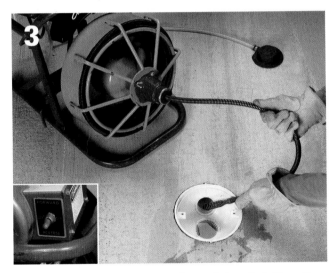

Wear close-fitting clothing and contain long hair. Place the power auger machine in a dry location within three feet of the drain opening. Plug the tool into a grounded, GFCI circuit. Put on eye protection and gloves; you will be holding a rotating metal cable and may be exposed to dangerous bacteria and caustic drain-cleaning chemicals. Position the footswitch where it is easy to actuate; visualize using the machine without having to overreach the rotating drum or exposed belts. Make sure the FOR/REV switch is in the Forward position (inset photo). Hand feed the cleaning tool and some cable into the drain or cleanout before turning the machine on.

Stationary power augers (as opposed to pistol-grip types) are controlled by a foot pedal called an actuator so you can turn the power on and off hands-free.

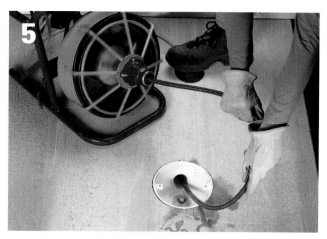

With both gloved hands on the cable, depress the foot actuator to start the machine. Gradually push the rotating cable into the drain opening. If the rotation slows or you cannot feed more cable into the drain, pull back on the cable before pushing it forward again. Don't force it. The cable needs to be rotating whenever the motor is running or it can kink and buckle, destroying the cable (although a clutch on the drum should prevent this). If the cleaning tool becomes stuck, turn the FOR/REV switch to Reverse and back the tool off the obstruction before switching back to Forward again.

Gradually work through the clog by pulling back on the cable whenever the machine starts to bog down and pushing it forward again when it gains new momentum. Again, never let the cable stop turning when the motor is running. When you have broken through the clog (or if you are using the spring head and believe you have snagged an object) withdraw the cable from the line. Manually pull the cable from the drain line while continuing to run the drum Forward. If it's practical, have a helper hose off the cable as its withdrawn and recoiled. When the cleaning tool is close to the drain opening, release the foot actuator and let the cable come to a stop before feeding the remaining cable into the drum by hand.

After clearing the drain pipe, run the auger through the trap. Finish cleaning the auger. Wrap Teflon tape clockwise onto the plug threads and replace the plug. Run hot water through a hose from the laundry sink or use a bucket to flush remaining debris through the trap and down the line.

Fixing a Water Heater

Standard tank water heaters are designed so that repairs are simple. All water heaters have convenient access panels that make it easy to replace worn-out parts. When buying new water heater parts, make sure the replacements match the specifications of your water heater. Most water heaters have a nameplate (page 392) that lists the information needed, including the pressure rating of the tank and the voltage and wattage ratings of the electric heating elements.

Many water heater problems can be avoided with routine yearly maintenance. Flush the water heater and test the pressure-relief valve once a year. Set the thermostat at a lower water temperature to prevent heat damage to the tank. (*Note: Water temperature may affect the efficiency of automatic dishwashers. Check manufacturer's directions for recommended water temperature.*) Water heaters last about 10 years on average, but with regular maintenance, a water heater can last 20 years or more.

Do not install an insulating jacket around a gas water heater. Insulation can block air supply and prevent the water heater from ventilating properly. Many water heater manufacturers prohibit the use of insulating jackets. To save energy, insulate the hot water pipes instead, using tube insulation sleeves available at home improvement centers.

The pressure-relief valve is an important safety device that should be checked at least once each year and replaced, if needed. When replacing the pressure-relief valve, shut off the water and drain several gallons of water from the tank.

Replacing a water heater is not a difficult project, but check with local codes for installation restrictions. Your community may require that a licensed plumber make gas hookups, for example, or that electrical water heaters be connected by an electrician.

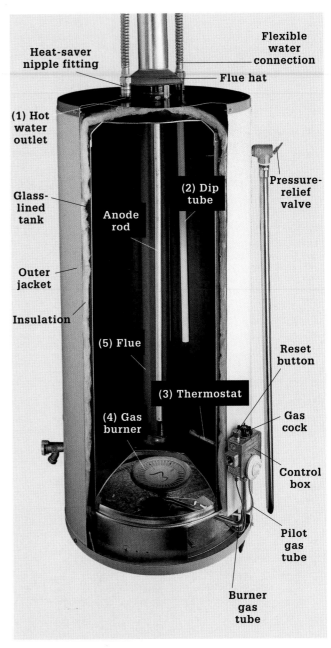

How a gas water heater works: Hot water leaves tank through the hot water outlet (1) as fresh, cold water enters the water heater through the dip tube (2). As the water temperature drops, the thermostat (3) opens the gas valve, and the gas burner (4) is lighted by pilot flame. Exhaust gases are vented through flue (5). When water temperature reaches preset temperature, the thermostat closes gas valve, extinguishing burner. The thermocouple protects against gas leaks by automatically shutting off gas if pilot flame goes out. Anode rod protects tank lining from rust by attracting corrosive elements in the water. Pressure-relief valve guards against ruptures caused by steam buildup in tank.

Problems	Repairs

No hot water, or not enough hot water.	1. Gas heater: Make sure gas is on, then relight pilot flame (page 389).
	   Electric heater: Make sure power is on, then reset thermostat (page 390).
	2. Flush water heater to remove sediment in tank (photo, below).
	3. Insulate hot water pipes to reduce heat loss.
	4. Gas heater: Clean gas burner & replace thermocouple (pages 388 to 389).
	   Electric heater: Replace heating element or thermostat (pages 390 to 391).
	5. Raise temperature setting of thermostat.

Pressure-relief valve leaks.	1. Lower the temperature setting (photo, below). 2. Install a new pressure-relief valve (page 394, steps 10 to 11). 3. Install a water hammer arrester (page 407).
Pilot flame will not stay lighted.	Clean gas burner & replace the thermocouple (pages 388 to 389).
Water heater leaks around base of tank.	Replace the water heater immediately (pages 392 to 399).

Tips for Maintaining a Water Heater ▶

Flush the water heater once a year by draining several gallons of water from the tank. Flushing removes sediment buildup that causes corrosion and reduces heating efficiency.

Lower the temperature setting on thermostat to 120° F. Lower temperature setting reduces damage to tank caused by overheating and also reduces energy use.

Fixing a Gas Water Heater

If a gas water heater does not heat water, first remove the outer and inner access panels and make sure the pilot is lighted. To relight a pilot, see steps 20 to 23, page 397. During operation, the outer and inner access panels must be in place. Operating the water heater without the access panels may allow air drafts to blow out the pilot flame.

If the pilot will not light, it is probably because the thermocouple is worn out. The thermocouple is a safety device designed to shut off the gas automatically if the pilot flame goes out. The thermocouple is a thin copper wire that runs from the control box to the gas burner. New thermocouples are inexpensive and can be installed in a few minutes.

If the gas burner does not light, even though the pilot flame is working, or if the gas burns with a yellow, smoky flame, the burner and the pilot gas tube should be cleaned. Clean the burner and gas tube annually to improve energy efficiency and extend the life of the water heater.

A gas water heater must be well ventilated. If you smell smoke or fumes coming from a water heater, shut off the water heater and make sure the exhaust duct is not clogged with soot. A rusted duct must be replaced.

Remember to shut off the gas before beginning work.

Tools & Materials ▸

Adjustable wrench
Vacuum cleaner
Needlenose pliers

Thin wires
Replacement thermocouple

How to Clean a Gas Burner & Replace a Thermocouple

Shut off gas by turning the gas cock on top of the control box to the OFF position. Wait 10 minutes for gas to dissipate.

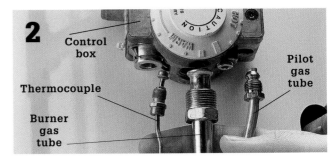

Disconnect the pilot gas tube, the burner gas tube, and the thermocouple from the bottom of the control box, using an adjustable wrench.

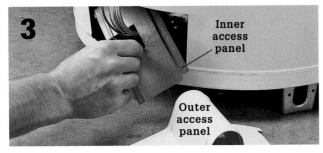

Remove the outer and inner access panels covering the burner chamber.

Pull down slightly on the pilot gas tube, the burner gas tube, and thermocouple wire to free them from the control box. Tilt the burner unit slightly and remove it from the burner chamber.

5 Burner jets
Gas tube nipple
Burner gas tube
Burner
Small opening

Unscrew burner from burner gas tube nipple. Clean small opening in nipple, using a piece of thin wire. Vacuum out burner jets and the burner chamber.

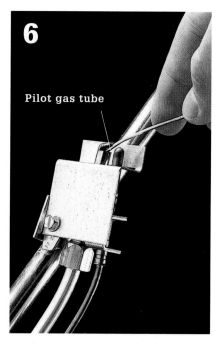

6 Pilot gas tube

Clean the pilot gas tube with a piece of wire. Vacuum out any loose particles. Screw burner onto gas tube nipple.

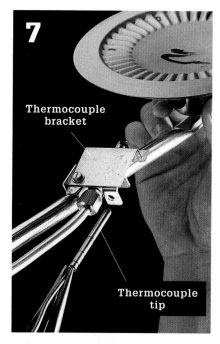

7 Thermocouple bracket
Thermocouple tip

Pull the old thermocouple from bracket. Install new thermocouple by pushing the tip into the bracket until it snaps into place.

8 Mounting bracket
Tab

Insert the burner unit into the chamber. Flat tab at end of burner should fit into slotted opening in mounting bracket at the bottom of the chamber.

9 Burner gas tube
Thermocouple
Pilot gas tube

Reconnect the gas tubes and the thermocouple to the control box. Turn on the gas and test for leaks (page 396, step 19). Light the pilot (page 397, steps 20 to 23).

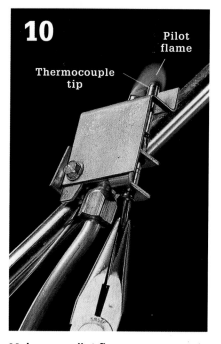

10 Pilot flame
Thermocouple tip

Make sure pilot flame wraps around tip of thermocouple. If needed, adjust thermocouple with needlenose pliers until tip is in flame. Replace the inner and outer access panels.

Fixing an Electric Water Heater

The most common problem with an electric water heater is a burned-out heating element. To determine which element has failed, turn on a hot water faucet and test the temperature. If the water heater produces water that is warm, but not hot, replace the top heating element. If the heater produces a small amount of very hot water, followed by cold water, replace the bottom heating element.

If replacing the heating element does not solve the problem, then replace the thermostat, found under convenient access panels on the side of the heater.

Remember to turn off the power and test for current before touching wires (page 398, step 4).

Tools & Materials ▸

Screwdriver
Gloves
Neon circuit tester
Channel-type pliers
Masking tape
Replacement heating element or thermostat
Replacement gasket
Pipe joint compound

How to Replace an Electric Thermostat

1

Turn off power at main service panel. Remove access panel on side of heater, and test for current (page 398, step 4).

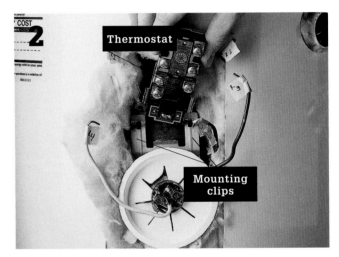

2

Disconnect thermostat wires, and label connections with masking tape. Pull old thermostat out of mounting clips. Snap new thermostat into place, and reconnect wires.

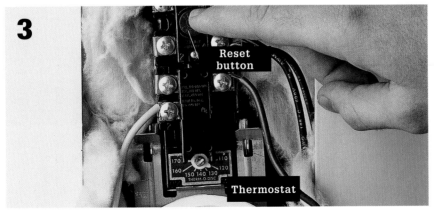

3

Press thermostat reset button, then use a screwdriver to set thermostat to desired temperature. Replace insulation and access panel. Turn on power.

How to Replace an Electric Heating Element

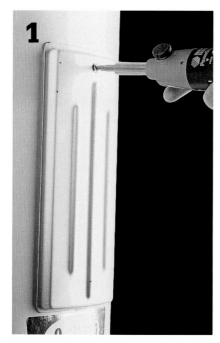

1

Remove access panel on side of water heater. Shut off power to water heater (page 390, step 1). Close the shutoff valves, then drain tank (page 393, step 3).

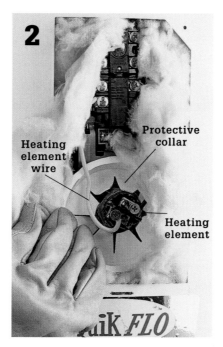

2

Heating element wire

Protective collar

Heating element

Wearing protective gloves, carefully move insulation aside. Caution: Test for current (page 398, step 4), then disconnect wires on heating element. Remove protective collar.

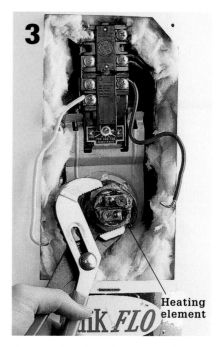

3

Heating element

Unscrew the heating element with channel-type pliers. Remove old gasket from around water heater opening. Coat both sides of new gasket with pipe joint compound.

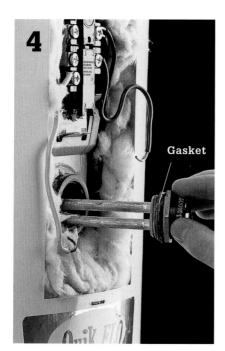

4

Gasket

Slide new gasket over heating element, and screw element into the tank. Tighten element with channel-type pliers.

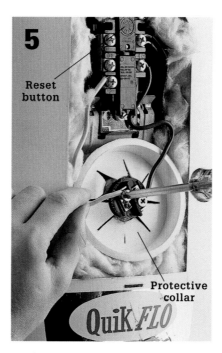

5

Reset button

Protective collar

Replace protective collar, and reconnect all wires. Turn on hot water faucets throughout house, then turn on water heater shutoff valves. When tap water runs steadily, close faucets.

6

Thermostat

170 °F   110
160   120
150 140 130
THERM-O-DISC

Use a screwdriver to set thermostat to desired temperature. Press thermostat reset buttons. Fold insulation over thermostat, and replace the access panel. Turn on power.

Replacing a Water Heater

A water heater that leaks should be replaced immediately to prevent expensive water damage. Leaks occur because the inner tank has rusted through.

When replacing an electric water heater, make sure the voltage of the new model is the same as the old heater. When replacing a gas water heater, maintain a clearance of 6" or more around the unit for ventilation. Water heaters are available with tank sizes ranging from 30 to 65 gallons. A 40- or 50-gallon heater should be large enough for a family of four.

Energy-efficient water heaters have polyurethane foam insulation and usually carry an extended warranty. These models are more expensive, but over the life of the water heater they cost less to own and operate.

The pressure-relief valve usually must be purchased separately. Make sure the new valve matches the working pressure rating of the tank.

Tools & Materials ▸

Pipe wrenches	Small wire brush	#4 gauge ⅜"	Teflon tape
Hacksaw	Propane torch	sheetmetal screws	Flexible
or tubing cutter	Adjustable wrench	Pressure-relief valve	water connectors
Screwdriver	Circuit tester	Threaded male	¾" copper pipe
Hammer	(electric heaters)	pipe adapters	Pipe joint compound
Appliance dolly	Bucket	Solder	Sponge
Level	Wood shims	Two heat-saver nipples	Masking tape

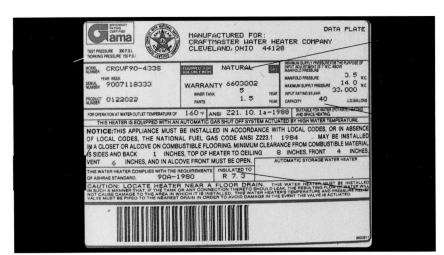

Nameplate on side of water heater lists tank capacity, insulation R-value, and working pressure (pounds per square inch). More efficient water heaters have an insulation R-value of 7 or higher. Nameplate for an electric water heater includes the voltage and the wattage capacity of the heating elements and thermostats. Water heaters also have a yellow energy guide label (photo, top) that lists typical yearly operating costs. Estimates are based on national averages. Energy costs in your area may vary.

How to Replace a Gas Water Heater

1

In-line gas valve

Shut off the gas by turning the handle of the in-line valve so it is perpendicular to gas line. Wait 10 minutes for gas to dissipate. Shut off the water supply at the shutoff valves.

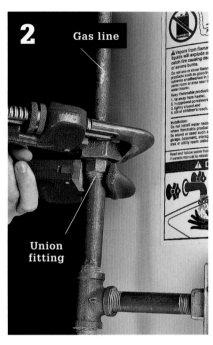

2

Gas line

Union fitting

Disconnect gas line at the union fitting or at the flare fitting below shutoff valve, using pipe wrenches. Disassemble and save the gas pipes and fittings.

3

Hose bib

Drain water from the water heater tank by opening the hose bib on the side of the tank. Drain the water into buckets, or attach a hose and empty the tank into a floor drain.

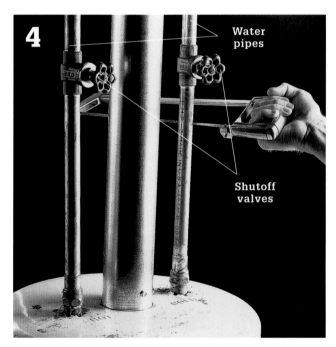

4

Water pipes

Shutoff valves

Disconnect the hot and cold water pipes above the water heater. If pipes are soldered copper, use a hacksaw or tubing cutter to cut through water pipes just below shutoff valves. Cuts must be straight.

5

Exhaust duct

Disconnect the exhaust duct by removing the sheetmetal screws. Remove the old water heater with an appliance dolly.

(continued)

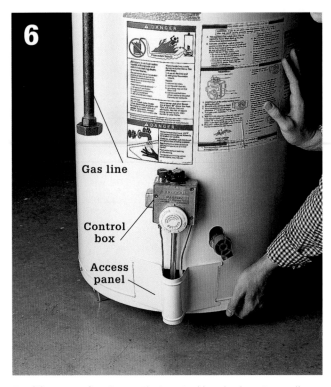

6

Gas line

Control
box

Access
panel

Position new heater so that control box is close to gas line, and access panel for burner chamber is not obstructed.

7

Level the water heater by placing wood shims under the legs.

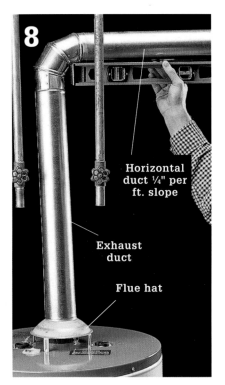

8

Horizontal
duct ¼" per
ft. slope

Exhaust
duct

Flue hat

Position flue hat so legs fit into slots on water heater, then slip exhaust duct over flue hat. Make sure horizontal duct slopes upward ¼" per ft. so fumes cannot back up into house.

9

Exhaust
duct

Flue hat

Attach the flue hat to the exhaust duct with #4 gauge ⅜" sheetmetal screws driven every 4".

10

Teflon tape

T & P
VALVE

Wrap threads of new pressure-relief valve with Teflon tape, and screw valve into tank opening with a pipe wrench.

11

Threaded
male
adapter

Drain
pipe

Attach a copper or CPVC drain pipe to the pressure-relief valve, using threaded male adapter. Pipe should reach to within 3" of floor.

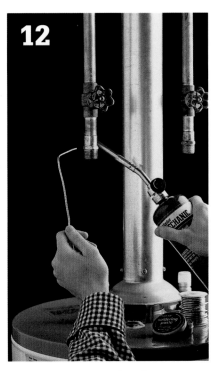

12

Solder threaded male adapters to the water pipes. Let pipes cool, then wrap Teflon tape around threads of adapters.

13

Wrap Teflon tape around the threads of two heat-saver nipples. The nipples are color-coded, and have water-direction arrows to ensure proper installation.

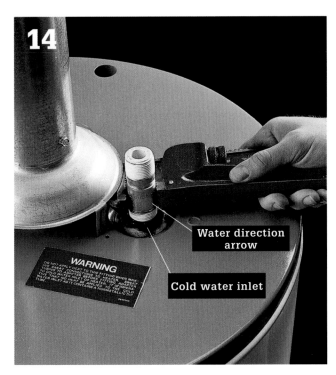

14

Water direction
arrow

Cold water inlet

WARNING

Attach blue-coded nipple fitting to cold water inlet and red-coded fitting to hot water outlet, using a pipe wrench. On cold water nipple, water direction arrow should face down; on hot water nipple, arrow should face up.

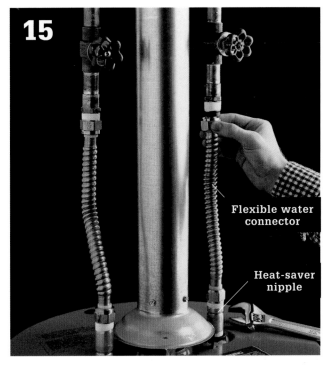

15

Flexible water
connector

Heat-saver
nipple

Connect the water lines to the heat-saver nipples with flexible water connectors. Tighten fittings with an adjustable wrench.

(continued)

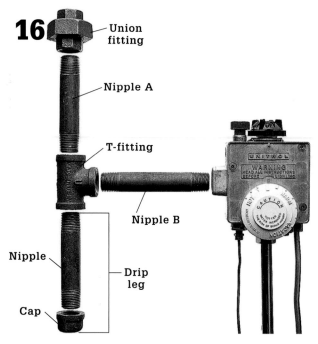

16 Union fitting

Nipple A

T-fitting

Nipple B

Nipple

Drip leg

Cap

Test-fit gas pipes and fittings from old water heater (step 2). One or two new black-iron nipples (A, B) may by necessary if new water heater is taller or shorter than old heater. Use black iron, not galvanized iron, for gas lines. Capped nipple is called a drip leg. The drip leg protects the gas burner by catching dirt particles.

17

Clean pipe threads with a small wire brush, and coat the threads with pipe joint compound. Assemble gas line in the following order: control box nipple (1), T-fitting (2), vertical nipple (3), union fitting (4), vertical nipple (5), cap (6).

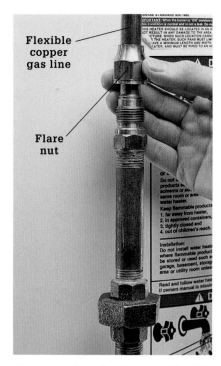

Flexible copper gas line

Flare nut

Alternate: If gas line is made of flexible copper, use a flare fitting to connect the gas line to the water heater.

18

Open the hot water faucets throughout house, then open the water heater inlet and outlet shutoff valves. When water runs steadily from faucets, close faucets.

19

Open the in-line valve on the gas line (step 1). Test for leaks by dabbing soapy water on each joint. Leaking gas will cause water to bubble. Tighten leaking joints with a pipe wrench.

Turn the gas cock on top of control box to the PILOT position. Set the temperature control on front of box to desired temperature.

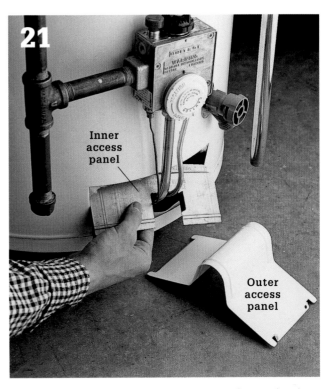

Remove the outer and inner access panels covering the burner chamber.

Light a match and hold flame next to the end of the pilot gas tube inside the burner chamber. Be sure to keep your face away from the opening.

While holding match next to end of pilot gas tube, press the reset button on top of control box. When pilot flame lights, continue to hold reset button for one minute. Turn gas cock to ON position, and replace the inner and outer access panels.

How to Replace a 220/240-volt Electric Water Heater

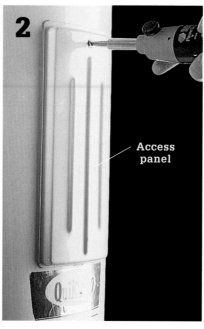

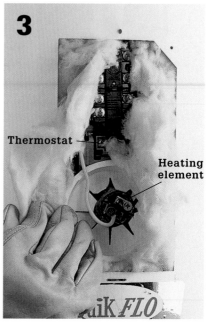

Turn off power to water heater by switching off circuit breaker (or removing fuse) at main service panel. Drain water heater and disconnect water pipes (page 393, steps 3 and 4).

Remove one of the heating element access panels on the side of the water heater.

Wearing protective gloves, fold back the insulation to expose the thermostat. *Caution: Do not touch bare wires until they have been tested for current.*

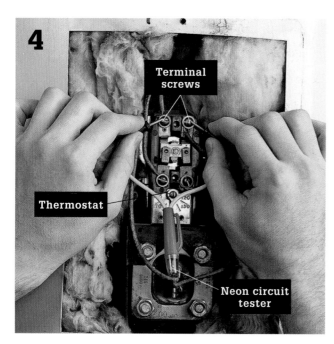

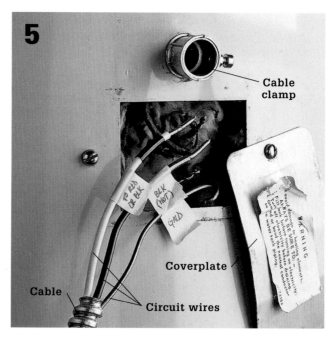

Test for current by touching probes of neon circuit tester to top pair of terminal screws on the thermostat. If tester lights, wires are not safe to work on; turn off main power switch and retest for current.

Remove coverplate on electrical box, found at side or top of water heater. Disconnect all wires, and label with masking tape for reference. Loosen cable clamp. Remove wires by pulling them through clamp. Remove old heater, then position new heater.

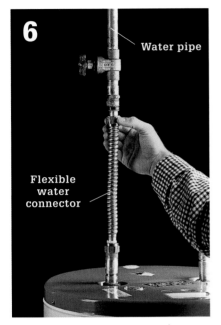

6

Water pipe

Flexible water connector

Connect water pipes and pressure-relief valve, following directions for gas water heaters (pages 395 to 396, steps 10 to 15). Open hot water faucets throughout the house, and turn on water. When water runs steadily, turn off faucets.

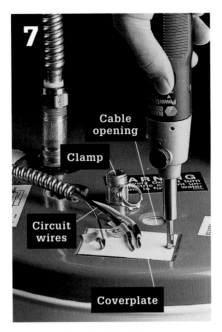

7

Cable opening

Clamp

Circuit wires

Coverplate

Remove the electrical box coverplate on new water heater. Thread the circuit wires through the clamp. Thread circuit wires through the cable opening on the water heater, and attach clamp to water heater.

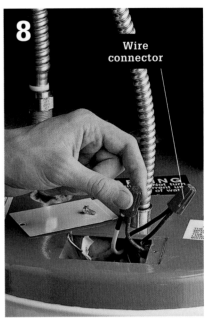

8

Wire connector

Connect the circuit wires to the water heater wires, using wire connectors.

9

Ground screw

Ground wire

Attach bare copper or green ground wire to ground screw. Replace coverplate.

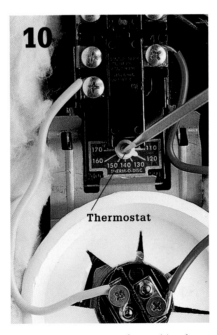

10

Thermostat

Remove access panels on side of water heater (steps 2 to 3), and use a screwdriver to set thermostats to desired water temperature.

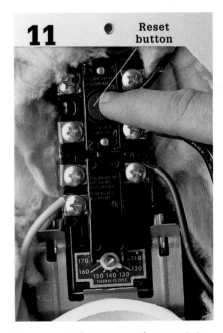

11

Reset button

Press reset button on thermostats. Replace the insulation and access panels. Turn on power.

Maintaining a Water Softener

A water softener lowers the content of "hard" minerals in water—magnesium and calcium—and replaces them with sodium or potassium to help prolong the life of pipes and appliances.

A water softener has just a few mechanical parts—valves to control water flow in and out of the tank, and a timer, which regulates the recharging of the mineral tank by the brine tank.

If your water becomes hard, the brine tank may just need additional salt or potassium pellets. Because household demands vary, check your supply every week to determine how often the salt or potassium supply should be replenished (typically every couple of months).

An improperly set timer can cause hard water. Adjust it to run more frequently to ensure a constant supply of soft water. Iron content also causes hard water. Measure the iron content of your water supply occasionally, or add a water filter to help reduce the iron flow into the water softener.

Repair problems generally arise in the brine line or the control unit. Inspect the brine line every two years for buildup of sediment from the water supply or foreign particles in the salt or potassium. If the control unit needs servicing, remove it and bring it to your nearest dealer. Follow the removal instructions in the owner's manual for your particular unit.

Tools & Materials ▸

Needlenose pliers
Screwdriver
Kitchen baster or funnel

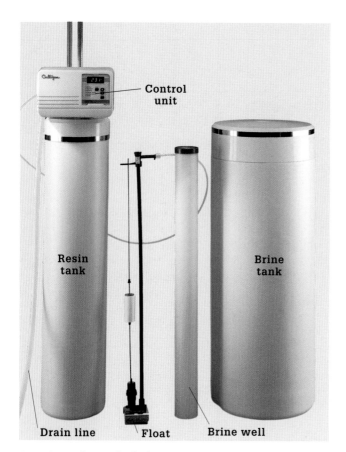

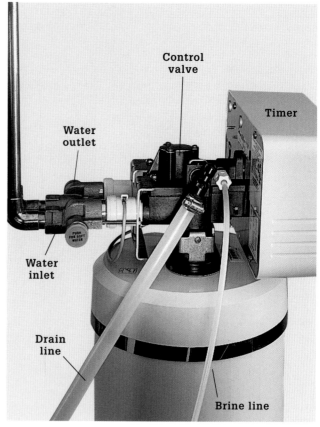

A water softener includes two tanks: a resin tank (left) and a brine tank (right). Inside the brine tank is the brine well and float (center).

How to Inspect & Clean Brine Connections

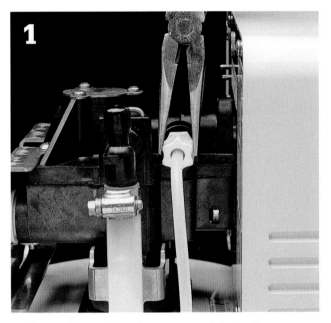

Unplug softener. Divert the water supply by turning the bypass valve, or closing the inlet valve and turning on the nearest faucet. Turn timer dial to backwash. With a needlenose pliers, remove the compression nut connecting the brine line to the control unit. Inspect line for obstructions.

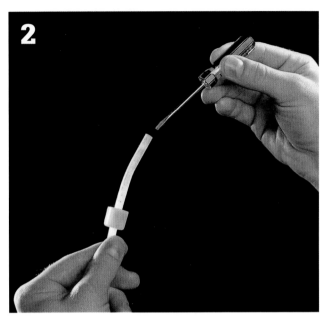

Remove particles or residue from the line, using a small screwdriver. Flush line with warm water—a funnel or kitchen baster is useful for this task—then reattach the brine line.

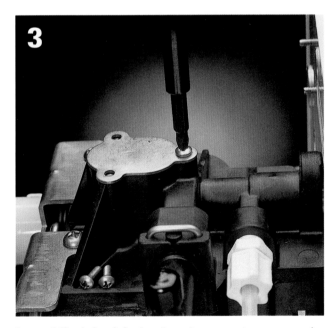

Inspect the brine injector. Do not reconnect power or make any changes to the supply or control dial. To gain access to the brine injector, which is often directly below the brine line connection, use a screwdriver to remove the cover. Unscrew injector from housing.

Pull off the injector filter screen covering the injector. Wash it with soap and water. Blow into injector or wipe it out with a soft cloth to clean. Do not use a sharp object that might scratch the metal and damage the injector. Reattach screen and screw injector back into place. Attach the cover. Return bypass valve to original position, or open inlet valve and turn off faucet. Reset the control dial and plug in softener.

Maintaining Septic Systems

About 15 percent of homes in the U.S. are not hooked up to a municipal sewer service. In these homes, the household waste is usually managed by a private septic system.

Septic systems consist of an underground holding tank and a drainage field. Sewage from the house is directed through the DWV system and into the septic tank. Once in the tank, the solid wastes separate from the liquid and settle to the bottom, where they're decomposed by microorganisms.

The breakdown of the wastes creates a liquid effluent. In a conventional system, the effluent flows from the tank into a sealed junction box. The junction box distributes the effluent to a drainage field—several perforated pipes lying on a bed of gravel or other loose-fill material. Seeping through holes in the pipes, the effluent is purified as it filters through layers of soil and rock on its return to the water table.

In a mound system, the drainage field is built in an elevated mound. A second tank, called a lift station, contains a pump which pumps the liquid effluent into the mounded drainage field. Mound systems are necessary where soil types or high water tables make a conventional drainage field unsuitable.

The storage and breakdown of sewage in the septic tank produces methane gas. Like a DWV system in a house with municipal sewer service, a septic system must have a vent pipe for the gases to escape at the roof of the house. Without this vent, the pressure in the tank would quickly increase to dangerous levels.

Undecomposed solids accumulate in the bottom of the tank, forming a growing layer of sludge. Over time, the tank reaches its capacity and the sludge must be pumped out. Most septic tanks need to be pumped out every one to three years, depending on tank capacity and the number of people who live in the home.

When neglected septic tanks become overfilled, the solid wastes do not separate from the liquid and instead pass through the tank and into the drainage field. There they clog the loose-fill material, barring the passage of effluent. When this happens, the field must be dug up and the loose-fill material replaced.

Septic systems rely on a natural process of decomposition and work best when allowed to function as designed. Don't try to help the process along by adding yeasts or other biological additives.

Regular tank maintenance and careful waste disposal should keep your septic system healthy for 20 years, or more. However, if the system has been neglected, it's possible you'll need to have the entire drainage field replaced.

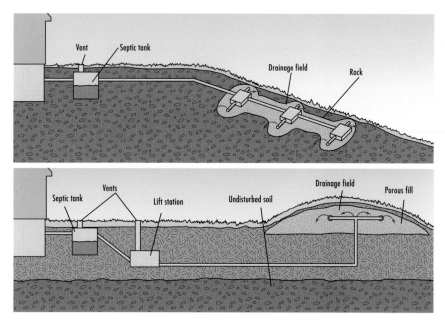

A conventional septic system (top) relies on gravity to move liquid from the tank to the drainage field. A mound system (bottom) uses a pump to move liquids to an elevated drainage field.

Have your tank inspected and emptied regularly.	A neglected tank will cause your system to fail, resulting in sewage backup and posing a serious risk to your family's health. Experts recommend pumping a septic tank every one to two years.
Avoid using chemicals.	Harsh chemicals and antibacterial agents kill the bacteria your system depends on. Keep these chemicals out of your toilets and house drains: Drain cleaner Paint and paint thinner Chemical cleaners Chlorine — including toilet bowl flush-cleaners Antibacterial soft-soaps
Limit kitchen wastes.	Grease and fat from food hinder the septic process by coating drain pipes, interfering with bacterial breakdown in the tank, and clogging the loose-fill material in the drain field. Food disposers overload your system with solid food particles, sometimes doubling the rate of sludge accumulation in the tank. Throw cooking grease and food scraps in the garbage or compost heap.
Limit water inflow.	Excess water speeds up the flow through the septic system. Repair leaky plumbing fixtures as soon as possible. The natural bacteria can't do its job, allowing too many solids to pass into the drain field. Route roof drains out of the house drain system. Don't drain a swimming pool or hot tub into the house drain.
Never use additives.	Biological additives designed to stimulate bacterial growth often harm more than they help. These additives agitate the anaerobic bacteria in the septic tank, and the increased activity forces undissolved solids into the drain field.

Troubleshooting Your Septic System

Once problems arise within a septic system, there isn't much a homeowner can do, but being able to identify signs of trouble may prolong the life of your system and will probably save you some money.

If your drains are working slowly, or not draining at all, there may be a clog in the main house drain, or the septic system may be backed up. Check for clogs first. Use a motorized auger (photo, right) to clear the main drain. Never use chemical drain cleaners.

If the house drain isn't clogged, the problem may be a clogged drain field, an absence of bacteria in the system, or a full septic tank.

In addition to slow drainage, common signs of trouble include the presence of dark-colored water on the surface of the drain field and a sewage odor in or around the home.

Any of these symptoms may indicate a serious problem. Human sewage is considered a hazardous waste, and there are strict regulations governing its removal. Servicing a septic system isn't something you should try to do yourself.

Septic tanks produce explosive methane gas and may contain deadly viruses. Contact a licensed sewer service to have your septic system inspected and serviced.

Fixing Burst or Frozen Pipes

When a pipe bursts, immediately turn off the water at the main shutoff valve. Make temporary repairs with a sleeve clamp repair kit (page opposite).

A burst pipe is usually caused by freezing water. Prevent freezes by insulating pipes that run in crawl spaces or other unheated areas.

Pipes that freeze, but do not burst, will block water flow to faucets or appliances. Frozen pipes are easily thawed, but determining the exact location of the blockage may be difficult. Leave blocked faucets or valves turned on. Trace supply pipes that lead to blocked faucet or valve, and look for places where the line runs close to exterior walls or unheated areas. Thaw pipes with a heat gun or hair dryer (below).

Old fittings or corroded pipe also may leak or rupture. Fix old pipes according to the guidelines described on pages 286 to 315.

Tools & Materials ▸

Heat gun
  or hair dryer
Gloves
Metal file

Screwdriver
Pipe insulation
Sleeve clamp
  repair kit

Begin any emergency repair by turning off water supply at main shutoff valve. The main shutoff valve is usually located near water meter.

How to Repair Pipes Blocked with Ice

Thaw pipes with a heat gun or hair dryer. Use heat gun on low setting, and keep nozzle moving to prevent overheating pipes.

Let pipes cool, then insulate with sleeve-type foam insulation to prevent freezing. Use pipe insulation in crawl spaces or other unheated areas.

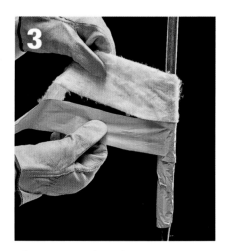

Alternate: Insulate pipes with fiberglass strip insulation and waterproof wrap. Wrap insulating strips loosely for best protection.

How to Temporarily Fix a Burst Pipe

Turn off water at main shutoff valve. Heat pipe gently with heat gun or hair dryer. Keep nozzle moving. Once frozen area is thawed, allow pipe to drain.

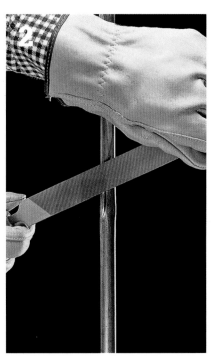

Smooth rough edges of rupture with metal file.

Place rubber sleeve of repair clamp around rupture. Make sure seam of sleeve is on opposite side of pipe from rupture.

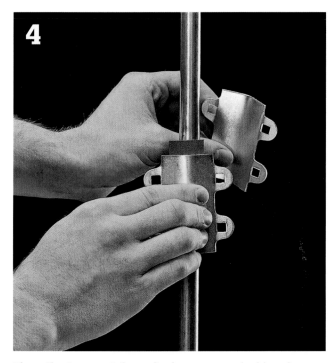

Place the two metal repair clamps around rubber sleeve.

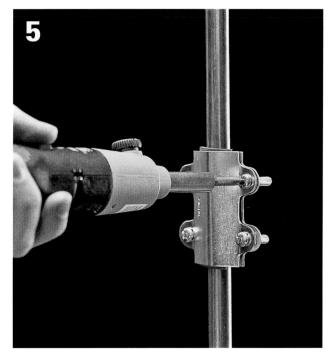

Tighten screws with screwdriver. Open water supply and watch for leaks. If repair clamp leaks, retighten screws. *Caution: Repairs made with a repair clamp kit are temporary. Replace ruptured section of pipe as soon as possible.*

Quieting Noisy Pipes

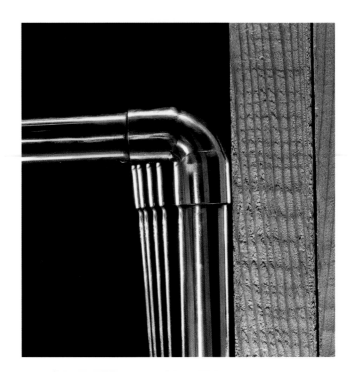

Pipes can make a loud banging noise when faucets are turned off or when valves on washing machines (or other automatic appliances) shut abruptly. The sudden stop of flowing water traps air and creates a shock wave, called water hammer, that slams through the water supply system. Some pipes may knock against wall studs or joists, creating additional noise.

Water hammer can be more than an annoyance. The shockwave can cause damage and eventually failure in pipes and fittings. If a pressure-relief valve on your water heater leaks, it may not be a faulty valve, but a pressure surge in the supply system.

You can eliminate water hammer by installing a simple device called a water hammer arrester in the supply line. Inexpensive point-of-use arresters are small enough to be installed easily near the noisy valve or appliance (the closer the better). They can be positioned horizontally or vertically or at an angle without any change in effectiveness. Unlike with old-style air chambers, water cannot fill a water hammer arrester, so they should be effective for the life of the system.

Pipes that bang against studs or joists can be quieted by cushioning them with pieces of pipe insulation. Make sure pipe hangers are snug and that pipes are well supported.

Tools & Materials ▸

Utility knife
Reciprocating saw
 or hacksaw
Propane torch
 (for sweating copper)
Pipe wrenches
 (for galvanized iron)

Foam rubber
 pipe insulation
Pipe and fittings,
 as needed

Install cushions made from pieces of foam rubber pipe insulation to prevent pipes from banging against wall studs or joists.

Loose pipes may bang or rub against joist hangers, creating unwanted noises. Use pieces of foam rubber pipe insulation to cushion pipes.

How to Install a Water Hammer Arrester

Shut off water supply and drain pipes. Measure and cut out a section of horizontal pipe for T-fitting.

Install a T-fitting as close to the valve as possible.

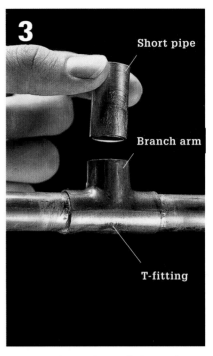

Install a short piece of pipe in the branch arm of the T-fitting. This short pipe will be used to attach a threaded fitting (step 4).

Install a threaded fitting. Use a fitting recommended by the manufacturer for your arrester.

Wrap the threads of the arrester in Teflon tape. Thread the arrester onto the fitting by hand. Tighten by holding the fitting with one adjustable wrench and turning the arrester with the other. Do not overtighten. Turn the water on and check for leaks.

Installing a Food Disposer

Food disposers are standard equipment in the modern home, and most of us have come to depend on them to macerate our plate leavings and crumbs so they can exit the house along with waste water from the sink drain. If your existing disposer needs replacing, you'll find that the job is relatively simple, especially if you select a replacement appliance that is the same model as the old one. In that case, you can probably reuse the exiting mounting assembly, drain sleeve and drain plumbing.

Most food disposers are classified as "continuous feed" because they can only operate when an ON/OFF switch n the wall is being actively held down. Let go of the switch, and the disposer stops. Each appliance has a power rating between ⅓ and 1 HP (horsepower). More powerful models bog down less under load and the motors last longer because they don't have to work as hard. They are also costlier, of course.

Disposers are hardwired to a switch mounted in an electrical box in the wall above the countertop. If your kitchen is not equipped for this, consult a wiring guide or hire an electrician. The actual electrical hookup of the appliance is quite simple (you only have to join two wires) but do hire an electrician if you are not comfortable with the job.

Tools & Materials ▸

Screwdriver	Drain auger
Channel-type pliers	Plumber's putty
Spud wrench	Wire caps
(optional)	Hose clamps
Hammer	Kitchen
Hacksaw or	drain supplies
tubing cutter	Threaded Y fitting

A properly functioning food disposer that's used correctly can actually help reduce clogs by ensuring that large bits of organic matter don't get into the drain system by accident.

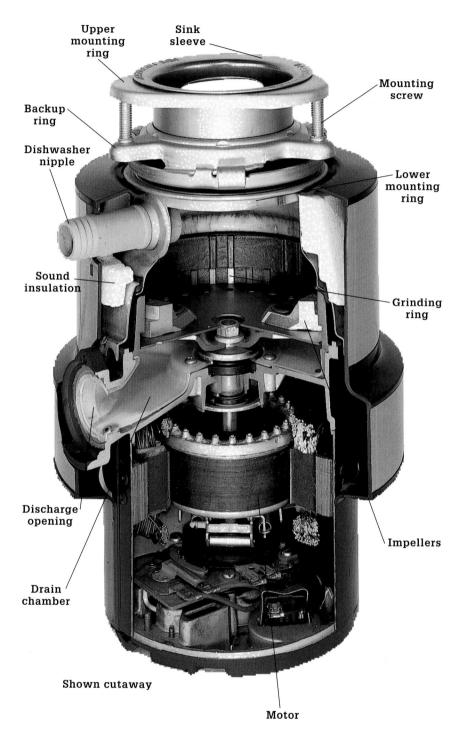

Upper mounting ring

Sink sleeve

Mounting screw

Backup ring

Dishwasher nipple

Lower mounting ring

Sound insulation

Grinding ring

Discharge opening

Impellers

Drain chamber

Shown cutaway

Motor

A food disposer grinds food waste so it can be flushed away through the sink drain system. A quality disposer has a ½ –horsepower, self-reversing motor that will not jam. Other features to look for include foam sound insulation, a cast iron grinding ring, and overload protection that allow the motor to be reset if it overheats. Better food disposers have a 5-year manufacturer's warranty.

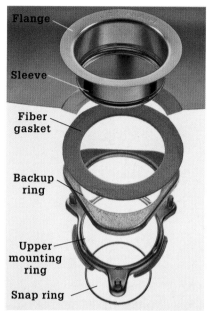

Flange

Sleeve

Fiber gasket

Backup ring

Upper mounting ring

Snap ring

The disposer is attached directly to the sink sleeve, which comes with the disposer and replaces the standard sink strainer. A snap ring fits into a groove around the sleeve of the strainer body to prevent the upper mounting ring and backup ring from sliding down while the upper mounting ring is tightened against the backup ring with mounting screws. A fiber gasket seals the connection from beneath the sink.

Kitchen and drain tees are required to have a baffle if the tee is connected to a dishwasher or disposer. The baffle is intended to prevent discharge from finding its way up the drain and into the sink. However, the baffle also reduces the drain flow capacity by half, which can cause the dishwasher or disposer to back up. You cannot, by most codes, simply replace the tee with another that has no baffle. The safest way to get around the problem is to run separate drains and traps to a Y fitting at the trap arm (as shown on previous page).

How to Install a Food Disposer

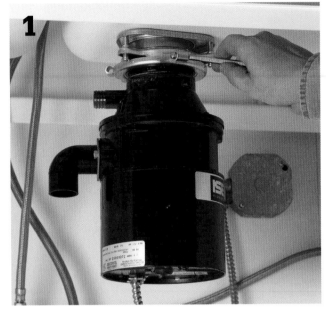

Remove the old disposer if you have one. You'll need to disconnect the drain pipes and traps first. If your old disposer has a special wrench for the mounting lugs, use it to loosen the lugs. Otherwise, use a screwdriver. If you do not have a helper, place a solid object directly beneath the disposer to support it before you begin removal. IMPORTANT: Shut off electrical power at the main service panel before you begin removal. Disconnect the wire leads, cap them and stuff them into the electrical box.

Tip ▸

Alternate: If you are installing a disposer in a sink that did not have one previously, remove the old sink strainer and drain tailpiece. Scrape up any old plumbers putty and clean the sink thoroughly around the drain opening with mineral spirits.

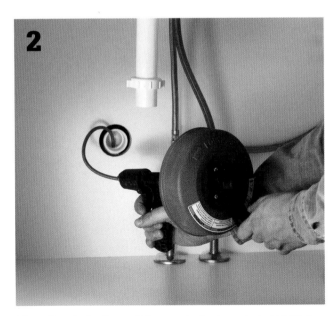

Clear the drain lines all the way to the branch drain before you begin the new installation. Remove the trap and trap arm first.

Disassemble the mounting assembly and then separate the upper and lower mounting rings and the backup ring. Also remove the snap ring from the sink sleeve. See photo, previous page.

Press the flange of the sink sleeve for your new disposer into a thin coil of plumbers putty that you have laid around the perimeter of the drain opening. The sleeve should be well-seated in the coil.

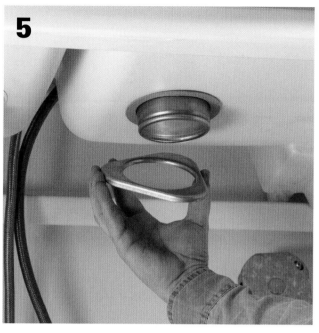

Slip the fiber gasket and then the backup ring onto the sink sleeve, working from inside the sink base cabinet. Make sure the backup ring is oriented the same way it was before you disassembled the mounting assembly.

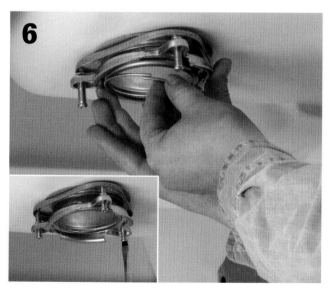

Insert the upper mounting ring onto the sleeve with the slotted ends of the screws facing away from the backup ring so you can access them. Then, holding all three parts at the top of the sleeve, slide the snap ring onto the sleeve until it snaps into the groove. Tighten the three mounting screws on the upper mounting ring until the tips press firmly against the backup ring (inset photo). It is the tension created by these screws that keeps the disposer steady and minimizes vibrating.

Make electrical connections before you mount the disposer unit on the mounting assembly. Shut OFF power at the service panel if you have turned it back on. Remove the access plate from the disposer. Attach the white and black feeder wires from the electrical box to the white and black wires (respectively) inside the disposer. Twist a small wire cap onto each connection and wrap it with electrical tape for good measure. Also attach the green ground wire from the box to the grounding terminal on your disposer.

(continued)

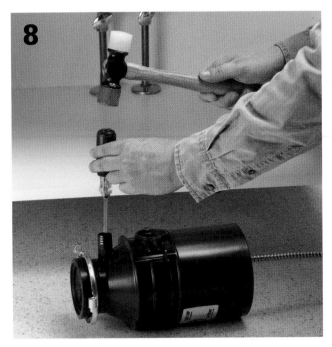

8

Knock out the plug in the disposer port IF you will be connecting your dishwasher to the disposer. If you have no dishwasher, leave the plug in. Insert a large flathead screwdriver into the port opening and rap it with a mallet. Retrieve the knock plug from inside the disposer canister.

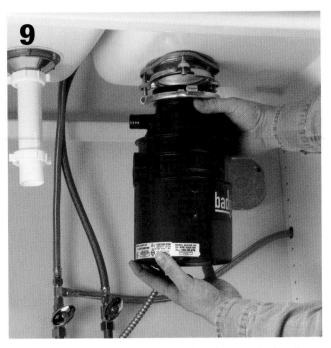

9

Hang the disposer from the mounting ring attached to the sink sleeve. To hang it, simply lift it up and position the unit so the three mounting ears are underneath the three mounting screws and then spin the unit so all three ears fit into the mounting assembly. Wait until after the plumbing hookups have been made to lock the unit in place.

10

Attach the discharge tube to the disposer according to the manufacturer's instructions. It is important to get a very good seal here, or the disposer will leak. Go ahead and spin the disposer if it helps you access the discharge port.

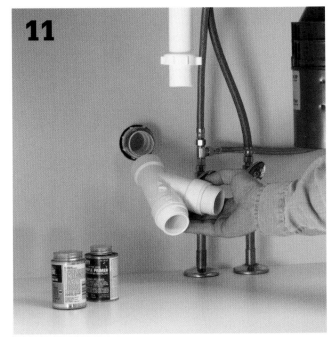

11

Attach a Y-fitting at the drain stubout. The Y-fitting should be sided to accept a drain line from the disposer and another form the sink (see Sidebar, page 35 for a discussion of why you should not simply run the disposer through the P-trap from the sink). Adjust the sink drain plumbing as needed to get from the sink P-trap to one opening of the Y-fitting.

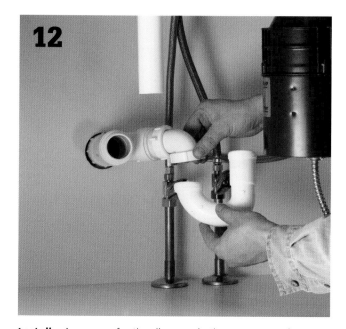

12

Install a trap arm for the disposer in the open port of the Y fitting at the wall stubout. Then, attach a P-trap or a combination of a tube extension and a P-trap so the low end of the trap will align with the bottom of the disposer discharge tube.

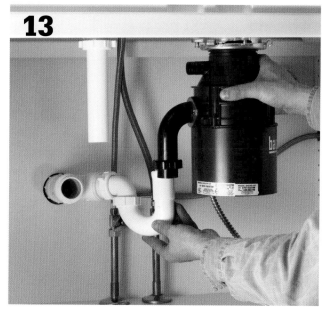

13

Spin the disposer so the end of the discharge tube is lined up over the open end of the P-trap and confirm that they will fit together correctly. If the discharge tube extends down too far, mark a line on it at the top of the P-trap and cut it there with a hack saw (inset). If the tube is too short, attach an extension with a threaded end. You may need to further shorten the discharge tube first to create enough room for the slip joint on the extension. Slide a slip nut and beveled compression washer onto the discharge tube and attach the tube to the P-trap.

14

Connect the dishwasher drain hose to the inlet port located at the top of the disposer unit. This may require a dishwasher hookup kit.

15

Lock the disposer into position on the mounting ring assembly once you have tested to make sure it is functioning correctly and without leaks. Lock it by turning one of the mounting lugs with a screwdriver until it makes contact with the locking notch.

Maintaining a Dishwasher

Dishwashers are durable, low-maintenance appliances. The few problems that do occur can be solved relatively easily. Replace a defective door gasket to eliminate leaks. If the gasket appears to be in good condition, adjust the door catch: loosen the retaining screws on the door catch, reposition it, and tighten the screws.

Replace a damaged or kinked drain hose to allow the unit to drain properly. Relocate water or waste lines that rest against the dishwasher to reduce excessive noise levels.

Clogged water lines can present more serious problems. A clogged screen or defective solenoid can keep the dishwasher from filling correctly. You can clean the inlet valve, which may solve the problem, but solenoid repair requires professional attention.

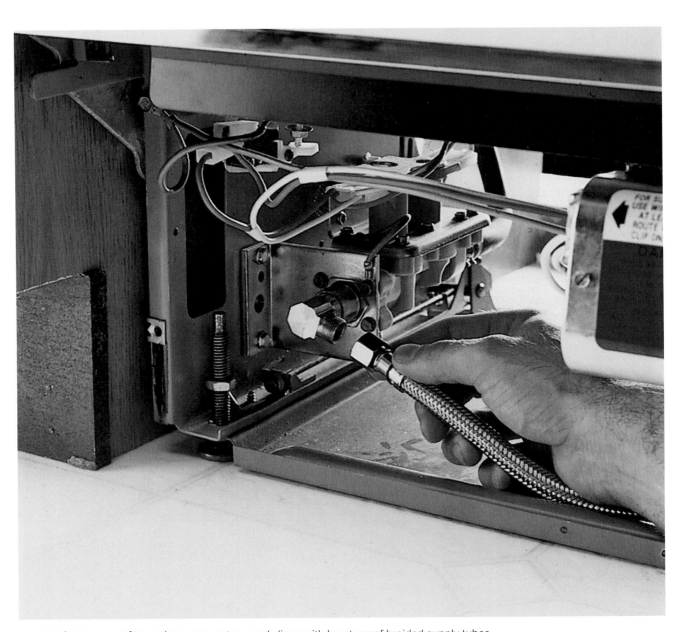

For maximum security, replace your water supply lines with burst-proof braided supply tubes.

How to Disconnect a Drain Hose

Turn off power and water supply, remove the lower panel of the unit (held in place by clips or screws). Place a baking pan or bowl under the pump to catch any water trapped in the drain hose. Loosen the hose clamp with pliers or a screwdriver. Remove hose from pump. Detach the other end of the hose from drain or garbage disposer beneath sink. Clean hose with water and bleach, or replace. Restore power and water supply. Test unit to make sure it drains properly.

How to Replace a Door Gasket

Inspect the gasket around the door. If it is cracked or damaged, replace it with a new one. Disconnect the electrical power at the main service panel. Pull out the bottom dish rack. Remove the old gasket, using a screwdriver to pry up the tabs or loosen the retaining screws that hold it in place. Soak the new gasket in warm soapy water to make it more pliable and to lubricate it. Install the new gasket by pressing or sliding it into its track. If the gasket has screws or clips, refasten as you go. Work from the center of the door to the ends.

How to Test a Valve & Replace the Valve Screen

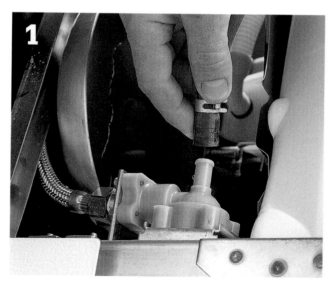

Turn off the power and water supply. Remove the access panel and locate the water supply connection. Disconnect wires from the inlet valve terminals. Attach continuity tester clip to one terminal and touch the probe to the other. If the tester does not glow, the solenoid is faulty and should be replaced. To replace the screen, place a shallow pan beneath the valve. Release the clamp and pull the fill tube from the valve outlet.

Disconnect the water supply tube. Loosen the valve bracket screws and remove valve. Remove the screen, using a small screwdriver. Replace the screen with a new one and reinstall the valve.

Your Electrical System

Electrical power that enters the home is produced by large power plants. Power plants are located in all parts of the country and generate electricity with turbines that are turned by water, wind, or steam. From these plants electricity enters large "step-up" transformers that increase voltage to half a million volts or more.

Electricity flows easily at these large voltages and travels through high-voltage transmission lines to communities that can be hundreds of miles from the power plants. "Step-down" transformers located at substations then reduce the voltage for distribution along street lines. On utility power poles, smaller transformers further reduce the voltage to ordinary 120-volt current for household use.

Lines carrying current to the house either run underground or are strung overhead and attached to a post called a service mast. Most homes built after 1950 have three wires running to the service head: two power lines, each carrying 120 volts of current, and a grounded neutral wire. Power from the two 120-volt lines may be combined at the service panel to supply current to large, 240-volt appliances like clothes dryers or electric water heaters.

Incoming power passes through an electric meter that measures power consumption. Power then enters the service panel, where it is distributed to circuits that run throughout the house. The service panel also contains fuses or circuit breakers that shut off power to the individual circuits in the event of a short circuit or an overload. Certain high-wattage appliances, like microwave ovens, are usually plugged into their own individual circuits to prevent overloads.

Voltage ratings determined by power companies and manufacturers have changed over the years. Current rated at 110 volts changed to 115 volts, then 120 volts. Current rated at 220 volts changed to 230 volts, then 240 volts. Similarly, ratings for receptacles, tools, light fixtures, and appliances have changed from 115 volts to 125 volts. These changes will not affect the performance of new devices connected to older wiring. For making electrical calculations, use a rating of 120 volts or 240 volts for your circuits.

Power plants supply electricity to thousands of homes and businesses. Step-up transformers increase the voltage produced at the plant, making the power flow more easily along high-voltage transmission lines.

Substations are located near the communities they serve. A typical substation takes current from high-voltage transmission lines and reduces it for distribution along street lines.

Utility pole transformers reduce the high-voltage current that flows through power lines along neighborhood streets. A utility pole transformer reduces voltage from 10,000 volts to the normal 120-volt current used in households.

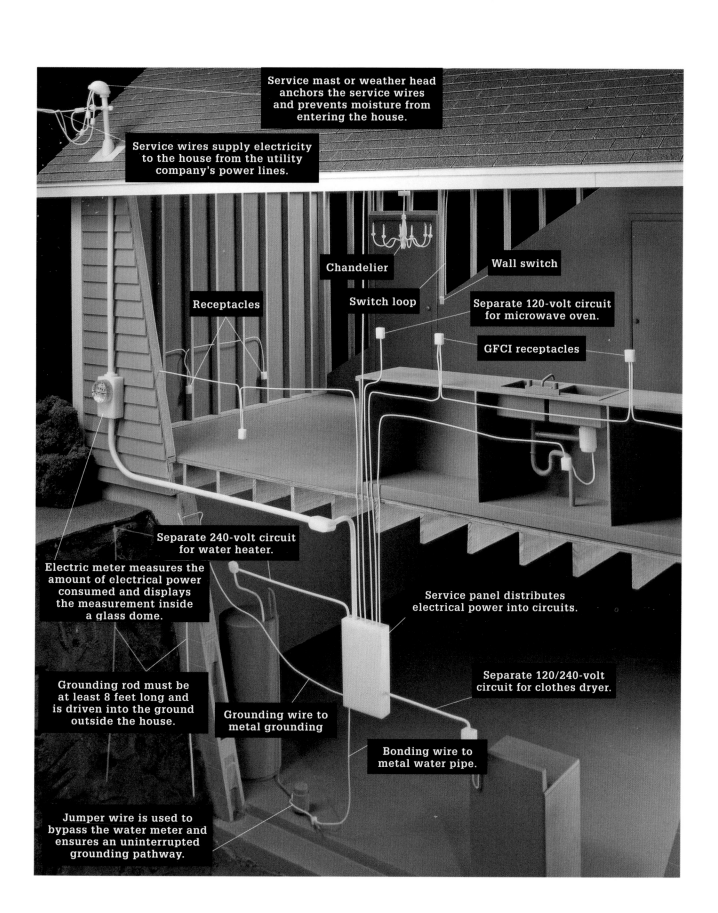

Service mast or weather head anchors the service wires and prevents moisture from entering the house.

Service wires supply electricity to the house from the utility company's power lines.

Chandelier

Wall switch

Receptacles

Switch loop

Separate 120-volt circuit for microwave oven.

GFCI receptacles

Separate 240-volt circuit for water heater.

Electric meter measures the amount of electrical power consumed and displays the measurement inside a glass dome.

Service panel distributes electrical power into circuits.

Grounding rod must be at least 8 feet long and is driven into the ground outside the house.

Grounding wire to metal grounding

Separate 120/240-volt circuit for clothes dryer.

Bonding wire to metal water pipe.

Jumper wire is used to bypass the water meter and ensures an uninterrupted grounding pathway.

Parts of the Electrical System

The service mast, anchors the service wires to the home. Three wires provide the standard 240-volt service necessary for the average home.

The electric meter measures the amount of electrical power consumed. It is usually attached to the side of the house, and connects to the service mast. A thin metal disc inside the meter rotates when power is used. The electric meter belongs to your local power utility company. If you suspect the meter is not functioning properly, contact the power company.

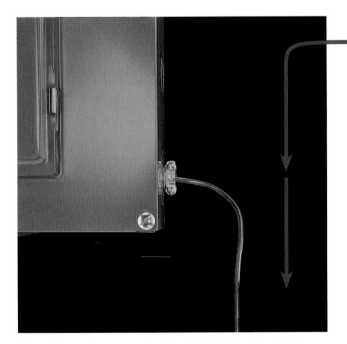

Grounding wire connects the electrical system to the earth through grounding rods or, in older systems, through a cold water pipe. In the event of an overload or short circuit, the grounding wire allows excess electrical power to find its way harmlessly to the earth.

Light fixtures attach directly to a household electrical system. They are usually controlled with wall switches. The two common types of light fixtures are incandescent and fluorescent.

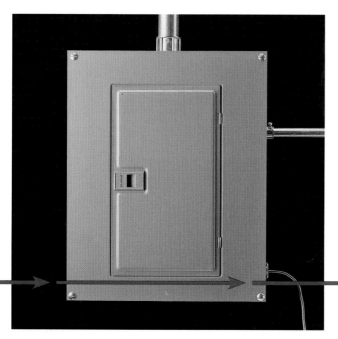

The main service panel, sometimes called a fuse box or breaker box, distributes power to individual circuits. Fuses or circuit breakers protect each circuit from short circuits and overloads. Fuses and circuit breakers also are used to shut off power to individual circuits while repairs are made.

Electrical boxes enclose wire connections. According to the National Electrical Code, all wire splices or connections must be contained entirely in a plastic or metal electrical box.

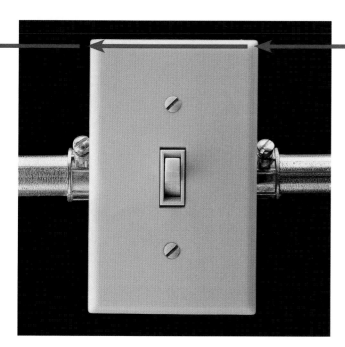

Switches control electrical current passing through hot circuit wires. Switches can be wired to control light fixtures, ceiling fans, appliances, and receptacles.

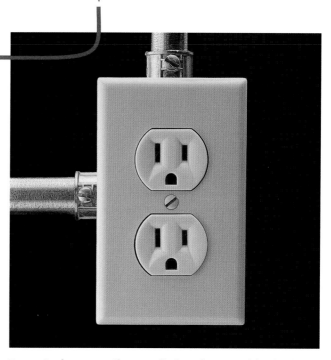

Receptacles, sometimes called outlets, provide plug-in access to electrical power. A 120-volt, 15-amp receptacle with a grounding hole is the most typical receptacle in wiring systems installed after 1965. Most receptacles have two plug-in locations and are called duplex receptacles.

Understanding Circuits

An electrical circuit is a continuous loop. Household circuits carry power from the main service panel, throughout the house, and back to the main service panel. Several switches, receptacles, light fixtures, or appliances may be connected to a single circuit.

Current enters a circuit loop on hot wires and returns along neutral wires. These wires are color coded for easy identification. Hot wires are black or red, and neutral wires are white or light gray. For safety, most circuits include a bare copper or green insulated grounding wire. The grounding wire conducts current in the event of a short circuit or overload, and helps reduce the chance of severe electrical shock. The service panel also has a grounding wire connected to a metal water pipe and metal grounding rod buried underground.

If a circuit carries too much power, it can overload. A fuse or a circuit breaker protects each circuit in case of overloads.

Current returns to the service panel along a neutral circuit wire. Current then becomes part of a main circuit and leaves the house on a large neutral service wire that returns it to the utility pole transformer.

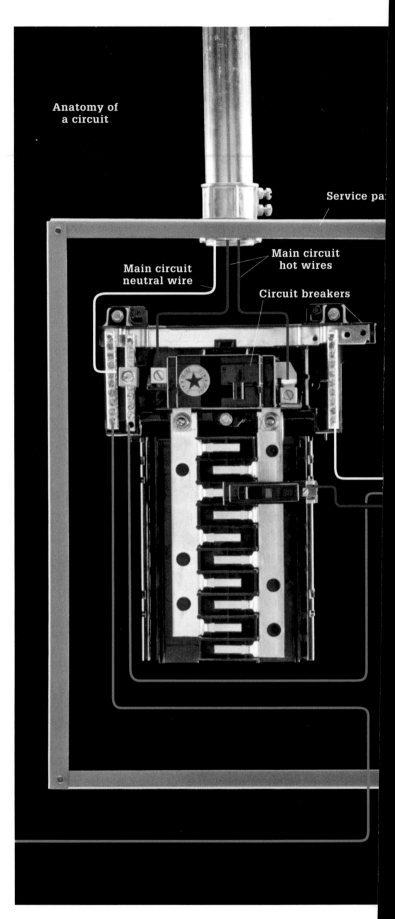

Anatomy of a circuit

Service pa[nel]

Main circuit neutral wire

Main circuit hot wires

Circuit breakers

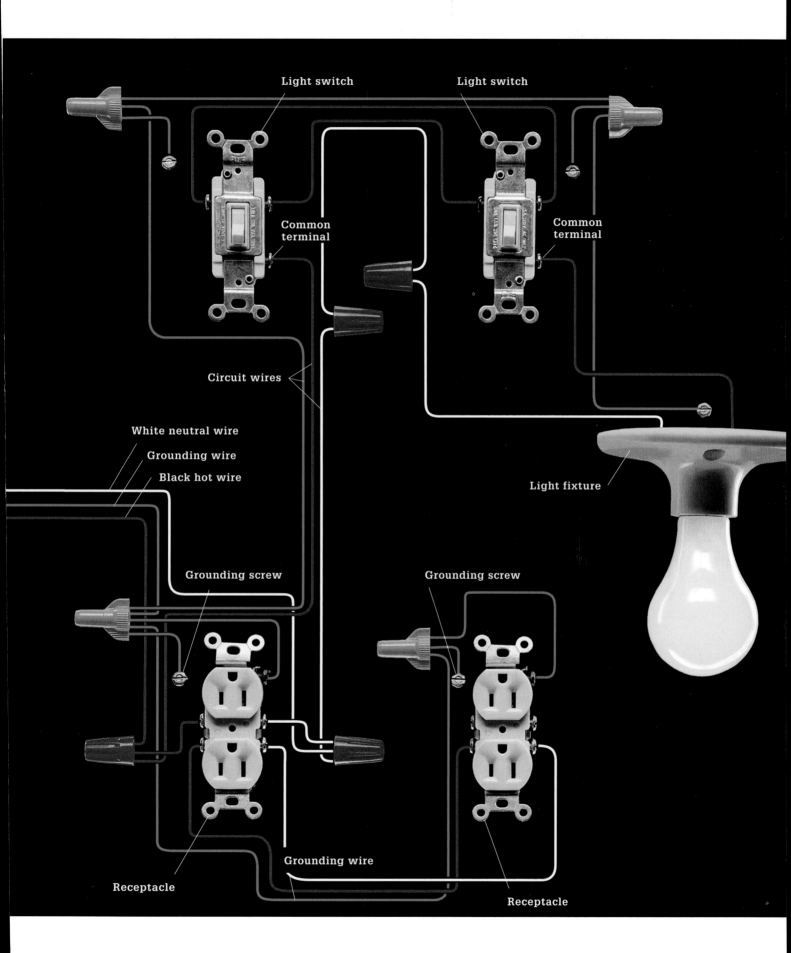

Light switch

Light switch

Common terminal

Common terminal

Circuit wires

White neutral wire

Grounding wire

Black hot wire

Light fixture

Grounding screw

Grounding screw

Receptacle

Grounding wire

Receptacle

Electricity & Safety

Safety should be the primary concern of anyone working with electricity. Although most household electrical repairs are simple and straightforward, always use caution and good judgment when working with electrical wiring or devices. Common sense can prevent accidents.

The basic rule of electrical safety is: Always turn off power to the area or device you are working on. At the main service panel, remove the fuse or shut off the circuit breaker that controls the circuit you are servicing. Then check to make sure the power is off by testing for power with a neon circuit tester. Restore power only when the repair or replacement project is complete.

Follow the safety tips shown on these pages. Never attempt an electrical project beyond your skill or confidence level. Never attempt to repair or replace your main service panel or service entrance head. These are jobs for a qualified electrician and require that the power company shuts off power to your house.

Shut off power to the proper circuit at the fuse box or main service panel before beginning work.

Make a map of your household electrical circuits to help you turn the proper circuits on and off for electrical repairs.

Close service panel door and post a warning sign to prevent others from turning on power while you are working on electrical projects.

Keep a flashlight near your main service panel. Check flashlight batteries regularly.

Always check for power at the fixture you are servicing before you begin any work.

Use only UL approved electrical parts or devices. These devices have been tested for safety by Underwriters Laboratories.

Wear rubber-soled shoes while working on electrical projects. On damp floors, stand on a rubber mat or dry wooden boards.

Use fiberglass or wood ladders when making routine household repairs near the service head.

Use GFCI receptacles (ground-fault circuit-interrupters) where specified by local and national electrical codes.

Protect children with receptacle caps or childproof receptacle covers.

Use extension cords only for temporary connections. Never place them underneath rugs or fasten them to walls, baseboards, or other surfaces.

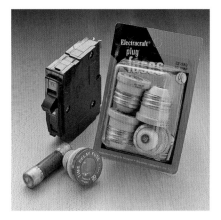

Use correct fuses or breakers in the main service panel. Never install a fuse or breaker that has a higher amperage rating than the circuit wires.

Do not touch metal pipes, faucets, or fixtures while working with electricity. The metal may provide a grounding path, allowing electrical current to flow through your body.

Never alter the prongs of a plug to fit a receptacle. If possible, install a new grounded receptacle.

Do not drill walls or ceilings without first shutting off electrical power to the circuits that may be hidden. Use double-insulated tools.

Fuses & Circuit Breakers

Fuses and circuit breakers are safety devices designed to protect the electrical system from short circuits and overloads. Fuses and circuit breakers are located in the main service panel.

Most service panels installed before 1965 rely on fuses to control and protect individual circuits. Screw-in plug fuses protect 120-volt circuits that power lights and receptacles. Cartridge fuses protect 240-volt appliance circuits and the main shutoff of the service panel.

Inside each fuse is a current-carrying metal alloy ribbon. If a circuit is overloaded, the metal ribbon melts and stops the flow of power. A fuse must match the amperage rating of the circuit. Never replace a fuse with one that has a larger amperage rating.

In most service panels installed after 1965, circuit breakers protect and control individual circuits. Single-pole circuit breakers protect 120-volt circuits, and double-pole circuit breakers protect 240-volt circuits. Amperage ratings for circuit breakers range from 15 to 100 amps.

Each circuit breaker has a permanent metal strip that heats up and bends when voltage passes through it. If a circuit is overloaded, the metal strip inside the breaker bends enough to "trip" the switch and stop the flow of power. If a circuit breaker trips frequently even though the power demand is small, the mechanism inside the breaker may be worn out. Worn circuit breakers should be replaced by an electrician.

When a fuse blows or a circuit breaker trips, it is usually because there are too many light fixtures and plug-in appliances drawing power through the circuit. Move some of the plug-in appliances to another circuit, then replace the fuse or reset the breaker. If the fuse blows or the breaker trips again immediately, there may be a short circuit in the system. Call a licensed electrician if you suspect a short circuit.

Tools & Materials ▸

Fuse puller and continuity tester
   (for cartridge fuses only)
Replacement fuse

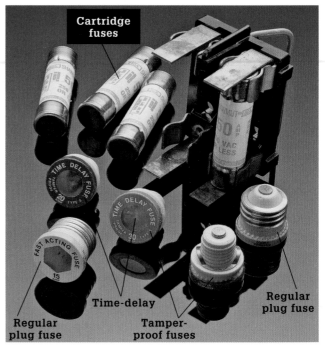

Fuses are used in older service panels. Plug fuses usually control 120-volt circuits rated for 15, 20, or 30 amps. Tamper-proof plug fuses have threads that fit only matching sockets, making it impossible to install a wrong-sized fuse. Time-delay fuses absorb temporary heavy power loads without blowing. Cartridge fuses control 240-volt circuits and range from 15 to 100 amps.

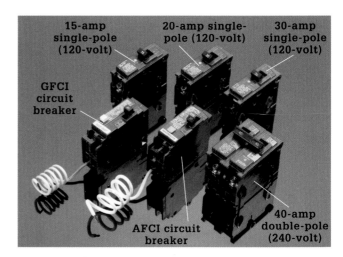

Circuit breakers are found in the majority of panels installed since the 1960s. Single-pole breakers control 120-volt circuits. Double-pole breakers rated for 15 to 100 amps control 240-volt circuits. Ground-fault circuit interrupter (GFCI) and arc-fault circuit interrupter (AFCI) breakers provide protection from shocks and fire-causing arcs for the entire circuit.

How to Identify & Replace a Blown Plug Fuse

Locate the blown fuse at the main service panel. If the metal ribbon inside is cleanly melted, the circuit was overloaded. If window is discolored, there was a short circuit in the system.

Unscrew the fuse, being careful to touch only the insulated rim of the fuse. Replace it with a fuse that has the same amperage rating.

How to Remove, Test & Replace a Cartridge Fuse

Remove cartridge fuses by gripping the handle of the fuse block and pulling sharply.

Remove the individual cartridge fuses from the block, using a fuse puller.

Test each fuse, using a continuity tester. If the tester glows, the fuse is good. If not, install a new fuse with the same amperage rating.

How to Reset a Circuit Breaker

Tripped circuit breaker

Open the service panel and locate the tripped breaker. The lever on the tripped breaker will be either in the OFF position, or in a position between ON and OFF.

Reset the tripped circuit breaker by pressing the circuit breaker lever all the way to the OFF position, then pressing it to the ON position.

Test AFCI and GFCI circuit breakers monthly by pushing the TEST button. Breaker should trip to the OFF position. If not, the breaker is faulty and must be replaced by an electrician.

Evaluating Old Wiring

If the wiring in your home is more than 30 years old, it may have a number of age-related problems. Many problems associated with older wiring can be found by inspecting electrical boxes for dirty wire connections, signs of arcing, cracked or damaged wire insulation, or dirt buildup.

However, it is difficult to identify problems with wiring that is hidden inside the walls. If old wires are dusty and have damaged insulation, they can "leak" electrical current. The amount of current that leaks through dust usually is very small, too small to trip a breaker or blow a fuse. Nevertheless, by allowing current to leave its normal path, these leaks consume power in much the same way that a dripping faucet wastes water.

This kind of electrical leak is called a high-resistance short circuit. A high-resistance short circuit can produce heat and should be considered a fire hazard.

It is possible to check for high-resistance short circuits by using your electric meter to test the wires of each circuit. The goal of the test is to determine if electricity is being consumed even if none of the lights and appliances are drawing power. To do this, you must turn on all wall switches to activate the hot circuit wires, then stop power consumption by removing lightbulbs and fluorescent tubes, and disconnecting all lamps and appliances.

Then examine the electric meter, usually located on the outside of the house near the service head. If the flat, circular rotor inside the meter is turning, it means that a high-resistance short circuit is causing an electrical leak somewhere in the wiring. High-resistance short circuits consume very small amounts of power, so you should watch the rotor for a full minute to detect any movement.

If the test shows there is a high-resistance short circuit in your wiring, contact a licensed electrician to have it repaired.

Tools & Materials ▸

Screwdriver
Wire connectors

Masking tape
Pen

How to Evaluate Old Wiring for High-resistance Short Circuits

1

Switch on all light fixtures.
Remember to turn on closet lights, basement lights, and exterior lights.

2

Stop all power consumption by removing all lightbulbs and fluorescent tubes. Turn off all thermostats.

3

Disconnect all plug-in lamps and appliances from the receptacles.

4

Shut off power to all permanently wired appliances by turning off the correct breakers or removing the correct fuses at the service panel. Permanently wired appliances include attic fans, water heaters, and ceiling fans.

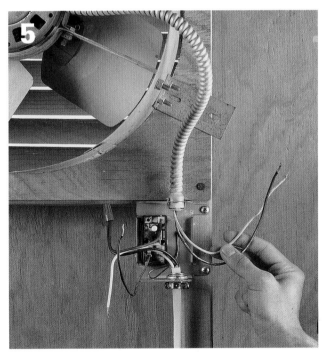

5

With the power turned off, disconnect circuit wires from each permanently wired appliance. Cap the wire ends with wire connectors. Next, turn on power and make sure all appliance wall switches are turned on.

(continued)

Watch the circular rotor located inside the electric meter for at least one minute. If the rotor does not move, then your wiring is in good condition. If the rotor moves, it means there is a high-resistance short circuit somewhere in the wiring system: proceed to step 7.

Turn off power to all circuits at the main service panel by switching off circuit breakers or removing fuses. Do not turn off main shutoff. Watch the rotor inside the meter. If rotor moves, then the high-resistance short circuit is located in the main service panel or service wiring. In this case, consult a licensed electrician. If rotor does not move, proceed to step 8.

Turn on individual circuits, one at a time, by switching on the circuit breaker or inserting the fuse. Watch for rotor movement in the electric meter. If rotor does not move, wiring is in good condition. Turn off power to the circuit, then proceed to the next circuit.

If the rotor is moving, then use masking tape to mark the faulty circuit. Turn off power to the circuit, then proceed to the next circuit.

If circuit contains three-way or four-way switches, flip the lever on each switch individually, and watch for rotor movement after each flip of a switch.

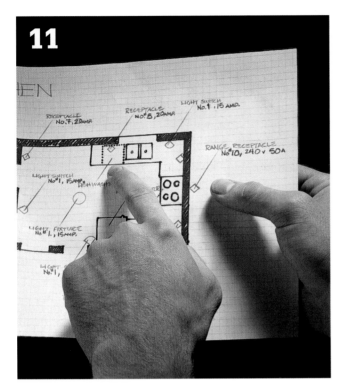

For each faulty circuit, identify the appliances, lights, switches, receptacles, and electrical junction boxes powered by the circuit. Use a map of your home wiring system as a guide.

Recheck all lights and appliances along each faulty circuit to make sure they are not consuming power. If they are, disconnect them and repeat test.

Inspect the electrical boxes along each faulty circuit for dirty wire connections, damaged wire insulation, dirt buildup, or signs of arcing.

If no problems are found in electrical boxes, then the high-resistance short circuit is in wiring contained inside the walls. In this case, consult a licensed electrician.

Inspector's Notebook

An electrical inspector visiting your home might identify a number of situations that are not "up to code." These situations may not be immediate problems. In fact, it is possible that the wiring in your home has remained trouble-free for many years.

Nevertheless, any wiring or device that is not up to code carries the potential for problems, often at risk to your home and your family. In addition, you may have trouble selling your home if it is not wired according to accepted methods.

Most local electrical codes are based on the National Electrical Code (NEC), a book updated and published every three years by the National Fire Protection Agency. This code book contains rules and regulations for the proper installation of electrical wiring and devices. Most public libraries carry reference copies of the NEC.

All electrical inspectors are required to be well versed in the NEC. Their job is to know the NEC regulations and to make sure these rules are followed in order to prevent fires and ensure safety. If you have questions regarding your home wiring system, your local inspector will be happy to answer them.

While a book like The Complete Photo Guide to Home Repair cannot possibly identify all potential wiring problems in your house, we have created the "Inspector's Notebook" to help you identify some of the most common wiring defects and show you how to correct them. When working on home wiring repair or replacement projects, refer to this section to help identify any conditions that may be hazardous.

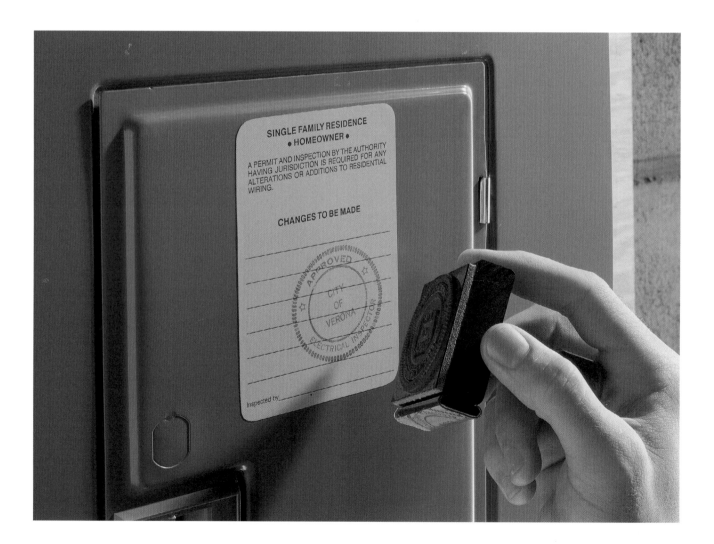

Service Panel Inspection

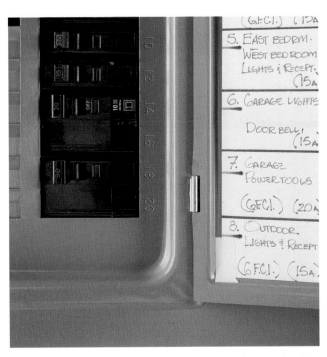

Problem: Rust stains are found inside the main service panel. This problem occurs because water seeps into the service head outside the house and drips down into the service panel.

Solution: Have an electrician examine the service head and the main service panel. If the panel or service wires have been damaged, new electrical service must be installed.

Problem: This problem is actually a very old and very dangerous solution. A penny or a knockout behind a fuse effectively bypasses the fuse, preventing an overloaded circuit from blowing the fuse. This is very dangerous and can lead to overheated wiring.

Solution: Remove the penny and replace the fuse. Have a licensed electrician examine the panel and circuit wiring. If the fuse has been bypassed for years, wiring may be dangerously compromised, and the circuit may need to be replaced.

(continued)

Problem: Two wires connected to one single-pole breaker is a sign of an overcrowded panel and also a dangerous code violation unless the breaker is approved for such a connection.

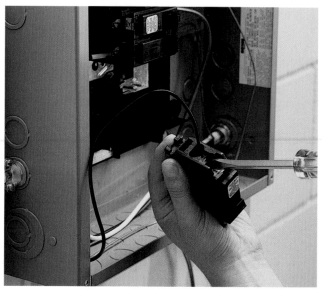

Solution: If there is room in the panel, install a separate breaker for the extra wire. If the panel is overcrowded have an electrician upgrade the panel or install a subpanel.

Recognizing Aluminum Wire ▸

Inexpensive aluminum wire was used in place of copper in many wiring systems installed during the late 1960s and early 1970s, when copper prices were high. Aluminum wire is identified by its silver color and by the AL stamp on the cable sheathing. A variation, copper-clad aluminum wire, has a thin coating of copper bonded to a solid aluminum core.

By the early 1970s, all-aluminum wire was found to pose a safety hazard if connected to a switch or receptacle with brass or copper screw terminals. Because aluminum expands and contracts at a different rate than copper or brass, the wire connections could become loose. In some instances, fires resulted.

Existing aluminum wiring in homes is considered safe if proper installation methods have been followed, and if the wires are connected to special switches and receptacles designed to be used with aluminum wire. If you have aluminum wire in your home, have a qualified electrical inspector review the system. Copper-coated aluminum wire is not a hazard.

For a short while, switches and receptacles with an Underwriters Laboratories (UL) wire

compatibility rating of AL-CU were used with both aluminum and copper wiring. However, these devices proved to be hazardous when connected to aluminum wire. AL-CU devices should not be used with aluminum wiring.

In 1971, switches and receptacles designed for use with aluminum wiring were introduced. They are marked CO/ALR. This mark is now the only approved rating for aluminum wires. If your home has aluminum wires connected to a switch or receptacle without a CO/ALR rating stamp, replace the device with a switch or receptacle rated CO/ALR.

A switch or receptacle that has no wire compatibility rating printed on the mounting strap or casing should not be used with aluminum wires. These devices are designed for use with copper wires only.

Inspecting the Grounding Jumper Wire

Problem: Grounding system jumper wire is missing or is disconnected. In most homes the grounding jumper wire attaches to water pipes on either side of the water meter. Because the ground pathway is broken, this is a dangerous situation that should be fixed immediately.

Solution: Attach a jumper wire to the water pipes on either side of the water meter, using pipe clamps. Use #6 gauge bare copper wire for services that are 150-amp or smaller. Use #4 gauge bare copper wire for 200-amp service.

Common Cable Problems

Problem: Cable running across joists or studs is attached to the edge of framing members. Electrical codes forbid this type of installation in exposed areas, like unfinished basements or walk-up attics.

Solution: Protect cable by drilling holes in framing members at least 2" from exposed edges, and threading the cable through the holes.

(continued)

Problem: Cable running along joists or studs hangs loosely. Loose cables can be pulled accidentally, causing damage to wires.

Solution: Anchor the cable to the side of the framing members at least 1¼" from the edge, using plastic staples. NM (nonmetallic) cable should be stapled every 4½ feet and within 12" of each electrical box.

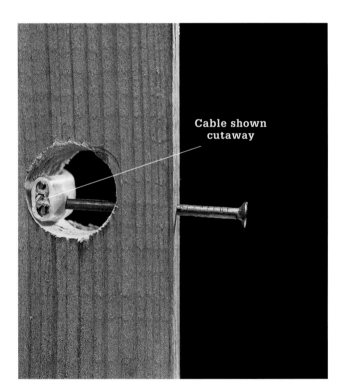

Cable shown cutaway

Problem: Cable threaded through studs or joists lies close to the edge of the framing members. NM (nonmetallic) cable (shown cutaway) can be damaged easily if nails or screws are driven into the framing members during remodeling projects.

Solution: Install metal nail guards to protect cable from damage. Nail guards are available at hardware stores and home centers.

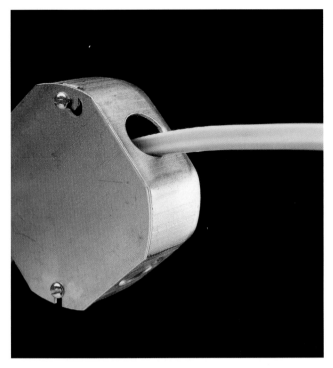

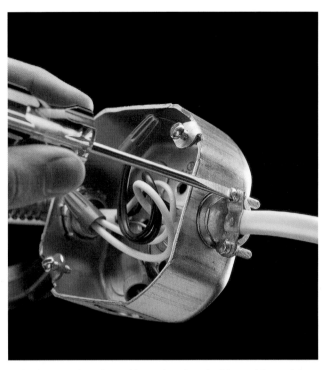

Problem: Unclamped cable enters a metal electrical box. Edges of the knockout can rub against the cable sheathing and damage the wires. *(Note: With plastic boxes, clamps are not required if cables are anchored to framing members within 12" of box.)*

Solution: Anchor the cable to the electrical box with a cable clamp. Several types of cable clamps are available at hardware stores and home centers.

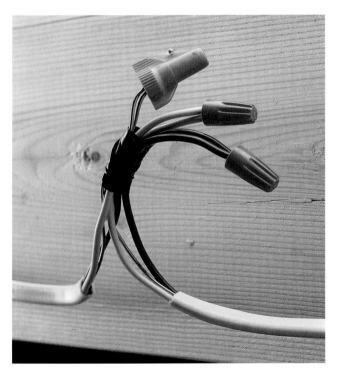

Problem: Cables are spliced outside an electrical box. Exposed splices can spark and create a risk of shock or fire.

Solution: Bring installation "up to code" by enclosing the splice inside a metal or plastic electrical box. Make sure the box is large enough for the number of wires it contains.

Checking Wire Connections

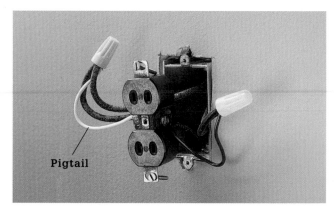

Problem: Two or more wires are attached to a single screw terminal. This type of connection is seen in older wiring but is now prohibited by the National Electrical Code.

Solution: Disconnect the wires from the screw terminal, then join them to a short length of wire (called a pigtail), using a wire connector. Connect the other end of the pigtail to the screw terminal.

Problem: Bare wire extends past a screw terminal. Exposed wire can cause a short circuit if it touches the metal box or another circuit wire.

Solution: Clip the wire, and reconnect it to the screw terminal. In a proper connection, the bare wire wraps completely around the screw terminal, and the plastic insulation just touches the screw head.

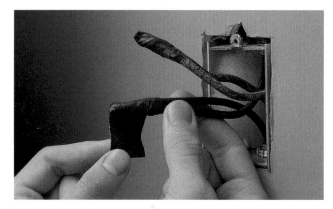

Problem: Wires are connected with electrical tape. Electrical tape was used frequently in older installations, but it can deteriorate over time, leaving bare wires exposed inside the electrical box.

Solution: Replace electrical tape with wire connectors. You may need to clip away a small portion of the wire so the bare end will be covered completely by the connector.

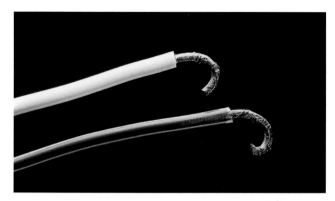

Problem: Nicks and scratches in bare wires interfere with the flow of current. This can cause the wires to overheat.

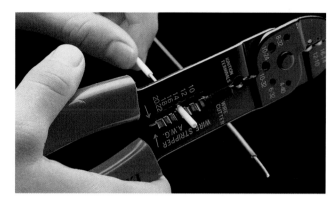

Solution: Clip away damaged portion of wire, then restrip about ¾" of insulation and reconnect the wire to the screw terminal.

Electrical Box Inspection

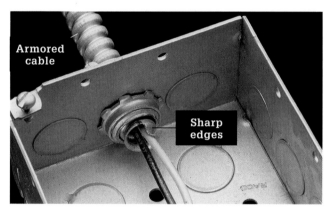

Problem: No protective sleeve on armored cable. Sharp edges of the cable can damage the wire insulation, creating a shock hazard and fire risk.

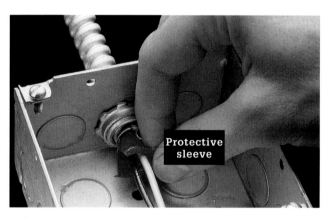

Solution: Protect the wire insulation by installing plastic or fiber sleeves around the wires. Sleeves are available at hardware stores. Wires that are damaged must be replaced.

Problem: Insulation on wires is cracked or damaged. If damaged insulation exposes bare wire, a short circuit can occur, posing a shock hazard and fire risk.

Solution: Wrap damaged insulation temporarily with plastic electrical tape. Damaged circuit wires should be replaced by an electrician.

(continued)

Problem: Open electrical boxes create a fire hazard if a short circuit causes sparks (arcing) inside the box.

Solution: Cover the open box with a solid metal coverplate, available at any hardware store. Electrical boxes must remain accessible and cannot be sealed inside ceilings or walls.

Problem: Short wires are difficult to handle. The National Electrical Code (NEC) requires that each wire in an electrical box have at least 6" of workable length.

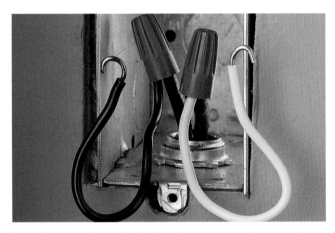

Solution: Lengthen circuit wires by connecting them to short pigtail wires, using wire connectors. Pigtails can be cut from scrap wire, but should be the same gauge and color as the circuit wires and at least 6" long.

Problem: Recessed electrical box is hazardous, especially if the wall or ceiling surface is made from a flammable material, like wood paneling. The National Electrical Code prohibits this type of installation.

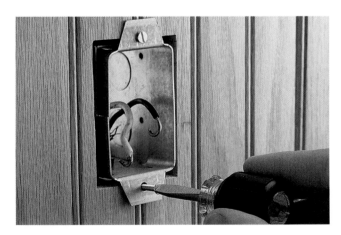

Solution: Add an extension ring to bring the face of the electrical box flush with the surface. Extension rings come in several sizes, and are available at hardware stores.

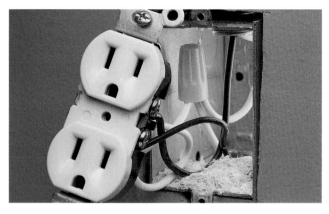

Problem: Open electrical boxes create a fire hazard if a short circuit causes sparks. Dust and dirt in electrical box can cause hazardous high-resistance short circuits (page 426). When making routine electrical repairs, always check the electrical boxes for dust and dirt buildup.

Solution: Vacuum electrical box clean, using a narrow nozzle attachment. Make sure power to box is turned off at main service panel before vacuuming.

Problem: Crowded electrical box (shown cutaway) makes electrical repairs difficult. This type of installation is prohibited because wires can be damaged easily when a receptacle or switch is installed.

Solution: Replace the electrical box with a deeper electrical box.

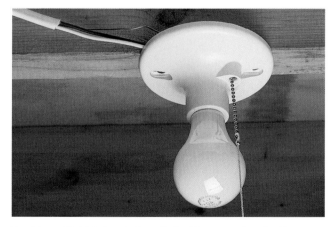

Problem: Light fixture is installed without an electrical box. This installation exposes the wiring connections, and provides no support for the light fixture.

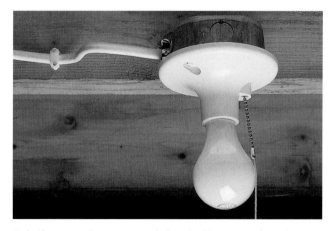

Solution: Install an approved electrical box to enclose the wire connections and support the light fixture.

Common Electrical Cord Problems

Problem: Lamp or appliance cord runs underneath a rug. Foot traffic can wear off insulation, creating a short circuit that can cause fire or shock.

Solution: Reposition the lamp or appliance so that cord is visible. Replace worn cords.

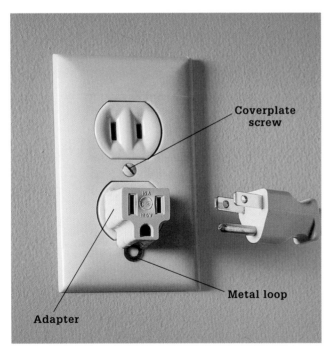

Coverplate screw

Metal loop

Adapter

GFCI receptacle

Problem: Three-prong appliance plugs do not fit two slot receptacle. Do not use three-prong adapters unless the metal loop on the adapter is tightly connected to the coverplate screw on receptacle.

Solution: Install a three-prong grounded receptacle if a means of grounding exists at the box. Install a GFCI (ground-fault circuit-interrupter) receptacle in kitchens and bathrooms, or if the electrical box is not grounded.

Problem: Lamp or appliance plug is cracked, or electrical cord is frayed near plug. Worn cords and plugs create a fire and shock hazard.

Solution: Cut away damaged portion of wire and install a new plug. Replacement plugs are available at appliance stores and home centers.

Problem: Extension cord is too small for the power load drawn by a tool or appliance. Undersized extension cords can overheat, melting the insulation and leaving bare wires exposed.

Solution: Use an extension cord with wattage and amperage ratings that meet or exceed the rating of the tool or appliance. Extension cords are for temporary use only. Never use an extension cord for a permanent installation.

Inspecting Receptacles & Switches

Problem: Octopus receptacle attachments used permanently can overload a circuit and cause overheating of the receptacle.

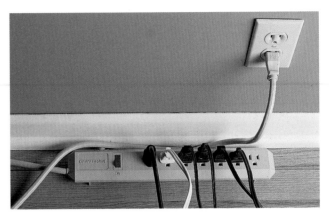

Solution: Use a multi-receptacle power strip with built-in overload protection. This is for temporary use only. If the need for extra receptacles is frequent, upgrade the wiring system.

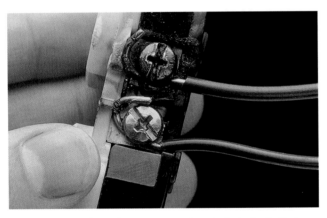

Problem: Scorch marks near screw terminals indicate that electrical arcing has occurred. Arcing usually is caused by loose wire connections.

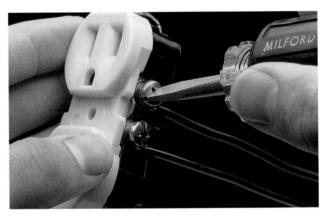

Solution: Clean wires with fine sandpaper, and replace the receptacle if it is badly damaged. Make sure wires are connected securely to screw terminals.

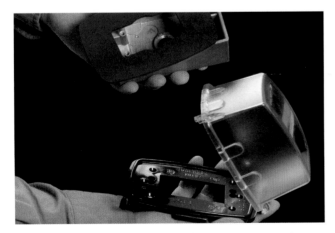

Problem: Exterior receptacle box allows water to enter box when receptacles slots are in use.

Solution: Replace the old receptacle box (no longer code compliant) with an in-use box that has a bubble cover to protect plugs from water while they are in the slots.

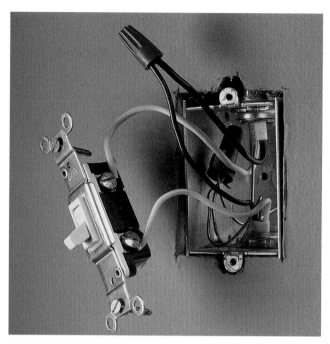

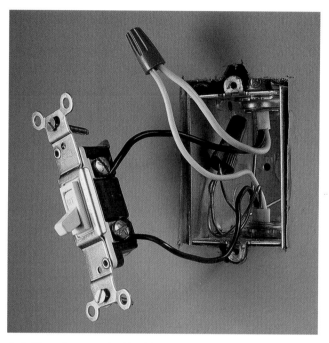

Problem: White neutral wires are connected to switch. Although switch appears to work correctly in this installation, it is dangerous because light fixture carries voltage when the switch is off.

Solution: Connect the black hot wires to the switch, and join the white wires together with a wire connector.

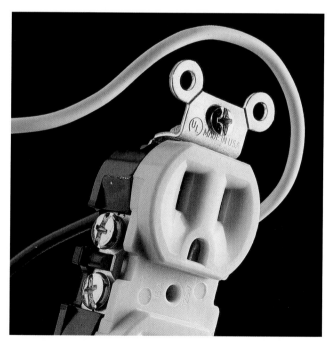

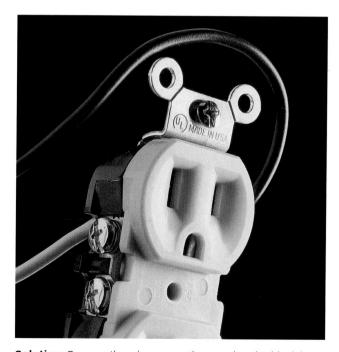

Problem: White neutral wires are connected to the brass screw terminals on the receptacle, and black hot wires are attached to silver screw terminals. This installation is hazardous because live voltage flows into the long neutral slot on the receptacle.

Solution: Reverse the wire connections so that the black hot wires are attached to brass screw terminals and white neutral wires are attached to silver screw terminals. Live voltage now flows into the short slot on the receptacle.

Common Receptacle Problems

Household receptacles, also called outlets, have no moving parts to wear out and usually last for many years without servicing. Most problems associated with receptacles are actually caused by faulty lamps and appliances, or their plugs and cords. However, the constant plugging in and removal of appliance cords can wear out the metal contacts inside a receptacle. Any receptacle that does not hold plugs firmly should be replaced. In addition, older receptacle made of hard plastic may harden and crack with age. They must be replaced when this happens.

A loose wire connection within the receptacle box is another possible problem. A loose connection can spark (called arcing), trip a circuit breaker, or cause heat to build up in the receptacle box, creating a potential fire hazard.

Wires can come loose for a number of reasons. Everyday vibrations caused by walking across floors, or from nearby street traffic, may cause a connection to shake loose. In addition, because wires heat and cool with normal use, the ends of the wires will expand and contract slightly. This movement also may cause the wires to come loose from the screw terminal connections.

Not all receptacles are created equally. When replacing, make sure to buy one with the same amp rating as the old one. Inadvertently installing a 20-amp receptacle in replacement of a 15-amp receptacle is a very common error.

See Inspector's Notebook ›

The earliest receptacles were modifications of the screw-in type light bulb. This receptacle was used in the early 1900s.

The polarized receptacle became standard in the 1920s. The different sized slots direct current flow for safety.

The ground-fault circuit-interrupter, or GFCI receptacle, is a modern safety device. When it detects slight changes in current, it instantly shuts off power.

Problem	Repair
Circuit breaker trips repeatedly, or fuse burns out immediately after being replaced.	1. Repair or replace worn or damaged lamp or appliance cord. 2. Move lamps or appliances to other circuits to prevent overloads. 3. Tighten any loose wire connections (page 455). 4. Clean dirty or oxidized wire ends (page 454).
Lamp or appliance does not work.	1. Make sure lamp or appliance is plugged in. 2. Replace burned-out bulbs. 3. Repair or replace worn or damaged lamp or appliance cord. 4. Tighten any loose wire connections (page 455). 5. Clean dirty or oxidized wire ends (page 454). 6. Repair or replace any faulty receptacle (pages 454 to 455).
Receptacle does not hold plugs firmly.	1. Repair or replace worn or damaged plugs. 2. Replace faulty receptacle (pages 454 to 455).
Receptacle is warm to the touch, buzzes, or sparks when plugs are inserted or removed.	1. Move lamps or appliances to other circuits to prevent overloads. 2. Tighten any loose wire connections (page 455). 3. Clean dirty or oxidized wire ends (page 454). 4. Replace faulty receptacle (pages 454 to 455).

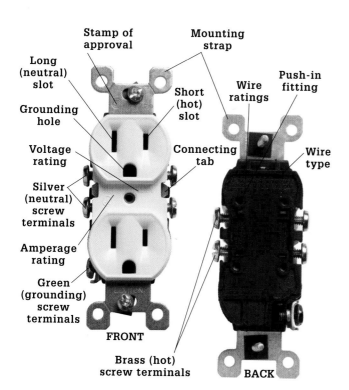

FRONT

BACK

Stamp of approval

Mounting strap

Long (neutral) slot

Short (hot) slot

Wire ratings

Push-in fitting

Grounding hole

Connecting tab

Wire type

Voltage rating

Silver (neutral) screw terminals

Amperage rating

Green (grounding) screw terminals

Brass (hot) screw terminals

The standard duplex receptacle has two halves for receiving plugs. Each half has a long (neutral) slot, a short (hot) slot, and a U-shaped grounding hole. The slots fit the wide prong, narrow prong, and grounding prong of a three-prong plug. This ensures that the connection between receptacle and plug will be polarized and grounded for safety.

Wires are attached to the receptacle at screw terminals or push-in fittings. A connecting tab between the screw terminals allows a variety of different wiring configurations. Receptacles also include mounting straps for attaching to electrical boxes.

Stamps of approval from testing agencies are found on the front and back of the receptacle. Look for the symbol UL or UND. LAB. INC. LIST to make sure the receptacle meets the strict standards of Underwriters Laboratories.

The receptacle is marked with ratings for maximum volts and amps. The common receptacle is marked 15A, 125V. Receptacles marked CU or COPPER are used with solid copper wire. Those marked CU-CLAD ONLY are used with copper-coated aluminum wire. Only receptacles marked CO/ALR may be used with solid aluminum wiring (page 432). Receptacles marked AL/CU no longer may be used with aluminum wire, according to code.

Receptacle Wiring

A 120-volt duplex receptacle can be wired to the electrical system in a number of ways. The most common are shown on these pages.

Wiring configurations may vary slightly from these photographs, depending on the kind of receptacles used, the type of cable, or the technique of the electrician who installed the wiring. To make dependable repairs or replacements, use masking tape and label each wire according to its location on the terminals of the existing receptacle.

Receptacles are wired as either end-of-run or middle-of-run. These two basic configurations are easily identified by counting the number of cables entering the receptacle box. End-of-run wiring has only one cable, indicating that the circuit ends. Middle-of-run wiring has two cables, indicating that the circuit continues on to other receptacles, switches, or fixtures.

A split-circuit receptacle is shown on the next page. Each half of a split-circuit receptacle is wired to a separate circuit. This allows two appliances of high wattage to be plugged into the same receptacle without blowing a fuse or tripping a breaker. This wiring configuration is similar to a receptacle that is controlled by a wall switch. Code requires a switch-controlled receptacle in any room that does not have a built-in light fixture operated by a wall switch.

Split-circuit and switch-controlled receptacles are connected to two hot wires, so use caution during repairs or replacements. Make sure the connecting tab between the hot screw terminals is removed.

Two-slot receptacles are common in older homes. There is no grounding wire attached to the receptacle, but the box may be grounded with armored cable or conduit.

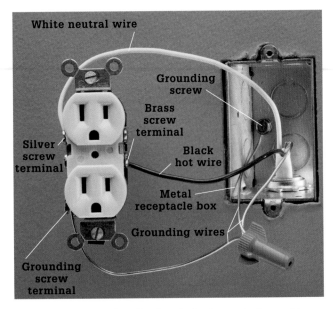

Single cable entering the box indicates end-of-run wiring. The black hot wire is attached to a brass screw terminal, and the white neutral wire is connected to a silver screw terminal. If the box is metal, the grounding wire is pigtailed to the grounding screws of the receptacle and the box. In a plastic box, the grounding wire is attached directly to the grounding screw terminal of the receptacle.

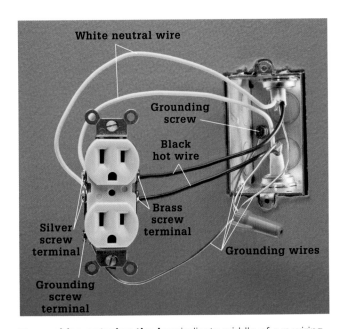

Two cables entering the box indicate middle-of-run wiring. Black hot wires are connected to brass screw terminals, and white neutral wires to silver screw terminals. The grounding wire is pigtailed to the grounding screws of the receptacle and the box.

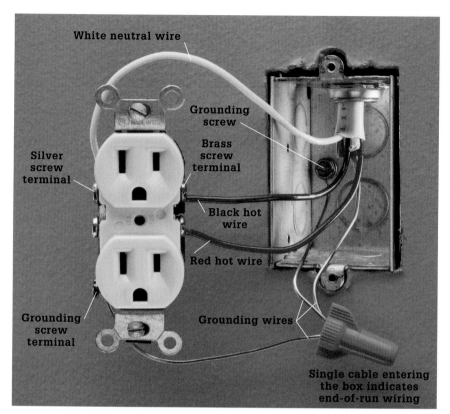

White neutral wire

Grounding screw

Brass screw terminal

Silver screw terminal

Black hot wire

Red hot wire

Grounding screw terminal

Grounding wires

Single cable entering the box indicates end-of-run wiring

Split-circuit receptacle is attached to a black hot wire, a red hot wire, a white neutral wire, and a bare grounding wire. The wiring is similar to a switch-controlled receptacle.

The hot wires are attached to the brass screw terminals, and the connecting tab or fin between the brass terminals is removed. The white wire is attached to a silver screw terminal, and the connecting tab on the neutral side remains intact. The grounding wire is pigtailed to the grounding screw terminal of the receptacle and to the grounding screw attached to the box.

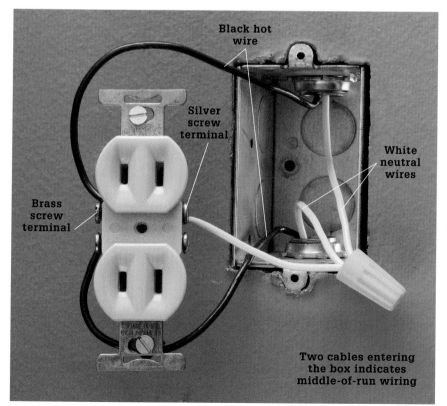

Black hot wire

Silver screw terminal

White neutral wires

Brass screw terminal

Two cables entering the box indicates middle-of-run wiring

Two-slot receptacle is often found in older homes. The black hot wires are connected to the brass screw terminals, and the white neutral wires are pigtailed to a silver screw terminal.

Two-slot receptacles may be replaced with three-slot types, but only if a means of grounding exists at the receptacle box. You can also replace a two-slot receptacle with a GFCI receptacle that's marked with a sticker indicating no equipment ground.

Basic Types of Receptacles

Several different types of receptacles are found in the typical home. Each has a unique arrangement of slots that accepts only a certain kind of plug, and each is designed for a specific job.

Household receptacles provide two types of voltage: normal and high voltage. Although voltage ratings have changed slightly over the years, normal receptacles should be rated for 110, 115, 120, or 125 volts. For purposes of replacement, these ratings are considered identical. High-voltage receptacles are rated at 220, 240, or 250 volts. These ratings are considered identical.

When replacing a receptacle, check the amperage rating of the circuit at the main service panel, and buy a receptacle with the correct amperage rating.

15 amps, 120 volts. Polarized two-slot receptacle is common in homes built before 1960. Slots are different sizes to accept polarized plugs.

15 amps, 120 volts. Three-slot grounded receptacle has two different size slots and a U-shaped hole for grounding. It is required in all new wiring installations.

20 amps, 120 volts. This three-slot grounded receptacle features a special T-shaped slot. It is installed for use with large appliances or portable tools that require 20 amps of current.

15 amps, 240 volts. This receptacle is used primarily for window air conditioners. It is available as a single unit or as half of a duplex receptacle with the other half wired for 120 volts.

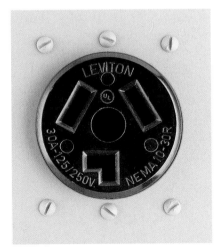

30 amps, 120/240 volts. This receptacle is used for clothes dryers. It provides high-voltage current for heating coils and 120-volt current to run lights and timers.

50 amps, 120/240 volts. This receptacle is used for ranges. The high-voltage current powers heating coils, and the 120-volt current runs clocks and lights.

Older Receptacles

Older receptacles may look different from more modern types, but most will stay in good working order. Follow these simple guidelines for evaluating or replacing older receptacles:

- Never replace an older receptacle with one of a different voltage or higher amperage rating.
- Any two-slot, unpolarized receptacle should be replaced with a two-slot polarized receptacle.
- If no means of grounding is available at the receptacle box, install a GFCI (page 457).
- If in doubt, seek the advice of a qualified electrician.

Never alter the prongs of a plug to fit an older receptacle. Altering the prongs may remove the grounding or polarizing features of the plug.

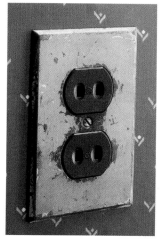

Unpolarized receptacles have slots that are the same length. Modern plug types may not fit these receptacles. Never modify the prongs of a polarized plug to fit the slots of an unpolarized receptacle.

Surface-mounted receptacles were popular in the 1940s and 1950s for their ease of installation. Wiring often ran in the back of hollowed-out base moldings. Surface-mounted receptacles are usually ungrounded.

Ceramic duplex receptacles were manufactured in the 1930s. They are polarized but ungrounded, and they are wired for 120 volts.

Twist-lock receptacles are designed to be used with plugs that are inserted and rotated. A small tab on the end of one of the prongs prevents the plug from being pulled from the receptacle.

Ceramic duplex receptacle has a unique hourglass shape. The receptacle shown above is rated for 250 volts but only 5 amps, and would not be allowed by today's electrical codes.

High-voltage Receptacles

High-voltage receptacles provide current to large appliances like clothes dryers, ranges, water heaters, and air conditioners. The slot configuration of a high-voltage receptacle (page 448) will not accept a plug rated for 120 volts.

A high-voltage receptacle can be wired in one of two ways. In a standard high-voltage receptacle, voltage is brought to the receptacle with two hot wires, each carrying a maximum of 120 volts. No white neutral wire is necessary, but a grounding wire should be attached to the receptacle and to the metal receptacle box. Conduit can also act as a ground from the metal receptacle box back to the service panel.

A clothes dryer or range also may require normal current (a maximum of 120 volts) to run lights, timers and clocks. If so, a white neutral wire will be attached to the receptacle. The appliance itself will split the incoming current into a 120-volt circuit and a 240-volt circuit.

Repair or replace a high-voltage receptacle using the techniques shown on pages 454 to 455. It is important to identify and tag all wires on the existing receptacle so that the new receptacle will be properly wired.

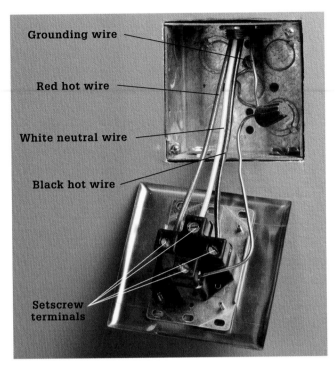

A receptacle rated for 120/240 volts has two incoming hot wires, each carrying 120 volts, a white neutral wire, and a bare copper grounding wire. Connections are made with setscrew terminals at the back of the receptacle.

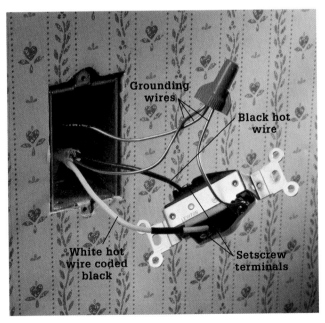

Standard receptacle rated for 240 volts has two incoming hot wires and no neutral wire. A grounding wire is pigtailed to the receptacle and to the metal receptacle box.

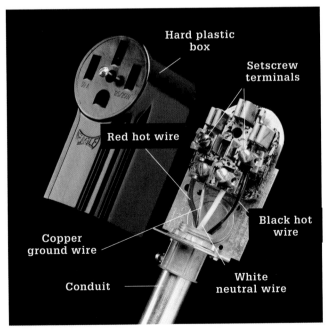

Surface-mounted receptacle rated for 240 volts has a hard plastic box that can be installed on concrete or block walls. Surface-mounted receptacles are often found in basements and utility rooms.

Childproof Receptacles & Other Accessories

Childproof your receptacles or adapt them for special uses by adding receptacle accessories. Before installing an accessory, be sure to read the manufacturer's instructions.

Homeowners with small children should add inexpensive caps or covers to guard against accidental electric shocks.

Plastic caps do not conduct electricity and are virtually impossible for small children to remove. A receptacle cover attaches directly to the receptacle and fits over plugs, preventing the cords from being removed.

Tamper resistant outlets are another way to prevent shocks. Thermoplastic shutters seal the slots of the outlet unless the two prongs of a plug are inserted at the same time, effectively keeping foreign objects out. Use plastic caps (inset) to protect standard outlets.

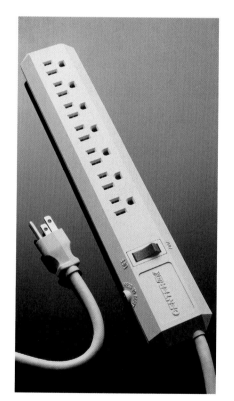

Install more than two plugs in a single duplex receptacle by using a multi-outlet power strip. A multi-outlet strip should have a built-in circuit breaker or fuse to protect against overloads.

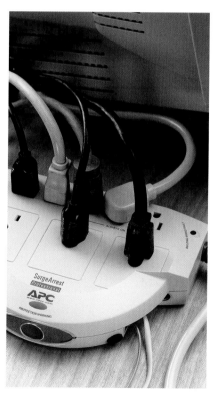

Protect electronic equipment, such as a home computer or stereo, with a surge protector. The surge protector prevents any damage to sensitive wiring or circuitry caused by sudden drops or surges in power.

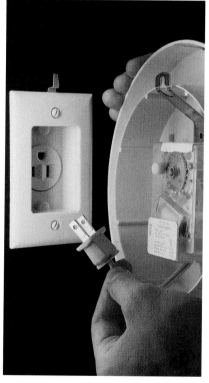

Recessed wall receptacle permits a plug-in clock to be hung flush against a wall surface.

Testing Receptacles for Power, Grounding & Polarity

For testing receptacles and other devices for power, grounding, and polarity, neon circuit testers are inexpensive and easy to use. But they are less sensitive than auto-ranging multimeters. In some cases, neon testers won't detect the presence of lower voltage in a circuit. This can lead you to believe that a circuit is shut off when it is not—a dangerous mistake. The small probes on a neon circuit tester also force you to get too close to live terminals and wires. For a quick check and confirmation, a neon circuit tester (or a plug-in tester) is adequate. But for the most reliable readings, buy and learn to use a multimeter.

The best multimeters are auto-ranging models with a digital readout. Unlike manual multimeters, auto-ranging models do not require you to preset the voltage range to get an accurate reading. Unlike neon testers, multimeters may be used for a host of additional diagnostic functions, such as testing fuses, measuring battery voltage, testing internal wiring in appliances, and checking light fixtures to determine if they're functional.

Tools & Materials ▸

Multimeter
Neon circuit tester
Plug-in tester
Screwdriver

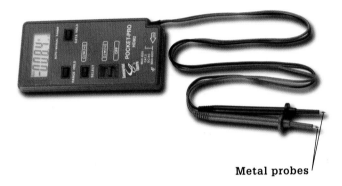

Metal probes

How to Use a Plug-in Tester

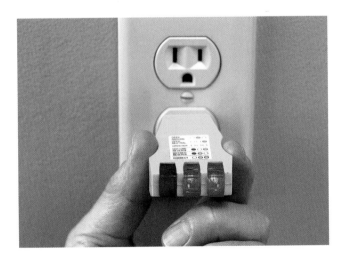

Use a plug-in tester to test a three-slot receptacle. With the power on, insert the tester into the suspect outlet. The face of the tester has three colored lights that will light up in different combinations, according to the outlet's problem. A reference chart is provided with tester, and many have a chart on the tester itself.

How to Test Quickly for Power

Use a neon circuit tester for quick testing to verify that power is not flowing to a receptacle before removing the cover plate. Insert one probe in each slot of the receptacle. If the bulb does not glow, remove the cover plate to access the receptacle and the screw terminals. Confirm that power is not flowing by testing the terminals with a multimeter.

How to Test a Receptacle for Power

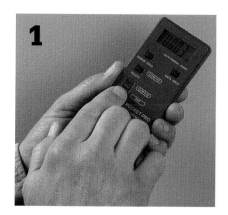

1

Set the selector dial for alternating-current voltage. Plug the black probe lead into the common jack on the multimeter (labeled COM). Plug the red probe lead into the V-labeled jack.

2

Insert the test ends of the probe into the receptacle slots. It does not make a difference which probe goes into which slot as long as they're in the same receptacle. If power is present and flowing normally, you will see a voltage reading (usually between 115 and 125 volts) on the readout screen.

3

If the multimeter reads 0 or gives a very low reading (less than 1 or 2 volts), power is not present in the receptacle and it is safe to remove the cover plate and work on the fixture (although it's always a good idea to confirm your reading by touching the probes directly to the screw terminals on the receptacles).

How to Test for Hot Wires

How to Test a Two-Slot Receptacle for Grounding

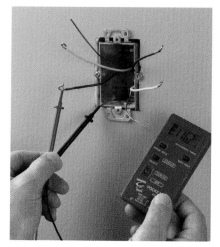

When a receptacle or switch is in the middle of a circuit, it is difficult to tell which wires are carrying current. Use a multimeter to check. With power off, remove the receptacle and separate the wires. Restore power. Touch one probe to the bare ground or the grounded metal box and touch the other probe to the end of each wire. The wire that shows current on the meter is hot.

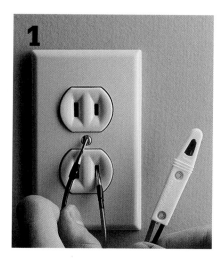

1

Confirm that the receptacle has power. Place one probe of a neon tester or multimeter in the short (hot) slot and the other on the coverplate screw (screw must be unpainted). If the tester shows current, the receptacle is grounded. If the tester doesn't show current, proceed to step 2.

2

Place one probe in the long (neutral) slot and the other on the coverplate screw. If the tester shows current, the hot and neutral wires are reversed. If not, the box is ungrounded.

Repairing & Replacing Receptacles

Receptacles are easy to repair. After shutting off power to the receptacle circuit, remove the coverplate and inspect the receptacle for any obvious problems such as a loose or broken connection, or wire ends that are dirty or oxidized. Remember that a problem at one receptacle may affect other receptacles in the same circuit. If the cause of a faulty receptacle is not readily apparent, test other receptacles in the circuit for power.

When replacing a receptacle, check the amperage rating of the circuit at the main service panel, and buy a replacement receptacle with the correct amperage rating.

When installing a new receptacle, always test for grounding. Never install a three-slot receptacle where no grounding exists. Instead, install a two-slot polarized or GFCI receptacle.

Tools & Materials ▸

Circuit tester
Screwdriver
Vacuum cleaner
 (if needed)

Fine sandpaper
Antioxidant paste
Masking tape
 (if needed)

How to Repair a Receptacle

Turn off power at the main service panel. Test the receptacle for power with a neon circuit tester (page 452). Test both ends of a duplex receptacle. Remove the coverplate, using a screwdriver.

Remove the mounting screws that hold the receptacle to the box. Carefully pull the receptacle from the box. Take care not to touch any bare wires.

Confirm that the power to the receptacle is off (page 452), using a neon circuit tester. If wires are attached to both sets of screw terminals, test both sets. The tester should not glow. If it does, you must turn off the correct circuit at the service panel.

4

Tighten all connections, using a screwdriver. Take care not to overtighten and strip the screws.

5

Check the box for dirt or dust and, if necessary, clean it with a vacuum cleaner and narrow nozzle attachment.

6

Reinstall the receptacle, and turn on power at the main service panel. Test the receptacle for power with a neon circuit tester. If the receptacle does not work, check other receptacles in the circuit before making a replacement.

How to Replace a Receptacle

1

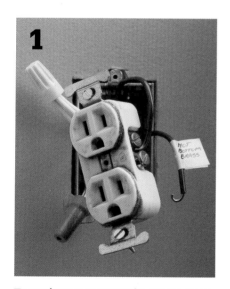

To replace a receptacle, repeat steps 1 to 3 on the opposite page. With the power off, label each wire for its location on the receptacle screw terminals, using masking tape and a felt-tipped pen.

2

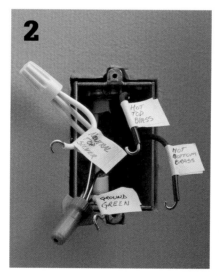

Disconnect all wires and remove the receptacle.

3

Replace the receptacle with one rated for the correct amperage and voltage. Replace coverplate, and turn on power. Test receptacle with a neon circuit tester or multimeter.

Installing GFCI Receptacles

The ground-fault circuit-interrupter (GFCI) receptacle protects against electrical shock caused by a faulty appliance, or a worn cord or plug. It senses small changes in current flow and can shut off power in as little as ⅟₄₀ of a second.

GFCIs are now required in bathrooms, kitchens, garages, crawl spaces, unfinished basements, and outdoor receptacle locations. Consult your local codes for any requirements regarding the installation of GFCI receptacles. Most GFCIs use standard screw terminal connections, but some have wire leads and are attached with wire connectors. Because the body of a GFCI receptacle is larger than a standard receptacle, small crowded electrical boxes may need to be replaced with more spacious boxes.

The GFCI receptacle may be wired to protect only itself (single location), or it can be wired to protect all receptacles, switches, and light fixtures from the GFCI "forward" to the end of the circuit (multiple locations).

Because the GFCI is so sensitive, it is most effective when wired to protect a single location. The more receptacles any one GFCI protects, the more susceptible it is to "phantom tripping," shutting off power because of tiny, normal fluctuations in current flow.

Tools & Materials ▸

Circuit tester   Wire connectors
Screwdriver   Masking tape

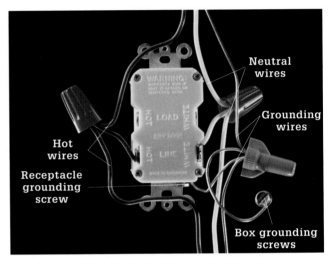

A GFCI wired for single-location protection (shown from the back) has hot and neutral wires connected only to the screw terminals marked LINE. A GFCI connected for single-location protection may be wired as either an end-of-run or middle-of-run configuration.

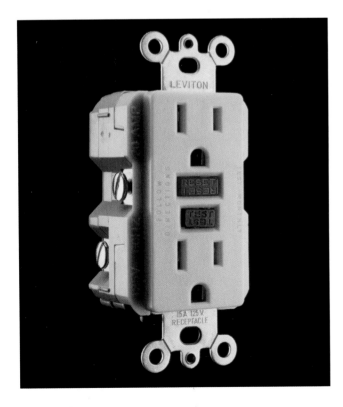

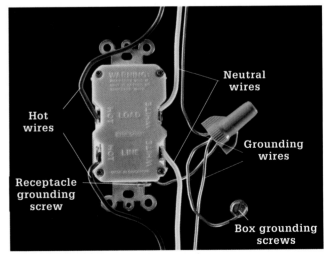

A GFCI wired for multiple-location protection (shown from the back) has one set of hot and neutral wires connected to the LINE pair of screw terminals, and the other set connected to the LOAD pair of screw terminals. A GFCI receptacle connected for multiple-location protection may be wired only as a middle-of-run configuration.

How to Install a GFCI for Single-location Protection

Shut off power to the receptacle at the main service panel. Test for power with a neon circuit tester (page 452). Be sure to check both halves of the receptacle.

Remove coverplate. Loosen mounting screws, and gently pull receptacle from the box. Do not touch wires. Confirm power is off with a circuit tester.

Disconnect all white neutral wires from the silver screw terminals of the old receptacle.

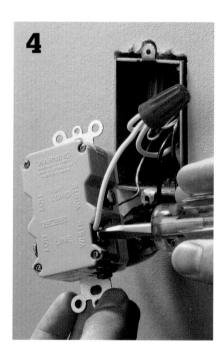

Pigtail all the white neutral wires together, and connect the pigtail to the terminal marked WHITE LINE on the GFCI (see photo on opposite page).

Disconnect all black hot wires from the brass screw terminals of the old receptacle. Pigtail these wires together, and connect them to the terminal marked HOT LINE on the GFCI.

If a grounding wire is available, connect it to the green grounding screw terminal of the GFCI. Mount the GFCI in the receptacle box, and reattach the coverplate. Restore power, and test the GFCI according to the manufacturer's instructions.

How to Install a GFCI for Multiple-location Protection

Use a map of your house circuits to determine a location for your GFCI. Indicate all receptacles that will be protected by the GFCI installation.

Turn off power to the correct circuit at the main service panel. Test all the receptacles in the circuit with a neon circuit tester to make sure the power is off. Always check both halves of each duplex receptacle.

Remove the coverplate from the receptacle that will be replaced with the GFCI. Loosen the mounting screws and gently pull the receptacle from its box. Take care not to touch any bare wires. Confirm the power is off with a neon circuit tester.

Disconnect all black hot wires. Carefully separate the hot wires and position them so that the bare ends do not touch anything. Restore power to the circuit at the main service panel. Determine which black wire is the "feed" wire by testing for hot wires. The feed wire brings power to the receptacle from the service panel. Use caution: This is a "live" wire test, during which the power is turned on temporarily.

When you have found the hot feed wire, turn off power at the main service panel. Identify the feed wire by marking it with masking tape.

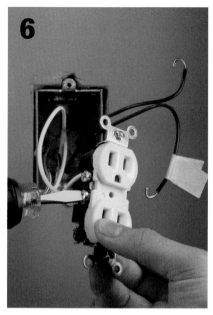

6

Disconnect the white neutral wires from the old receptacle. Identify the white feed wire and label it with masking tape. The white feed wire will be the one that shares the same cable as the black feed wire.

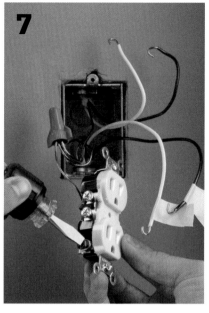

7

Disconnect the grounding wire from the grounding screw terminal of the old receptacle. Remove the old receptacle. Connect the grounding wire to the grounding screw terminal of the GFCI.

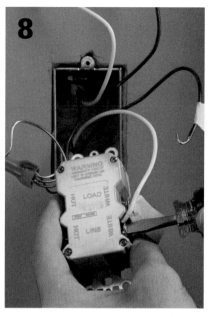

8

Connect the white feed wire to the terminal marked WHITE LINE on the GFCI. Connect the black feed wire to the terminal marked HOT LINE on the GFCI.

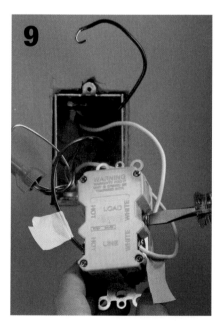

9

Connect the other white neutral wire to the terminal marked WHITE LOAD on the GFCI.

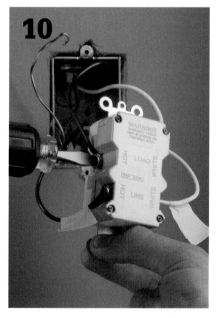

10

Connect the other black hot wire to the terminal marked HOT LOAD on the GFCI.

11

Carefully tuck all wires into the receptacle box. Mount the GFCI in the box and attach the coverplate. Turn on power to the circuit at the main service panel. Test the GFCI according to the manufacturer's instructions.

Common Wall-switch Problems

An average wall switch is turned on and off more than 1,000 times each year. Because switches receive constant use, wire connections can loosen and switch parts gradually wear out. If a switch no longer operates smoothly, it must be repaired or replaced.

The methods for repairing or replacing a switch vary slightly, depending on the switch type and its location along an electrical circuit. When working on a switch, use the photographs on pages 448 to 449 to identify your switch type and its wiring configuration. Individual switch styles may vary from manufacturer to manufacturer, but the basic switch types are universal.

It is possible to replace most ordinary wall switches with a specialty switch, like a timer switch or an electronic switch. When installing a specialty switch, make sure it is compatible with the wiring configuration of the switch box.

Tools & Materials ▶

Common Cable Problems
   (pages 433 to 435)
Checking Wire Connections
   (pages 435 to 436)
Inspecting Receptacles & Switches
   (pages 442 to 443)

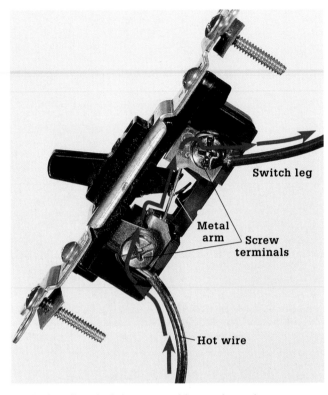

Typical wall switch has a movable metal arm that opens and closes the electrical circuit. When the switch is ON, the arm completes the circuit and power flows between the screw terminals and through the black hot wire to the light fixture. When the switch is OFF, the arm lifts away to interrupt the circuit, and no power flows. Switch problems can occur if the screw terminals are not tight or if the metal arm inside the switch wears out.

Rotary snap switches are found in many installations completed between 1900 and 1920. Handle is twisted clockwise to turn light on and off. The switch is enclosed in a ceramic housing.

Push-button switches were widely used from 1920 until about 1940. Many switches of this type are still in operation. Reproductions of this switch type are available for restoration projects.

Toggle switches were introduced in the 1930s. This early design has a switch mechanism that is mounted in a ceramic housing sealed with a layer of insulating paper.

Problem	Repair
Fuse burns out or circuit breaker trips when the switch is turned on.	1. Tighten any loose wire connections on switch (pages 474 to 475). 2. Move lamps or plug-in appliances to other circuits to prevent overloads. 3. Test switch, and replace, if needed (pages 474 to 475). 4. Repair or replace faulty fixture (pages 480 to 499) or faulty appliance.
Light fixture or permanently installed appliance does not work.	1. Replace burned-out lightbulb. 2. Check for blown fuse or tripped circuit breaker to make sure circuit is operating (page 425). 3. Check for loose wire connections on switch (pages 474 to 475). 4. Test switch, and replace, if needed (pages 474 to 475). 5. Repair or replace light fixture (pages 480 to 499) or appliance.
Light fixture flickers.	1. Tighten lightbulb in the socket. 2. Check for loose wire connections on switch (pages 474 to 475). 3. Repair or replace light fixture or switch (pages 480 to 499).
Switch buzzes or is warm to the touch.	1. Check for loose wire connections on switch (pages 474 to 475). 2. Test switch, and replace, if needed (pages 480 to 499). 3. Move lamps or appliances to other circuits to reduce demand.
Switch lever does not stay in position.	Replace worn-out switch (pages 474 to 475).

Toggle switches were improved during the 1950s, and are now the most commonly used type. This switch type was the first to use a sealed plastic housing that protects the inner switch mechanism from dust and moisture.

Mercury switches became common in the early 1960s. They conduct electrical current by means of a sealed vial of mercury. Although more expensive than other types, mercury switches are durable: some are guaranteed for 50 years.

Electronic motion-sensor switch has an infrared eye that senses movement and automatically turns on lights when a person enters a room. Motion-sensor switches can provide added security against intruders.

Wall-switch Basics

Wall switches are available in three general types. To repair or replace a switch, it is important to identify its type.

Single-pole switches are used to control a set of lights from one location. Three-way switches are used to control a set of lights from two different locations and are always installed in pairs. Four-way switches are used in combination with a pair of three-way switches to control a set of lights from three or more locations.

Identify switch types by counting the screw terminals. Single-pole switches have two screw terminals, three-way switches have three screw terminals, and four-way switches have four.

Most switches include a grounding screw terminal, which is identified by its green color.

When replacing a switch, choose a new switch that has the same number of screw terminals as the old one. The location of the screws on the switch body varies, depending on the manufacturer, but these differences will not affect the switch operation.

Whenever possible, connect switches using the screw terminals rather than push-in fittings. Some specialty switches (pages 468 to 469) have wire leads instead of screw terminals. They are connected to circuit wires with wire connectors.

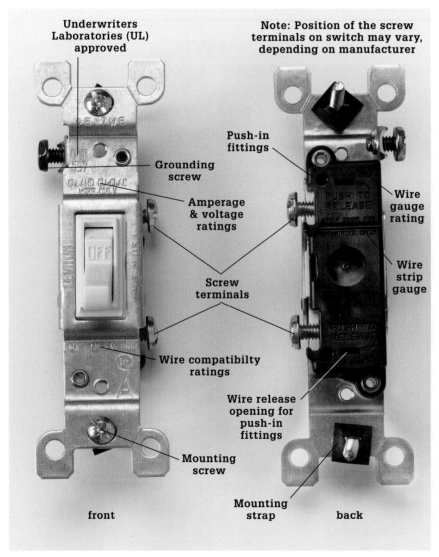

Underwriters Laboratories (UL) approved

Note: Position of the screw terminals on switch may vary, depending on manufacturer

Push-in fittings

Grounding screw

Amperage & voltage ratings

Screw terminals

Wire gauge rating

Wire strip gauge

Wire compatibilty ratings

Wire release opening for push-in fittings

Mounting screw

Mounting strap

front

back

A wall switch is connected to circuit wires with screw terminals or with push-in fittings on the back of the switch. A switch may have a stamped strip gauge that indicates how much insulation must be stripped from the circuit wires to make the connections.

The switch body is attached to a metal mounting strap that allows it to be mounted in an electrical box. Several rating stamps are found on the strap and on the back of the switch. The abbreviation UL or UND. LAB. INC. LIST means that the switch meets the safety standards of the Underwriters Laboratories. Switches also are stamped with maximum voltage and amperage ratings. Standard wall switches are rated 15A, 120V. Voltage ratings of 110, 120, and 125 are considered to be identical for purposes of identification.

For standard wall switch installations, choose a switch that has a wire gauge rating of #12 or #14. For wire systems with solid-core copper wiring, use only switches marked COPPER or CU. For aluminum wiring (page 432), use only switches marked CO/ALR. Switches marked AL/CU can no longer be used with aluminum wiring, according to the National Electrical Code.

Single-pole Wall Switches

A single-pole switch is the most common type of wall switch. It has ON-OFF markings on the switch lever and is used to control a set of lights, an appliance, or a receptacle from a single location. A single-pole switch has two screw terminals and a grounding screw. When installing a single-pole switch, check to make sure the ON marking shows when the switch lever is in the up position.

In a correctly wired single-pole switch, a hot circuit wire is attached to each screw terminal. However, the color and number of wires inside the switch box will vary, depending on the location of the switch along the electrical circuit.

If two cables enter the box, then the switch lies in the middle of the circuit. In this installation, both of the hot wires attached to the switch are black.

If only one cable enters the box, then the switch lies at the end of the circuit. In this installation (sometimes called a switch loop), one of the hot wires is black, but the other hot wire usually is white. A white hot wire sometimes is coded with black tape or paint.

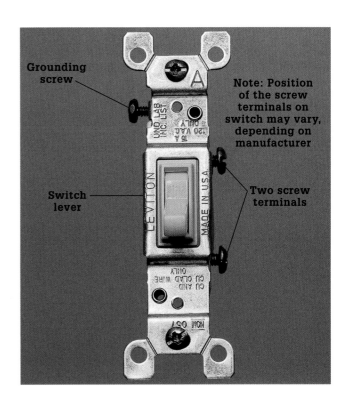

Note: Position of the screw terminals on switch may vary, depending on manufacturer

Typical Single-pole Switch Installations

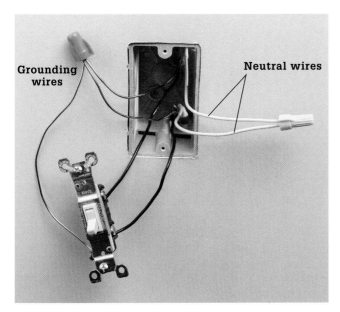

Two cables enter the box when a switch is located in the middle of a circuit. Each cable has a white and a black insulated wire, plus a bare copper grounding wire. The black wires are hot and are connected to the screw terminals on the switch. The white wires are neutral and are joined together with a wire connector. Grounding wires are pigtailed to the switch.

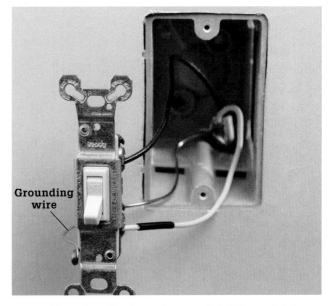

One cable enters the box when a switch is located at the end of a circuit. The cable has a white and a black insulated wire, plus a bare copper grounding wire. In this installation, both of the insulated wires are hot. The white wire may be labeled with black tape or paint to identify it as a hot wire. The grounding wire is connected to the switch grounding screw.

Three-way Wall Switches

Three-way switches have three screw terminals and do not have ON-OFF markings. Three-way switches are always installed in pairs and are used to control a set of lights from two locations.

One of the screw terminals on a three-way switch is darker than the others. This screw is the common screw terminal. The position of the common screw terminal on the switch body may vary, depending on the manufacturer. Before disconnecting a three-way switch, always label the wire that is connected to the common screw terminal. It must be reconnected to the common screw terminal on the new switch.

The two lighter-colored screw terminals on a three-way switch are called the traveler screw terminals. The traveler terminals are interchangeable, so there is no need to label the wires attached to them.

Because three-way switches are installed in pairs, it sometimes is difficult to determine which of the switches is causing a problem. The switch that receives greater use is more likely to fail, but you may need to inspect both switches to find the source of the problem.

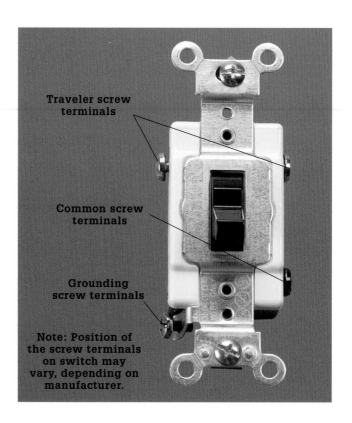

Traveler screw terminals

Common screw terminals

Grounding screw terminals

Note: Position of the screw terminals on switch may vary, depending on manufacturer.

Typical Three-way Switch Installations

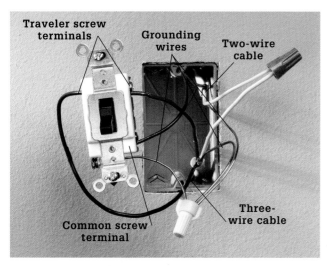

Traveler screw terminals

Grounding wires

Two-wire cable

Common screw terminal

Three-wire cable

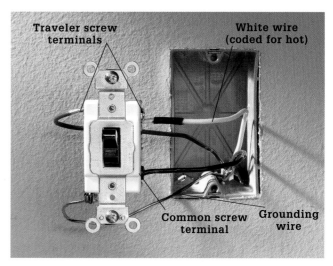

Traveler screw terminals

White wire (coded for hot)

Common screw terminal

Grounding wire

Two cables enter the box if the switch lies in the middle of a circuit. One cable has two wires, plus a bare copper grounding wire; the other cable has three wires, plus a ground. The black wire from the two-wire cable is connected to the dark, common screw terminal. The red and black wires from the three-wire cable are connected to the traveler screw terminals. The white neutral wires are joined together with a wire connector, and the grounding wires are pigtailed to the grounded metal box.

One cable enters the box if the switch lies at the end of the circuit. The cable has a black wire, red wire, and white wire, plus a bare copper grounding wire. The black wire must be connected to the common screw terminal, which is darker than the other two screw terminals. The white and red wires are connected to the two traveler screw terminals. The white wire is taped to indicate that it is hot. The bare copper grounding wire is connected to the grounded metal box.

Four-way Wall Switches

Four-way switches have four screw terminals and do not have ON-OFF markings. Four-way switches are always installed between a pair of three-way switches. This switch combination makes it possible to control a set of lights from three or more locations. Four-way switches are common in homes where large rooms contain multiple living areas, such as a kitchen opening into a dining room. Switch problems in a four-way installation can be caused by loose connections or worn parts in a four-way switch or in one of the three-way switches (facing page).

In a typical installation, there will be a pair of three-way cables that enter the box for the four-way switch. With most switches, the white and red wires from one cable should be attached to the bottom or top pair of screw terminals, and the white and red wires from the other cable should be attached to the remaining pair of screw terminals. However, not all switches are configured the same way, and wiring configurations in the box may vary, so always study the wiring diagram that comes with the switch.

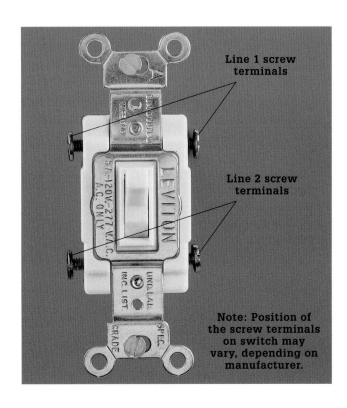

Line 1 screw terminals

Line 2 screw terminals

Note: Position of the screw terminals on switch may vary, depending on manufacturer.

Typical Four-way Switch Installation

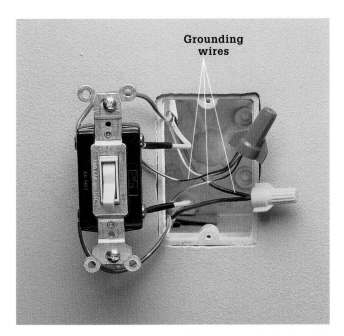

Grounding wires

Four wires are connected to a four-way switch. The red and white wires from one cable are attached to the top pair of screw terminals, while the red and white wires from the other cable are attached to the bottom screw terminals.

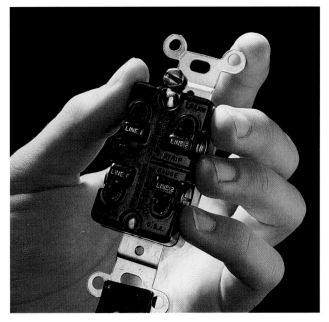

Switch variation: Some four-way switches have a wiring guide stamped on the back to help simplify installation. For the switch shown above, one pair of color-matched circuit wires will be connected to the screw terminals marked LINE 1, while the other pair of wires will be attached to the screw terminals marked LINE 2.

Double Switches

A double switch has two switch levers in a single housing. It is used to control two light fixtures or appliances from the same switch box.

In most installations, both halves of the switch are powered by the same circuit. In these single-circuit installations, three wires are connected to the double switch. One wire, called the "feed" wire, supplies power to both halves of the switch. The other wires carry power out to the individual light fixtures or appliances.

In rare installations, each half of the switch is powered by a separate circuit. In these separate-circuit installations, four wires are connected to the switch, and the metal connecting tab joining two of the screw terminals is removed (photo below).

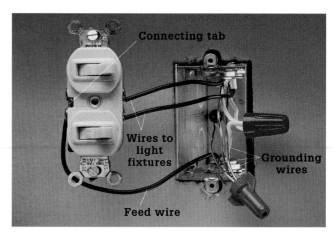

Single-circuit wiring: Three black wires are attached to the switch. The black feed wire bringing power into the box is connected to the side of the switch that has a connecting tab. The wires carrying power out to the light fixtures or appliances are connected to the side of the switch that does not have a connecting tab. The white neutral wires are connected together with a wire connector.

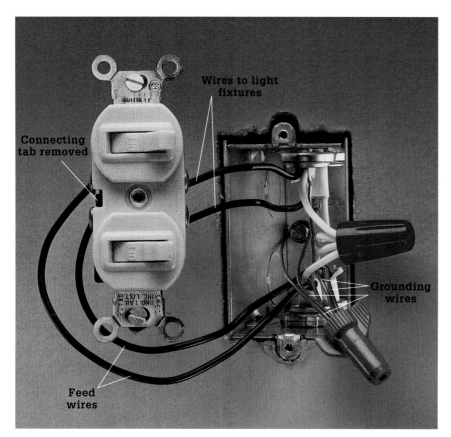

Separate-circuit wiring: Four black wires are attached to the switch. Feed wires from the power source are attached to the side of switch that has a connecting tab, and the connecting tab is removed (photo, right). Wires carrying power from the switch to light fixtures or appliances are connected to the side of the switch that does not have a connecting tab. White neutral wires are connected together with a wire connector.

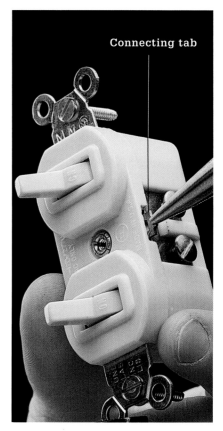

Remove the connecting tab on a double switch when wired in a separate-circuit installation. The tab can be removed with needlenose pliers or a screwdriver.

Pilot-light Switches

A pilot-light switch has a built-in bulb that glows when power flows through the switch to a light fixture or appliance. Pilot-light switches often are installed for convenience if a light fixture or appliance cannot be seen from the switch location. Basement lights, garage lights, and attic exhaust fans frequently are controlled by pilot-light switches.

A pilot-light switch requires a neutral wire connection. A switch box that contains a single two-wire cable has only hot wires and cannot be fitted with a pilot-light switch.

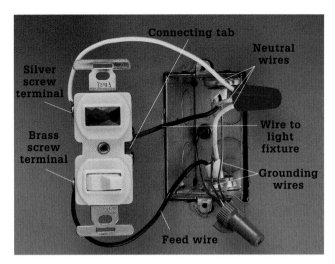

Pilot-light switch wiring: Three wires are connected to the switch. One black wire is the feed wire that brings power into the box. It is connected to the brass screw terminal on the side of the switch that does not have a connecting tab. The white neutral wires are pigtailed to the silver screw terminal. Black wire carrying power out to light fixture or appliance is connected to screw terminal on side of the switch that has a connecting tab.

Switch/receptacles

A switch/receptacle combines a grounded receptacle with a single-pole wall switch. In a room that does not have enough wall receptacles, electrical service can be improved by replacing a single-pole switch with a switch/receptacle.

A switch/receptacle requires a neutral wire connection. A switch box that contains a single two-wire cable has only hot wires and cannot be fitted with a switch/receptacle.

A switch/receptacle can be installed in one of two ways. In the most common installations, the receptacle is hot even when the switch is off (photo, right).

In rare installations, a switch/receptacle is wired so the receptacle is hot only when the switch is on. In this installation, the hot wires are reversed, so that the feed wire is attached to the brass screw terminal on the side of the switch that does not have a connecting tab.

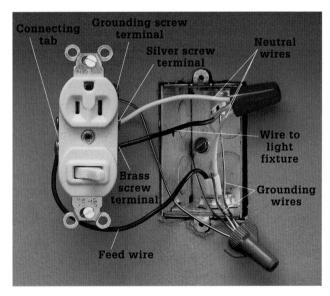

Switch/receptacle wiring: Three wires are connected to the switch/receptacle. One of the hot wires is the feed wire that brings power into the box. It is connected to the side of the switch that has a connecting tab. The other hot wire carries power out to the light fixture or appliance. It is connected to the brass screw terminal on the side that does not have a connecting tab. The white neutral wire is pigtailed to the silver screw terminal. The grounding wires must be pigtailed to the green grounding screw on the switch/receptacle and to the grounded metal box.

Specialty Switches

Your house may have several types of specialty switches. Dimmer switches (pages 478 to 479) are used frequently to control light intensity in dining and recreation areas. Timer switches and time-delay switches (below) are used to control light fixtures and exhaust fans automatically. Electronic switches (facing page) provide added convenience and home security, and are easy to install. Electronic switches are durable, and they rarely need repair.

Most specialty switches have preattached wire leads instead of screw terminals and are connected to circuit wires with wire connectors. Some motor-driven timer switches require a neutral wire connection and cannot be installed in switch boxes that have only one cable with two hot wires.

If a specialty switch is not operating correctly, you may be able to test it with a continuity tester. Timer switches and time-delay switches can be tested for continuity, but dimmer switches cannot be tested. With electronic switches, the manual switch can be tested for continuity, but the automatic features cannot be tested.

Timer Switches

Timer switches have an electrically powered control dial that can be set to turn lights on and off automatically once each day. They are commonly used to control outdoor light fixtures.

Timer switches have three preattached wire leads. The black wire lead is connected to the hot feed wire that brings power into the box, and the red lead is connected to the wire carrying power out to the light fixture. The remaining wire lead is the neutral lead. It must be connected to any neutral circuit wires. A switch box that contains only one cable has no neutral wires, so it cannot be fitted with a timer switch.

After a power failure, the dial on a timer switch must be reset to the proper time.

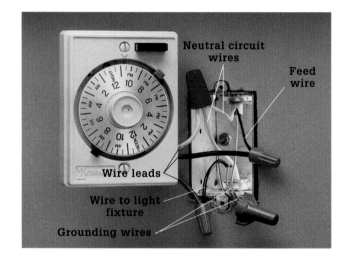

Time-delay Switches

A time-delay switch has a spring-driven dial that is wound by hand. The dial can be set to turn off a light fixture after a delay ranging from 1 to 60 minutes. Time-delay switches often are used for exhaust fans, bathroom vent fans, and heat lamps.

The black wire leads on the switch are connected to the hot circuit wires. If the switch box contains white neutral wires, these are connected together with a wire connector. The bare copper grounding wires are pigtailed to the grounded metal box.

A time-delay switch needs no neutral wire connection, so it can be fitted in a switch box that contains either one or two cables.

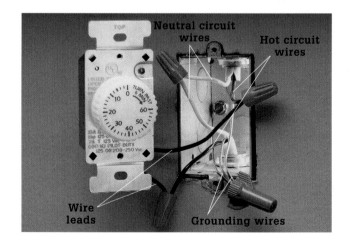

Automatic Switches

An automatic switch uses a narrow infrared beam to detect movement. When a hand passes within a few inches of the beam, an electronic signal turns the switch on or off. Some automatic switches have a manual dimming feature.

Automatic switches can be installed wherever a standard single-pole switch is used. Automatic switches are especially convenient for children and persons with disabilities.

Automatic switches require no neutral wire connections. For this reason, an automatic switch can be installed in a switch box containing either one or two cables. The wire leads on the switch are connected to hot circuit wires with wire connectors.

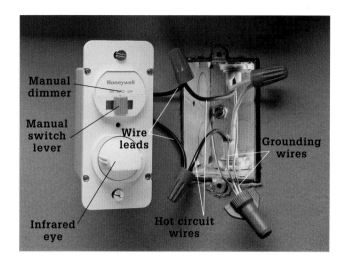

Motion-sensor Security Switches

A motion-sensor switch uses a wide-angle infrared beam to detect movement over a large area and turns on a light fixture automatically. A time-delay feature turns off lights after movement stops.

Most motion-sensor switches have an override feature that allows the switch to be operated manually. Better switches include an adjustable sensitivity control and a variable time-delay shutoff control.

Motion-sensor switches require no neutral wire connections. They can be installed in switch boxes containing either one or two cables. The wire leads on the switch are connected to hot circuit wires.

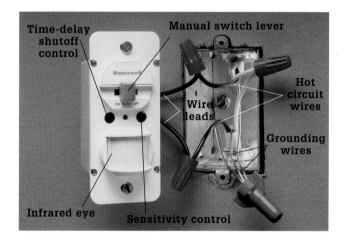

Programmable Switches

Programmable switches have digital controls and can provide four on-off cycles each day. They frequently are used to provide security when a homeowner is absent. Law enforcement experts say that programmed lighting is a proven crime deterrent. For best protection, programmable switches should be set to a random on-off pattern.

Programmable switches require no neutral wire connections. They can be installed in switch boxes containing either one or two cables. The wire leads on the switch are connected to hot circuit wires with wire connectors.

Testing Switches for Continuity

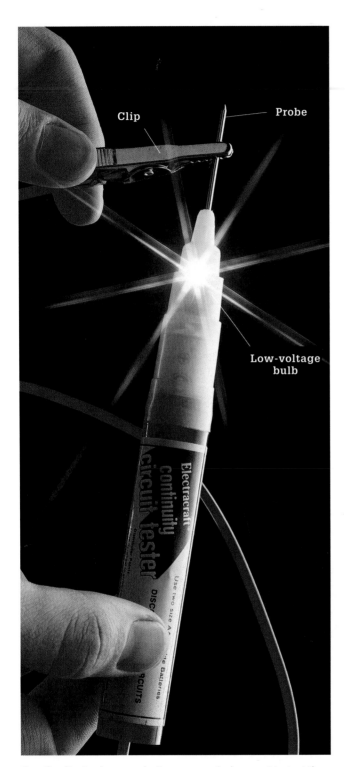

A switch that does not work properly may have worn or broken internal parts. Test for internal wear with a battery-operated continuity tester. The continuity tester detects any break in the metal pathway inside the switch. Replace the switch if the continuity tester shows the switch to be faulty.

Never use a continuity tester on wires that might carry live current. Always shut off the power and disconnect the switch before testing for continuity.

Some specialty switches, like dimmers, cannot be tested for continuity. Electronic switches can be tested for manual operation using a continuity tester, but the automatic operation of these switches cannot be tested.

Tools & Materials ▸

Continuity tester

How to Test a Single-pole Wall Switch

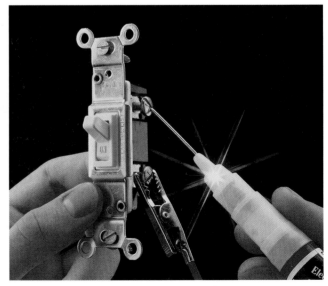

Attach clip of tester to one of the screw terminals. Touch the tester probe to the other screw terminal. Flip switch lever from ON to OFF. If switch is good, tester glows when lever is ON, but not when OFF.

Continuity tester uses battery-generated current to test the metal pathways running through switches and other electrical fixtures. Always "test" the tester before use. Touch the tester clip to the metal probe. The tester should glow. If not, then the battery or lightbulb is dead and must be replaced.

How to Test a Three-way Wall Switch

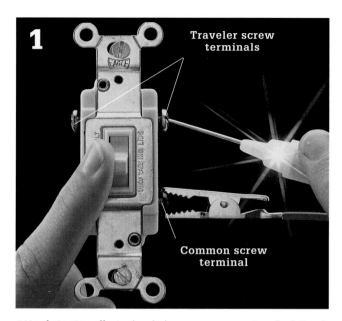

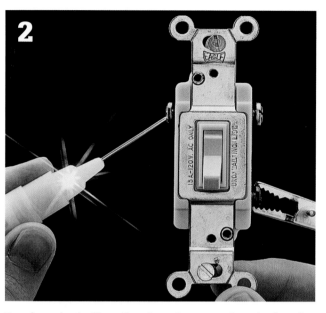

Attach tester clip to the dark common screw terminal. Touch the tester probe to one of the traveler screw terminals, and flip switch lever back and forth. If switch is good, the tester should glow when the lever is in one position, but not both.

Touch probe to the other traveler screw terminal, and flip the switch lever back and forth. If switch is good, the tester will glow only when the switch lever is in the position opposite from the positive test in step 1.

How to Test a Four-way Wall Switch

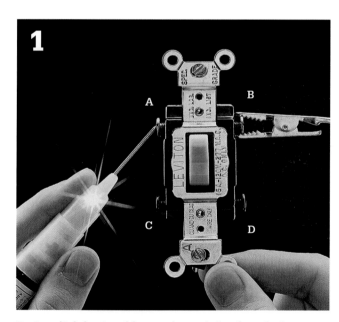

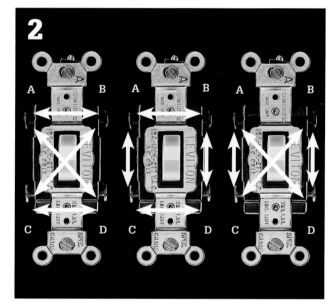

Test switch by touching probe and clip of continuity tester to each pair of screw terminals (A-B, C-D, A-D, B-C, A-C, B-D). The test should show continuous pathways between two different pairs of screw terminals. Flip lever to opposite position, and repeat test. Test should show continuous pathways between two different pairs of screw terminals.

If switch is good, test will show a total of four continuous pathways between screw terminals—two pathways for each lever position. If not, then switch is faulty and must be replaced. (The arrangement of the pathways may differ, depending on the switch manufacturer. The photo above shows the three possible pathway arrangements.)

How to Test a Pilot-light Switch

Test pilot light by flipping the switch lever to the ON position. Check to see if the light fixture or appliance is working. If the pilot light does not glow even though the switch operates the light fixture or appliance, then the pilot light is defective and the unit must be replaced.

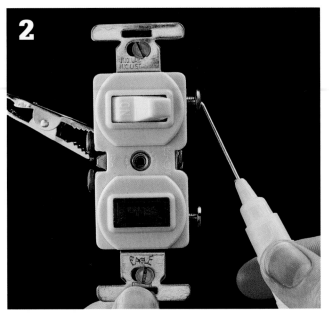

Test the switch by disconnecting the unit. With the switch lever in the ON position, attach the tester clip to the top screw terminal on one side of the switch. Touch tester probe to top screw terminal on opposite side of the switch. If switch is good, tester will glow when switch is ON, but not when OFF.

How to Test a Timer Switch

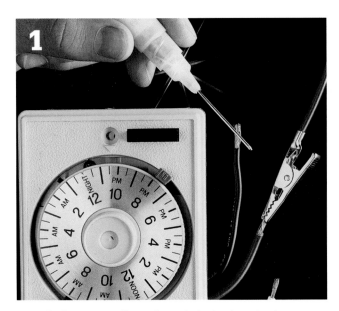

Attach the tester clip to the red wire lead on the timer switch, and touch the tester probe to the black hot lead. Rotate the timer dial clockwise until the ON tab passes the arrow marker. Tester should glow. If it does not, the switch is faulty and must be replaced.

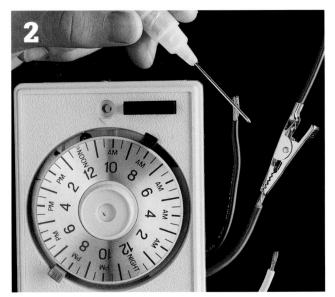

Rotate the dial clockwise until the OFF tab passes the arrow marker. Tester should not glow. If it does, the switch is faulty and must be replaced.

How to Test Switch/receptacle

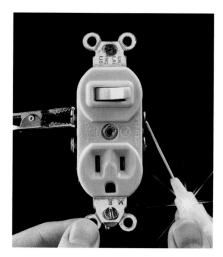

Attach tester clip to one of the top screw terminals. Touch the tester probe to the top screw terminal on the opposite side. Flip the switch lever from ON to OFF position. If the switch is working correctly, the tester will glow when the switch lever is ON, but not when OFF.

How to Test a Double Switch

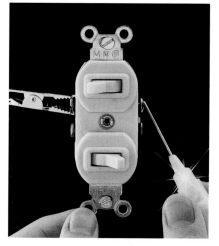

Test each half of switch by attaching the tester clip to one screw terminal and touching the probe to the opposite side. Flip switch lever from ON to OFF position. If switch is good, tester glows when the switch lever is ON, but not when OFF. Repeat test with the remaining pair of screw terminals. If either half tests faulty, replace the unit.

How to Test a Time-delay Switch

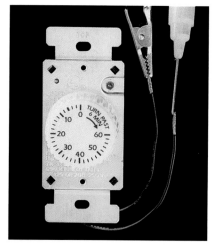

Attach tester clip to one of the wire leads, and touch the tester probe to the other lead. Set the timer for a few minutes. If switch is working correctly, the tester will glow until the time expires.

How to Test Manual Operation of Electronic Switches

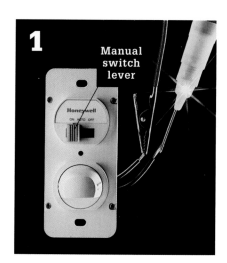

Automatic switch: Attach the tester clip to a black wire lead, and touch the tester probe to the other black lead. Flip the manual switch lever from ON to OFF position. If switch is working correctly, tester will glow when the switch lever is ON, but not when OFF.

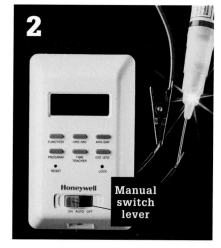

Programmable switch: Attach the tester clip to a wire lead, and touch the tester probe to the other lead. Flip the manual switch lever from ON to OFF position. If the switch is working correctly, the tester will glow when the switch lever is ON, but not when OFF.

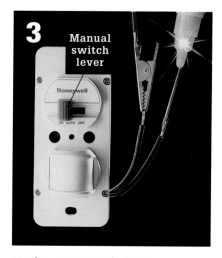

Motion-sensor switch: Attach the tester clip to a wire lead, and touch the tester probe to the other lead. Flip the manual switch lever from ON to OFF position. If the switch is working correctly, the tester will glow when the switch lever is ON, but not when OFF.

Fixing & Replacing Wall Switches

Most switch problems are caused by loose wire connections. If a fuse blows or a circuit breaker trips when a switch is turned on, a loose wire may be touching the metal box. Loose wires also can cause switches to overheat or buzz.

Switches sometimes fail because internal parts wear out. To check for wear, the switch must be removed entirely and tested for continuity (pages 470 to 471). If the continuity test shows the switch is faulty, replace it.

Tools & Materials ▸

Screwdriver
Circuit tester
Continuity tester
Combination tool
Fine sandpaper

Antioxidant paste
(for aluminum
wiring)
Masking tape

How to Fix or Replace a Single-pole Wall Switch

Turn off the power to the switch at the main service panel, then remove the switch coverplate.

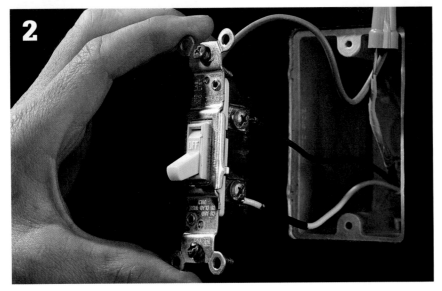

Remove the mounting screws holding the switch to the electrical box. Holding the mounting straps carefully, pull the switch from the box. Be careful not to touch any bare wires or screw terminals until the switch has been tested for power.

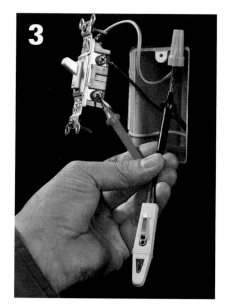

3

Test for power by touching one probe of the neon circuit tester to the grounded metal box or to the bare copper grounding wire, and touching other probe to each screw terminal. Tester should not glow. If it does, there is still power entering the box. Return to service panel, and turn off correct circuit.

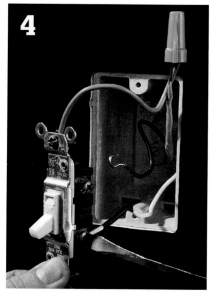

4

Disconnect the circuit wires and remove the switch. Test the switch for continuity, and buy a replacement if the switch is faulty. If circuit wires are too short, lengthen them by adding pigtail wires (page 438).

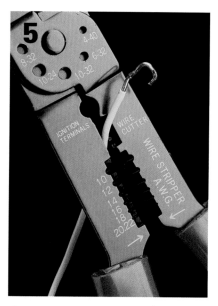

5

If wires are broken or nicked, clip off damaged portion, using a combination tool. Strip wires so there is about ¾" of bare wire at the end of each wire.

6

Clean the bare copper wires with fine sandpaper if they appear darkened or dirty. If wires are aluminum, apply an antioxidant paste before connecting the wires.

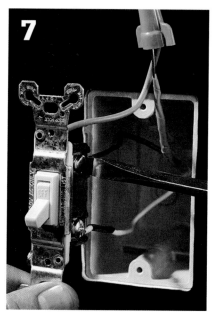

7

Connect the wires to the screw terminals on the switch. Tighten the screws firmly, but do not overtighten. Overtightening may strip the screw threads.

8

Remount the switch, carefully tucking the wires inside the box. Reattach the switch coverplate, and turn on the power to the switch at the main service panel.

How to Fix or Replace a Three-way Wall Switch

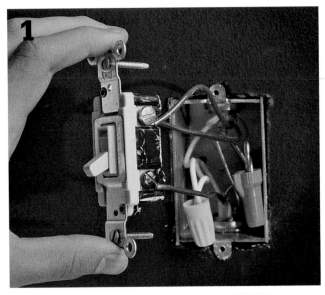

Turn off the power to the switch at the main service panel, then remove the switch coverplate and mounting screws. Holding the mounting strap carefully, pull the switch from the box. Be careful not to touch the bare wires or screw terminals until they have been tested for power.

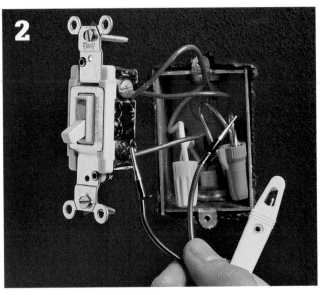

Test for power by touching one probe of the neon circuit tester to the grounded metal box or to the bare copper grounding wire, and touching the other probe to each screw terminal. Tester should not glow. If it does, there is still power entering the box. Return to the service panel, and turn off the correct circuit.

Locate dark common screw terminal, and use masking tape to label the "common" wire attached to it. Disconnect wires and remove switch. Test switch for continuity (pages 470 to 471). If it tests faulty, buy a replacement. Inspect wires for nicks and scratches. If necessary, clip damaged wires and strip them.

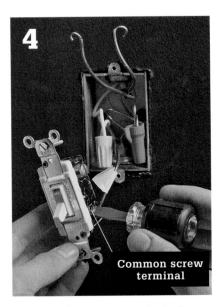

Connect the common wire to the dark common screw terminal on the switch. On most three-way switches the common screw terminal is black. Or it may be labeled with the word COMMON stamped on the back of the switch. If the switch has a grounding screw, connect it to the circuit grounding wires with a pigtail.

Connect the remaining two circuit wires to the screw terminals. These wires are interchangeable and can be connected to either screw terminal. Carefully tuck the wires into the box. Remount the switch, and attach the coverplate. Turn on the power at the main service panel.

How to Fix or Replace a Four-way Wall Switch

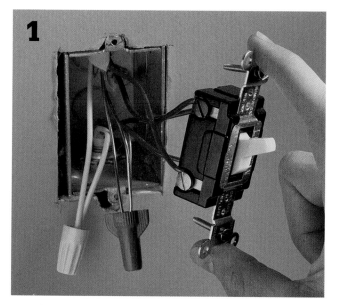

Turn off the power to the switch at the main service panel, then remove the switch coverplate and mounting screws. Holding the mounting strap carefully, pull the switch from the box. Be careful not to touch any bare wires or screw terminals until they have been tested for power.

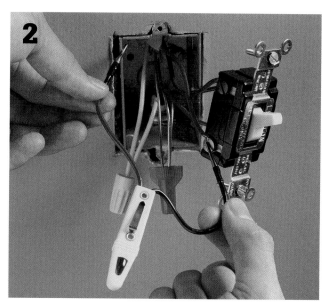

Test for power by touching one probe of the neon circuit tester to the grounded metal box or bare copper grounding wire, and touching the other probe to each of the screw terminals. Tester should not glow. If it does, there is still power entering the box. Return to the service panel, and turn off the correct circuit.

Disconnect the wires and inspect them for nicks and scratches. If necessary, clip damaged wires and strip them. Test the switch for continuity (pages 471 to 472). Buy a replacement if the switch tests faulty.

Connect two wires from one incoming cable to the top set of screw terminals.

Attach remaining wires to the other set of screw terminals. Pigtail the grounding wires to the grounding screw. Carefully tuck the wires inside the switch box, then remount the switch and coverplate. Turn on power at main service panel.

Installing Dimmer Switches

A dimmer switch makes it possible to vary the brightness of a light fixture. Dimmers are often installed in dining rooms, recreation areas, or bedrooms.

Any standard single-pole switch can be replaced with a dimmer, as long as the switch box is of adequate size. Dimmer switches have larger bodies than standard switches. They also generate a small amount of heat that must dissipate. For these reasons, dimmers should not be installed in undersized electrical boxes or in boxes that are crowded with circuit wires. Always follow the manufacturer's specifications for installation.

In lighting configurations that use three-way switches (page 462), replace the standard switches with special three-way dimmers. If replacing both the switches with dimmers, buy a packaged pair of three-way dimmers designed to work together.

Dimmer switches are available in several styles (photo, left). All types have wire leads instead of screw terminals, and they are connected to circuit wires using wire connectors. Some types have a green grounding lead that should be connected to the grounded metal box or to the bare copper grounding wires.

Tools & Materials ▶

Screwdriver
Circuit tester
Needlenose pliers
Wire connectors
Masking tape

Toggle-type dimmer resembles standard switches. Toggle dimmers are available in both single-pole and three-way designs.

Dial-type dimmer is the most common style. Rotating the dial changes the light intensity.

Slide-action dimmer has an illuminated face that makes the switch easy to locate in the dark.

Automatic dimmer has an electronic sensor that adjusts the light fixture to compensate for the changing levels of natural light. An automatic dimmer also can be operated manually.

How to Install a Dimmer Switch

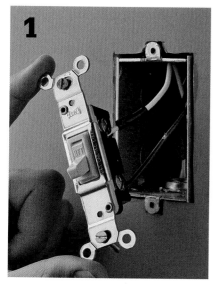

Turn off power to switch at the main service panel, then remove the coverplate and mounting screws. Holding the mounting straps carefully, pull switch from the box. Be careful not to touch bare wires or screw terminals until they have been tested for power.

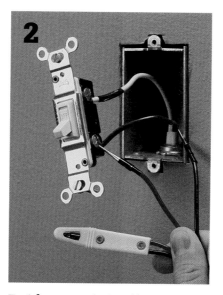

Test for power by touching one probe of neon circuit tester to the grounded metal box or to the bare copper grounding wires, and touching other probe to each screw terminal. Tester should not glow. If it does, there is still power entering the box. Return to the service panel and turn off the correct circuit.

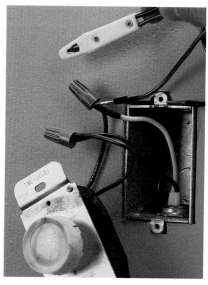

If replacing an old dimmer, test for power by touching one probe of circuit tester to the grounded metal box or bare copper grounding wires, and inserting the other probe into each wire connector. Tester should not glow. If it does, there is still power entering the box. Return to the service panel, and turn off the correct circuit.

Disconnect the circuit wires and remove the switch. Straighten the circuit wires, and clip the ends, leaving about ½" of the bare wire end exposed.

Hot circuit wires

Wire leads

Connect the wire leads on the dimmer switch to the circuit wires, using wire connectors. The switch leads are interchangeable and can be attached to either of the two circuit wires.

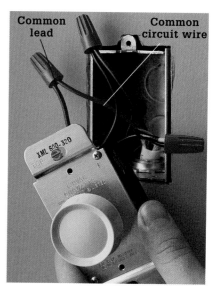

Common lead

Common circuit wire

Three-way dimmer has an additional wire lead. This "common" lead is connected to the common circuit wire. When replacing a standard three-way switch with a dimmer, the common circuit wire is attached to the darkest screw terminal on the old switch.

Repairing & Replacing Incandescent Light Fixtures

Incandescent light fixtures are attached permanently to ceilings or walls. They include wall-hung sconces, ceiling-hung globe fixtures, recessed light fixtures, and chandeliers. Most incandescent light fixtures are easy to repair, using basic tools and inexpensive parts.

If a light fixture fails, always make sure the lightbulb is screwed in tightly and is not burned out. A faulty lightbulb is the most common cause of light fixture failure. If the light fixture is controlled by a wall switch, also check the switch as a possible source of problems.

Light fixtures can fail because the sockets or built-in switches wear out. Some fixtures have sockets and switches that can be removed for minor repairs. These parts are held to the base of the fixture with mounting screws or clips. Other fixtures have sockets and switches that are joined permanently to the base. If this type of fixture fails, purchase and install a new light fixture.

Damage to light fixtures often occurs because homeowners install lightbulbs with wattage ratings that are too high. Prevent overheating and light fixture failures by using only lightbulbs that match the wattage ratings printed on the fixtures.

Techniques for repairing fluorescent lights are different from those for incandescent lights. Refer to pages 494 to 497 to repair or replace a fluorescent light fixture.

Tools & Materials ▶

Circuit tester
Screwdriver
Continuity tester
Combination tool
Replacement parts, as needed

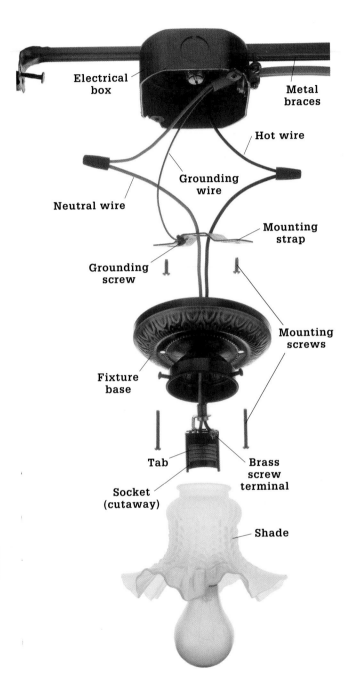

In a typical incandescent light fixture, a black hot wire is connected to a brass screw terminal on the socket. Power flows to a small tab at the bottom of the metal socket and through a metal filament inside the bulb. The power heats the filament and causes it to glow. The current then flows through the threaded portion of the socket and through the white neutral wire back to the main service panel.

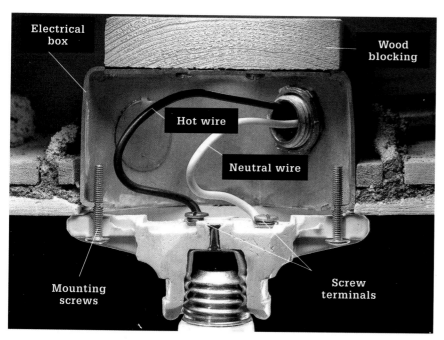

Electrical box

Wood blocking

Hot wire

Neutral wire

Mounting screws

Screw terminals

Before 1959, incandescent light fixtures (shown cut away) often were mounted directly to an electrical box or to plaster lath. Electrical codes now require that fixtures be attached to mounting straps that are anchored to the electrical boxes (page 484). If you have a light fixture attached to plaster lath, install an approved electrical box with a mounting strap to support the fixture.

Problem	Repair
Wall- or ceiling-mounted fixture flickers or does not light.	1. Check for faulty lightbulb. 2. Check wall switch, and repair or replace, if needed (pages 474 to 477). 3. Check for loose wire connections in electrical box. 4. Test socket, and replace, if needed (pages 482 to 483). 5. Replace light fixture (page 484).
Built-in switch on fixture does not work.	1. Check for faulty lightbulb. 2. Check for loose wire connections on switch. 3. Replace switch (pages 474 to 477). 4. Replace light fixture (page 484).
Chandelier flickers or does not light.	1. Check for faulty lightbulb. 2. Check wall switch, and repair or replace, if needed (pages 474 to 477). 3. Check for loose wire connections in electrical box. 4. Test sockets and fixture wires, and replace, if needed (pages 482 to 483).
Recessed fixture flickers or does not light.	1. Check for faulty lightbulb. 2. Check wall switch, and repair or replace, if needed (pages 474 to 477). 3. Check for loose wire connections in electrical box. 4. Test fixture, and replace, if needed (page 484).

How to Remove a Light Fixture & Test a Socket

Turn off the power to the light fixture at the main service panel. Remove the lightbulb and any shade or globe, then remove the mounting screws holding the fixture base to the electrical box or mounting strap. Carefully pull the fixture base away from box.

Test for power by touching one probe of a neon circuit tester to green grounding screw, then inserting other probe into each wire connector. Tester should not glow. If it does, there is still power entering box. Return to the service panel, and turn off power to correct circuit.

Disconnect the light fixture base by loosening the screw terminals. If fixture has wire leads instead of screw terminals, remove the light fixture base by unscrewing the wire connectors.

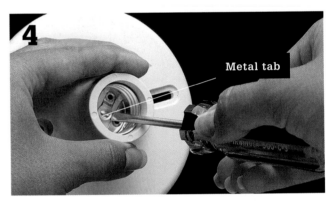

Adjust the metal tab at the bottom of the fixture socket by prying it up slightly with a small screwdriver. This adjustment will improve the contact between the socket and the lightbulb.

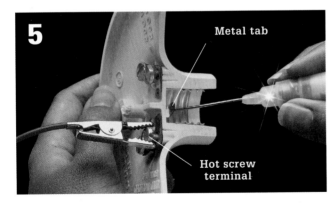

Test the socket (shown cutaway) by attaching the clip of a continuity tester to the hot screw terminal (or black wire lead) and touching probe of tester to metal tab in bottom of socket. Tester should glow. If not, socket is faulty and must be replaced.

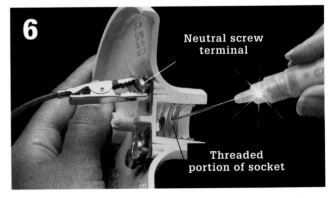

Attach tester clip to neutral screw terminal (or white wire lead), and touch probe to threaded portion of socket. Tester should glow. If not, socket is faulty and must be replaced. If socket is permanently attached, replace the fixture (page 484).

How to Replace a Socket

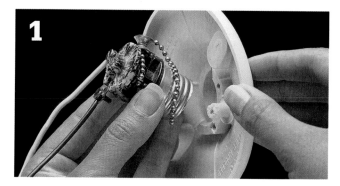

Remove light fixture (steps 1 to 3, page 482). Remove the socket from the fixture. Socket may be held by a screw, clip, or retaining ring. Disconnect wires attached to the socket.

Purchase an identical replacement socket. Connect white wire to silver screw terminal on socket, and connect black wire to brass screw terminal. Attach socket to fixture base, and reinstall fixture.

How to Test & Replace a Built-in Light Switch

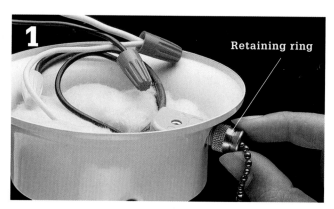

Remove light fixture (steps 1 to 3, page 482). Unscrew the retaining ring holding the switch.

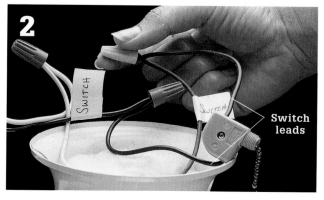

Label the wires connected to the switch leads. Disconnect the switch leads and remove switch.

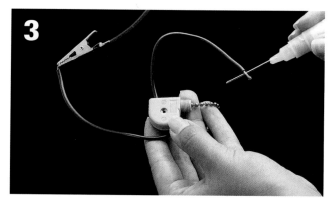

Test switch by attaching clip of continuity tester to one of the switch leads and holding tester probe to the other lead. Operate switch control. If switch is good, tester will glow when switch is in one position, but not both.

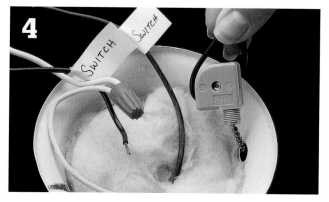

If the switch is faulty, purchase and install an exact duplicate switch. Remount the light fixture, and turn on the power at the main service panel.

How to Replace an Incandescent Light Fixture

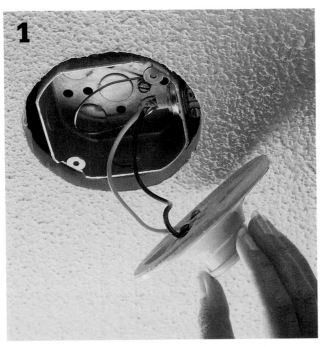

Turn off the power, and remove the old light fixture, following the directions for standard light fixtures (page 482, steps 1 to 3) or chandeliers (pages 488 to 489, steps 1 to 4).

Attach a mounting strap to the electrical box, if box does not already have one. The mounting strap, included with the new light fixture, has a preinstalled grounding screw.

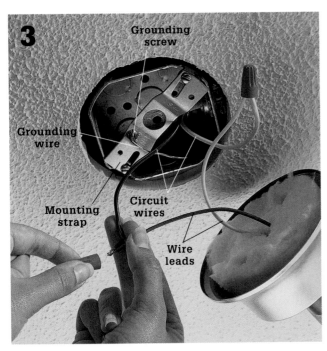

Connect the circuit wires to the base of the new fixture, using wire connectors. Connect the white wire lead to the white circuit wire, and the black wire lead to the black circuit wire. Pigtail the bare copper grounding wire to the grounding screw on the mounting strap.

Attach the light fixture base to the mounting strap, using the mounting screws. Attach the globe, and install a lightbulb with a wattage rating that is the same as or lower than the rating indicated on the fixture. Turn on the power at the main service panel.

Repairing & Replacing Recessed Light Fixtures

Most problems with recessed light fixtures occur because heat builds up inside the metal canister and melts the insulation on the socket wires. On some recessed light fixtures, sockets with damaged wires can be removed and replaced. However, most newer fixtures have sockets that cannot be removed. With this type, you will need to buy a new fixture if the socket wires are damaged.

When buying a new recessed light fixture, choose a replacement that matches the old fixture. Install the new fixture in the metal mounting frame that is already in place.

Unless the fixture is rated IC (insulated covered), make sure building insulation is at least 3" away from the canister to dissipate heat.

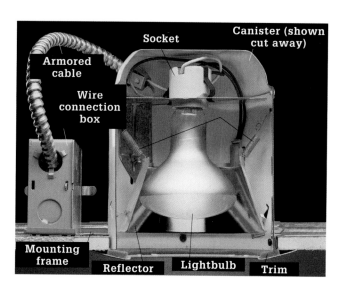

Socket · Canister (shown cut away) · Armored cable · Wire connection box · Mounting frame · Reflector · Lightbulb · Trim

How to Remove & Test a Recessed Light Fixture

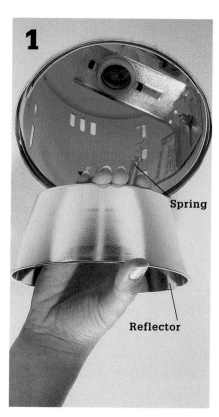

1

Spring

Reflector

Turn off the power to the light fixture at the main service panel. Remove the trim, lightbulb, and reflector. The reflector is held to the canister with small springs or mounting clips.

2

Loosen the screws or clips holding the canister to the mounting frame. Carefully raise the canister and set it away from the frame opening.

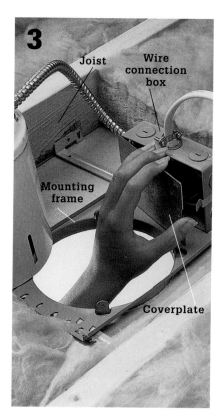

3

Joist · Wire connection box · Mounting frame · Coverplate

Remove the coverplate on the wire connection box. The box is attached to the mounting frame between the ceiling joists.

(continued)

4

Test for power by touching one probe of neon circuit tester to grounded wire connection box and inserting other probe into each wire connector. Tester should not glow. If it does, there is still power entering box. Return to the service panel and turn off correct circuit.

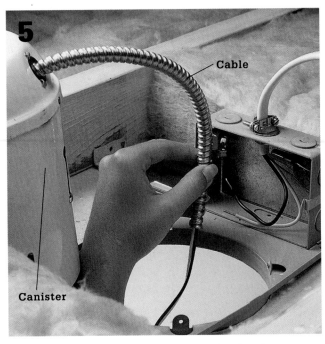

5

Cable

Canister

Disconnect the white and black circuit wires by removing the wire connectors. Pull the armored cable from the wire connection box. Remove the canister through the frame opening.

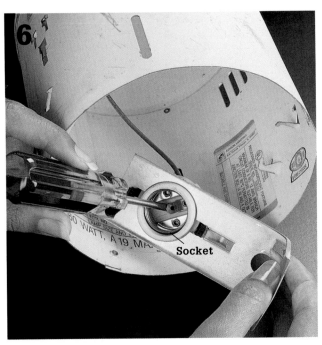

6

Socket

Adjust the metal tab at the bottom of the fixture socket by prying it up slightly with a small screwdriver. This adjustment will improve contact with the lightbulb.

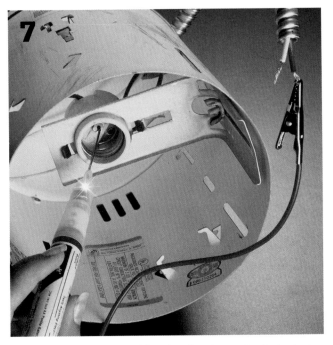

7

Test the socket by attaching the clip of a continuity tester to the black fixture wire and touching tester probe to the metal tab in bottom of the socket. Attach the tester clip to white fixture wire, and touch probe to the threaded metal socket. Tester should glow for both tests. If not, then socket is faulty. Replace the socket (page 483), or install a new light fixture (next page).

How to Replace a Recessed Light Fixture

Remove the old light fixture (pages 485 to 486). Buy a new fixture that matches the old fixture. Although the new light fixture comes with its own mounting frame, it is easier to mount the new fixture using the frame that is already in place.

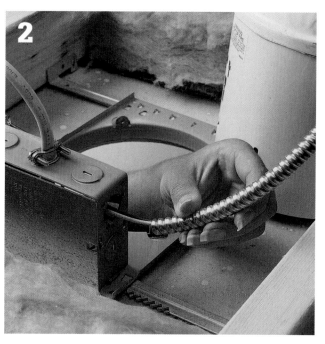

Set the fixture canister inside the ceiling cavity, and thread the fixture wires through the opening in the wire connection box. Push the armored cable into the wire connection box to secure it.

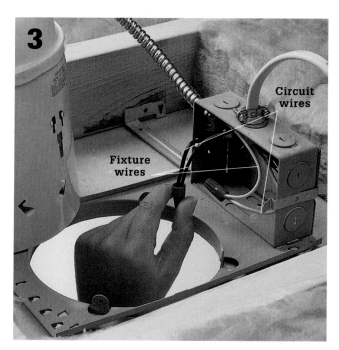

Connect the white fixture wire to the white circuit wire, and the black fixture wire to the black circuit wire, using wire connectors. Attach the coverplate to the wire connection box. Make sure any building insulation is at least 3" from canister and wire connection box.

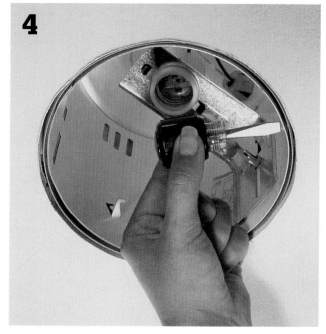

Position the canister inside the mounting frame, and attach the mounting screws or clips. Attach the reflector and trim. Install a lightbulb with a wattage rating that is the same as or lower than rating indicated on the fixture. Turn on power at main service panel.

Repairing Chandeliers

Repairing a chandelier requires special care. Because chandeliers are heavy, it is a good idea to work with a helper when removing a chandelier. Support the fixture to prevent its weight from pulling against the wires.

Chandeliers have two fixture wires that are threaded through the support chain from the electrical box to the hollow base of the chandelier. The socket wires connect to the fixture wires inside this base.

Fixture wires are identified as hot and neutral. Look closely for a raised stripe on one of the wires. This is the neutral wire that is connected to the white circuit wire and white socket wire. The other, smooth, fixture wire is hot and is connected to the black wires.

If you have a new chandelier, it may have a grounding wire that runs through the support chain to the electrical box. If this wire is present, make sure it is connected to the grounding wires in the electrical box.

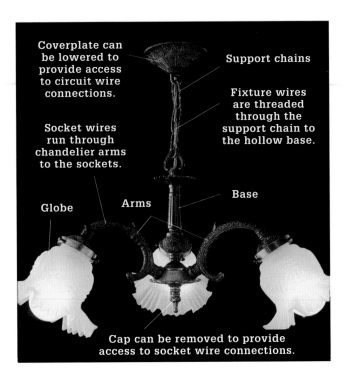

Coverplate can be lowered to provide access to circuit wire connections.

Support chains

Fixture wires are threaded through the support chain to the hollow base.

Socket wires run through chandelier arms to the sockets.

Globe

Arms

Base

Cap can be removed to provide access to socket wire connections.

How to Repair a Chandelier

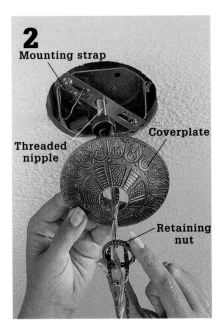

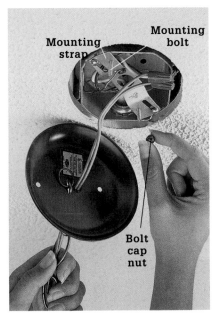

Label any lights that are not working, using masking tape. Turn off power to the fixture at the main service panel. Remove lightbulbs and all shades or globes.

Unscrew the retaining nut and lower the decorative coverplate away from the electrical box. Most chandeliers are supported by a threaded nipple attached to a mounting strap.

Mounting variation: Some chandeliers are supported only by the coverplate that is bolted to the electrical box mounting strap. These types do not have a threaded nipple.

3

Test for power by touching one probe of neon circuit tester to the green grounding screw and inserting other probe into each wire connector. Tester should not glow. If it does, there is still power entering box. Return to service panel, and turn off power to correct circuit.

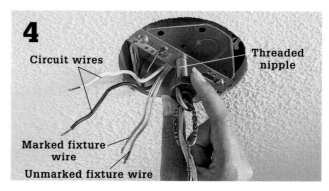

4

Disconnect fixture wires by removing the wire connectors. Marked fixture wire is neutral, and is connected to white circuit wire. Unmarked fixture wire is hot, and is connected to black circuit wire. Unscrew threaded nipple, and carefully place chandelier on a flat surface.

5

Remove the cap from the bottom of the chandelier, exposing the wire connections inside the hollow base. Disconnect the black socket wires from the unmarked fixture wire, and disconnect the white socket wires from the marked fixture wire.

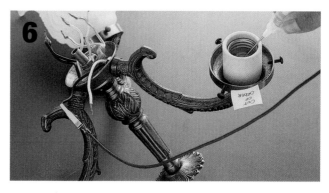

6

Test socket by attaching clip of continuity tester to black socket wire and touching probe to tab in socket. Repeat test with threaded portion of socket and white socket wire. Tester should glow for both tests. If not, the socket is faulty and must be replaced.

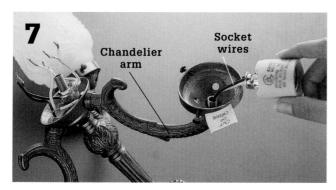

7

Remove a faulty socket by loosening any mounting screws or clips, and pulling the socket and socket wires out of the fixture arm. Purchase and install a new chandelier socket, threading the socket wires through the fixture arm.

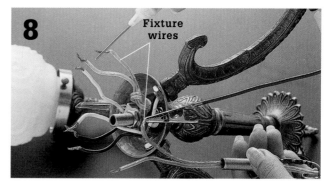

8

Test each fixture wire by attaching clip of continuity tester to one end of wire and touching probe to other end. If tester does not glow, wire is faulty and must be replaced. Install new wires, if needed, then reassemble and rehang the chandelier.

Repairing Track Lights

Like other light fixtures, track lights are connected to an electrical box in the ceiling. The circuit wires in the box provide power to the entire track, and the current runs along two metal power strips inside the track. Each fixture on the track has a contact arm with metal contacts that draw current from the strips to power the fixture.

Common fixture problems are dirty or corroded contacts or power strips, and bad sockets. Track lights are easy to work on because you can quickly remove individual fixtures to get to the source of the problem.

Tools & Materials ▸

Screwdriver
Continuity tester
Combination tool

Fine sandpaper
Crimp-style
   wire connectors

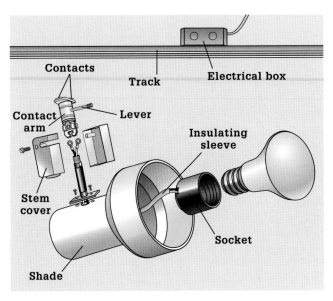

Track lights are powered by an electrical box connected to the middle of, or at the end of, a track. With multiple track sections, special connectors provide the links to power the entire system.

How to Clean Track Light Contacts

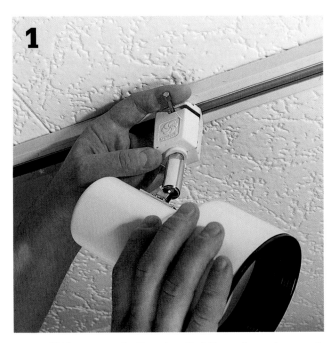

1

Turn off the power to the circuit at the main service panel. Shift the lever on the fixture stem to release the fixture from the track. Use fine sandpaper to clean the metal power strips inside the track in the general area where the fixture hangs.

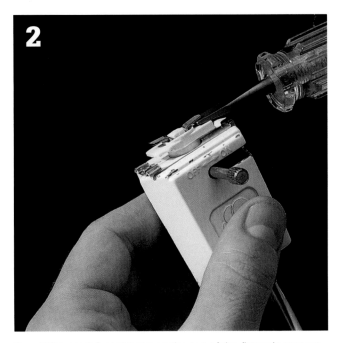

2

Sand the metal contacts on the top of the fixture's contact arm, then use a screwdriver to pry up the tabs slightly. Reattach the fixture to the track, and restore the power. If the fixture doesn't light, test the socket (next page).

How to Test & Replace a Track Light Socket

Turn off the power to the circuit at the main service panel. Remove the problem fixture from the track. Loosen the screws on the stem cover, and remove the cover.

Remove the screws securing the socket, and test the socket with a continuity tester. Attach the clip to the brass track contact, and touch the tester probe to the black wire connection on the socket. Repeat the test with the white contact and white wire connection. If the tester fails to light in either test, replace the socket.

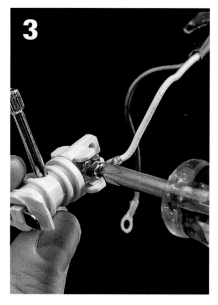

To remove the old socket, pull the contact arm from the stem housing, and disconnect the socket wires from the screw terminals. Pull the socket and wires from the shade. If the wires have an insulating sleeve, remove it and set it aside.

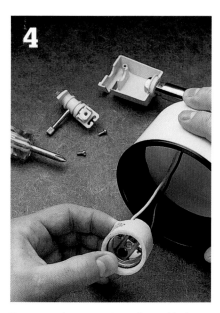

Buy a replacement socket with the same wattage rating as the old one. Feed the wires of the new socket into the shade and up through the stem. Attach the socket to the shade.

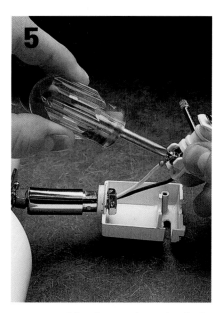

Use a combination tool to strip ¼" of insulation from each wire end, and attach a crimp-style wire connector to each wire. Fasten the connectors to the proper screw terminals on the contact arm.

Reinstall the socket and contact arm, and reattach the stem cover. Remount the fixture.

Repairing Ceiling Fans

Ceiling fans contain rapidly moving parts, making them more susceptible to trouble than many other electrical fixtures. Installation is a relatively simple matter, but repairing a ceiling fan can be very frustrating. The most common problems you'll encounter are balance and noise issues and switch failure, usually precipitated by the pull chain breaking. In most cases, both problems can be corrected without removing the fan from the ceiling. But if you have difficulty on ladders or simply don't care to work overhead, consider removing the fan when replacing the switch.

Tools & Materials ▸

Screwdriver
Combination tool
Replacement switch

Ceiling fans are subject to a great deal of vibration and stress, so it's not uncommon for switches and motors to fail. Minimize wear and tear by making sure blades are in balance so the fan doesn't wobble.

How to Troubleshoot Blade Wobble

1

Start by checking and tightening all hardware used to attach the blades to the mounting arms and the mounting arms to the motor. Hardware tends to loosen over time and this is frequently the cause of wobble.

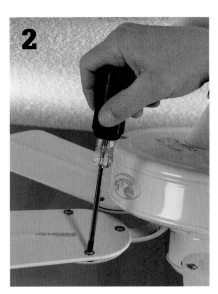

2

If wobble persists, try switching around two of the blades. Often, this is all it takes to get the fan back into balance. If a blade is damaged or warped, replace it.

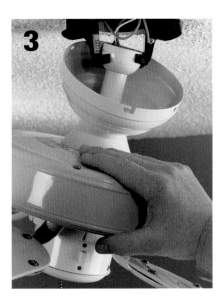

3

If the blades are tight and you still have wobble, turn the power off at the panel, remove the fan canopy, and inspect the mounting brace and the connection between the mounting pole and the fan motor. If any connections are loose, tighten them and then replace the canopy.

How to Replace a Pull-chain Switch on a Ceiling Fan

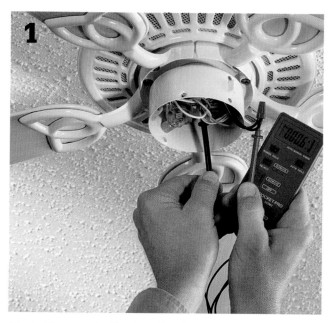

Shut off power to the fan circuit at the panel, and then detach the bottom of the fan unit to expose the wires inside. Test the wires by placing one probe of a tester into the wire connecter that joins the black wires and the other to the grounding screw.

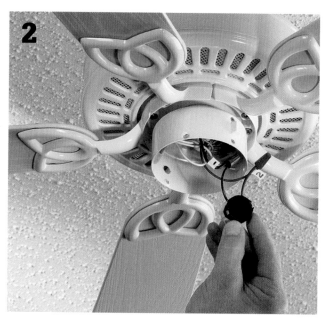

Locate the plastic switch unit (the part that the pull chain used to be attached to if it broke off). You'll need to replace the switch, which may be attached to the power source with wire connectors or soldered connection that require you to cut the wires. Fans have four to eight feed wires, depending on the number of speed settings. Label the wires before you remove the old switch (this is very important). Remove the old switch.

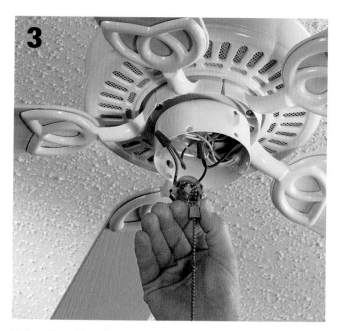

Using the old switch as a reference, purchase an identical new switch. Hook up the new switch using the same wiring configuration as on the old model. On newer fans, this probably require inserting the wires from the fan into the switch and crimping them (most switches come with installation instructions).

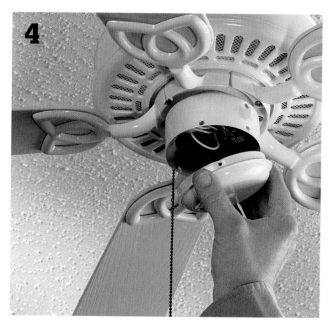

Secure the new switch in the housing and make sure all wires are tucked neatly inside. Restore power and test the switch before replacing the cap. (If you have improperly wired the switch, it may run only at one or two speeds, so test all settings). Reattach the base cap.

Repairing & Replacing Fluorescent Lights

Fluorescent lights are relatively trouble-free and use less energy than incandescent lights. A typical fluorescent tube lasts about three years and produces two to four times as much light per watt as a standard incandescent light bulb.

The most frequent problem with a fluorescent light fixture is a worn-out tube. If a fluorescent light fixture begins to flicker, or does not light fully, remove and examine the tube. If the tube has bent or broken pins, or black discoloration near the ends, replace it. Light gray discoloration is normal in working fluorescent tubes. When replacing an old tube, read the wattage rating printed on the glass surface, and buy a new tube with a matching rating. Never dispose of old tubes by breaking them. Fluorescent tubes contain a small amount of hazardous mercury. Check with your local environmental control agency or health department for disposal guidelines.

Fluorescent light fixtures also can malfunction if the sockets are cracked or worn. Inexpensive replacement sockets are available at any hardware store and can be installed in a few minutes.

If a fixture does not work even after the tube and sockets have been serviced, the ballast probably is defective. Faulty ballasts may leak a black, oily substance and can cause a fluorescent light fixture to make a loud humming sound. Although ballasts can be replaced, always check prices before buying a new ballast. It may be cheaper to purchase and install a new fluorescent fixture rather than to replace the ballast in an old fluorescent light fixture.

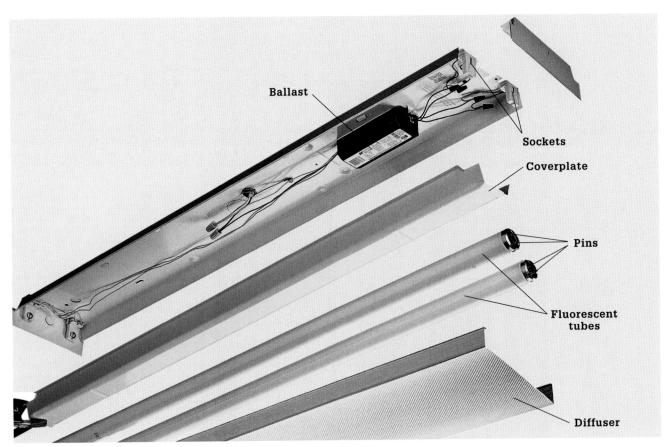

A fluorescent light works by directing electrical current through a special gas-filled tube that glows when energized. A white translucent diffuser protects the fluorescent tube and softens the light. A coverplate protects a special transformer, called a ballast. The ballast regulates the flow of 120-volt household current to the sockets. The sockets transfer power to metal pins that extend into the tube.

Problem	Repair
Tube flickers, or lights partially.	1. Rotate tube to make sure it is seated properly in the sockets. 2. Replace tube (page 496) and the starter (where present) if tube is discolored or if pins are bent or broken. 3. Replace the ballast (page 498) if replacement cost is reasonable. Otherwise, replace the entire fixture (page 499).
Tube does not light.	1. Check wall switch, and repair or replace, if needed (pages 474 to 477). 2. Rotate the tube to make sure it is seated properly in sockets. 3. Replace tube (page 496) and the starter (where present) if tube is discolored or if pins are bent or broken. 4. Replace sockets if they are chipped or if tube does not seat properly (page 497). 5. Replace the ballast (page 498) or the entire fixture (page 499).
Noticeable black substance around ballast.	Replace ballast (page 498) if replacement cost is reasonable. Otherwise, replace the entire fixture (page 499).
Fixture hums.	Replace ballast (page 498) if replacement cost is reasonable. Otherwise, replace the entire fixture (page 499).

 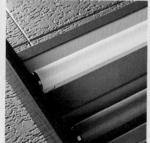  

Tools & Materials ▸

Screwdriver
Ratchet wrench
Combination tool
Circuit tester
Replacement tubes
Starters, or ballast (if needed)
Replacement fluorescent light
    fixture (if needed)

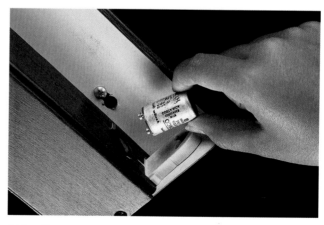

Older fluorescent lights may have a small cylindrical device, called a starter, located near one of the sockets. When a tube begins to flicker, replace both the tube and the starter. Turn off the power, then remove the starter by pushing it slightly and turning counterclockwise. Install a replacement that matches the old starter.

How to Replace a Fluorescent Tube

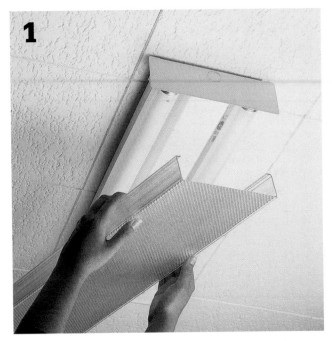

Turn off power to the light fixture at the main service panel. Remove the diffuser to expose the fluorescent tube.

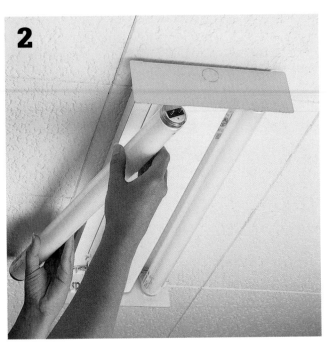

Remove the fluorescent tube by rotating it ¼ turn in either direction and sliding the tube out of the sockets. Inspect the pins at the end of the tube. Tubes with bent or broken pins should be replaced.

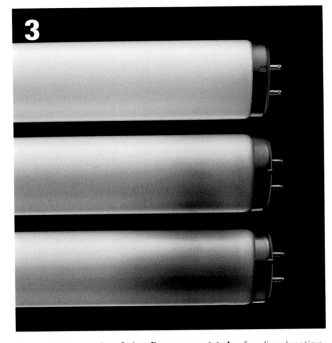

Inspect the ends of the fluorescent tube for discoloration. New tube in good working order (top) shows no discoloration. Normal, working tube (middle) may have gray color. A worn-out tube (bottom) shows black discoloration.

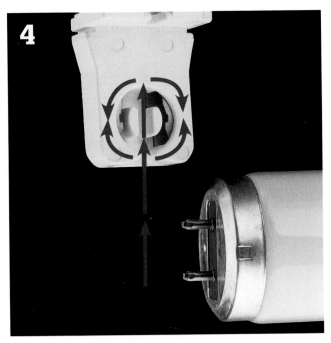

Install a new tube with the same wattage rating as the old tube. Insert the tube so that pins slide fully into sockets, then twist tube ¼ turn in either direction until it is locked securely. Reattach the diffuser, and turn on the power at the main service panel.

How to Replace a Socket

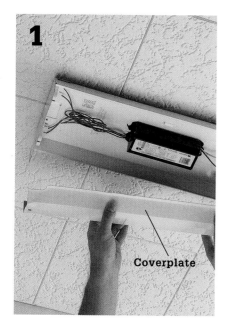

1

Turn off the power at the main service panel. Remove the diffuser, fluorescent tube, and the coverplate.

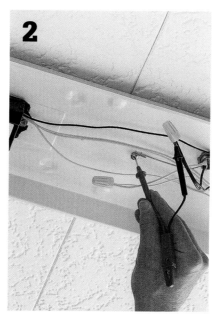

2

Test for power by touching one probe of a neon circuit tester to the grounding screw and inserting the other probe into each wire connector. Tester should not glow. If it does, power is still entering the box. Return to the service panel, and turn off correct circuit.

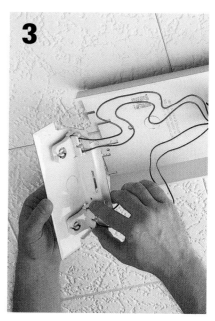

3

Remove the faulty socket from the fixture housing. Some sockets slide out, while others must be unscrewed.

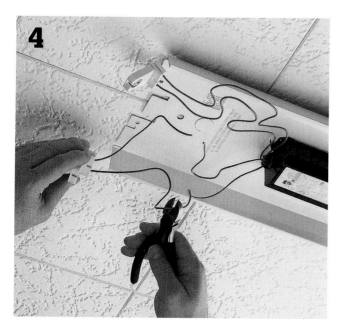

4

Disconnect wires attached to socket. For push-in fittings (above) remove the wires by inserting a small screwdriver into the release openings. Some sockets have screw terminal connections, while others have preattached wires that must be cut before the socket can be removed.

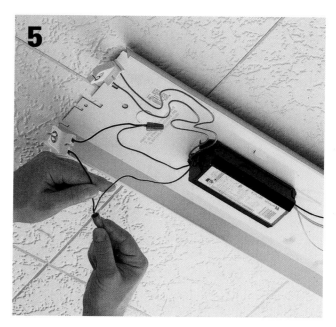

5

Purchase and install a new socket. If socket has preattached wire leads, connect the leads to the ballast wires using wire connectors. Replace coverplate, then the fluorescent tube, making sure that it seats properly. Replace the diffuser. Restore power to the fixture at the main service panel.

How to Replace a Ballast

1

Turn off the power at the main service panel, then remove the diffuser, fluorescent tube, and coverplate. Test for power, using a neon circuit tester.

2

Remove the sockets from the fixture housing by sliding them out, or by removing the mounting screws and lifting the sockets out.

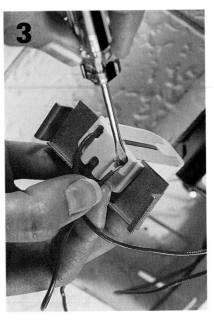

3

Disconnect the wires attached to the sockets by pushing a small screwdriver into the release openings (above), by loosening the screw terminals, or by cutting wires to within 2" of sockets.

4

Remove the old ballast, using a ratchet wrench or screwdriver. Make sure to support the ballast so it does not fall.

5

Install a new ballast that has the same ratings as the old ballast.

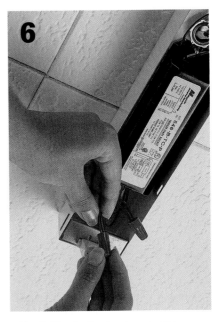

6

Attach the ballast wires to the socket wires, using wire connectors, screw terminal connections, or push-in fittings. Reinstall the coverplate, fluorescent tube, and diffuser. Turn on power to the light fixture at the main service panel.

How to Replace a Fluorescent Light Fixture

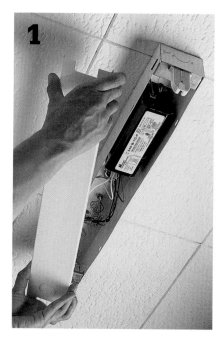

Turn off power to the light fixture at the main service panel. Remove the diffuser, tube, and coverplate. Test for power, using a neon circuit tester.

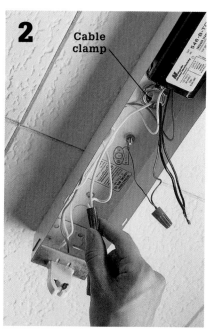

Cable clamp

Disconnect the insulated circuit wires and the bare copper grounding wire from the light fixture. Loosen the cable clamp holding the circuit wires.

Unbolt the fixture from the wall or ceiling, and carefully remove it. Make sure to support the fixture so it does not fall.

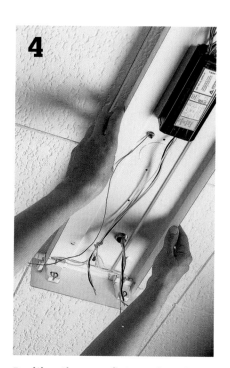

Position the new fixture, threading the circuit wires through the knockout opening in the back of the fixture. Bolt the fixture in place so it is firmly anchored to framing members.

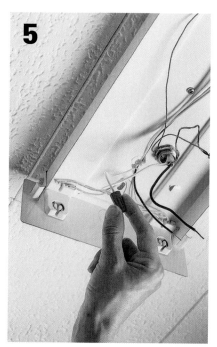

Connect the circuit wires to the fixture wires, using wire connectors. Follow the wiring diagram included with the new fixture. Tighten the cable clamp holding the circuit wires.

Attach the fixture coverplate, then install the fluorescent tubes, and attach the diffuser. Turn on power to the fixture at the main service panel.

Replacing a Plug

Replace an electrical plug whenever you notice bent or loose prongs, a cracked or damaged casing, or a missing insulating faceplate. A damaged plug poses a shock and fire hazard.

Replacement plugs are available in different styles to match common appliance cords. Always choose a replacement that is similar to the original plug. Flat-cord and quick-connect plugs are used with light-duty appliances, like lamps and radios. Round-cord plugs are used with larger appliances, including those that have three-prong grounding plugs.

Some tools and appliances use polarized plugs. A polarized plug has one wide prong and one narrow prong, corresponding to the hot and neutral slots found in a standard receptacle.

If there is room in the plug body, tie the individual wires in an underwriter's knot to secure the plug to the cord.

Tools & Materials ▸

Combination tool   Screwdriver
Needlenose pliers   Replacement plug

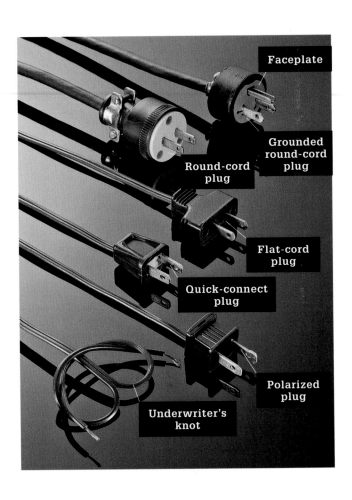

Faceplate

Grounded round-cord plug

Round-cord plug

Flat-cord plug

Quick-connect plug

Underwriter's knot

Polarized plug

How to Install a Quick-connect Plug

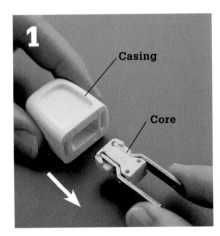

Squeeze the prongs of the new quick-connect plug together slightly and pull the plug core from the casing. Cut the old plug from the flat-cord wire with a combination tool, leaving a clean cut end.

Casing

Core

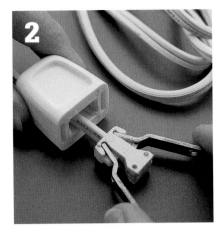

Feed unstripped wire through rear of plug casing. Spread prongs, then insert wire into opening in rear of core. Squeeze prongs together; spikes inside core penetrate cord. Slide casing over core until it snaps into place.

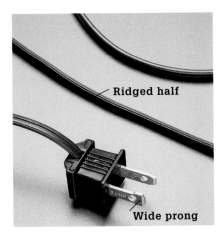

Ridged half

Wide prong

Variation: When replacing a polarized plug, make sure that the ridged half of the cord lines up with the wider (neutral) prong of the plug.

How to Replace a Round-cord Plug

Cut off round cord near the old plug, using a combination tool. Remove the insulating faceplate on the new plug, and feed cord through rear of plug. Strip about 3" of outer insulation from the round cord. Strip ¾" insulation from the individual wires.

Tie an underwriter's knot with the black and white wires. Make sure the knot is located close to the edge of the stripped outer insulation. Pull the cord so that the knot slides into the plug body.

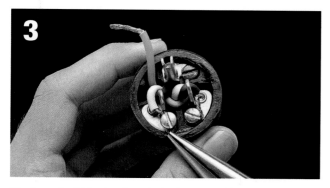

Hook end of black wire clockwise around brass screw and white wire around silver screw. On a three-prong plug, attach third wire to grounding screw. If necessary, excess grounding wire can be cut away.

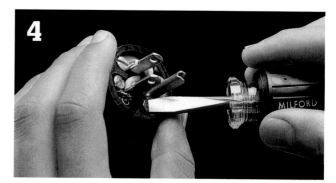

Tighten the screws securely, making sure the copper wires do not touch each other. Replace the insulating faceplate.

How to Replace a Flat-cord Plug

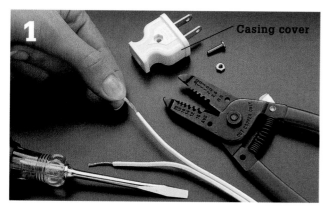

Cut old plug from cord using a combination tool. Pull apart the two halves of the flat cord so that about 2" of wire are separated. Strip ¾" insulation from each half. Remove casing cover on new plug.

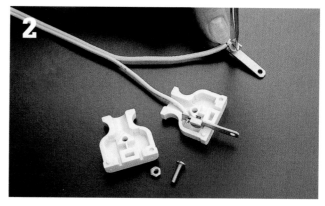

Hook ends of wires clockwise around the screw terminals, and tighten the screw terminals securely. Reassemble the plug casing. Some plugs may have an insulating faceplate that must be installed.

Replacing a Lamp Socket

Next to the cord plug, the most common source of trouble in a lamp is a worn lightbulb socket. When a lamp socket assembly fails, the problem is usually with the socket-switch unit, although replacement sockets may include other parts you do not need.

Lamp failure is not always caused by a bad socket. You can avoid unnecessary repairs by checking the lamp cord, plug, and lightbulb before replacing the socket.

Tools & Materials ▸

Replacement socket
Continuity tester
Screwdriver

Socket-mounted switch types are usually interchangeable: choose a replacement you prefer. Clockwise from top left: twist knob, remote switch, pull chain, push lever.

Tip ▸

When replacing a lamp socket, you can improve a standard ON-OFF lamp by installing a three-way socket.

How to Repair or Replace a Lamp Socket

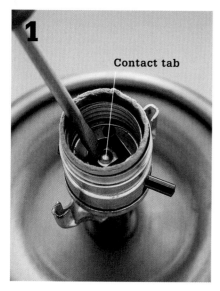

1

Contact tab

Unplug lamp. Remove shade, lightbulb, and harp (shade bracket). Scrape contact tab clean with a small screwdriver. Pry contact tab up slightly if flattened inside socket. Replace bulb, plug in lamp, and test. If lamp does not work, unplug, remove bulb, and continue with next step.

2

Outer shell

Insulating sleeve

Squeeze outer shell of socket near PRESS marking, and lift it off. On older lamps, socket may be held by screws found at the base of the screw socket. Slip off cardboard insulating sleeve. If sleeve is damaged, replace entire socket.

3

Check for loose wire connections on screw terminals. Refasten any loose connections, then reassemble lamp, and test. If connections are not loose, remove the wires, lift out the socket, and continue with the next step.

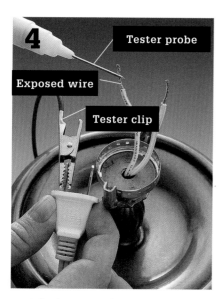

4

Tester probe

Exposed wire

Tester clip

Test for lamp cord problems with continuity tester. Place clip of tester on one prong of plug. Touch probe to one exposed wire, then to the other wire. Repeat test with other prong of plug. If tester fails to light for either prong, then replace the cord and plug. Retest the lamp.

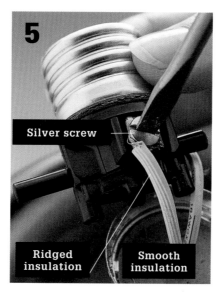

5

Silver screw

Ridged insulation

Smooth insulation

If cord and plug are functional, then choose a replacement socket marked with the same amp and volt ratings as the old socket. One half of flat-cord lamp wire is covered by insulation that is ridged or marked: attach this wire to the silver screw terminal. Connect other wire to brass screw.

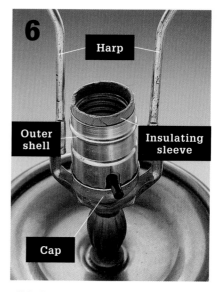

6

Harp

Outer shell

Insulating sleeve

Cap

Slide insulating sleeve and outer shell over socket so that socket and screw terminals are fully covered and switch fits into sleeve slot. Press socket assembly down into cap until socket locks into place. Replace harp, lightbulb, and shade.

Installing an Electrical Box

Install an electrical box any time you find exposed wire connections or cable splices. Exposed connections sometimes can be found in older homes, where wires attach to light fixtures. Exposed splices (page 435) can be found in areas where NM (nonmetallic) cable runs through uncovered joists or wall studs, such as in an unfinished basement or utility room.

When installing an electrical box, make sure there is enough cable to provide about 8" of wire inside the box. If the wires are too short, you can add pigtails to lengthen them (page 438). If the electrical box is metal, make sure the circuit grounding wires are pigtailed to the box.

Tools & Materials ▶

Circuit tester
Screwdriver
Hammer
Screws or nails
Electrical box

Cable clamps
Locknuts
Pigtail wire
Wire connectors

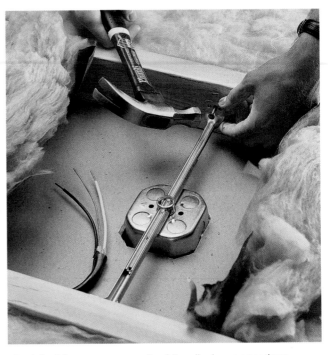

Electrical boxes are required for all wire connections. The box protects wood and other flammable materials from electrical sparks (arcing). Electrical boxes should always be anchored to joists or studs.

How to Install an Electrical Box for Cable Splices

Turn off power to circuit wires at the main service panel. Carefully remove any tape or wire connectors from the exposed splice. Avoid contact with the bare wire ends until the wires have been tested for power.

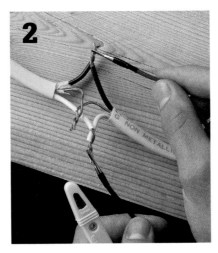

Test for power. Touch one probe of a circuit tester to the black hot wires, and touch other probe to the white neutral wires. The tester should not glow. If it does, the wires are still hot. Shut off power to correct circuit at the main service panel. Disconnect the spliced wires.

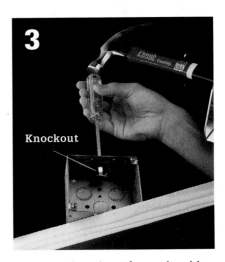

Knockout

Open one knockout for each cable that will enter the box, using a hammer and screwdriver. Any unopened knockouts should remain sealed.

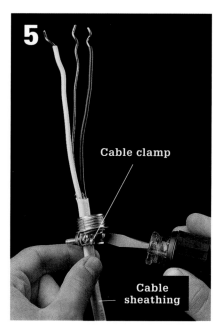

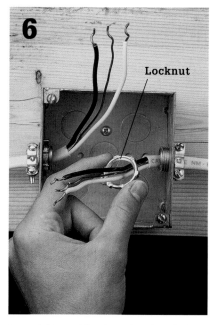

Anchor the electrical box to a wooden framing member, using screws or nails.

Thread each cable through a cable clamp. Tighten the clamp with a screwdriver. Do not overtighten. Overtightening can damage cable sheathing.

Insert the cables into the electrical box, and screw a locknut onto each cable clamp.

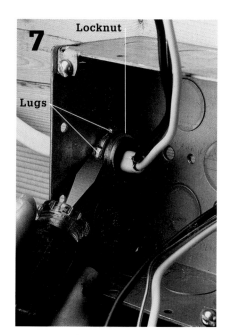

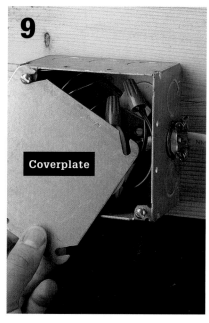

Tighten the locknuts by pushing against the lugs with the blade of a screwdriver.

Use wire connectors to reconnect the wires. Pigtail the copper grounding wires to the green grounding screw in the back of the box.

Carefully tuck the wires into the box, and attach the coverplate. Turn on the power to the circuit at the main service panel. Make sure the box remains accessible, and is not covered with finished walls or ceilings.

Fixing & Replacing Doorbells

Most doorbell problems are caused by loose wire connections or worn-out switches. Reconnecting loose wires or replacing a switch requires only a few minutes. Doorbell problems also can occur if the chime unit becomes dirty or worn, or if the low-voltage transformer burns out. Both parts are easy to replace. Because doorbells operate at low voltage, the switches and the chime unit can be serviced without turning off power to the system. However, when replacing a transformer, always turn off the power at the main service panel.

Most houses have other low-voltage transformers in addition to the doorbell transformer. These transformers control heating and air-conditioning thermostats, or other low-voltage systems. When testing and repairing a doorbell system, it is important to identify the correct transformer. A doorbell transformer has a voltage rating of 24 volts or less. This rating is printed on the face of the transformer. A doorbell transformer often is located near the main service panel and in some homes is attached directly to the service panel. The transformer that controls a heating/ air-conditioning thermostat system is located near the furnace and has a voltage rating of 24 volts or more.

Occasionally, a doorbell problem is caused by a broken low-voltage wire somewhere in the system. You can test for wire breaks with a battery-operated multi-tester. If the test indicates a break, new low-voltage wires must be installed between the transformer and the switches, or between the switches and chime unit. Replacing low-voltage wires is not a difficult job, but it can be time-consuming. You may choose to have an electrician do this work.

Tools & Materials ▶

Continuity tester
Screwdriver
Multimeter
Needlenose pliers
Cotton swab
Rubbing alcohol

Replacement
doorbell switch
(if needed)
Masking tape
Replacement chime
unit (if needed)

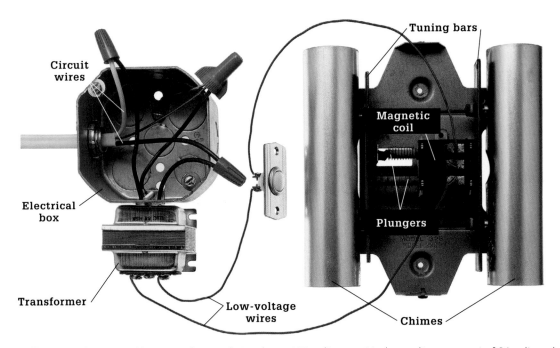

Home doorbell system is powered by a transformer that reduces 120-volt current to low-voltage current of 24 volts or less. Current flows from the transformer to one or more push-button switches. When pushed, the switch activates a magnet coil inside the chime unit, causing a plunger to strike a musical tuning bar.

How to Test a Doorbell System

1

Remove the mounting screws holding the doorbell switch to the house. Shut off power at the service panel.

2

Carefully pull the switch away from the wall.

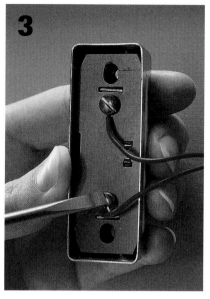

3

Check wire connections on the switch. If wires are loose, reconnect them to the screw terminals. Test the doorbell by pressing the button. If the doorbell still does not work, disconnect the switch and test it with a continuity tester.

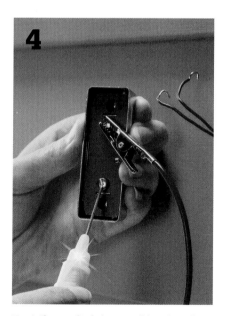

4

Test the switch by attaching the clip of a continuity tester to one screw terminal and touching the probe to the other screw terminal. Press the switch button. Tester should glow. If not, then the switch is faulty and must be replaced.

5

Twist the doorbell switch wires together temporarily to test the other parts of the doorbell system.

6

Transformer

Locate the doorbell transformer, often located near the main service panel. Transformer may be attached to an electrical box, or may be attached directly to the side of the service panel.

(continued)

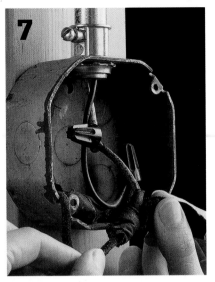

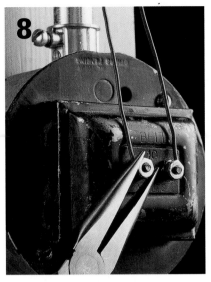

Identify the doorbell transformer by reading its voltage rating. Doorbell transformers have a voltage rating of 24 volts or less. Turn off power to transformer at main service panel. Remove cover on electrical box, and test wires for power (page 507, step 3). Reconnect any loose wires. Replace taped connections with wire connectors.

Reattach coverplate. Inspect the low-voltage wire connections, and reconnect any loose wires, using needlenose pliers. Turn on power to the transformer at the main service panel.

Touch the probes of the multi-tester to the low-voltage screw terminals on the transformer. Set the dial of the multimeter to the 50-volt (AC) range if the meter is not auto ranging. If transformer is operating properly, the meter will detect power within 2 volts of transformer's rating. If not, the transformer is faulty and must be replaced.

Test the chime unit. Remove the coverplate on the doorbell chime unit. Inspect the low-voltage wire connections, and reconnect any loose wires.

Test that the chime unit is receiving current. Touch probes of a multimeter to screw terminals marked TRANSFORMER and FRONT. If the multimeter detects power within 2 volts of the transformer rating, then the unit is receiving proper current. If it detects no power or very low power, there is a break in the low-voltage wiring, and new wires must be installed.

Clean the chime plungers with a cotton swab dipped in rubbing alcohol. Reassemble doorbell switches, then test the system by pushing one of the switches. If doorbell still does not work, then the chime unit is faulty and must be replaced.

How to Replace a Doorbell Switch

1

Remove the doorbell switch mounting screws, and carefully pull the switch away from the wall. Shut off power at the service panel.

2

Disconnect wires from switch. Tape wires to the wall to prevent them from slipping into the wall cavity.

3

Purchase a new doorbell switch, and connect wires to screw terminals on new switch. (Wires are interchangeable and can be connected to either terminal.) Anchor the switch to the wall.

How to Replace a Doorbell Chime Unit

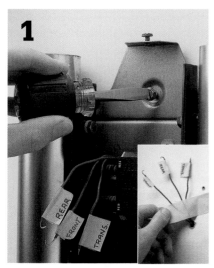

1

Turn off power to the doorbell at the main panel. Remove the coverplate from the old chime. Label the low-voltage wires FRONT, REAR, or TRANS to identify their screw terminal locations. Disconnect the wires. Remove the old chime unit. Tape the wires to the wall to prevent them from slipping into the wall cavity (inset).

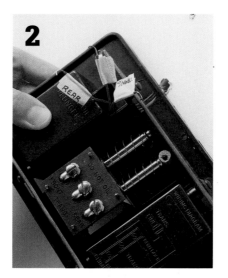

2

Purchase a new chime unit that matches the voltage rating of the old unit. Thread the low-voltage wires through the base of the new chime unit. Attach the chime unit to the wall, using the mounting screws included with the installation kit.

3

Connect the low-voltage wires to the screw terminals on the new chime unit. Attach the coverplate and turn on the power at the main service panel.

Installing Hardwired Smoke, Carbon Monoxide (CO) & Heat Alarms

Smoke and carbon monoxide (CO) alarms are an essential safety component of any living facility. All national fire protection codes require that new homes have a hard-wired smoke alarm in every sleeping room and on every level of a residence, including basements, attics, and attached garages. Smoke alarms must have a circuit with AFCI protection when installed in bedrooms.

Most authorities also recommend CO detectors on every level of the house and in every sleeping area.

Heat alarms, which detect heat instead of smoke, are often specified for locations like utility rooms, basements, or unfinished attics where conditions may cause nuisance tripping of smoke alarms.

Hard-wired alarms operate on your household electrical current, but have battery backups in case of a power outage. On new homes, all smoke alarms must be wired in a series so that every alarm sounds regardless of the fire's location. When wiring a series of alarms, be sure to use alarms of the same brand to ensure compatiility. Always check local codes before starting the job.

Ceiling-installed alarms should be four inches away from the nearest wall. Don't install smoke alarms near windows, doors, or ducts where drafts might interfere with their operation.

Tools & Materials ▸

Screwdriver	Cable clamps (if boxes
Combination tool	are not self-clamping)
Fish tape	2- and 3-wire 14-gauge
Drywall saw	NM cable
Wall or ceiling	Alarms
outlet boxes	Wire connectors
	15-amp single-pole breaker

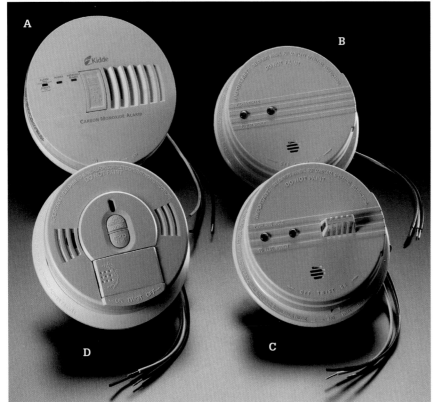

Hardwired carbon monoxide detectors (A) are triggered by the presence of carbon monoxide gas. Smoke detectors are available in photoelectric and ionizing models. In ionizing detectors (B), a small amount of current flows in an ionization chamber. When smoke enters the chamber, it interrupts the current, triggering the alarm. Photoelectric detectors (C) rely on a beam of light, which, when interrupted by smoke, triggers an alarm. Heat alarms (D) sound an alarm when they detect areas of high heat in the room.

How to Connect a Series of Hardwired Smoke Alarms

1

3-wire cable to next detector in series

2-wire cable from service panel

Pull 14/2 NM cable from the service panel into the first ceiling electrical box in the smoke alarm series. Pull 14/3 NM cable between the remaining alarm outlet boxes. Use cable clamps to secure the cable in each outlet box. Remove sheathing and strip insulation from wires.

2

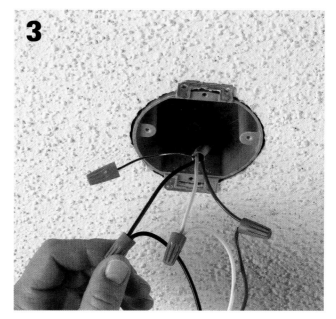

3

Wire the first alarm in the series. Use a wire connector to connect the ground wires. Splice the black circuit wire with the alarm's black lead and the black wire going to the next alarm in the series. Splice the white circuit wire with the alarm's white wire and the white (neutral) wire going to the next alarm in the series. Splice the red traveler wire with the odd-colored alarm wire (in this case, the red wire).

Wire the remaining alarms in the series by connecting the like-colored wires in each outlet box. Always connect the red traveler wire to the odd-colored (in this case, red) alarm wire. This red traveler wire connects all the alarms together so that when one alarm sounds, all the alarms sound. If the alarm doesn't have a grounding wire, cap the ground with a wire connector. When all alarms are wired, install and connect the new 15-amp breaker.

Repairing & Replacing Phone Jacks

Although the telephone company owns the wires that bring telephone service to the house, repair and new installation can take place in any part of the telephone system that extends past the company's demarcation jack. The demarcation jack is usually located in a basement or utility area, although it may also be mounted on a baseboard in a home's living quarters.

Because the voltage running through telephone wires is very low, there is little danger of shock when working on the wiring. Still, it is best not to work in wet conditions when repairing any wiring. Also, do not work on a phone system if you wear a cardiac pacemaker, because the mild electrical currents in phone lines can interfere with the device.

Common telephone repairs include replacing a loose or broken modular connection (page 513), installing a modular jack in place of an outdated jack (page 514), and installing a junction box (page 515) that allows additional phone jacks to be run anywhere in the house.

A phone can be plugged directly into the demarcation jack to find out if a problem lies in the house wiring or in the phone company's wires and equipment. If there is no dial tone at the demarcation jack, the problem lies outside the home and should be fixed by the phone company. If there is a dial tone, however, this means that any problem lies inside the house.

Note: As the needs for Internet service and network data links in the home become increasingly important, larger and stronger telecommunication cables are needed in place of standard two-way telephone lines.

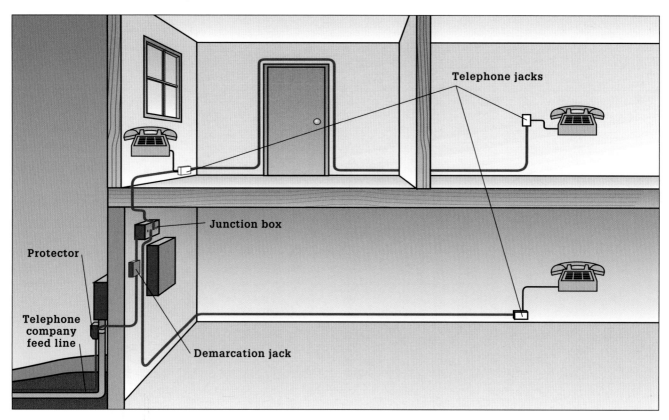

Two methods are used to wire phone systems. Relatively new systems are wired using the home run method (shown above), in which a wire distribution hub, or junction box, feeds individual lines to various phone jacks in the house. A junction box allows new jacks to easily be added by running new wires from the box to the new location. If one line becomes damaged, the other jacks will still operate. Older systems use a continuous loop method. With this method, various jacks are installed along a single loop of wire running throughout the house. A continuous loop is easier to install but less reliable since a single problem in the wire can render all the jacks inoperable.

Troubleshooting Phone Problems ▸

Problems	Possible causes	Solutions
Dead air; no sound on line.	Wires may be crossed.	Make sure bare copper wires inside jack aren't touching.
Static on line.	Wires may be wet.	Check for moisture in phone jacks. Check all connections.
Buzzing on line.	Wires may be touching metal. Wires may be connected to wrong terminals.	Check all wires and connections. Check color coding of connections.

How to Replace a Modular Connector

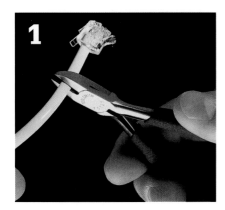

Remove the telephone cord from the wall jack and telephone. Use wire cutters to snip off the cord just below the connector to be replaced. Make sure to trim the cord at a straight angle.

Insert the cord into the stripper section of the tool. Squeeze the handle just enough to sever the outer insulation. Tug on the cord to pull the wires free of the insulation. Make sure not to cut the inner insulation on the individual wires.

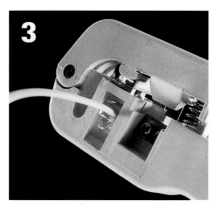

Insert the individual wires into a plastic connector in the opposite sequence from that at the other end of the cord. Make sure the wires are flush with the top of connector and touching the metal contacts. Use a crimper tool to secure the connector to the wires.

Wire Assignments ▸

Most phone cords have four wires: red, green, yellow, and black. But there are two other possible color schemes. Use the following as a guide to connecting the wires:

The red terminal will accept:
• a red wire
• a blue wire
• a blue wire w/white stripe

The green terminal will accept:
• a green wire
• a white wire w/blue stripe

The yellow terminal will accept:
• a yellow wire
• an orange wire
• an orange wire w/white stripe

The black terminal will accept:
• a black wire
• a white wire w/orange stripe

If there are extra wires in the cord (usually these will be green and white), they can be tucked into the jack and left unconnected. The phone company will use these wires to connect additional phone lines if you should ever need them.

How to Install a Modular Jack

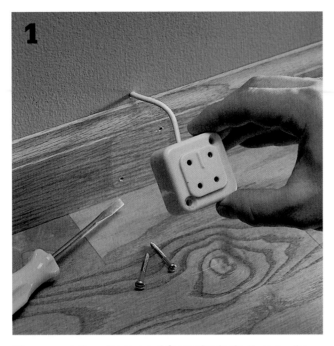

1

Disconnect the phone cord from the jack. Unscrew the phone jack from the wall or baseboard with a screwdriver. Gently pull the jack away from the wall.

2

Disconnect the individual wires from the terminals on the jack. Clip off the bare copper ends of the wire, using a wire cutter.

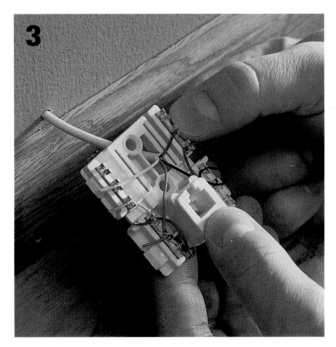

3

Remove casing from the connection block on the new modular jack, and feed phone cables through the back of the base piece. Force each colored wire into one of the metal slots on the terminal block that has a wire of the same or acceptable color (page 513). About ½" of wire should extend through the slot.

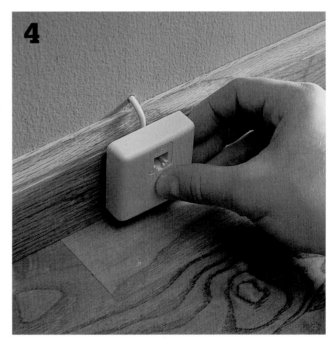

4

Screw the connection block to the wall with the screw included with the jack, and snap coverplate in place. Attach a phone to the new jack, and test it to make sure it works.

How to Install a Telephone Junction Box

Select a location that allows the cable for the junction box to reach the demarcation jack. Snap off the cover of the junction box. Attach the box to a wall, baseboard, or framing member, using the mounting screws that are included with it. Run phone cable to the demarcation jack. Secure to wall or framing members with staples every 24".

Trim all but 5" of cable, and strip off 3" of outer insulation, using a crimper. Strip 1" of inner insulation from each of the four individual wires, using a utility knife. Loop the bare copper wires clockwise around demarcation jack screw terminals, matching the colors. Tighten screws. *Note: Some junction boxes have attached cords with modular connections that plug directly into demarcation jacks.*

Loosen one terminal screw on each of the four color-coded sections of the junction box. Insert each wire into a slot in the corresponding section. About ½" of wire should extend through the slot.

For each phone extension line, attach the cable to the junction box following the same procedure used for the cable running to the demarcation jack. Screw the terminals down tight, then bend the wires upright so they don't touch each other. Snap the cover back on the junction box.

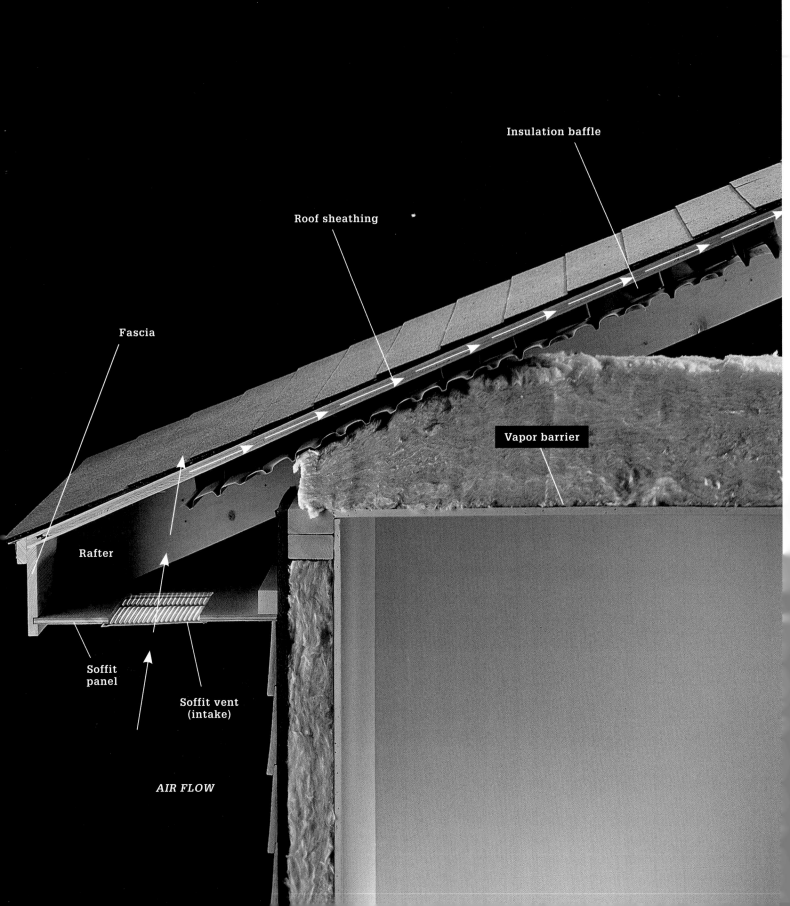

Insulation baffle

Roof sheathing

Fascia

Vapor barrier

Rafter

Soffit
panel

Soffit vent
(intake)

AIR FLOW

Roof vent
(outtake)

Unheated
attic space

Attic insulation blanket
(between ceiling joists)

Heated room space

Shown cutaway for clarity

Heating,
Ventilation &
Air Conditioning

In this chapter:

- Maintaining Gas Forced-air Systems
- Maintaining Hot Water & Steam Systems
- Identifying & Repairing Exhaust Leaks
- Repairing Electric Baseboard Heaters
- Repairing Wall-mounted Electric Heaters
- Fixing & Replacing Thermostats
- Installing a Ridge Vent
- Installing New Vents

Maintaining Gas Forced-air Systems

Gas forced-air systems are widely used in cool climates worldwide. A gas forced-air furnace—running on natural gas or liquid propane (LP)—draws in surrounding air, channels it across a set of heated plates, known as a heat exchanger, and then uses a blower to circulate the air throughout the house (illustration). A chamber on top of the furnace, known as a plenum, leads the warmed air from the furnace to a network of ducts that carry the warm air to heat registers or vents mounted on walls or ceilings. To keep the cycle going, return ducts carry cooled air from each room back to the furnace so it can be reheated and recirculated. Older systems use gravity to carry warm air throughout the house and cool air back to the furnace.

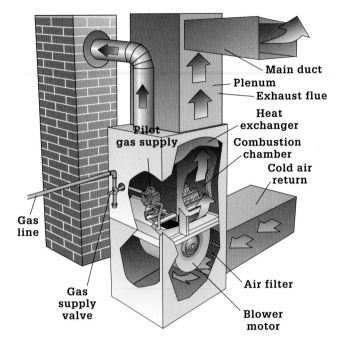

Identifying the plenum and cold air return, as well as the main duct leading to the rooms in your home, is a good way to begin familiarizing yourself with your forced-air system.

Balancing a Forced-air System

Most forced-air systems have dampers within the ducts that let you control how much air flows to various parts of the house. These are separate from the registers used to manage airflow within each room. Adjusting the dampers is called balancing the system.

Start by locating the dampers (illustration). When a damper handle or wing nut is parallel to the duct, it is wide open, allowing maximum airflow. When the handle is perpendicular to the duct, it is closed.

To balance your system, start by setting the thermostat as you would for the times when you're at home. Close the dampers that lead to the room with the thermostat. Wait a few hours, and go to the rooms that are farthest from the furnace. If those rooms are too warm, leave them until later, when more dampers are open. Check the other rooms for comfort. After each damper adjustment, wait a few hours for the air temperature to stabilize.

Once you're satisfied with the heat each room receives, use a permanent marker on each duct to indicate the correct setting for each damper (photo 1). Repeat the process in the summer for air conditioning, making a second set of marks to indicate the correct damper settings for cooling.

Mark damper positions on each duct, and indicate which room is affected by the settings. Open or close the damper using a screwdriver or by turning the wing nut (inset).

Maintaining a Forced-air System

You can handle most routine furnace maintenance yourself. Generally, the newer the furnace, the simpler the maintenance, since a number of heavy-maintenance components have been eliminated on newer models.

Most furnaces installed since the 1980s do not have a thermocouple-controlled pilot light. In fact, the standing pilot light found on older furnaces has been eliminated completely. In most cases, it's been replaced with either an intermittent pilot light that's lit only when there's a call for heat from the thermostat, or a glowing element, known as a hot-surface igniter. An intermittent pilot light must be repaired by a professional technician, should it fail. You can replace a hot-surface igniter yourself.

Use this section to identify and complete the maintenance procedures that apply to the furnace in your home.

Before doing any maintenance, always turn off the furnace's main gas supply and the pilot gas supply, if your furnace has a separate one. Then, switch off the furnace's main power switch and the power to the furnace at the main service panel. Check your owner's manual for any warnings or special instructions concerning your furnace. Then, clear the area, so you have a safe work space.

Start with the most important and simplest furnace maintenance procedure—inspecting the air filter. There are many types of filters. Read the section below to find out how to clean yours and how often it must be changed.

Tools & Materials ▸

Standard screwdriver
Ratchet wrench
Nut driver
Open-end wrench set
Straightedge

Channel-type pliers
Pilot jet tool
Parts brush
Mild liquid detergent
Light machine oil

Replacing the Air Filter

The air filter on your forced-air furnace is designed to capture dust, pollen, and other airborne particles. The filter must be cleaned regularly, according to the manufacturer's specifications, and should be inspected once a month. Locate the filter compartment and remove the access cover (photo 1). The location of the compartment depends on the furnace type and the style of filter. Many filters fit in a slot between the return air duct and blower. A few styles are located inside the main furnace compartment. An electrostatic filter is installed in a separate unit attached to the furnace.

Slide the filter out of its compartment, taking care not to catch it on the sides of the blower housing. Hold the filter up to a light (photo 2). If the filter blocks much of the light, replace it. Electrostatic filters can be reused after cleaning.

Many filters are located between the return air duct and the blower, and rest in a slot or bracket.

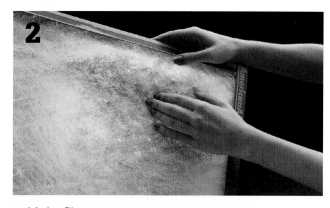

Hold the filter up to a bright light for inspection.

Maintaining the Blower Motor

Inspect the blower motor before the start of the heating season. Inspect it again before the start of the cooling season if your central air conditioning uses the same blower.

Turn off the power to the furnace. Remove the access panel to the blower housing and inspect the motor (photo 1). Some motors have oil ports and an adjustable, replaceable drive belt. Others are self-lubricating and have a direct-drive mechanism. Wipe the motor clean with a damp cloth and check for oil fill ports. The access panel may include a diagram indicating their location. Remove the covers to the ports (if equipped) and add a few drops of light machine oil (photo 2). Place the covers on the ports.

With the power still off, inspect the drive belt. If it is cracked, worn, glazed, or brittle, replace it. Check the belt tension by pushing down gently midway between the pulleys (photo 3). The belt should flex about 1". To tighten or loosen the belt, locate the pulley tension adjustment nut on the blower motor (photo 4). Loosen the locknut, and turn the adjustment nut slightly. Check the belt tension, and readjust as required until the tension is correct.

If the belt is out of alignment or the bearings are worn, adjusting the tension will not solve the problem. With the power off, hold a straightedge so it's flush with the edge of both pulleys (photo 5). To align the belt, locate the mounting bolts on the motor's sliding bracket (photo 6). Loosen the bolts, and move the motor carefully until the pulleys are aligned. Tighten the bolts and check the tension and alignment again. Repeat until the pulley is aligned and the tension adjusted. Replace the furnace access panels. Restore power and switch on the furnace.

Remove the access panel to the blower housing and inspect the motor.

Remove the covers to the oil ports and add a few drops to each port.

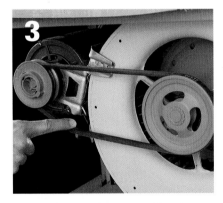

Check the tension by pushing down on the middle of the belt.

Loosen the pulley tension adjustment nut slightly to tighten the belt.

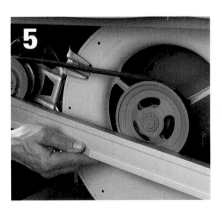

Check the pulley alignment, using a straightedge.

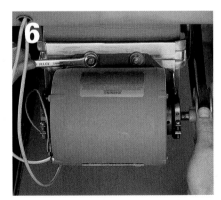

Loosen the bolts that hold the motor on its sliding bracket, and move the motor carefully until the pulleys are aligned.

Inspecting the Pilot & Thermocouple

The pilot light (it's actually a flame used to ignite gas flowing through the burners) plays a large role in the efficiency of the entire system, and a clean-burning pilot saves money, improves indoor air quality, and extends furnace life.

If your furnace has a standing pilot light, always check the flame before the start of the heating season to ensure that it's burning cleanly and with the proper mix of air and fuel. Start by removing the main furnace access panel. If you can't see the pilot flame clearly, turn off the gas supply (photo 1) and the pilot gas shutoff switch (if equipped). Wait 10 minutes for the pilot to cool, and remove the pilot cover. Relight the pilot, following the instructions on the control housing or access cover. If the pilot won't stay lit, shut off the gas supply once again and inspect the thermocouple.

Inspect the flame (photo 2). If the flame is too weak (left flame), it will be blue and may barely touch the thermocouple. If the flame is too strong (center flame), it will also be blue, but may be noisy and lift off the pilot. A well-adjusted flame (right flame) will be blue with a yellow tip, and cover ½" at the end of the thermocouple. Turn the pilot adjustment screw (photo 3) on the control housing or gas valve to reduce the pressure. If it's weak, turn the screw in the other direction to increase the pressure. If the flame appears weak and yellow even after adjustment, remove the pilot jet and clean the orifice (page 523).

If the pilot in your furnace or boiler goes out quickly, and you have made sure the gas supply is sufficient, you may need to replace the thermocouple. Turn off the gas supply. Using an open-end wrench, loosen the thermocouple tube fitting from the control housing or gas valve. Unscrew the thermocouple from the pilot housing and install a new one (photo 4). Tighten it with a wrench just until it's snug.

Turn off the main gas supply and the pilot gas supply (if your furnace has a separate one).

Adjust the flame so it is steady, has a yellow tip, and covers the thermocouple's tip (right).

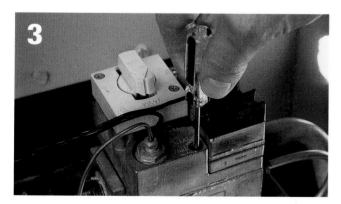

Turn the screw to adjust the height of the flame so it covers the top of the thermocouple.

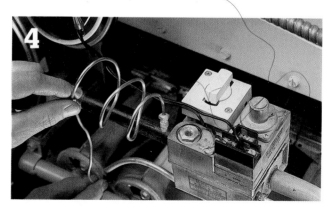

Remove the thermocouple from the control housing and install a new one.

Cleaning & Adjusting the Pilot Light

If the thermocouple and burners in your furnace or boiler appear to be working correctly, but the pilot flame is inconsistent or weak, remove the pilot jet and clean or replace it. Turn off the power and close the gas supply, including the gas supply to the pilot if your unit has a separate one. Wait at least 30 minutes for the parts to cool. Using an open-end wrench, remove the thermocouple from the pilot housing (photo 1).

Use two wrenches to hold the gas line in place, then loosen the nut that connects it to the control housing. Unscrew and remove the pilot housing, then carefully remove the pilot jet from the housing (photo 2).

Clean the outside of the pilot jet with a parts brush, and carefully clean the inside with a pilot jet tool. Take care not to scratch the inside of the jet, as this will affect its performance. If the pilot jet is severely corroded or difficult to clean, replace it.

Thread the pilot jet back into the pilot housing, and reinstall the housing. Reattach the gas line, turning the connecting nut while holding the line steady. Reinstall the thermocouple. Reopen the gas supply and turn the power back on, then light the pilot.

Loosen the connecting nut on the gas line with an open-end wrench.

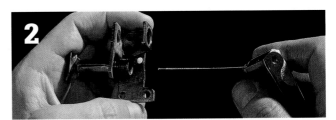

Remove the pilot jet from the housing and clean it with a pilot jet tool.

Inspecting the Burner Flame

Once you've set the pilot flame, check the burner flame. The burner flame should be blue, with a bluish green flame at the center and occasional streaks of yellow (photo 1). If it appears too blue or too yellow, adjust the air shutter at the end of the burner tube (photo 2). Start by setting the thermostat high

so that the furnace continues to burn. Wearing protective gloves, loosen the air shutter locking screw. Open the shutter wide, then close it slowly until the flame color is right. Retighten the locking screw. Repeat the procedure for each remaining burner. Reset the thermostat.

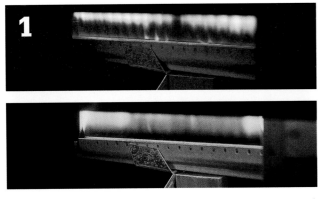

Compare your burner flame with the two above. Yours should be blue-green, with streaks of yellow (top).

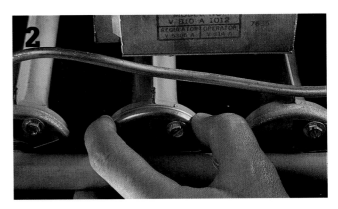

If the shutters are adjustable, you can set them yourself. Otherwise, call a professional for service.

Cleaning the Burners

Burners work by mixing together gas and air that is then ignited by a pilot flame or a heated element. Gas is delivered by a manifold and enters each burner tube through a small orifice, known as a spud. Burners and spuds gradually become encrusted with soot and other products of the combustion process and must be cleaned occasionally to keep them working efficiently.

To clean the burners, turn off the furnace's main shutoff, and switch off the power to the furnace at the main service panel. Shut off the gas supply, including the pilot gas supply if your unit has a separate one. Wait at least 30 minutes for the parts to cool. Remove the burner tubes by unscrewing them from their retaining brackets (photo 1), by pulling out the metal pan that holds them, or by loosening the screws that attach the gas manifold to the furnace. On some furnaces, you need to remove the pilot housing to reach the burners.

Twist each burner carefully to remove it from its spud (photo 2). Fill a laundry tub with water and soak the burners. Carefully clean the outside of the burner tubes and the burner ports with a soft-bristled brush. Replace any tubes that are cracked, bent, or severely corroded.

Inspect the spuds: clean burners won't work effectively if the spuds are dirty or damaged. Use a ratchet wrench to loosen and remove each spud (photo 3). Clean the outside of each spud with a soft-bristled brush. Then, use a pilot jet tool to clean the inside of each spud (photo 4). The tool is designed for cleaning small orifices, but take special care to avoid scratching or enlarging a spud's opening. Reinstall the spuds in the manifold. Tighten them just until they're snug. Once the burner tubes are dry, install them on the spuds, and attach them to the burner tube brackets or burner pan. Connect the pilot housing, if equipped. Turn the power and gas supply back on. On furnaces with a standing pilot, relight the pilot flame.

Remove the screws holding the burners to their brackets or to a slide-out pan.

If a burner is difficult to remove, twist it carefully from side to side while lifting and pulling.

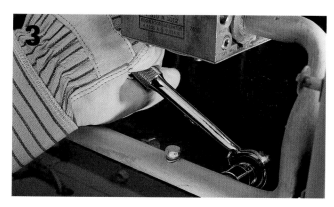

To avoid bending or damaging the spud threads, hold the manifold steady with one hand as you remove each spud.

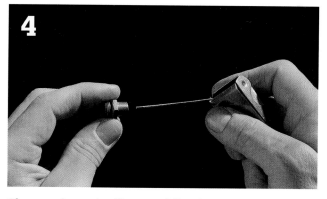

Clean each spud orifice carefully with a pilot jet tool, taking care not to scratch or enlarge the orifice.

Servicing Electronic Ignition Furnaces

Newer furnaces include an intermittent pilot light or hot-surface igniter as well as an electronic control center, with warning lights to help you recognize problems.

On some newer models, the temperature difference between the supply and return ducts needs to be within a narrow range to avoid damaging the heat exchanger. To find out whether this applies to your furnace, check the information plate on the burner compartment—it may include an indication of the acceptable range.

Each season, check the differential by slipping the probe of a pocket thermometer into a slit in an expansion joint in the supply duct (photo 1). Record the reading and compare it with the temperature in the return air duct. Call a professional technician if the difference between the two numbers falls outside the recommended range.

Your furnace may contain an intermittent pilot, which is lighted with a spark when signaled by the thermostat. An intermittent pilot consumes gas only when necessary, reducing home fuel costs. If the electronic ignition fails to spark, call a technician for service.

Some furnace models ignite the gas with a glowing element, known as a hot-surface igniter. If the igniter fails, replace it. Remove the main furnace panel and locate the igniter just beyond the ignition end of the burner tubes. Disconnect the igniter plug and remove the nut on the mounting bracket with a nut driver or ratchet wrench (photo 2). Replace the igniter.

If the igniter still doesn't function properly, check with the manufacturer: you may need to replace the control center. Detach the wires from the old control center one at a time and attach them to the replacement (photo 3). Then, disconnect the old control center, using a screwdriver, and connect the new one (photo 4).

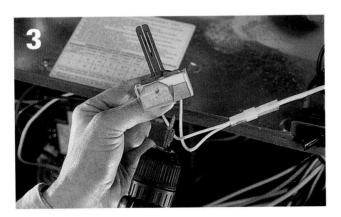

Remove the control center wires one at a time and switch them over to the new control center.

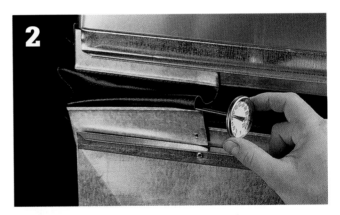

Check the temperature inside the supply duct and compare it with the temperature in the return duct.

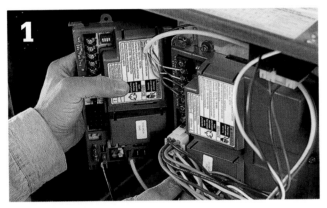

Disconnect the faulty hot-surface igniter from the mounting bracket.

Unscrew the control center's mounting screws and install the replacement unit.

Maintaining a High-efficiency Gas Furnace

A high-efficiency gas furnace is defined as a furnace that's at least 90% "efficient," as determined by an annual fuel utilization efficiency (AFUE) rating.

Furnaces made as late as 1992 can have ratings as low as 60%. A standard, mid-efficient unit sold today is about 80% percent, while high-efficiency units can be as high as 96% efficient.

Like other furnaces, high-efficiency gas furnaces require maintenance. The air filters must be cleaned regularly—electronic filters need to be cleaned on a monthly basis, and disposable filters should be changed every three months (photo 1).

If the drain line cannot drain properly, moisture can build up inside the heat exchanger and restrict gas flow. Inspect the drain line to make sure it's free of kinks. Some furnaces have several drain connections that should be inspected.

Clean the drain line once a year by disconnecting it from the furnace and forcing water from a garden hose through the line (photo 2). If the drain line is black plastic, remove it at a connection point, then reattach once it's clean. If the line is white, then it's PVC, and you'll need to reconnect it to the unit with a coupling after cleaning it.

Some furnaces have a removable condensate trap. If your unit has one, remove it at the beginning of the winter season and clean it out with water. Check the trap periodically throughout the season and dump the water as necessary.

Check the vent pipes and furnace unit for signs of corrosion (photo 3). The water produced by the furnace is acidic and will corrode metal quickly. If pipes are leaking, they must be replaced.

Make sure the areas around the air intake and exhaust are unobstructed. Plants, bushes, and other materials that block the intake and exhaust can cause the furnace to shut down (photo 4).

Clean electronic filters every month, then reinsert them in your furnace.

Clean the drain line once a year by running water through it from a garden hose.

Inspect the areas around vent pipes for signs of corrosion. Corroded pipes will need to be replaced.

Remove any debris and materials that could block the air intake and exhaust.

Maintaining a Furnace Humidifier

Furnace humidifiers are an effective means of increasing the humidity in your home. There are two types of furnace humidifiers, drum-style and drip-style. They attach to the furnace's warm air or return air duct.

A drum-style humidifier picks up water from a reservoir or pan, using a rotating drum covered with an absorbent pad. Air flows through the pad and the water evaporates, raising the humidity level. In a drip-style humidifier, water drips into a stationary evaporator pad through which the air passes.

Drip-style humidifiers typically consume more water, since excess water runs off the bottom of the pad and into a drain. However, they stay cleaner and require far less maintenance, because the flow of water greatly reduces scum buildup. Drum-style humidifiers must be cleaned more often to keep mold from growing in the standing water.

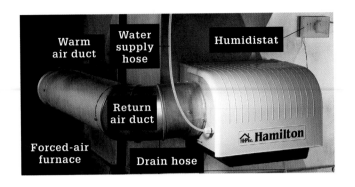

Tools & Materials ▸

Tape measure
Open-end wrench set
Chisel
Putty knife

Vinegar
Replacement
  evaporator pad
  (if required)

Maintaining a Drip-style Humidifier

A drip-style humidifier should be inspected monthly. The evaporator pad should be replaced at the end of every heating season.

To service a drip-style humidifier, shut off the power, and turn off the water supply. Slide your finger under the plastic water outlet and lift up to pop off the outlet. Remove the distribution tray by pushing down on the tray while pushing out on the plastic frame (photo 1). Use a chisel to scrape out any mineral deposits from the V-notches on the tray (photo 2).

Slide the evaporator pad from the frame (photo 3). Twist and flex the evaporator pad to loosen the deposits, using a putty knife to scrape them away, if necessary. If the pad itself crumbles, replace it.

Disconnect the drain hose. Flex it, then flush it with cold water (photo 4). Reassemble the humidifier and attach the drain hose. Turn on the electricity and the water supply.

Remove the distribution tray from the humidifier.

Use a chisel to scrape mineral deposits from the V-notches.

Remove the evaporator pad from the frame.

Disconnect the drain hose and flush it with cold water.

Maintaining a Drum-style Humidifier

Drum-style evaporator pads should be cleaned monthly and replaced at the end of each heating season. Turn off the power to the heating and cooling system and the water at the water supply valve. Then, loosen the nuts or release the clips that hold the humidifier cover in place, and remove the cover.

Lift out the drum-style evaporator, by holding both ends (photo 1). If the pad is hard, clean or replace it.

Separate the pad from the drum shaft by removing the clip on the center spindle and pulling apart the two parts of the drum shaft (photo 2).

Soak the pad in a 1:3 mixture of water and vinegar. Squeeze the pad to rinse it. If the pad remains hard or appears damaged, replace it. With the pad in place, use a tape measure to check the depth of the water in the pan (photo 3). Your owner's manual may indicate the correct water depth. If not, see if the pad dips into the water in each rotation and comes up wet, and whether there is a mineral line on the side of the tray wall, indicating where the water level should be.

To adjust the water level either up or down, loosen the screw on the float mount (photo 4). To raise the water level, raise the float height and then tighten the screw. To lower the level, lower the float, then tighten the screw. Wait 30 minutes and check the water level and evaporator pad again. If water leaks from the supply tube fitting, tighten the nut with an open-end wrench (photo 5).

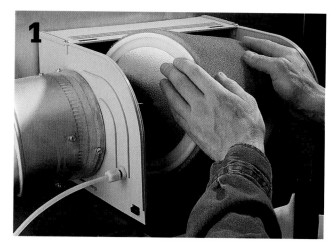

Remove the drum-style evaporator by lifting it from its slots.

Separate the two parts of the drum shaft by removing the clip and pulling the two pieces apart.

Make sure the pad soaks in the water. Mineral deposits left on the wall will indicate the original water level.

Loosen the locknut on the water line with an open-end wrench.

Adjust the float height and retighten the locknut.

Maintaining Hot Water & Steam Systems

Hot water and steam systems, also known as hydronic systems, feature a boiler that heats water and circulates it through a closed network of pipes to a set of radiators or convectors. Because water expands and contracts as it heats and cools, these systems include expansion tanks to ensure a constant volume of water circulating through the pipes.

Hot water and steam systems warm the surrounding air through a process called convection. Hot water radiators (photo 1) are linked to the system by pipes connected near the bottom of the radiator. As water cools inside the radiator, it is drawn back to the boiler for reheating. The radiators in steam systems (photo 2) have pipes connected near the top of the radiator. These radiators can be very hot to the touch. Convectors (photo 3) are smaller and lighter and may be used to replace hot water radiators, or to extend an existing hot water system.

Although the delivery of hot water or steam to the rooms in your house is considered a closed system, some air will make its way into the system. Steam radiators have an automatic release valve that periodically releases hot, moist air. Hot water radiators contain a bleed valve that must periodically be opened to release trapped air. It is usually necessary to bleed convector systems using a valve near the boiler.

Today's hot water and steam systems are often fueled by natural gas. Older systems may use fuel oil. Fuel oil systems require more frequent maintenance of the filter (page 529) and blower (page 530).

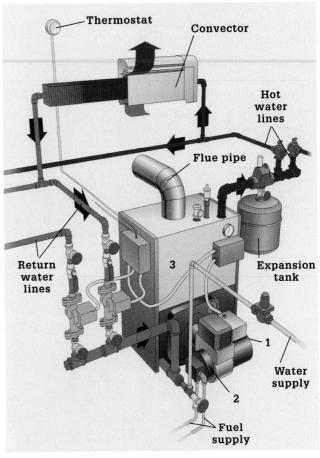

A blower draws in air through the air intake (1) while a fuel pump (2) maintains a constant supply of fuel oil. The mixture is ignited by a high-voltage spark as it enters the combustion chamber (3) and heats water.

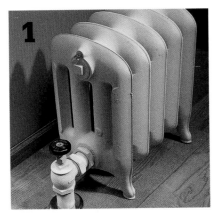

Hot-water radiators circulate heated water through pipes. As it cools, water is drawn back to the boiler for reheating.

Steam radiators operate at a higher temperature. Steam cools in the radiators, returns to a liquid state, and then flows back to the boiler.

Space-saving hot water convectors work on the same principle as radiators, but use thin sheet-metal fins to transfer heat to the air.

Servicing the Oil Filter & Strainer

Replacing the oil filter is the best routine maintenance you can do for your hot water or steam heating system.

Surround the base of the boiler with a drop cloth and newspaper. Shut off the power to the boiler at the main service panel and at the boiler shutoff switch, usually located near the boiler. Then, close the fuel line supply valve and wait 30 minutes for all parts to cool.

Wearing disposable gloves, unscrew the top of the filter cartridge (photo 1). Remove the cartridge with a twisting motion and turn it over to dump the old filter into a plastic bag (photo 2). Remove the gasket from the cartridge and wipe out the inside, first with a cloth dipped in solvent, then with a dry cloth. Install a new filter and gasket (photo 3). Position the cartridge under the cover and screw it back in place.

Use an open-end wrench to remove the bolts from the pump cover (photo 4). Leave the oil line attached, and remove the gasket and mesh strainer from the cover (photo 5). Clean the strainer with solvent and a parts brush. If it's badly worn or damaged, replace it. Wipe the cover with a clean cloth. Place the clean strainer or replacement strainer in the cover and install a new gasket. Fasten the cover bolts in place. Restart the boiler.

Tools & Materials ▸

Open-end wrench set	Replacement
Parts brush	oil filter and
Gloves	cartridge gasket
Drop cloth	Strainer gasket
Solvent	Cloth

Have a disposable plastic bag ready, and unscrew the top of the filter cartridge.

Twist the cartridge to remove it from the oil supply line. Ask your waste removal company for disposal instructions.

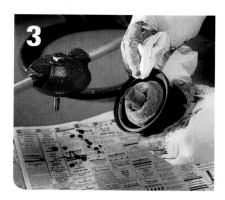

Wipe the edge of the cartridge, first with a solvent-dipped rag and then with a dry rag.

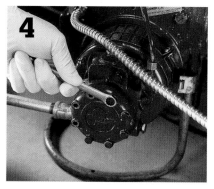

Leave the pump cover attached to the fuel line when you remove it.

Remove the mesh strainer carefully. Even a heavily soiled one can often be reused after a good cleaning.

Cleaning & Lubricating the Blower

Clean fuel and a reliable air supply are critical to your boiler's performance. Clean the air intake on your boiler every month and lubricate the motor every two months during the heating season.

Turn off the power to the boiler. Brush any dust and debris from the air intake with a narrow, medium-bristle brush (photo 1). Use an open-end wrench or screwdriver, as required, to loosen the transformer. With the transformer still attached, move it aside to reach the blower fan (photo 2). Use the brush and a damp cloth to remove dirt and debris from the fan blades (photo 3).

Most boiler blowers have a port on top or cups at each end for adding lubricating oil. Check your owner's manual or consult the manufacturer on the best lubricating oil for your blower. Before removing the plugs or opening the cups, clean the outside of the motor with a damp cloth (photo 4) to keep dirt and

debris from getting into the motor. Remove the plug from the opening or the lid from each cup, using a wrench or screwdriver, as required. Add a few drops of lubricating oil (photo 5).

If the motor doesn't have oil ports or cups, it's probably a self-lubricating type (photo 6). Check your owner's manual to be sure.

Tools & Materials ▸

Open-end wrench set
Screwdrivers
  (standard
  and Phillips)

Medium-bristle brush
Drop cloth
Boiler lubricating oil
Cloth

To clean the air intake, use a brush designed for cleaning the condensing coils on a refrigerator.

If the transformer attaches to the blower housing with a hinge, simply swing it out of the way. If it comes loose, be careful not to strain the wire connections.

The blades on most blower fans are thin and hard to reach, so use a long brush carefully: a bent fan blade makes much more noise than a dirty one.

To prevent dust or dirt from getting in the motor while you add oil, clean off the surface with a damp cloth before opening the ports or cups.

Add lubricating oil to the ports or cups. The motor housing may indicate what kind of oil to use.

If the motor doesn't have cups or openings for adding lubricating oil, it's probably sealed and may not need extra lubrication.

Draining & Filling a System

Sediment gradually accumulates in any water-based system, reducing the system's efficiency and damaging internal parts. Draining the boiler every season reduces the accumulation of sediment. Be aware that draining the system can take a long time, and the water often has an unpleasant odor. This doesn't indicate a problem. Drain the system during warm weather, and open the windows and run a fan to reduce any odor.

Start by shutting off the boiler and allowing the hot system to cool. Attach a garden hose to the drain at the bottom of the boiler (photo 1), and place the other end in a floor drain or utility sink. Open a bleed valve on the highest radiator in the house (page 532).

When water stops draining, open a bleed valve on a radiator closer to the boiler. When the flow stops, locate the valve or gauge on top of the boiler, and remove it with a wrench (photo 2).

Make sure the system is cool before you add water. Close the drain valve on the boiler. Insert a funnel into the gauge fitting and add rust inhibitor, available from heating supply dealers (photo 3). Check the container for special instructions. Reinstall the valve or gauge in the top of the boiler, close all radiator bleed valves, and slowly reopen the water supply to the boiler.

When the water pressure gauge reads 5 psi, bleed the air from the radiators on the first floor, then do the same on the upper floors. Let the boiler reach 20 psi before you turn the power on (photo 4). Allow 12 hours for water to circulate fully, then bleed the radiators again.

Tools & Materials ▶

Open-end wrench set	Plastic bucket
Pipe wrenches	Drop cloth
Garden hose	Boiler rust inhibitor
Funnel	

Use a garden hose to drain water from the boiler. Keep the drain end of the hose lower than the drain cock on the boiler.

If the valve or gauge on top of the boiler is attached to a separate fitting, hold the fitting still with one wrench while removing the valve or gauge with another.

Using a funnel, add a recommended rust inhibitor to the boiler through the valve or gauge fitting.

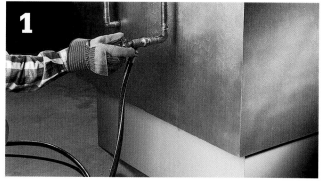

The boiler should reach a pressure of 20 psi before you turn the power back on.

Bleeding a Hot Water System

Hot water systems operate more quietly and efficiently if you bleed them of trapped air once a year. To bleed a hot water system, the boiler must be on. Start with the radiator that's highest in the house and farthest from the boiler. Place a cloth under the bleed valve, and open the valve slowly (photo 1). Close it as soon as water squirts out. Some bleed valves have knobs, which open with a half turn; others must be opened with a screwdriver or valve key, available at hardware stores.

Steam radiators have automatic bleed valves. To clear a clogged valve, close the shutoff at the radiator and let unit cool. Unscrew the bleed valve and clear the orifice with a fine wire or needle (photo 2).

Older hot water convector systems may have bleed valves on or near the convectors. Bleed these convectors as you would radiators.

Most convector systems today don't have bleed valves. For these, locate the hose bib where the return water line reaches the boiler. Close the gate valve between the bib and the boiler. Attach a short section of hose to the bib and immerse the other end in a bucket of water. Open the bib while adding water to the boiler by opening the supply valve. The supply valve is located on the supply pipe, usually the smallest pipe in the system. Flush the system until no air bubbles come out of the hose in the bucket (photo 3). Open the gate valve to bleed any remaining air. Close the hose bib before restarting the boiler.

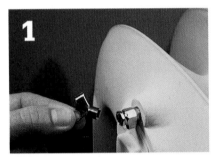

If you can't find a key for your radiators, a local hardware store or home center may have a replacement.

If the radiator isn't heating, clear the orifice with a fine wire or needle.

A convector-based heating system is usually bled at the boiler by holding a hose underwater and flushing the system until there are no more air bubbles coming from the hose.

Replace Radiator Control Valves ▸

A radiator control valve that won't operate should be replaced. To replace the valve, you'll first need to drain the system (page 531). Then use a pipe wrench to disconnect the nut on the outlet side of the valve, then disconnect the valve body from the supply pipe (photo 1, right). Thread the tailpiece of the new valve into the radiator. Thread the valve body onto the supply pipe. Make sure the arrow on the valve body points in the direction of the water flow. Thread the connecting nut on the tailpiece onto the outlet side of the valve (photo 2). When you recharge the system, open the bleed valve on the radiator until a trickle of water runs out.

Use a pipe wrench to remove the control valve (left). Thread the tailpiece of the new valve into the radiator (right).

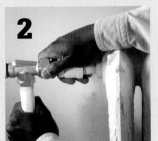

Fasten the valve to the supply tube, then secure the connecting nut on the tailpiece to the valve.

Identifying & Repairing Exhaust Leaks

Leaks in the exhaust flue, around the burner mounting flange, combustion chamber cover plate, or fire door are potential sources of carbon monoxide. Any leak that might allow carbon monoxide to enter your home should be repaired immediately.

Holes and rusted portions are visible signs of a damaged flue. Smaller leaks can be found by turning on the burner and holding a lighted candle along the joints in the flue and the seams of the burner mounting flange, combustion chamber cover plate, and fire door. The flame is drawn toward the joint or seam when there is a leak.

Tools & Materials ▸

Wire brush
Putty knife
Long candle
Power drill/screwdriver
Replacement
 flue sections
Refractory
 furnace cement

Hold a lighted candle to the joints on the flue and seams around the burner to find leaks.

Sealing an Exhaust Leak

To seal a leak at a seam, turn off the burner and let the boiler cool. Then, use a wire brush to remove any dirt or rust that has accumulated around the leak (photo 1).

Seal the leak by applying refractory furnace cement with a putty knife (photo 2). To stop a mounting flange leak, loosen the retaining bolts located at the edges of the flange. Scrape away the decayed gasket and apply refractory furnace cement at the edge. Then, tighten the bolts.

To test your repair, turn on the boiler and hold a lighted candle to the repair area. The candle flame should not flicker or waver.

Use a wire brush to clean off any rust or dirt deposits that have accumulated on the surface.

With a putty knife, apply refractory furnace cement to seal the leak.

Repairing Electric Baseboard Heaters

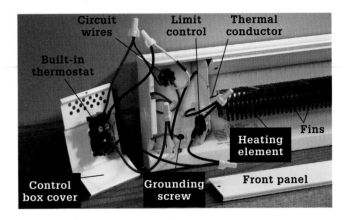

Baseboard heaters are simple electrical units consisting of a heating element with attached metal fins for transferring heat, and a limit control—a switch that prevents the element from overheating. To control the temperature, some models have a built-in thermostat; others are controlled by a line voltage, or zone thermostat (page 544)—a wall-mounted thermostat that is wired directly to the heater.

Most heaters are wired to a 240-volt circuit, which means both the black and white circuit wires are hot and carry voltage. Others use 120 volts and are wired to a circuit or plugged into a standard receptacle. The tests for all three types are nearly the same.

If the heater is wired to a household circuit, shut off the power at the main service panel, and test for power before proceeding (left).

Note: Wiring for heaters and thermostats varies. For the best—and safest—results, check the manufacturer's wiring instructions, and label all wires before disconnecting.

Tools & Materials ▸

Screwdriver
Multimeter
Vacuum or brush
Needlenose pliers

Replacement parts
Masking tape
Pen

How to Test for Power Before Making Repairs

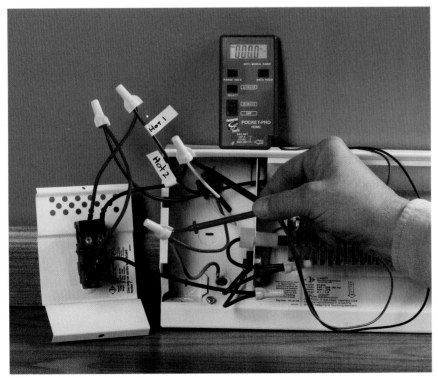

Turn off the power to the heater at the main service panel. Remove the heater's control box cover, and label the black hot circuit wire. Insert one probe of a neon circuit tester or multimeter into the wire connector at the end of the circuit wire, and touch the other probe to the grounding screw on the heater casing. Then, label the other circuit wire (with a 240-volt heater, this wire will also carry voltage). Insert the tester probe into its wire connector, and touch the other probe to the grounding screw. Finally, insert one probe into each of the wire connectors you've just tested. If the tester shows current for any of the tests, the power is still on. Return to the service panel, and turn off the correct circuit.

How to Test & Service an Electric Baseboard Heater

Begin by testing the limit control. Shut off the power at the main service panel, and confirm it is off by testing the unit (page 534). Pull a limit control lead from its terminal. Set multimeter to test continuity. Touch one probe to each limit control terminal. If the tester shows continuity, it means the limit control is working correctly, and you should move on to testing the thermostat (step 2). If the tester does not show continuity, remove the limit control and thermal conductor from the unit, and replace it with a duplicate part from the manufacturer.

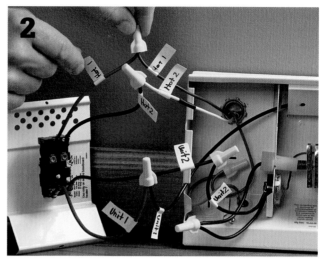

To test the thermostat, start by labeling each thermostat lead and wire connected to it, giving both wires the same name. Designate circuit wires and their respective leads as HOT, and heater wires and their respective leads as UNIT.

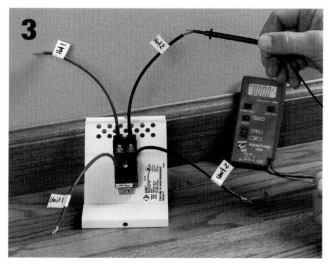

Disconnect wires, and remove thermostat. Turn thermostat dial to highest (hottest) setting. Set multimeter to test continuity. Touch one probe to a HOT wire lead and the other to each UNIT wire. The tester should indicate continuity in one of the connections. Repeat test for the other HOT wire lead and each UNIT wire. If there is continuity for both HOT wires, move on to step 4. If the thermostat fails either test, replace with duplicate part from manufacturer.

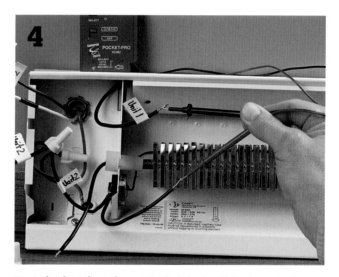

Test the heating element. Find the heating element wire that connects to a thermostat lead. (This wire may come from the far end of the element.) Unscrew wire connector, and separate wires. Set a multimeter to test continuity. Touch one probe to the free heating element wire and the other to the wire running from limit control to the other end of the element. Multitester should indicate continuity, meaning element is sound and the problem may lie in the circuit. If not, the element is bad, and the entire unit should be replaced.

Repairing Wall-mounted Electric Heaters

Wall-mounted electric heaters are installed between studs in an interior wall, typically in small areas, such as entryways or bathroom additions, where no other heat source is available. They work on the same principles as electric baseboard heaters (pages 534 to 535), generating heat by running electrical current through a heating element.

Wall-mounted heaters often contain a fan to help distribute heat to the room. If the heater won't turn on or shut off when the room temperature changes or when you turn the control knob, minor repairs may solve the problem.

The heater may have one or two limit controls near the heating element. They are designed to shut off the heater if it overheats. If there is a slight burning smell and the heater doesn't shut itself off, one or both limit controls may be faulty.

If the heater doesn't respond when adjusting the control knob, the thermostat may be faulty. Starting at OFF, turn the thermostat knob, and listen for a click. If the unit doesn't click, test the thermostat for continuity, using a multi-tester. Replace the thermostat if it is faulty.

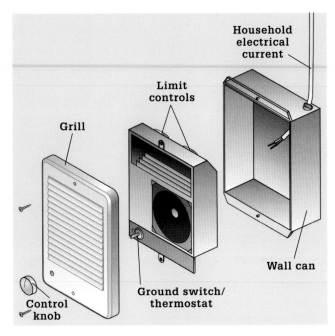

Inspect a wall-mounted heater before the start of the heating season. Dirt and dust can build up around the heating element, resulting in a burning smell when the heater is back in service. A careful cleaning with a soft-bristled brush is important for safe, reliable use.

How to Remove the Heater and Check for Power

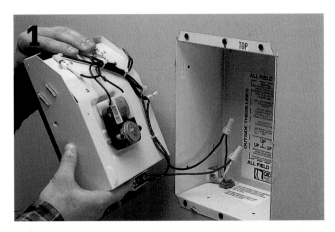

To remove and test the heater, shut off the power to the heater at the main service panel. Remove the control knob. Loosen the mounting screws on the grill, and slide the heater out of the wall can. Lift the top out first, disengaging the tabs at the base.

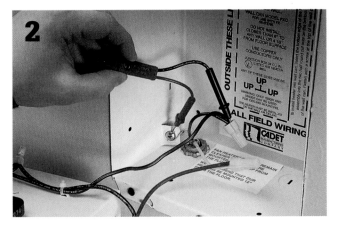

Insert one end of a neon circuit tester into the wire connector holding the black circuit wire, and touch the other probe to the grounding screw. Repeat, touching the probes to the white circuit connector and grounding screw. Finally, insert one probe into each of the wire connectors. The tester should not glow for any of these tests. If it does, shut off the correct circuit breaker on the main service panel. Repeat the tests until the tester does not glow.

How to Test & Replace a Limit Control

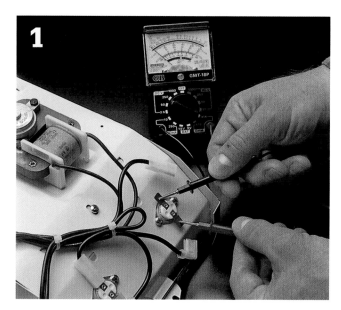

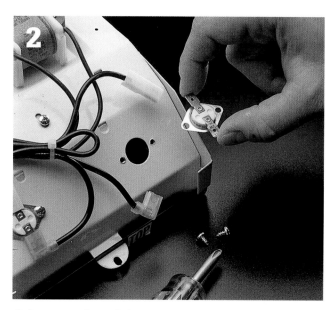

Shut off the power to the heater at the main service panel, and check for power. Use needlenose pliers to remove a single limit control lead from its terminal on the back of the heater, and test for continuity with a multimeter. Touch one probe of the multimeter to each limit control terminal. Repeat the test for the other limit control.

If the tester doesn't indicate continuity, remove the limit control and thermal conductor assembly from the heater. When purchasing a replacement, bring the old limit control with you for identification. Install the new limit control, and reassemble the heater.

How to Test & Replace a Thermostat

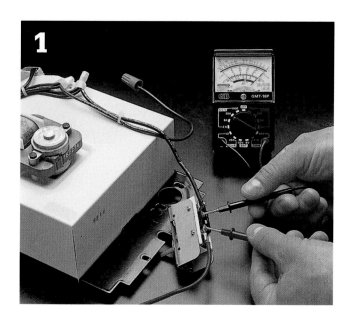

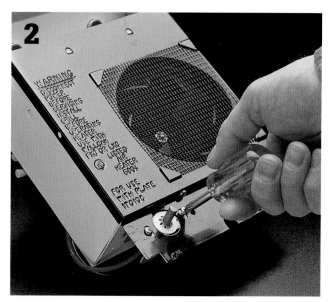

Shut off the power to the heater at the main service panel, and check for power. Disconnect one lead from the back of the control switch/thermostat unit by prying it loose with a needlenose pliers or unscrewing it. With the multimeter set to test for continuity, place one probe on each terminal.

If the multimeter doesn't indicate continuity, remove the other lead, and unscrew the control switch/thermostat unit from the base of the heater. Install an identical replacement unit.

Servicing Thermostats

A thermostat is a temperature-sensitive switch that automatically controls home heating and air-conditioning systems. There are two types of thermostats used to control heating and air-conditioning systems. Low-voltage thermostats control whole-house heating and air conditioning from one central location. Line-voltage thermostats are used in zone heating systems, where each room has its own heating unit and thermostat.

A low-voltage thermostat is powered by a transformer that reduces 120-volt current to about 24 volts. A low-voltage thermostat is very durable, but failures can occur if wire connections become loose or dirty, if thermostat parts become corroded, or if a transformer wears out. Some thermostat systems have two transformers. One transformer controls the heating unit, and the other controls the air-conditioning unit.

Line-voltage thermostats are powered by the same circuit as the heating unit, usually a 240-volt circuit. Always make sure to turn off the power before servicing a line-voltage thermostat.

A thermostat can be replaced in about one hour. Many homeowners choose to replace standard low-voltage or line-voltage thermostats with programmable setback thermostats. These programmable thermostats can cut energy use by up to 35%.

When buying a new thermostat, make sure the new unit is compatible with your heating/air-conditioning system. For reference, take along the brand name and model number of the old thermostat and of your heating/air-conditioning units. When buying a new low-voltage transformer, choose a replacement with voltage and amperage ratings that match the old thermostat.

Tools & Materials ▸

Soft-bristled paint brush
Multimeter, screwdriver
Combination tool
Continuity tester
Masking tape
Short piece of wire

Electronic programmable thermostats can be set to make up to four temperature changes each day. They are available in low-voltage designs (right) for central heating/cooling systems and in line-voltage designs (left) for electric baseboard heating. Most electronic programmable thermostats have an internal battery that saves the program in case of a power failure.

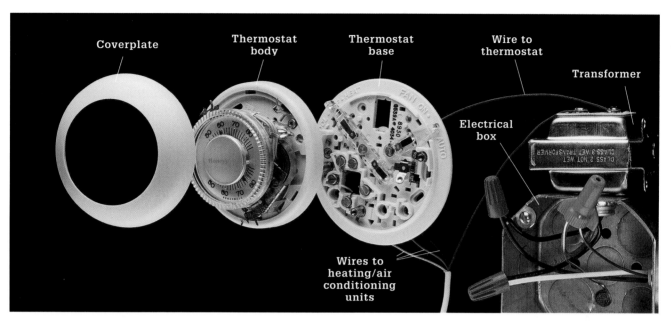

Coverplate · Thermostat body · Thermostat base · Wire to thermostat · Transformer · Electrical box · Wires to heating/air conditioning units

Low-voltage thermostat system has a transformer that is either connected to an electrical junction box or mounted inside a furnace access panel. Very thin wires (18 to 22 gauge) send current to the thermostat. The thermostat constantly monitors room temperatures, and sends electrical signals to the heating/cooling unit through additional wires. The number of wires connected to the thermostat varies from two to six, depending on the type of heating/air conditioning system. In the common four-wire system shown above, power is supplied to the thermostat through a single wire attached to screw terminal R. Wires attached to other screw terminals relay signals to the furnace heating unit, the air-conditioning unit, and the blower unit. Before removing a thermostat, make sure to label each wire to identify its screw terminal location.

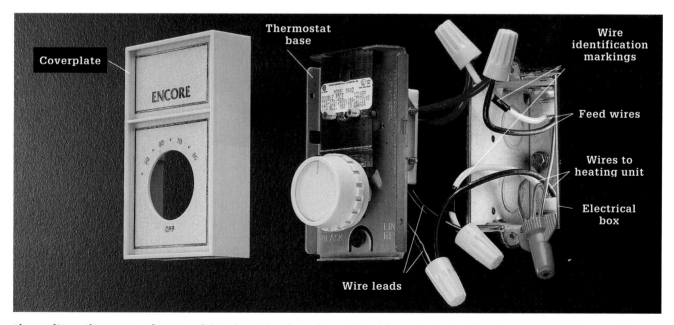

Coverplate · Thermostat base · Wire identification markings · Feed wires · Wires to heating unit · Electrical box · Wire leads

Line-voltage thermostat for 240-volt baseboard heating unit usually has four wire leads, although some models have only two leads. On a four-wire thermostat, the two red wire leads (sometimes marked LINE or L) are attached to the two hot feed wires bringing power into the box from the service panel. The black wire leads (sometimes marked LOAD) are connected to the circuit wires that carry power to the heating unit.

How to Inspect & Test a Low-voltage Thermostat System

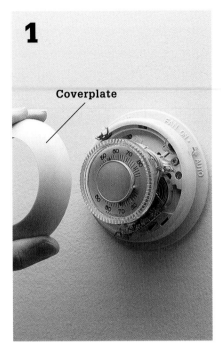

1

Coverplate

Turn off power to the heating/ air-conditioning system at the main service panel. Remove the thermostat coverplate.

2

Clean dust from the thermostat parts using a small, soft-bristled paint brush.

3

Mounting screws

Remove the thermostat body by loosening the mounting screws with a screwdriver.

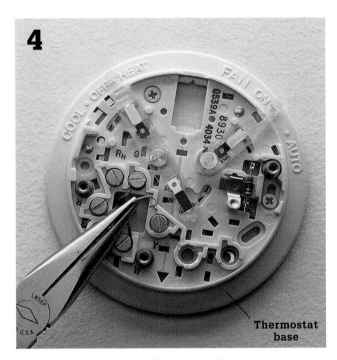

4

Thermostat base

Inspect the wire connections on the thermostat base. Reattach any loose wires. If wires are broken or corroded, they should be clipped, stripped, and reattached to the screw terminals.

5

Locate the low-voltage transformer that powers the thermostat. This transformer usually is located near the heating/air-conditioning system or inside a furnace access panel. Tighten any loose wire connections.

6

Set a multimeter to the 50-volt (AC) range. Turn on power to the heating/air-conditioning system at the main service panel.

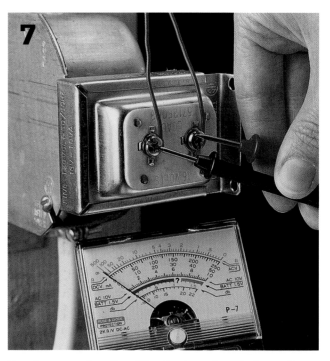

7

Touch one probe of multimeter to each of the low-voltage screw terminals. If tester does not detect current, then the transformer is defective and must be replaced (page 543).

8

Turn on power to heating system. Set thermostat control levers to AUTO and HEAT.

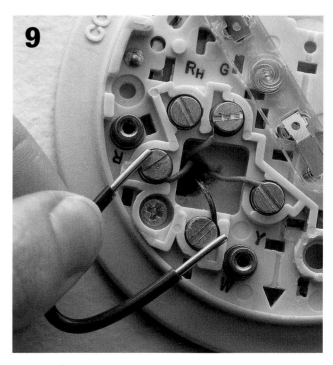

9

Strip ½" from each end of a short piece of insulated wire. Touch one end of the wire to terminal marked W and the other end to terminal marked R. If heating system begins to run, then the thermostat is faulty and must be replaced (page 542).

How to Install a Programmable Low-voltage Thermostat

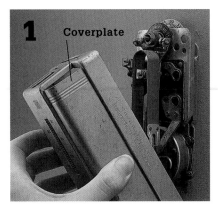

1 Coverplate

Turn off power to the heating/air-conditioning system at the main service panel. Remove the thermostat coverplate.

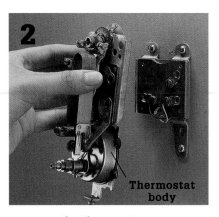

2 Thermostat body

Unscrew the thermostat mounting screws, and remove the thermostat body.

3

Label the low-voltage wires to identify their screw terminal locations, using masking tape. Disconnect all low-voltage wires.

4

Remove the thermostat base by loosening the mounting screws. Tape the wires against the wall to make sure they do not fall into the wall cavity.

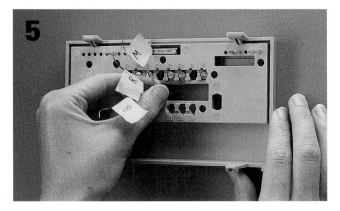

5

Thread the low-voltage wires through base of new thermostat. Mount the thermostat base on the wall, using the screws included with the thermostat.

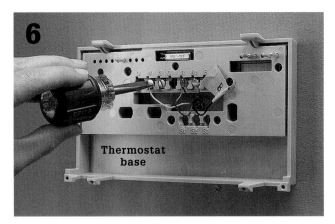

6 Thermostat base

Connect the low-voltage wires to the screw terminals on the thermostat base. Use the manufacturer's connection chart as a guide.

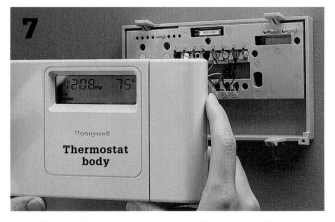

7 Thermostat body

Install batteries in thermostat body, then attach the body to thermostat base. Turn on power, and program the thermostat as desired.

How to Replace a Low-voltage Transformer

Turn off power to the heating/air-conditioning system at the main service panel. Remove the coverplate on the transformer electrical box.

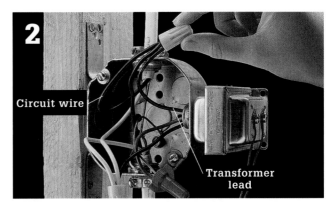

Carefully remove the wire connector joining the black circuit wire to the transformer lead. Be careful not to touch bare wires.

Test for power by touching one probe of neon circuit tester to grounded metal box and other probe to exposed wires. Remove wire connector from white wires and repeat test. Tester should not glow for either test. If it does, power is still entering box. Return to service panel, and turn off correct circuit.

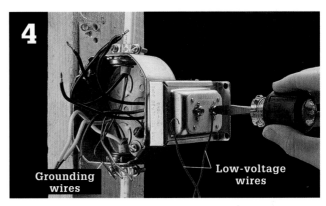

Disconnect the grounding wires inside the box, then disconnect low-voltage wires attached to the screw terminals on the transformer. Unscrew the transformer mounting bracket inside the box, and remove transformer. Purchase a new transformer with the same voltage rating as the old transformer.

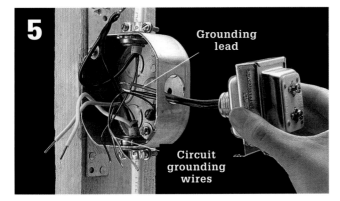

Attach new transformer to electrical box. Reconnect circuit wires to transformer leads. Connect circuit grounding wires to transformer grounding lead.

Connect the low-voltage wires to the transformer, and reattach the electrical box coverplate. Turn on the power at the main service panel.

How to Test & Replace a Line-voltage Thermostat

Turn off power to the heating unit at the main service panel. Remove the thermostat coverplate.

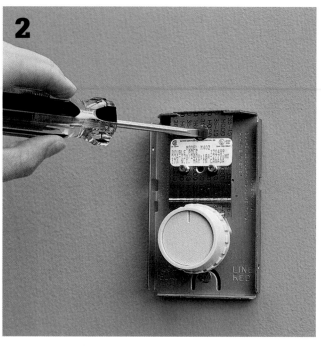

Loosen the thermostat mounting screws, and carefully pull the thermostat from the electrical box.

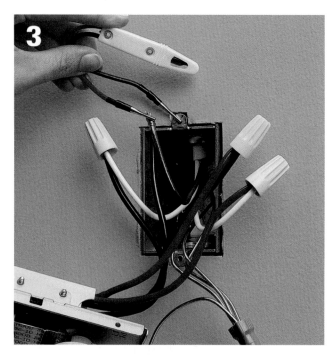

Unscrew one wire connector. Test for power by touching one probe of neon circuit tester to grounded metal box and touching other probe to exposed wires. Tester should not glow. Repeat test with other wire connections. Tester should not glow. If it does, then power is still entering box. Return to service panel, and turn off correct circuit.

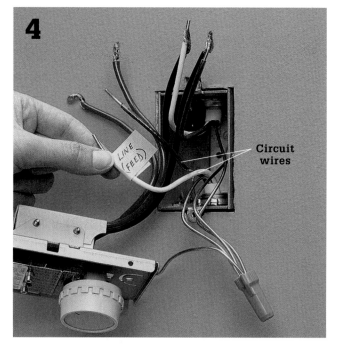

Circuit wires

Identify the two circuit wires that are attached to the thermostat leads marked LINE. The circuit wires attached to the LINE leads bring power into the box and are known as feed wires. Label the feed wires with masking tape, then disconnect all wires.

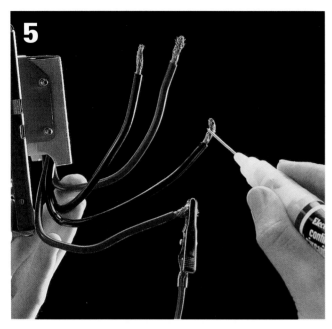

5

Test thermostat by attaching the clip of a continuity tester to one of the two leads marked LINE then touching probe to wire lead marked LOAD on same side of thermostat. Turn temperature dial from HIGH to LOW. Tester should glow in both positions. Repeat test with other pair of wire leads. If tester does not glow for both positions, thermostat is faulty and must be replaced.

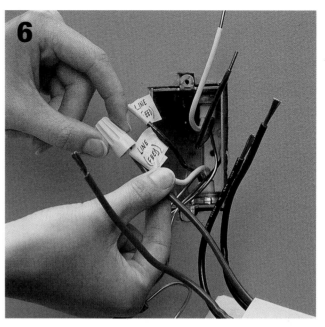

6

Replace a faulty thermostat with a new thermostat that has the same voltage and amperage ratings as the old one. Connect the new thermostat by attaching the circuit feed wires to the wire leads marked LINE, using wire connectors.

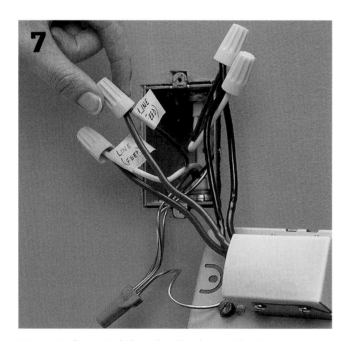

7

Connect the remaining circuit wires to the thermostat leads marked LOAD, using wire connectors. Connect the grounding wires together with a wire connector.

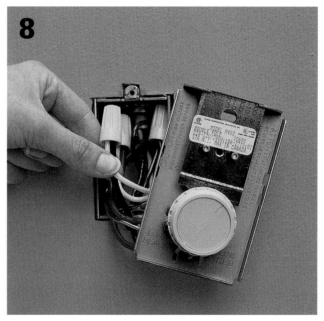

8

Carefully fold the wires inside the electrical box, then attach the thermostat mounting screws and the coverplate. Turn on the power at the main service panel. If new thermostat is programmable, set the program as desired.

Installing a Ridge Vent

If you need attic ventilation, installing a continuous ridge vent will get the job done. Since they're installed along the entire ridge of the roof, they provide an even flow of air along the entire underside of the roof decking. Combined with continuous soffit vents, this is the most effective type of ventilation system.

Since the vents are installed along the ridge, they're practically invisible, eliminating any disruptions to the roof. Other vent types, such as roof louvers and turbines, often distract from the roof's aesthetics.

Installing one continuous ridge vent is quicker and easier than installing other types of vents that need to be placed in several locations across the roof. It also saves you from having to make numerous cuts in your finished roof, which can disturb surrounding shingles.

Tools & Materials ▸

Hammer	Flat pry bar
Circular saw	Ridge vents
Tape measure	1½" roofing nails
Chalk line	

Continuous ridge vents work in conjunction with the soffits to allow airflow under the roof decking. Installed at the roof peak and covered with cap shingles, ridge vents are less conspicuous than other roof vents.

How to Install a Ridge Vent

Remove the ridge caps, using a flat pry bar. Measure down from the peak the width of the manufacturer's recommended opening, and mark each end of the roof. Snap a chalk line between the marks. Repeat for the other side of the peak. Remove any nails in your path.

Set the blade depth of a circular saw to cut the sheathing, but not the rafters. Cut along each chalk line, staying 12" from the edges of the roof. Remove the cut sheathing, using a pry bar.

Measure down from the peak half the width of the ridge vent, and make a mark on both ends of the roof. Snap a line between the marks. Do this on both sides of the peak.

Center the ridge vent over the peak, aligning the edges with the chalk lines. Install using roofing nails that are long enough to penetrate the roof sheathing. *Tip: If a chimney extends through the peak, leave 12" of sheathing around the chimney.*

Butt sections of ridge vents together and nail the ends. Install vents across the entire peak, including the 12" sections at each end of the roof that were not cut away.

Place ridge cap shingles over the ridge vents. Nail them with two 1½" roofing nails per cap. Overlap the caps as you would on a normal ridge. If the caps you removed in step 1 are still in good shape, you can reuse them. Otherwise, use new ones.

Installing New Vents

If you need more ventilation for your attic, but you don't want to replace your entire soffits or embark on a roofing project, you can add vents to your existing wood soffits and roof.

This project shows how to add soffit vents for air intake, and how to add roof vents for air outtake. These additional vents increase the airflow under your roof, helping to eliminate heat buildup in your attic.

Tools & Materials ▸

Hammer
Pry bar
Chalk line
Caulk gun
Tape measure
Drill
Jigsaw
Utility knife
Chalk line

Rubber-gasket nails
Roof cement
Stainless
   steel screws
Soffit vent covers
Roof vents
Siliconized
   acrylic caulk
Screwdriver

Adding vents to wood soffits and the roof can increase airflow in the attic.

How to Install New Vents

Examine the eaves area from inside your attic to make sure there is nothing obstructing air flow from the soffits. If insulation is blocking the air passage, install insulation baffles.

Draw a cutout for the soffit vent cover on the soffit panel. Center the vents between the fascia and the side of the house. The cover outline should be ¼" smaller on all sides than the soffit vent cover.

Drill a starter hole, then cut the vent openings with a jigsaw.

Caulk the flanges of the vent cover. Screw the vent cover to the soffit. *Tip: For visual effect, install new vent covers with the louvers pointing in the same direction.*

Ridge pole

Mark the location for the roof vent by driving a nail through the roof sheathing. Center the nail between rafters, 16" to 24" from the ridge pole.

Center a vent cover over the nail on the outside of the roof. Outline the base flange of the vent cover on the shingles, then remove shingles in an area 2" inside the outline. Mark the roof vent hole, using the marker nail as a centerpoint. Cut the hole, using a reciprocating saw or jigsaw.

Apply roof cement to the underside of the base flange. Set the vent cover in position, slipping the flange under the shingles, centered over the vent-hole cutout.

Secure the roof vent to the sheathing with rubber-gasket nails on all sides of the flange. Tack down any loose shingles. Do not nail through the flange when attaching shingles.

Reference Charts

Metric Conversions

To Convert:	To:	Multiply by:
Inches	Millimeters	25.4
Inches	Centimeters	25.4
Feet	Meters	0.305
Yards	Meters	0.914
Square inches	Square centimeters	6.45
Square feet	Square meters	0.093
Square yards	Square meters	0.836
Ounces	Milliliters	30.0
Pints (U.S.)	Liters	0.473 (Imp. 0.568)
Quarts (U.S.)	Liters	0.946 (Imp. 1.136)
Gallons (U.S.)	Liters	3.785 (Imp. 4.546)
Ounces	Grams	28.4
Pounds	Kilograms	0.454

To Convert:	To:	Multiply by:
Millimeters	Inches	0.039
Centimeters	Inches	0.394
Meters	Feet	3.28
Meters	Yards	1.09
Square centimeters	Square inches	0.155
Square meters	Square feet	10.8
Square meters	Square yards	1.2
Milliliters	Ounces	.033
Liters	Pints (U.S.)	2.114 (Imp. 1.76)
Liters	Quarts (U.S.)	1.057 (Imp. 0.88)
Liters	Gallons (U.S.)	0.264 (Imp. 0.22)
Grams	Ounces	0.035
Kilograms	Pounds	2.2

Converting Temperatures

Convert degrees Fahrenheit (F) to degrees Celsius (C) by following this simple formula: Subtract 32 from the Fahrenheit temperature reading. Then, multiply that number by $\frac{5}{9}$. For example, 77°F - 32 = 45. 45 × $\frac{5}{9}$ = 25°C.

To convert degrees Celsius to degrees Fahrenheit, multiply the Celsius temperature reading by $\frac{9}{5}$. Then, add 32. For example, 25°C × $\frac{9}{5}$ = 45. 45 + 32 = 77°F.

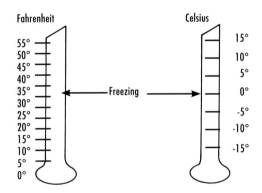

Metric Plywood Panels

Metric plywood panels are commonly available in two sizes: 1,200 mm × 2,400 mm and 1,220 mm × 2,400 mm, which is roughly equivalent to a 4 × 8-ft. sheet. Standard and Select sheathing panels come in standard thicknesses, while Sanded grade panels are available in special thicknesses.

Standard Sheathing Grade		Sanded Grade	
7.5 mm	($\frac{5}{16}$ in.)	6 mm	($\frac{4}{17}$ in.)
9.5 mm	($\frac{3}{8}$ in.)	8 mm	($\frac{5}{16}$ in.)
12.5 mm	($\frac{1}{2}$ in.)	11 mm	($\frac{7}{16}$ in.)
15.5 mm	($\frac{5}{8}$ in.)	14 mm	($\frac{9}{16}$ in.)
18.5 mm	($\frac{3}{4}$ in.)	17 mm	($\frac{2}{3}$ in.)
20.5 mm	($\frac{13}{16}$ in.)	19 mm	($\frac{3}{4}$ in.)
22.5 mm	($\frac{7}{8}$ in.)	21 mm	($\frac{13}{16}$ in.)
25.5 mm	(1 in.)	24 mm	($\frac{15}{16}$ in.)

Lumber Dimensions

Nominal - U.S.	Actual - U.S. (in inches)	Metric
1 × 2	$\frac{3}{4}$ × 1$\frac{1}{2}$	19 × 38 mm
1 × 3	$\frac{3}{4}$ × 2$\frac{1}{2}$	19 × 64 mm
1 × 4	$\frac{3}{4}$ × 3$\frac{1}{2}$	19 × 89 mm
1 × 5	$\frac{3}{4}$ × 4$\frac{1}{2}$	19 × 114 mm
1 × 6	$\frac{3}{4}$ × 5$\frac{1}{2}$	19 × 140 mm
1 × 7	$\frac{3}{4}$ × 6$\frac{1}{4}$	19 × 159 mm
1 × 8	$\frac{3}{4}$ × 7$\frac{1}{4}$	19 × 184 mm
1 × 10	$\frac{3}{4}$ × 9$\frac{1}{4}$	19 × 235 mm
1 × 12	$\frac{3}{4}$ × 11$\frac{1}{4}$	19 × 286 mm
1$\frac{1}{4}$ × 4	1 × 3$\frac{1}{2}$	25 × 89 mm
1$\frac{1}{4}$ × 6	1 × 5$\frac{1}{2}$	25 × 140 mm
1$\frac{1}{4}$ × 8	1 × 7$\frac{1}{4}$	25 × 184 mm
1$\frac{1}{4}$ × 10	1 × 9$\frac{1}{4}$	25 × 235 mm
1$\frac{1}{4}$ × 12	1 × 11$\frac{1}{4}$	25 × 286 mm
1$\frac{1}{2}$ × 4	1$\frac{1}{4}$ × 3$\frac{1}{2}$	32 × 89 mm
1$\frac{1}{2}$ × 6	1$\frac{1}{4}$ × 5$\frac{1}{2}$	32 × 140 mm
1$\frac{1}{2}$ × 8	1$\frac{1}{4}$ × 7$\frac{1}{4}$	32 × 184 mm
1$\frac{1}{2}$ × 10	1$\frac{1}{4}$ × 9$\frac{1}{4}$	32 × 235 mm
1$\frac{1}{2}$ × 12	1$\frac{1}{4}$ × 11$\frac{1}{4}$	32 × 286 mm
2 × 4	1$\frac{1}{2}$ × 3$\frac{1}{2}$	38 × 89 mm
2 × 6	1$\frac{1}{2}$ × 5$\frac{1}{2}$	38 × 140 mm
2 × 8	1$\frac{1}{2}$ × 7$\frac{1}{4}$	38 × 184 mm
2 × 10	1$\frac{1}{2}$ × 9$\frac{1}{4}$	38 × 235 mm
2 × 12	1$\frac{1}{2}$ × 11$\frac{1}{4}$	38 × 286 mm
3 × 6	2$\frac{1}{2}$ × 5$\frac{1}{2}$	64 × 140 mm
4 × 4	3$\frac{1}{2}$ × 3$\frac{1}{2}$	89 × 89 mm
4 × 6	3$\frac{1}{2}$ × 5$\frac{1}{2}$	89 × 140 mm

Liquid Measurement Equivalents

1 Pint	= 16 Fluid Ounces	= 2 Cups
1 Quart	= 32 Fluid Ounces	= 2 Pints
1 Gallon	= 128 Fluid Ounces	= 4 Quarts

Drill Bit Guide

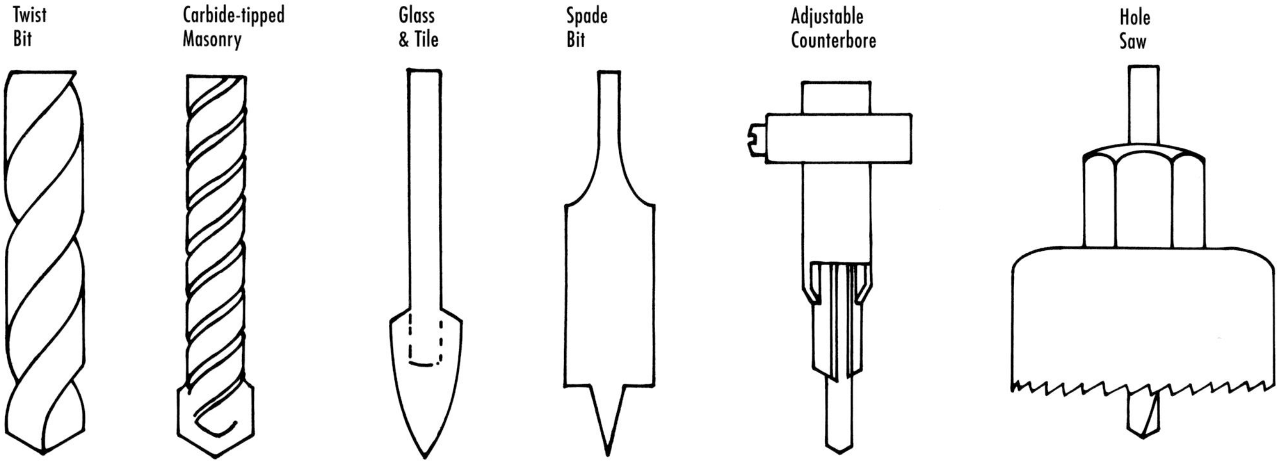
Twist
Bit
Carbide-tipped
Masonry
Glass
& Tile
Spade
Bit
Adjustable
Counterbore
Hole
Saw

Nails

Nail lengths are identified by numbers from 4 to 60 followed by the letter "d," which stands for "penny." For general framing and repair work, use common or box nails. Common nails are best suited to framing work where strength is important. Box nails are smaller in diameter than common nails, which makes them easier to drive and less likely to split wood. Use box nails for light work and thin materials. Most common and box nails have a cement or vinyl coating that improves their holding power.

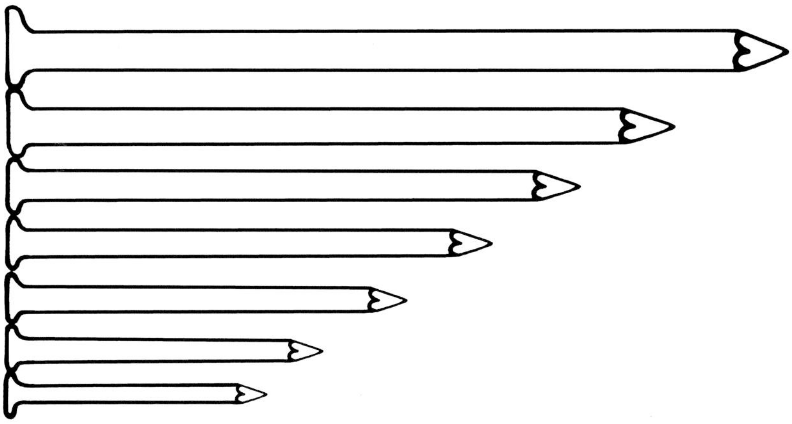

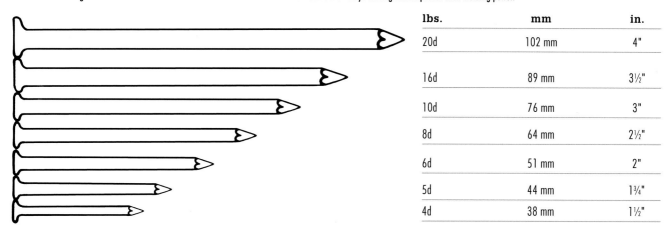

lbs.	mm	in.
20d	102 mm	4"
16d	89 mm	3½"
10d	76 mm	3"
8d	64 mm	2½"
6d	51 mm	2"
5d	44 mm	1¾"
4d	38 mm	1½"

Counterbore, Shank & Pilot Hole Diameters

Screw Size	Counterbore Diameter for Screw Head (in inches)	Clearance Hole for Screw Shank (in inches)	Pilot Hole Diameter: Hard Wood (in inches)	Pilot Hole Diameter: Soft Wood (in inches)
#1	.146 (9/64)	5/64	3/64	1/32
#2	1/4	3/32	3/64	1/32
#3	1/4	7/64	1/16	3/64
#4	1/4	1/8	1/16	3/64
#5	1/4	1/8	5/64	1/16
#6	5/16	9/64	3/32	5/64
#7	5/16	5/32	3/32	5/64
#8	3/8	11/64	1/8	3/32
#9	3/8	11/64	1/8	3/32
#10	3/8	3/16	1/8	7/64
#11	1/2	3/16	5/32	9/64
#12	1/2	7/32	9/64	1/8

Index

Also From CREATIVE PUBLISHING international

Complete Guide to Attics & Basements

Complete Guide to Basic Woodworking

Complete Guide Build Your Kids a Treehouse

Complete Guide to Carpentry for Homeowners

Complete Guide to Contemporary Sheds

Complete Guide to Creative Landscapes

Complete Guide to Custom Shelves & Built-Ins

Complete Guide to Decorating with Ceramic Tile

Complete Guide to Decks

Complete Guide to DIY Projects for Luxurious Living

Complete Guide to Dream Bathrooms

Complete Guide to Dream Kitchens

Complete Guide to Finishing Walls & Ceilings

Complete Guide to Floor Décor

Complete Guide to Gazebos & Arbors

Complete Guide to Home Plumbing

Complete Guide to Home Wiring

Complete Guide to Landscape Construction

Complete Guide Maintain Your Pool & Spa

Complete Guide to Masonry & Stonework

Complete Guide to Outdoor Wood Projects

Complete Guide to Painting & Decorating

Complete Guide to Patios

Complete Guide to Roofing & Siding

Complete Guide to Trim & Finish Carpentry

Complete Guide to Windows & Entryways

Complete Guide to Wood Storage Projects

Complete Guide to Yard & Garden Features

Complete Outdoor Builder

Complete Photo Guide to Home Repair

Complete Photo Guide to Home Improvement

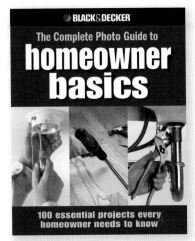

ISBN 1-58923-376-X

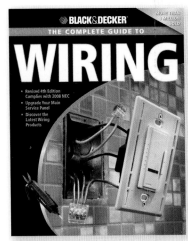

ISBN 1-58923-413-0

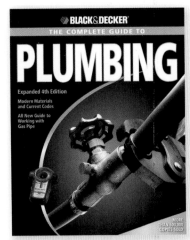

ISBN 1-58923-378-6

Creative Publishing
international

400 First Avenue North • Suite 300 • Minneapolis, MN 55401 • www.creativepub.com